# TAKING SIDES

Clashing Views on Controversial

# Issues in Childhood and Society

**FOURTH EDITION**

**Selected, Edited, and with Introductions by**

**Diana S. DelCampo**
*New Mexico State University*

**and**

**Robert L. DelCampo**
*New Mexico State University*

**McGraw-Hill/Dushkin**
**A Division of The McGraw-Hill Companies**

Photo Acknowledgment
Cover image: © 2002 by PhotoDisc, Inc.

Cover Art Acknowledgment
Charles Vitelli



Manufactured in the United States of America

Fourth Edition

123456789BAHBAH5432

Library of Congress Cataloging-in-Publication Data
Main entry under title:
Taking sides: clashing views on controversial issues in childhood and society/selected, edited, and with introductions by Diana S. DelCampo and Robert L. DelCampo.—4th ed.
Includes bibliographical references and index.
1. Children—United States. 2. Child welfare—United States. I. DelCampo, Diana S., *comp.* II. DelCampo, Robert L., *comp.*
305.23

0-07-248052-1
ISSN: 1094-7558

Printed on Recycled Paper

# Preface

Children are society's most valuable resource, and however clichéd that idea may be, there can be no doubt about the urgency of the issues confronting children today and the people who care for them and care about them. Each day we are bombarded with media reports on issues affecting children—complex issues related to child care, schooling, violence, morality, gangs, divorce; the list goes on. In this book we look at 17 of those controversial issues and ask you to think about them, perhaps for the first time, perhaps in ways you may not have previously considered.

For the student who likes to memorize facts and learn *the* right answer, the controversies in this book could be most unsettling! However, a good education should include the nurturing of your ability to think critically and to be an active learner. This book endeavors to put you on the path toward further developing these skills. As you read each side of an issue and grapple with the points made by the authors, you will be moved to consider the merits of each position. In the process, you may adopt the point of view of one side, or the other, or formulate an opinion completely your own on the issue. And when you attend class, you will be exposed to your classmates' and instructor's ideas on the issue as well. This may further challenge you to reconsider and defend your position, which is the essence of critical thinking and a primary purpose of this book.

**Plan of the book** *Taking Sides: Clashing Views on Controversial Issues in Childhood and Society*, fourth edition, is designed to be used for courses in child development, human development, or parenting. The issues can be studied consecutively or in any order, as each is designed to be independent of the other. We have included 17 issues encompassing 34 selections from a wide variety of sources and authors. Each part of the book deals with one of four developmental phases of childhood: infancy, early childhood, middle childhood, and adolescence. Within each part are issues related to aspects of child development at that stage. Each issue has an *introduction,* which provides some background about the controversy, briefly describes the authors, and gives a brief summary of the positions reflected in the issue. Each issue concludes with a *postscript,* which contains some final thoughts on the issue and offers a bibliography of related readings should you want to explore the topic further.

A listing of all the *contributors* to this volume is included at the back of the book to give you additional information on the scholars, practitioners, educators, policymakers, and social critics whose views are debated here.

**Changes to this edition** The fourth edition of *Taking Sides: Clashing Views on Controversial Issues in Childhood and Society* includes some important changes from the third edition. Three completely new issues have been added: *Is Institutional Child Care Beneficial to Children?* (Issue 1); *Does Transracial Adoption Harm a Child's Development?* (Issue 4); and *Are Fathers Really Necessary?* (Issue 6). In addition, for one of the issues, *Is Television Violence Viewing Harmful for Children?* (Issue 8), we have retained the topic from the previous edition but have replaced both of the selections in order to bring the debate up-to-date and to focus more clearly on the controversy. As a result, there are 8 new readings. The issue introductions and postscripts have also been revised and updated.

In addition to changes in topics and selections, the *On the Internet* page that precedes each part opener has been updated. For these pages, several relevant sites on the World Wide Web have been identified and annotated.

**A word to the instructor** An *Instructor's Manual With Test Questions* (both multiple-choice and essay) is available through the publisher for the instructor using this volume of *Taking Sides.* A general guidebook, *Using Taking Sides in the Classroom,* which discusses methods and techniques for integrating the pro-con approach into any classroom setting, is also available. An online version of *Using Taking Sides in the Classroom* and a correspondence service for Taking Sides adopters can be found at `http://www.dushkin.com/usingts/`.

*Taking Sides: Clashing Views on Controversial Issues in Childhood and Society* is only one title in the Taking Sides series. If you are interested in seeing the table of contents for any of the other titles, please visit the Taking Sides Web site at `http://www.dushkin.com/takingsides/`.

**Acknowledgments** We would like to thank New Mexico State University students, Cleo Cerna, Faith Ybarra, and Miya Hoshijo for assisting with the fourth edition of the book. We thank those professors who adopted the third edition of this book and took the time to make suggestions for this edition:

**John Barroso**
*University of Pittsburgh*

**Laura Bennett-Murphy**
*Otterbein College*

**Judith Hudson**
*Rutgers University*

**Margaret Ruddy**
*College of New Jersey*

**Julie Wolfe Sakin**
*University of Maryland*

**Leo Sandy**
*Plymouth State College*

**C. Sharpe**
*Santa Barbara City College*

**Susan Siaw**
*California State University-Pomona*

**Jeanine Stewart**
*Washington and Lee University*

**Douglas Trimble**
*Northwestern College*

We also want to extend warm thanks to Theodore Knight, list manager of the Taking Sides series, and Juliana Gribbins, developmental editor, at McGraw-Hill/Dushkin.

We look forward to receiving feedback and comments on this fourth edition of *Taking Sides: Clashing Views on Controversial Issues in Childhood and Society* from both faculty and students who experience the book. We can be reached via the Internet (ddelcamp@nmsu.edu or rdelcamp@nmsu.edu), or you can write us in care of the Taking Sides series at McGraw-Hill/Dushkin.

**Diana S. DelCampo**
*New Mexico State University*

**Robert L. DelCampo**
*New Mexico State University*

# Contents In Brief

# Contents

**NO: Elizabeth H. Thilo and Susan F. Townsend,** from "What Are the Pitfalls of Early Discharge?" *Contemporary OB/GYN* (January 1997) *60*

John R. Britton, Helen L. Britton, and Susan A. Beebe, all affiliated with the Department of Pediatrics at the University of Utah Medical Center in Salt Lake City, review the available data on the appropriate time to discharge a newborn and summarize some of the studies that promote early discharge. Elizabeth H. Thilo, an associate professor of pediatrics, and Susan F. Townsend, an assistant professor of pediatrics, contend that the recently recommended 48-hour hospital stay for newborns may still not be long enough to catch some of the medical problems that infants can develop.

### Issue 4. Does Transracial Adoption Harm a Child's Development? 68

**YES: Leslie Doty Hollingsworth,** from "Symbolic Interactionism, African American Families, and the Transracial Adoption Controversy," *Social Work* (September 1999) *70*

**NO: Rudolph Alexander, Jr. and Carla M. Curtis,** from "A Review of Empirical Research Involving the Transracial Adoption of African American Children," *Journal of Black Psychology* (May 1996) *80*

Leslie Doty Hollingsworth, assistant professor at the University of Michigan, contends that socialization within an African American family is a unique and distinct experience for children. As a consequence, children not socialized in these families cannot effectively embrace African American definitions of self and family. Rudolph Alexander, Jr. and Carla M. Curtis, both professors at Ohio State University, offer research maintaining that African American children are not psychologically harmed by transracial adoptions.

## PART 2 EARLY CHILDHOOD 93

### Issue 5. Is Spanking Detrimental to Children? 94

**YES: Murray A. Straus,** from "Spanking and the Making of a Violent Society," *Pediatrics* (October 1996) *96*

**NO: Robert E. Larzelere,** from "A Review of the Outcomes of Parental Use of Nonabusive or Customary Physical Punishment," *Pediatrics* (October 1996) *108*

Murray A. Straus, codirector of the Family Research Laboratory at the University of New Hampshire, argues that spanking with any frequency teaches children aggressiveness and is associated with subsequent violent behavior. Robert E. Larzelere, director of Residential Research at Boys Town, Nebraska, agrees that no professional believes that abusive physical punishment of children is acceptable but contends that spankings, or nonabusive physical punishment, which have been used by parents for years, should not be considered detrimental to children.

### Issue 6. Are Fathers Really Necessary? 118

**YES: W. J. Doherty, Edward F. Kouneski, and Martha F. Erickson,** from "Responsible Fathering: An Overview and Conceptual Framework," *Journal of Marriage and the Family* (May 1998) *120*

**NO: Alexis J. Walker and Lori A. McGraw,** from "Who Is Responsible for Responsible Fathering?" *Journal of Marriage and the Family* (May 2000) *133*

Professor of family social science W. J. Doherty, psychologist Edward F. Kouneski, and Martha F. Erickson, director of the University of Minnesota's Children, Youth and Family Consortium, explore the contextual influences on fathering and conclude that a quality marriage in the optimal context promotes responsible fathering. Professor of human development and family sciences Alexis J. Walker and Lori A. McGraw, 4-H program coordinator at Oregon State University, contend that there is no empirical evidence that children need active fathers in their lives.

**Issue 7. Does Divorce Create Long-Term Negative Effects for Children? 146**

**YES: Karl Zinsmeister,** from "Divorce's Toll on Children," *The American Enterprise* (May/June 1996) *148*

**NO: David Gately and Andrew I. Schwebel,** from "Favorable Outcomes in Children After Parental Divorce," *Journal of Divorce and Remarriage* (vol. 18, nos. 3–4, 1992) *155*

Karl Zinsmeister, editor in chief of the *American Enterprise*, argues that divorce causes damage from which children never recover and that the conflict within a marriage will not cause the same amount of problems for children that the breakup of a marriage creates. Educators David Gately and Andrew I. Schwebel contend that children of divorce are not doomed to failure; they often display positive characteristics, such as enhanced levels of maturity, self-esteem, empathy, and adaptability.

**Issue 8. Is Television Violence Viewing Harmful for Children? 170**

**YES: Merrilyn O. Johnson,** from "Television Violence and Its Effect on Children," *Journal of Pediatric Nursing* (April 1996) *172*

**NO: Jib Fowles,** from "The Whipping Boy: The Hidden Conflicts Underlying the Campaign Against Violent TV," *Reason* (March 2001) *179*

Merrilyn O. Johnson, MSN, RN, is from the nursing Ph.D. collaborative program at the Medical University of South Carolina and the University of South Carolina, Columbia. She argues that the negative impact of television viewing is so great that it should be included in health professionals' assessments of children and families. Jib Fowles, a professor of communication at the University of Houston, asserts that although television violence has increased steadily, the violent crime rate has in fact decreased.

**PART 3 MIDDLE CHILDHOOD 191**

**Issue 9. Are Boys Better in Math Than Girls? 192**

**YES: Carol J. Mills, Karen E. Ablard, and Heinrich Stumpf,** from "Gender Differences in Academically Talented Young Students' Mathematical Reasoning: Patterns Across Age and Subskills," *Journal of Educational Psychology* (vol. 85, no. 2, 1993) *194*

**NO: American Association of University Women,** from *How Schools Shortchange Girls: A Study of Major Findings on Girls and Education* (American Association of University Women, 1992) *206*

Carol J. Mills, Karen E. Ablard, and Heinrich Stumpf, associates of the Center for Talented Youth Research at Johns Hopkins University, argue that boys perform better than girls on tests for math reasoning ability. A report developed by the Center for Research on Women at Wellesley College for the American Association of University Women concludes that the differences in math achievement between boys and girls are not significant and are narrowing.

## Issue 10. Are Stepfamilies Inherently Problematic for Children? 216

**YES: David Popenoe,** from "The Evolution of Marriage and the Problem of Stepfamilies: A Biosocial Perspective," in Alan Booth and Judy Dunn, eds., *Stepfamilies: Who Benefits? Who Does Not?* (Lawrence Erlbaum, 1994) *218*

**NO: Lawrence A. Kurdek,** from "Remarriages and Stepfamilies Are Not Inherently Problematic," in Alan Booth and Judy Dunn, eds., *Stepfamilies: Who Benefits? Who Does Not?* (Lawrence Erlbaum, 1994) *226*

Professor of sociology David Popenoe contends that children from single-parent families and stepfamilies are more likely to have emotional problems and health problems and to do poorly in school than children from intact families with two biological parents. Psychologist Lawrence A. Kurdek maintains that multiple-divorce families, not stepfamilies, differ from two-parent families and that stepfamilies are not inherently problematic for children.

## Issue 11. Will School Vouchers Improve Children's Education? 232

**YES: Kevin Walthers,** from "Saying Yes to Vouchers: Perception, Choice, and the Educational Response," *NASSP Bulletin* (September 1995) *234*

**NO: John F. Lewis,** from "Saying No to Vouchers: What Is the Price of Democracy?" *NASSP Bulletin* (September 1995) *242*

Teacher Kevin Walthers argues that the pro-school-voucher movement has emerged because parents and taxpayers seriously question the efficacy of the public education system. He cites professionalism among teachers, declining academic standards for students, and disenchantment among taxpayers and parents as justification for changing how public education is administered. Attorney John F. Lewis counters that the perceived problems of the schools—such as drug use, premarital pregnancy, crime, and violence—are really societal problems *in* the schools, not problems *with* the schools. Lewis contends that public education has, in fact, improved over the last few decades.

## Issue 15. Is the Welfare of Disadvantaged Children Improving? 316

**YES: Lisbeth B. Schorr,** from "Making the Most of What We Already Know," *Public Welfare* (Spring 1994) *318*

**NO: William J. Bennett,** from "What to Do About the Children," *Commentary* (March 1995) *326*

Lisbeth B. Schorr, director of the Harvard University Project on Effective Services, contends that organized intervention programs are working to circumvent social problems such as teen pregnancy, juvenile crime, and school dropout rates. William J. Bennett, former secretary of education and former director of the Office of National Drug Control Policy, sees the decline of the two-parent family and moral confusion as the primary reasons for children's poor living conditions.

## Issue 16. Is Abstinence Education the Best Sex Education? 338

**YES: Thomas Lickona,** from "Where Sex Education Went Wrong," *Educational Leadership* (November 1993) *340*

**NO: Peggy Brick and Deborah M. Roffman,** from " 'Abstinence, No Buts' Is Simplistic," *Educational Leadership* (November 1993) *349*

Thomas Lickona, a developmental psychologist, states that Americans need to promote a higher standard of sexual morality in society through "directive" sex education, which promotes abstinence before marriage. Peggy Brick, director of education at Planned Parenthood of Northern New Jersey, and Deborah M. Roffman, a sexuality educator and consultant, refute the directive approach to sex education and argue that a comprehensive approach to sex education is more effective.

## Issue 17. Can Memories of Childhood Sexual Abuse Be Recovered? 356

**YES: May Benatar,** from "Running Away From Sexual Abuse: Denial Revisited," *Families in Society: The Journal of Contemporary Human Services* (May 1995) *358*

**NO: Susan P. Robbins,** from "Wading Through the Muddy Waters of Recovered Memory," *Families in Society: The Journal of Contemporary Human Services* (October 1995) *367*

May Benatar, a clinical social worker, argues that the mass media and contemporary culture question the accuracy and truthfulness of survivors of sexual abuse. By doing this the long-term effects of these abuses tend to be minimized. Susan P. Robbins, an associate professor of social work, contends that the reason some professionals are skeptical of recovered memories is that there is no research that supports the accuracy of recovered memory. She cautions that the indiscriminate acceptance of recovered memories can lead to a serious backlash of disbelief when legitimate cases of abuse are reported.

Contributors 380
Index 384

# Introduction

## Children in Society

Diana S. DelCampo

Robert L. DelCampo

Childhood can be a wondrous time when days are filled with play and new discoveries, nights provide rest and security, and dedicated, loving parents nurture their children and meet their needs. Some children do indeed experience the full joy of childhood; however, regretfully, there are other, more sobering scenarios: There are children who do not have nurturing adults to guide them, who go to bed hungry, and some who do not even have homes. Most typically, childhood experiences fall between these two extremes. So there is a wide variety of experiences that can impact the developing child, and larger social forces are at work as well. Ask yourself as you debate the issues in this book the extent to which society must collectively address and resolve them. This a vital function of society because children are society's future.

In order to understand and appreciate children in contemporary society, it may be useful to briefly review how society's views of children have changed over time. Most child development texts review the history of adult perceptions of children in western European society. Would it surprise you to know that in ancient times children were sometimes killed as religious sacrifices and buried in the walls of buildings? People believed that this practice would strengthen a building's structure. Up until the fourth century, parents were legally allowed to kill their newborns if the children were not in good health at birth. They were also permitted to do away with a child if they already had too many children, if the child was female, or if the child was illegitimate. In 374 A.D., the Romans outlawed infanticide, hoping that this would end the killing. Since parents could no longer legally kill their children, unwanted infants began to be abandoned. This practice endured for over 1,000 years. It was not until the 1600s that child abandonment was outlawed throughout most of Europe.

During the seventeenth century, foundling homes were established to provide for the needs of unwanted children. During this period, children were considered to be miniature adults. They were dressed like adults and were expected to act as adults would act. By contemporary standards, parents took a rather casual attitude toward their children. This was probably due to the high child mortality rate at the time. Since parents thought it likely that their children would die in infancy or childhood, they did not get as emotionally close to their young children as parents typically do today. It was not until the end of the century that society began to look upon children as different from adults.

Early in the 1700s, European societal attitudes about children underwent further change. Children were no longer considered to be miniature adults, and literature written specifically for children began to emerge. By the end of the century, children who went to school were grouped by age, reflecting an awareness of stages of growth. The eighteenth century also marked the rise of the systematic study of children, which centered around the moral development of children and child-rearing problems.

It was not until the beginning of the twentieth century that three distinct age groupings emerged in the study of human development: infancy through age four or five; childhood to late puberty or early adulthood; and adulthood. This time period also marked the beginnings of the distinct field of child study. Early child study emphasized descriptive accounts of individual children and was mainly concerned with aspects of physical growth. As the century progressed, the term *child study* was changed to *research in child development.* Mothering became an important concept in the study of early child development, and the psychological aspects of development began to be examined more rigorously. Today, in the beginning of the twenty-first century, research in child development focuses on issues related to family systems and the larger social issues that affect child development.

## Nature-Nurture Controversy

There are many things that impact individuals as they progress through the human life cycle. People, places, events, illnesses, education, success, failure—have you ever thought about the number of experiences each of us encounters in our lives? If one were to place all of the variables that influence human development into two general categories, those categories would be heredity and environment. As you may know, your genetic blueprint was determined at the moment of conception with chromosomes contributed by your father and mother. In a sense, for many of us, environment is also determined at the moment of conception. A good portion of the major elements of what makes up one's environment is often determined before a person is born. The society in which one will live, one's cultural and ethnic heritage, and one's family and subsequent socioeconomic status, for example, are usually predetermined for a child.

For this edition of *Taking Sides: Clashing Views on Controversial Issues in Childhood and Society,* we have selected articles that look at children in general and how they affect or are affected by the issues raised, rather than give you, the reader, clinical case examples of issues related to a certain child or children. For the purposes of this book, we make three assumptions: (1) When we discuss a child's environment, we are usually describing elements of the society in which a child is growing, developing, and otherwise being socialized; (2) All child development occurs within this social context; and (3) Children cannot help but affect and be affected by the societal forces that surround them. In most university classes, students derive a certain sense of security in receiving definitions of terms that are used frequently in a given class. We offer the following one for *society,* which we have adapted from Gelles's 1995 textbook *Contemporary Families*:

> Society is a collection of people who interact within socially structured relationships. The only way that societies can survive their original members is by replacing them. These "replacements" are the children about whom the issues in this book are concerned.

Determining an appropriate group of societal issues and fitting them into the confines of only one work on children and society is a challenging task. Consider, for example, the diversity of contemporary society. We live in a sea of divergent and unique subcultures and ethnicities. Categorizing and describing the myriad values, customs, and belief systems of these groups could fill many volumes. In America and Canada, for example, there are many ethnic subgroups of citizens, such as English, Irish, Italians, Polish, Germans, Greeks, Russians, Scots, who are considered to be of Anglo descent. There are people of native descent, who are affiliated with scores of different tribes and subtribes. Some Canadian and American citizens trace their heritages to a variety of Asian countries, including China, Japan, Vietnam, Cambodia, Thailand, and the Philippines. Even among blacks, there are those who trace their roots to the Caribbean region and those who identify with different regions of Africa.

In light of the above, it may be reasoned that there are really no "typical" children in society! Although there are strong arguments supporting similarities within each of these general groups, there is a wide array of subgroupings and differences in customs and beliefs. As a consequence, when reading a book such as this one, it is important to be mindful of the extent to which differences might exist for those who may be of another race, ethnicity, religion, or socioeconomic status than the target group of children about which a selection focuses. It would also be prudent to consider geographic locale—rural, urban, northeastern, southwestern—when considering the relevance of a given argument to a specific subgroup of children.

## Children in Contemporary Society

It is worth understanding children's points of view as they are molded by society. It can be astonishing to take a step back and observe children as they undergo the socialization process in contemporary society. They come into the world totally helpless, unable to feed, care for, or protect themselves. As they grow and develop, children undertake the process of acquiring a sense of identity and learning the rules of the society in which they live. This process of socialization is fostered by many of the subsystems of society that provide prescriptions for behavior in particular areas of life. These subsystems include the family, the peer group, the school system, religion, and the media.

One important consideration is that up to about age five, children are oblivious to most racial, ethnic, religious, or socioeconomic differences. Typically, children can only realize differences in external appearance. One implication of this fact is that children can be much more amenable to learning and embracing a variety of cultural behaviors, attitudes, and even languages when they are young. Only as children move into middle childhood do they begin to recognize and understand other, more subtle differences. It is important to note that although young children may be oblivious to these differences, they are nonetheless impacted by them in the way they are socialized by their parents, families, and the significant others in their lives. This is done through family rituals, traditions, and outings; religious ceremonies; types of food prepared in the home; location where children live; and things that are found in the home, such as books, magazines, music, and so on.

Societal influences on children do not stop within the family system. As children grow, other institutions in society, such as schools, the economy, politics, and religion, expand their life experiences. Controversy arises as to how children react to these experiences. Consider, for example, what happens to children when both parents are employed outside the home. There are factions in our society who adamantly ascribe many of the problems associated with children to the fact that many parents are overly involved with work at the expense of time with their children. They contend that one parent (usually the mother) should stay home with the children, especially when they are young. Children who care for themselves after school and the quality of after-school child care are also hotly contested, related issues.

Few readers of this book will be unfamiliar with the attacks on the mass media for its portrayal of violence in movies, television programming, and video games targeted at children. Again, researchers, clinicians, teachers, policymakers, and others fall on both sides of what should be done to address this.

As children move toward adolescence and become more independent, concerns regarding identity, values, morals, and sexual behavior become issues of controversy. Homosexuality, for example, which often is first evidenced by a person in adolescence, is considered by many to be a learned and abhorrent form of sexual expression. Others believe that there are people who are predisposed to homosexuality for reasons that are as yet unclear.

Events in contemporary society have a direct or indirect impact on children, despite attempts to protect them. Violence, inflation, war, poverty, AIDS, racism, and new technology are just a few of the phenomena that shape the society in which our children are socialized.

## Researching Children

In finding answers to controversial topics, policymakers and the public alike often look to research literature for clues. The typical college student might think of researching a topic as going to the library or logging onto the Internet and looking up information on a subject, reading that information, formulating a conclusion or opinion about the topic, and writing a paper that conveys the student's findings. This is not the type of research about which we are referring!

The type of research that we refer to here is called empirical research. This means that there is some question or group of interrelated questions to be answered about a topic. Data are then collected relative to the topic, which typically sheds light on how one goes about answering the question.

Data collection in research on children is undertaken from a variety of approaches. It could entail things like observing children at play in preschool or interacting with their parents at home. This is called observing children in a natural setting. With this method, observers must code behavior in the same way each and every time it is seen. Most of the information we have today on physical growth and developmental stages was acquired through observation by child development pioneers such as Arnold Gessell and Louise Bates Ames. You can imagine how time-consuming this form of study must be.

Another type of data collection is called an experiment. Experimental researchers systematically control how certain things happen in a situation and then observe the results. In this type of research, an experimental group and a control group are chosen. Both groups are examined to determine that they are the same before the experiment begins. The experimental group then receives some kind of treatment, while the control group receives no treatment. Then tests are conducted to see what kind of change, if any, has occurred between the two groups.

Interviewing children with a structured set of questions or giving children a structured questionnaire on a given research topic are other ways of collecting data. Projective techniques, where children might reveal their first thoughts about a picture or word, is also a form of the interview method.

The study of children can be organized in a variety of ways. One is by stages. The parts of this book (infancy, early childhood, middle childhood, and adolescence) are one type of stage organization. Another way to organize research endeavors is by topics. Topics are usually organized within the context of social, emotional, intellectual, physical, creative, and even spiritual aspects of development.

The time frames used to gather data on children also varies. In longitudinal data collection, information is collected from the same subjects over a long period of time. For example, one could examine the effects of preschool education on performance in elementary school by following and testing the same children during the preschool years and all the way through the elementary years. Because this type of research can take years to complete, a shorter method, cross-sectional research, could be used. In the previous example, one group of preschoolers would be compared to a similar group of elementary school children in order to answer the research question.

There are ethical considerations in studying children that some other disciplines may not face. Children should never be manipulated or put in danger in designing an experiment to answer research questions. Similarly, experiments that would not be in a child's best interests should not be conducted. Studies of abuse and neglect, for example, rely on retrospective techniques in which children who have already been abused report what has previously happened to them. No ethical researcher would ever put children at risk in order to observe the effects of abuse on children. Because of these ethical constraints, it can be frustrating for a researcher to fully answer questions raised in a research project. Additionally, it may take years to demonstrate the effectiveness of intervention for a particular social problem. Consequently, research on children and resultant intervention initiatives rarely offer "quick fixes" to the problems of children and society.

## Future Directions

The study of children in society can begin to offer solutions to many of the more pressing societal problems. Quality child care, parenting skills education, stress reduction, affordable housing, job training, and humane political policies are a few ideas for solutions to some of the controversies that will be raised in this book.

The imbalance between work and family in the United States has created problems in the economy as well as in the family system. Workers are expected to produce quality goods and services but they receive little social support in raising their families. Employers must acknowledge the strain that workers feel as they are pulled between work and family responsibilities. Health insurance, family-friendly work policies, flexible work schedules, parental and dependent care leave, exercise facilities, quality child care and sick child care, on-site or nearby one-stop service centers with post offices, grocery stores, and dry cleaners would be ways of providing support for families in the workplace.

Schools contribute to the problems of child-care arrangements by keeping to an antiquated schedule that was first developed to meet the needs of the farm family. Years ago, schools were let out in the early afternoon and all summer so that children could help with the crops, livestock, and other farm-related chores before sunset. However, ours has been a predominantly industrial society for a large part of the twentieth century and into the twenty-first century. As a result, a different type of schedule is required. Many concerned families advocate activities for children after school and schools that are open all year long to match the schedules of workers. The economy has changed and families have changed; why have educational institutions remained static?

The majority of children somehow manage to grow and develop successfully in a variety of family forms, but the stressors on all families are constantly increasing, which may, in turn, decrease the likelihood of continued success. Parents worry that the cost of a college education will be more than they can afford; parents worry about their children and AIDS, violence, and drugs; parents are concerned that in adulthood their children will not be able to live as well as they have lived. Families need emotional support, and parents need opportunities to learn stress management and parenting skills.

Society can promote the optimal growth and development of its children by taking responsibility for them. There is an old saying, "It takes a village to raise a child." Our society can raise its children by establishing policies in schools, workplaces, and other institutions that reflect the importance of nurturing children.

# On the Internet . . .

## Families and Work Institute

This Web site provides resources from the Families and Work Institute, which conducts policy research on issues related to the changing workforce and operates a national clearinghouse on work and family life.

http://www.familiesandworkinst.org

## Babyworld

Babyworld provides extensive information on caring for infants. There are also links to numerous related sites.

http://www.babyworld.co.uk

## The National Parent Information Network (NPIN)

The National Parent Information Network contains resources related to many of the controversial issues faced by parents raising children in contemporary society. In addition to articles and resources, discussion groups are available.

http://npin.org

## Zero to Three: National Center for Infants, Toddlers, and Families

Zero to Three: National Center for Infants, Toddlers, and Families is a national organization dedicated solely to infants, toddlers, and their families. It is headed by recognized experts in the field and provides technical assistance to communities, states, and the federal government. The site provides information that the organization gathers and disseminates through its publications.

http://www.zerotothree.org

## National Center for Health Statistics (NCHS)

This Web site provides access to National Center for Health Statistics (NCHS) information, including what's new, products, data warehouse, news releases, and fact sheets.

http://www.cdc.gov/nchswww/

## American Academy of Pediatrics (AAP)

The American Academy of Pediatrics (AAP) and its member pediatricians dedicate their efforts and resources to the health, safety, and well-being of infants, children, adolescents, and young adults.

http://www.aap.org

# PART 1

# Infancy

*Infancy and toddlerhood encompass the time period from birth to age two or three. During this time, the most dramatic growth of a child's life takes place. Traditionally, much of the literature on infancy has dealt with the physical aspects of development; more recently, however, researchers, practitioners, and policymakers have begun to be concerned with the interaction of brain development on later learning and the social and emotional aspects of the infant's development. The issues examined in this section focus on how the family and social institutions influence children's development from the time they are born.*

- Is Institutional Child Care Beneficial to Children?
- Does Maternal Employment Have a Negative Effect on Infant Development?
- Should Hospitals Continue Early Discharge Policies for Newborns?
- Does Transracial Adoption Harm a Child's Development?

# ISSUE 1

## Is Institutional Child Care Beneficial to Children?

**YES: Greg Parks**, from "The High/Scope Perry Preschool Project," *Juvenile Justice Bulletin* (October 2000)

**NO: T. Berry Brazelton and Stanley I. Greenspan**, from *The Irreducible Needs of Children: What Every Child Must Have to Grow, Learn, and Flourish* (Perseus Publishing, 2000)

### ISSUE SUMMARY

**YES:** Greg Parks, an intern program specialist at the Office of Juvenile Justice and Delinquency Prevention, details the results of the Perry Preschool Project. Parks contends that evaluations of the program show significant benefits in adulthood for the children who attended the preschool.

**NO:** Pediatrician T. Berry Brazelton and Stanley I. Greenspan, clinical professor of psychiatry and pediatrics at George Washington University Medical School, question the practice by many families of placing their children into the institutional settings of child-care centers.

Increasingly, parents are placing their children in some kind of child care during the day so that they are free to work to support the family economically. This is true not only for single parents but also for parents in a two-parent household who must work in order to live even modestly. In the past, the majority of children in child care were cared for in a family setting by a relative or a home day care with a few children. Today, many families have no relatives close by to whom they can turn for help. In addition, mothers used to take as much time as possible after the birth of a baby to stay at home during a large part of the child's infancy. Things have changed; many women return to work within six weeks of giving birth and, when faced with choices for child care, find that they must place their infant in an institutional or chain-type day care facility.

These day care centers usually serve children of varying ages, from infancy to four or five years of age, and often have after-school programs for elementary school children. These centers often have many rooms and are housed in a large building with as many as 20 caregivers. Child-caregivers must meet licensing standards, but because of the low pay and no benefits, the child-care industry is plagued with a high turnover rate. Thus, caregivers might change many times during a child's stay, depending upon the center's pay structure and the administration's philosophy of quality care. These types of centers look somewhat institutional because of their large building size, numerous rooms, and large number of personnel. Many object to the institutional-type child-care centers because they do not have the home-type atmosphere that one usually associates with the care of very young children.

What is a parent to do? Parents must work to support their families, and they must find a safe place to leave their children. Is a large institutional-like setting appropriate for infants and toddlers who need the security of a close, warm environment? Will these young children be harmed by having several caregivers within a week, or is institutional child care the best environment for children? This is the dilemma discussed in the following two selections. T. Berry Brazelton and Stanley I. Greenspan, long respected in the world of child development, voice their concerns about America's youngest children being enrolled in day care at an alarmingly high rate. In contrast, the Perry Preschool Project results, which are detailed by Greg Parks, indicate that child care is beneficial for children. Longitudinal data from the Perry Preschool Project spans over 40 years and shows the program to have been beneficial for the children who attended the center.

**Greg Parks**

# The High/Scope Perry Preschool Project

The Office of Juvenile Justice and Delinquency Prevention (OJJDP) recently published *Costs and Benefits of Early Childhood Intervention* (Greenwood, 1999), a Fact Sheet reviewing the benefits of early childhood intervention in the prevention of later delinquency. Among the most notable and longstanding secondary prevention programs considered was the High/Scope Perry Preschool Project of Ypsilanti, MI.[1] This [selection] examines this successful program model, which demonstrates a potential link between early childhood intervention and delinquency prevention.

The High/Scope Perry Preschool Project is a well-established early childhood intervention that has been in operation for almost 40 years. A review of the program's findings is useful at this time in light of the field's growing knowledge of risk factors associated with juvenile delinquency, including early childhood risk factors that may be diminished by secondary prevention programs targeted at high-risk populations. Juvenile justice research has made great strides in identifying risk factors that may be precursors to delinquency. Although the problem of delinquency increases with the number of risk factors, specific risk factors appear to vary according to a child's stage of development and may be reduced with appropriate preventive measures. These developmental differences for risk factors indicate the need for targeted interventions that address specific age-related factors (Wasserman and Miller, 1998). Given this link between early risk factors and later delinquency, it is important for practitioners to plan intervention programs for high-risk youth early in a youth's life so that he or she can develop a strong foundation for later development.

## Background

The High/Scope Perry Preschool Project, which began in 1962, is the focus of an ongoing longitudinal study—conducted by the High/Scope Educational Research Foundation—of 123 high-risk African American children.[2] Participants were of low socioeconomic status, had low IQ scores (between 70 and 85, the range for borderline mental impairment) with no organic deficiencies (i.e., biologically based mental impairment), and were at high risk of failing school. Fifty-eight of these 3- and 4-year-old children were assigned to the program

From Greg Parks, "The High/Scope Perry Preschool Project," *Juvenile Justice Bulletin,* a publication of The Office of Juvenile Justice and Delinquency Prevention (October 2000). References omitted.

group, and 65 of these children were assigned to a control group that did not go through the program. The groups were matched according to age, IQ, socioeconomic status, and gender. There were no differences between the groups with regard to father absence, parent education level, family size, household density, or birth order. Researchers collected followup data annually when the children were between ages 4 and 11 and at ages 14, 15, and 19 and collected age 27 data from 1986 to 1991 (Schweinhart, Barnes, and Weikart, 1993; Schweinhart and Weikart, 1995).[3]

The High/Scope Perry Preschool Project's high-quality educational approach is based on an active learning model that emphasizes participants' intellectual and social development. Children attended the preschool Monday through Friday for 2.5 hours per day over a 2-year period. During that same period, a staff-to-child ratio of one adult for every five or six children enabled teachers to visit each child's family in their home for 1.5 hours each week. In addition, parents participated in monthly small group meetings with other parents, facilitated by program staff.

Although it was initiated as an educational intervention, the High/Scope Perry Preschool Project has demonstrated a number of other positive outcomes, including a significantly lower rate of crime and delinquency and lower incidence of teenage pregnancy and welfare dependency. Overall, the program group has demonstrated significantly higher rates of prosocial behavior, academic achievement, employment, income, and family stability as compared with the control group. The success of this and similar programs demonstrates intervention and delinquency prevention in terms of both social outcome and cost-effectiveness and has a number of useful implications for policy, practice, and ongoing research. This Bulletin reviews the program outcomes, describes the early childhood risk factors that can be targeted with intervention, and explores the relationship between program components and risk factors.

## Program Outcomes

Outcomes of the High/Scope Perry Preschool longitudinal study can be divided into three major categories: social responsibility, scholastic success, and socioeconomic success (Schweinhart et al., 1985). Social responsibility variables include delinquency, marital status, and pregnancy. Scholastic success is determined by a number of factors including graduation rate, grade point average, and postsecondary education, whereas socioeconomic success is measured in terms of employment, earnings, and welfare assistance. Cost-benefit is included as an additional outcome because of the long-term savings to society as a result of program success.

### Social Responsibility

**Delinquency** Data collected from police and court records show that juvenile delinquency was significantly lower for the High/Scope Perry Preschool program group as compared with the control group, including fewer arrests and fewer juvenile court petitions (Schweinhart, Barnes, and Weikart, 1993;

Schweinhart and Weikart, 1995). Only 31 percent of the program group had ever been arrested, compared with 51 percent of the control group. In addition to police and court records, data collected from respondents at age 19 were used as an overall indicator of delinquency. When study participants were 19 years old, researchers found significant differences between the program and control groups. The program group had fewer arrests overall than the control group (averages of 1.3 versus 2.3 arrests per person), fewer felony arrests (averages of 0.7 versus 2.0 arrests per person), and fewer juvenile court petitions filed (averages of 0.2 versus 0.4 petitions per person).

Like the criminal record data, a misconduct scale based on teacher-report data and self-report data from the 19-year-old respondents demonstrates a significant difference between the program and control groups, as reflected by the following results for the program group:

- Lower overall scores for total misconduct and serious misconduct at ages 15 and 19.
- Lower incidence of fighting and other violent behavior.
- Lower incidence of property damage.
- Fewer police contacts.

Data collected from respondents at age 27 indicate significant differences between the program group and control group for adult arrests: the control group underwent more than twice as many arrests as the program group (averages of 4.0 versus 1.8 arrests per person). Thirty-six percent of the control group accounted for 98 felony arrests between ages 19 and 27, while 27 percent of the program group accounted for 40 felony arrests during the same period. Thirty-five percent of the control group were considered frequent offenders (defined as five or more arrests), compared with only 7 percent of the program group. In addition, 25 percent of the control group had been arrested for drug-related offenses, versus 7 percent of the program group. The control group also averaged more months on probation (6.6 versus 3.2 months) and had more than twice as many of its members placed on probation or parole for longer than 18 months (20 percent versus 9 percent).

**Marital status and pregnancy** Marital status among the males was the same for both groups, with 26 percent married at age 27, although program group males, on average, had been married for a longer period (6.2 versus 3.3 years). Marital status among the females differed significantly, with 40 percent of program group females married, compared with 8 percent of the control group females. Although fewer females in the program group were parents (64 percent versus 75 percent), significantly more of them were married, cohabiting parents (28 percent versus 8 percent). Fifty-seven percent of mothers in the program group gave birth out of wedlock, compared with 83 percent of mothers in the control group. In measures related to family stability, the program group scored significantly higher on a measure of closeness to family and friends (66 percent versus 48 percent) and the ability to maintain persistence at tasks (i.e., work or study hard all day) (47 percent versus 33 percent).

## Scholastic Success

Participants in the High/Scope Perry Preschool study were characterized by better academic performance than those in the control group, as measured by higher graduation rates, better grades, higher standardized test scores, and fewer instances of placement in special education classes. In addition, the program group spent more time on homework and demonstrated more positive attitudes toward school at ages 15 and 19. More parents of program group members had positive attitudes regarding their children's educational experiences and were hopeful that their children would obtain college degrees. The program group demonstrated significant academic differences in the following areas:

- **Special education for mental impairment.** Only 15 percent of the program group had been placed in special education programs for mental impairment, compared with 34 percent of the control group.
- **Test scores.** Each year from ages 7 to 14, the mean achievement test scores of the program group were noticeably higher than those of the control group (an average difference of 16 percent). The difference in the final achievement test scores of the two groups at age 14 was particularly significant: the program group's scores were 29 percent higher than those of the control group.
- **Grade point average.** The mean high school grade point average of the program group was higher than that of the control group (2.09 versus 1.68).
- **Graduation from high school.** Seventy-one percent of the program group graduated from high school, compared with 54 percent of the control group. The difference was largely accounted for by graduation rates among females (84 percent and 35 percent, respectively).

## Socioeconomic Success

Data collected at ages 19 and 27 indicate that the program group has been more successful socioeconomically than the control group. The data for age 19 reveal that significantly more program group members were employed (50 percent versus 32 percent) and self-reporting (45 percent versus 25 percent). These data also reflect that fewer program group members received welfare assistance (18 percent versus 32 percent). The data for age 27 reveal a continuation of significant economic differences characterized by more economic stability among the program group members, as measured by the following indicators:

- **Public assistance.** Fifteen percent of the program group were receiving public assistance, versus 32 percent of the control group.
- **Monthly earnings.** Twenty-nine percent of the program group had monthly earnings of $2,000 or more, versus 7 percent of the control group (36 percent versus 11 percent, respectively, when comparing only employed members in each group).

- **Household earnings.** When the income of the spouses of the study participants was taken into account, 47 percent of the program group had household income earnings of $3,000 or more per month, versus 17 percent of the control group.
- **Home ownership.** Thirty-six percent of the program group owned a home, versus 13 percent of the control group.
- **Automobile ownership.** Thirty percent of the program group owned a second car, versus 13 percent of the control group.

## Cost-Benefit Analysis

A cost-benefit analysis of the High/Scope Perry Preschool study indicates a savings to the public of more than seven times the initial investment per child, with a return of $7.16 for every dollar spent (Barnett, 1983). When adjusted for inflation and a 3-percent discount rate, the investment in early childhood prevention resulted in a taxpayer return of $88,433 per child from the following sources:

- Savings in welfare assistance (prior to welfare reform).
- Savings in special education.
- Savings to the criminal justice system.
- Savings to crime victims.
- Increased tax revenue from higher earnings.

An independent reanalysis is provided in a recent RAND Corporation report (Karoly et al., 1998). This report found that eliminating the largest and least reliable savings category (savings to crime victims) still left a return of more than twice the initial investment. Savings to crime victims make up 65 percent of the total investment return in the earlier analysis (Barnett, 1993). Although victim savings should be considered a significant outcome and societal benefit of early childhood intervention, this factor is also distinct from the other factors that can be estimated based on direct governmental costs and savings. With victim savings factored out of the analysis, the largest savings category is in criminal justice costs (40 percent), followed by increased taxable revenue (26 percent), reduced educational services (25 percent), and reduced welfare costs (9 percent).

# Early Childhood Risk Factors for Delinquency

An understanding of early childhood risk factors for delinquency is helpful to interpreting the success of the High/Scope Perry Preschool Project. One factor identified with risk for delinquency is poor language skills. (Stattin and Klackenberg-Larsson, 1993). As a component of overall mental development, language functions as an indicator of later intelligence and is a critical factor in the relationship between intelligence and delinquency. Additional early risk factors include poor attachment to caregivers (Egeland and Farber, 1984; Shaw and Bell, 1993), poor parenting skills (Hawkins et al., 1998; Loeber and Stouthamer-Loeber, 1986), and multiple family stressors (Fergusson and Lynskey, 1996; Shaw et al., 1998). These risk factors may not only directly affect delinquency but may also indirectly influence other factors that interact with delinquency, such as school- and community-related risk factors.

As demonstrated in the Prenatal and Early Childhood Nurse Home Visitation Program supported by OJJDP (Olds, Hill, and Rumsey, 1998), prenatal and early postnatal prevention are shown to reduce risk factors that contribute to the development of antisocial behavior in childhood. Early childhood intervention during the preschool years also offers an opportunity to halt the developmental trajectory toward delinquency and related behavioral disorders. Family support services help develop parenting skills, attachment, and coping mechanisms that have a positive effect on family stressors. A multicomponent approach to enhancing child development promotes protective factors and reduces risk factors by addressing the many systems and influences that affect a child's development.

## Program Components and Related Risk Factors for Delinquency

The components of the High/Scope Perry Preschool Project affect a number of the early childhood risk factors associated with later delinquency and other behavioral problems. In addition to directly reinforcing early developmental processes in the educational setting, the program strengthens positive parenting skills.

The High/Scope Educational Research Foundation explains the effectiveness of the High/Scope Perry Preschool model in terms of empowerment, which includes developing skills for success by enabling children to be active and independent learners, helping parents to support the development of their children, and providing teachers with effective training and support (Schweinhart and Weikart, 1995).

Because an ongoing home-school relationship enhances socialization, involving parents early in the educational process is critical to the later success of participants in an early childhood intervention such as High/Scope Perry Preschool (Seitz, 1990). Weekly home visits by teachers and regular parent group meetings promote the strengthening of parent-child relationships and increase parent involvement in the educational process. A more recent OJJDP longitudinal study, the Rochester Youth Development Study (Thornberry et al., 1998), confirmed a significant relationship between parents' involvement in their children's lives and reduced delinquency.

In addition to enhancing parent attachment, parent involvement, and parenting skills, early childhood intervention aimed at both parents and children influences a child's attachment to school and later commitment to school success (Thornberry et al., 1998). Findings from the Rochester study confirm earlier research linking poor school attachment, commitment, and achievement to delinquent behavior and drug use (Krohn et al., 1995; Smith et al., 1995). Another OJJDP study, the Seattle Social Development Project (Hill et al., 1999), found that a lack of success in elementary school was linked to later gang membership. Even in the midst of multiple other factors placing youth at high risk for delinquency, school success (as indicated by higher standardized test scores, school commitment, attachment to teachers, college aspirations, and parent expectations) appears to be a protective factor against delinquency (Smith et al., 1995). Academic achievement outcomes of the High/Scope Perry Preschool study indicate that the program group was more successful than the control group in school-related factors that appear to protect against delinquency.

The positive outcomes of the High/Scope Perry Preschool study are the result of a cumulative effect that begins with increased school readiness (Berrueta-Clement et al., 1987; Zigler, Taussig, and Black, 1992). School readiness results in positive reinforcement from teachers in the early grades followed by enhanced academic performance in subsequent grades and an overall stronger commitment to school. A correlational analysis of the High/Scope Perry Preschool data reveals a strong association between school motivation in the early years and literacy scores at age 19 (Schweinhart, Barnes, and Weikart, 1993). School motivation is also higher correlated with the highest year of schooling completed, which is associated with higher monthly earnings in adulthood and fewer lifetime arrests.

## Program and Policy Implications

The outcomes of the High/Scope Perry Preschool study demonstrate the value of prevention and early intervention efforts in promoting protective factors that reduce delinquency. The program was developed for high-risk children who stood to benefit the most from such an intervention. The intervention also affected multiple risk factors and was carried out in multiple domains (i.e., home and school). In an extensive review of early childhood interventions, Yoshikawa (1995) concluded that the combination of an early educational component with family support, as exemplified by the High/Scope Perry Preschool Project, is a determining factor in long-term effects on antisocial behavior. Other combination programs that have demonstrated long-term effects on delinquency include the Yale Child Welfare Project (Seitz and Apfel, 1994), Houston Parent Child Development Center (Johnson and Walker, 1987), and Syracuse Family Development Research Program (Lally, Mangione, and Honig, 1988). Single-component models, such as those that address only educational factors, have not been shown to demonstrate significant results.

In addition to the need to target appropriate populations and address multiple risk factors in multiple domains, program quality is essential to success. The High/Scope Perry Preschool model is based on a high-quality educational approach that assumes a low staff-to-child ratio, an active learning curriculum, and a home visitation component that engages parents in the educational process. Furthermore, teachers are well educated, adequately compensated, and well supported in their tasks.

Head Start, perhaps the largest and best-known early childhood intervention program, has recently made efforts to expand and improve its effectiveness by emphasizing family support, staff training, and performance standards (U.S. Department of Health and Human Services, 1999). The 1994 legislation reauthorizing Head Start incorporated a number of recommendations from the Advisory Committee on Head Start Quality and Expansion (1993), including increased parent involvement, a lower staff-to-child ratio, and increased mental health services.[4] Head Start has increased the emphasis on curriculum and child outcomes as a result of this reauthorization and has formed Head Start Quality Research Centers to respond to the need for additional research in the area of early childhood intervention. Further research is clearly needed to build on the limited existing knowledge base and assess the effectiveness of programs across various demographic groups, risk factors, and co-occurring factors that are related to delinquency, such as mental health issues and substance abuse (Yoshikawa, 1995).

Although the High/Scope Perry Preschool study's sample size was small in proportion to its eventual influence, its strong experimental design has contributed to its prominence in the field of early childhood education. Subsequent early childhood research that is carefully controlled and longitudinal in design remains limited. The limited research involving similar models that combine educational and family support components, however, supports the positive outcomes of the High/Scope Perry Preschool model. Subsequent independent evaluations of the programs that have implemented the High/Scope model have rated those programs significantly higher than comparison programs, with 58 percent of High/Scope programs versus 40 percent of comparison programs being rated as high quality (Epstein, 1993). In addition, 72 percent of children in High/Scope programs versus 57 percent of children in comparison programs scored high on measures of emotional, social, cognitive, and motor development.

Some targeted, multicomponent early childhood interventions have been demonstrated to exceed their costs in eventual savings and benefit to the public. However, implementing an effective prevention strategy requires a commitment to provide empirically based quality programming and to invest the up-front resources that will result in long-term savings and positive social change in the lives of children and families. The High/Scope Perry Preschool Project provides one such model for early childhood intervention that has proven successful when executed with quality and commitment to long-term results. The complexity of juvenile delinquency requires multiple strategies that address the problem at various stages of development; early childhood intervention is one promising component in the context of a more comprehensive approach, as recommended in OJJDP's *Comprehensive Strategy for Serious, Violent, and Chronic Juvenile Offenders* (Wilson and Howell, 1993). The High/Scope Perry Preschool model is worthy of consideration as an effective early childhood intervention as communities attempt to implement a comprehensive strategy that includes prevention, intervention, and graduated sanctions (Howell, 1995; Wilson and Howell, 1993).

## Notes

1. Unlike primary prevention programs, which are directed at the general population, secondary prevention programs target children at risk for school failure or delinquency.
2. The original Perry Preschool no longer exists, but the High/Scope Educational Research Foundation–founded in 1970 by Perry Preschool researcher David Weikart –continues to collect followup data from the participants of the 1962 study. The foundation is an independent organization dedicated to nonprofit research, development, training, and public advocacy. Its principal goals are to promote the learning and development of children worldwide from infancy through adolescence and to support and train educators and parents as they help children learn. In a High/Scope program, students should learn through active involvement with materials, events, and ideas. The Foundation disseminates the High/Scope Preschool model worldwide.
3. Researchers are currently collecting followup data from the original program participants. Called the High/Scope Perry Preschool Midlife Study, researchers have already interviewed 30 of the 39- to 41-year-old participants. The interview emphasized health and the performance of the program participants' children. The researchers expect to complete the data collection by the end of 2001. This study is funded by the McCormick Tribune Foundation in Chicago, IL.
4. Head Start Act Amendments of 1994. Pub. L. No. 103-252, tit. 1 § 108, Stat. 624 (1994).

T. Berry Brazelton and
Stanley I. Greenspan

# The Irreducible Needs of Children

Children who are living with their biological parent or parents and are deprived of the ordinary experiences that would enable them to be warm, loving, and caring are often in families with multiple problems, such as mental illness or severe antisocial patterns in one or both parents. The children aren't provided opportunities for nurturance, interaction, or learning. Here, too, we see chaotic, impulsive, self-absorbed, aimless children with severe language, social, and emotional difficulties.

In reading this, one may sigh with a sense of relief thinking that in your community such patterns of multiple foster care placements or neglect and abuse are very rare. But there is another trend occurring, both in the United States and around the world—a new type of institutional care. This type of care is part of every community. Approximately 50 percent of young children are now reared for significant parts of the day by persons other than their biological parents. Here, we're not talking about after-school programs for school-aged children. We're talking about infants and toddlers in the first three years of life. From the 1970s through the 1990s, there has been a transformation of the attitudes of families towards raising their own children. During this time, there has been a huge increase in the number of families giving up the care of babies, toddlers, and preschoolers to others for 35 or more hours a week. In other words, large numbers of infants, toddlers, and preschoolers are spending the lion's share of their days in nonparental care.

More important than mere numbers are reports regarding the quality of this care. These are not encouraging. The most comprehensive study of the quality of day care reported that the vast majority of center-based care was not of high quality (over 85 percent was not of high quality for preschool children and over 90 percent was not of high quality for infants and toddlers). Similar reports have emerged around other non-parental child care arrangements, such as family day care. In addition, most states in the United States have very weak regulations governing care. New findings regarding daycare options for mothers on welfare are especially alarming. These "Wave 1 Findings" are from the Growing Up in Poverty Project 2000. These findings suggest that day care for

From T. Berry Brazelton and Stanley I. Greenspan, *The Irreducible Needs of Children: What Every Child Must Have to Grow, Learn, and Flourish* (Perseus Publishing, 2000).  Notes omitted.

such families is of very poor quality (eg. instances of toddlers wandering aimlessly about). The findings about overall lack of care suggest that quality of care is an important contributor to a child's development.

The day care debate gets confused however by focusing only on research reports that maintain it's the quality of care that counts, not whether children are in institutional day care or family day care or cared for by parents. The reports stress that the quality of nurturance, interaction, and sensitivity to the child's cues are what's associated with their development status. It is true, and makes common sense, that quality would be an important variable and certainly, as indicated above, there's no guarantee that biological parents will always provide good quality care. But, what tends to get obscured in these academic discussions is the fact that at present most nonparental care (as revealed in a number of studies, including the study that documented that quality counts) is not of high quality.

We do know that quality child care is essential to the optimal development of small children. In our present setup, as indicated above, only 10% or less of infants and toddlers have access to high quality day care. The rest wind up with care that anyone with real options would not trust. Nor do the parents of these children. When a parent must leave a small child in less than optimal child care, that parent is bound to grieve. The grieving can take many forms: denial, detachment from the child, and anger and/or depression at the workplace that demands the separation. If we want motivated workers we need to offer them optimal child care or flexible hours that permit parental sharing of care.

With over half the nation's children receiving one form or another of nonparental care, the question is whether we want to allow a type of care that is not providing children the needed nurturance and social and intellectual interaction. We have to ask whether this nurturance is possible in settings where caregivers are caring for four or more babies (and later six or more toddlers), are paid minimal wage, and given little training and little incentive to avoid staff turnover (among those who can get better jobs)....

Even when children are cared for at home for the first few years, there still are worrisome trends. There has been a shift towards more impersonal, rather than emotionally nurturing types of care-giving for infants, toddlers, preschoolers, and children. A recent report from the Kaiser Foundation revealed that on average, children are spending five to six hours a day in front of the TV or computer screen. During this time, children are not receiving nurturing warmth or age-appropriate social or intellectual interactions.

But this is just one sign of the movement towards impersonal care. Many families are overly scheduled. Both parents are working to make ends meet or to improve the family's economics, leaving little relaxed family time. Education is becoming more impersonal as it is, more technologically oriented, losing the personal touch. Families in their own relationships with one another are also moving towards more impersonal modes of communication. E-mails are replacing lunches together and time in front of the screen is replacing many other forms of personal interaction. Recreation as well as work is taking place in a more impersonal atmosphere, with less interaction among and within families.

One of us (S.I.G.) was recently struck by how pervasive this shift is towards impersonal modes of care. A visit within the same week to two very different settings attempting to provide nurturing care revealed some striking similarities in what might be called "institutional love."

In the first setting, a woman sat in the corner of the room looking at the floor. Around her crawled four babies who seemed to relate only to their own bodies and the objects they can see or touch. One of them got her hand caught in a toy. The woman went to her, pulled her hand free, said, "O.K." and then moved silently back to her chair. Another baby banged on his half-filled bottle of milk. The woman picked him up, put him stiffly on her lap and faced him towards the wall while the baby sucked down the rest of his milk. When the baby was finished, she put him back on the floor without a word. The room was quiet. There were no signs of the familiar gestures, sounds, and expressions that tie people together.

Was this an overwhelmed, economically disadvantaged mother in a worrisome family situation? Or an over-stressed home day care facility in a poor neighborhood? No, in fact this was a scene in an upper-middle class day care center for infants and toddlers. The woman was an aide earning the minimum wage. The director of the private, well-run, fully accredited center said, "She is the norm."

In another room in the same center, a smiling woman animatedly exchanged words, grunts, smiles, laughs, and gestures with five toddlers as they rolled trucks back and forth and giggled at one another. The children pointed at, crawled over, and made sounds at each other and the woman caring for them. Using subtle movements of hand, face, and voice she engaged all five toddlers at once.

"Who is she?" S.I.G. asked.

"Oh, she is the assistant director, substituting for one of the aides who is sick," replied the director.

"Is it possible to have more of the staff that cares directly for the babies show her warmth and interactive skills?" S.I.G. asked.

"Occasionally we have caregivers similar to her, but in general we don't and people with her skills quickly get to higher levels. We can't afford to pay someone like her to spend time with the infants," the director responded.

A few days later, in the second setting, S.I.G. saw similarly unresponsive aides sitting in their chairs. One was telling an elderly woman, "Sit down and stop babbling or you won't get your ice cream." In another room, six other elderly women were sitting and staring silently into space while two more aides sat behind their table looking bored and indifferent. A woman pleaded unsuccessfully for a back rub and later confessed, "I just need some human touch." Another woman brightened up when an aide talked to her and was unnecessarily thankful for the little conversation.

This setting is one of the city's best institutions for the elderly. Here, too, the food, cleanliness and medical care are excellent.

This is "institutional love." It is provided at either end of the lifespan for both the poor and the well-to-do, for those who, because of their age and helplessness, need to depend on others for their care. We all know what this kind of care is like. What we don't want to think about is that this care is what we are providing for those we love.

Surely, one may rationalize, with enough money we can have good services. In fact, in some workplaces parental involvement in on-site day care creates a sense of an extended family. "Cooperative" nursery schools benefit from parent participation. A compassionate head nurse in a home for the elderly may instill a personal touch. But, sadly, these are the exceptions. The irony is that if we as a society keep this up, in 80 years the current infants will be back in these impersonal surroundings and it will feel strangely familiar.

One of us (S.I.G.) has questioned whether we are creating a new view of human nature reflected in our impersonal child care policies and interaction patterns, a concrete, materialistic one. In this view, we are more concerned with the brain than the mind and with biology and genetics than experience....

## Ongoing Nurturing Relationships

### Day Care

***SIG:*** If parents have options and are able to provide high-quality care themselves, I find it best not to have infants or toddlers (in the first two years) in full-time, 30–40-plus-hour-a-week day care. Current research and my own clinical observations suggest that most day-care centers do not provide high-quality care. The quality of interaction between caregivers and babies is often less than optimal. Also, the current ratios of four babies per caregiver in the first year and six in the second year, coupled with high staff turnover, minimum wages, insufficient training, and the expectable change of caregivers each year, make it difficult to provide high-quality, ongoing, nurturing care in those early years.

The question is, are parents able to' shift back to caring for their babies and using day care less?

***TBB:*** I would prefer if day care for babies and toddlers weren't necessary, but I think that there is a large portion of the population right now who can't take the full-time care of their infants.

***SIG:*** Is one reason why parents can't do this a difference in the way people are growing up these days?

***TBB:*** Expectations are changing. It's like what is happening to marriage in a society where the divorce rate is going up to 50 percent. The expectations for marriage have changed. I think the same thing is happening to the way mothers perceive staying at home. In an earlier generation, most mothers were expected to stay at home, and it was easier for them to do so. Now we've changed that expectation entirely, and it's hard to reverse it.

***SIG:*** From the child's point of view, however, let's look at the first year of life in full-time day care—40 or more hours a week. How do you think babies develop relationships in this circumstance?

***TBB:*** Babies can make can make multiple attachments that are meaningful. Certainly I would hope that the parents come first and the baby makes secondary attachments to everybody else. I visited a day-care center recently at a time when all the mothers were there. After a while, only one mother was left and all the children gravitated to her. I turned to the very talented day-care people there and said, "They really seem to desert you, don't they?" They said, "When there's a mother here, we don't even exist." The children were already differentiating among caregivers. It doesn't even have to be their mother; it just has to be a mother.

***SIG:*** That's not so great. In a number of day-care centers, when the children are mobile, I see a lot of emotionally hungry children. Children come up to any new adult and hang on. Some of that reaching out for any mother is simply reaching out to anyone who will give them some attention. It's a little indiscriminate. We see that in institutions such as orphanages where there is emotional deprivation. A minute here and there of reciprocal interaction, sometimes around feeding or diapering, is not enough to provide the needed security and sense of being cared for.

If we are going to give parents flexible options, we need both to improve day care and to reduce the number of hours per week children spend in day-care situations.

***TBB:*** Again, I think it needs to be a case-by-case decision, weighing this or that, rather than simply telling people what to do. Some parents are better parents if there is an outlet for them. But we do need to provide the child with an optimal secondary caregiver.

***SIG:*** When I talk to college students, I often ask them how they see their lives in terms of having children. As they think about a career and getting married, are they taking into account child-rearing, as well as the demands of a profession? Are they engaged to a neurosurgeon or are they going to be neurosurgeons themselves? Are they planning on having several children? Having two neurosurgeons in the family along with four children may be more difficult and demanding than they can possibly imagine. On the other hand, if two people are getting married and both want careers, and one of them is a writer and the other a psychologist, they may have more control of their time. Each one could work two-thirds time or one could work halftime and they could get child care for the limited remaining hours. But a lot of these potential parents haven't thought this out. They want children and a good career and see no problem. What they're being led to believe now is that full-time day care in the first years of life is as good as if not better than what they can provide: "I'll have a baby, take a two month leave of absence, put the baby in day care, and I'll be a lawyer and my spouse will be a lawyer. We'll work until 8:00 at night. We'll pick up the baby, come home, and play for an hour." In families like this I see children not getting their basic needs for nurturing met.

***TBB:*** When I see a family like that I see a lot of grieving. That kind of treatment of the child is ignoring the child's interests to such an extent that there must be a lot of denial. Something is so painful that these parents have to hide behind defenses.

***SIG:*** But do we support this type of denial or help parents out of it? As new parents make their decisions early on, some parents intuitively plan for the flexibility to be home more; sometimes it's the mom and sometimes it's the dad who stays home. The parents who are more ambivalent and tend to use denial often look around for guidance. But they're getting a lot of misinformation. They're told it doesn't make a difference. If parents-to-be knew more about this need for a continuous, close relationship, they might plan more realistically. They would see how hard it is to have such relationships with two full-time jobs and full-time day care. If parents see the options, they could make choices. If they have a caregiver at home and pick well, they have a greater likelihood, if they can afford it, of having the same caregiver being with them for a number of years. In day care, by design, the caregivers change each year. Turnover is so great, though, that there may be another change or two changes even within one year. There may be three changes of caregivers by the time a baby has had a year of day care. Minimum wages, lack of training, and so on contribute to this. The caregiver in a day-care setting is not like a *meta peleth* in a kibbutz in Israel, who is a stable person in a child's life, with him for four or five years. It doesn't have to be the mother. It could be the father or the grandfather or grandmother. The child needs a caregiver in his or her life who's going to be there for the long haul.

***TBB:*** To improve day care, I see three babies per adult as the absolute maximum for the first year of life. But now the norm is four babies per caregiver. Imagine a mother with triplets and how hard it is for her to care for all three babies at the same time.

***SIG:*** Would you recommend, Berry, that a baby should keep the same caregivers for the first three or four years? One group of caregivers, for example, would follow a group of children who started as infants on up through their toddler years.

***TBB:*** This would work as long as the caregiver really liked each baby, but suppose she didn't like one? Couldn't it be moved to another caregiver's group? Caregivers and babies, like parents, could be evaluated for "goodness of fit" between them. Also, when you go up into the second and third years, and taking care of four children becomes possible, a fourth child will be added to the group of three. The fourth baby wouldn't necessarily get the same caregivers.

***SIG:*** The extra children in the group might come from outside, perhaps from home. To make this work, you'd have to have expanding entry into day care at the second and third years, with each class being larger than the last. More children are in day care by age three than in the first two years of life. Then we have to create incentives for the staff of day-care centers to stay on, giving better wages and training.

***TBB:*** We have to increase wages to a decent level, and we need to improve their status. At present, they are thought of as "baby-sitters" with some scorn.

***SIG:*** That's what we need to correct. We need to get across all that's involved in meaningful care of a child: creating ongoing dialogues, reflecting and accepting a variety of emotions. You can sometimes find people who are warm and nourishing and emotionally responsive, even though they haven't been given a chance to educate themselves. Sometimes you can find young people who want to get experience with children and who are naturally sensitive and flexible.

***TBB:*** Day-care staff need constant refueling. It's a demanding job, taking care of somebody else's children. If parents and day-care personnel could handle their natural, inevitable gatekeeping, parents could become peer "fuelers" of the day-care personnel. The team (of parents and child care worker) could share the child's optimal development.

***SIG:*** We need to see all this from the point of view of prevention. It's a public health issue.

***TBB:*** When Congress was talking about that $22 billion for improving child care, I got a chance to go down to Washington, and told them that if they just turn the money over to the states, it will all get eaten up. You'd do better to give the money to states tied to choices based on the quality child care that we know how to produce, and to let them pick their choices. When it came to laying out choices that will work for the child, they said, "Oh, we have to do some research." I told them there was already plenty of research. What we need now is just the will to put the research into practice. They asked if I could tell them what programs work. I said not by myself, but I certainly could gather a bunch of colleagues who could tell you which ones we guarantee would work.

State governments can eat up revenues for child care at the top, if we're not careful. The one sector that could make a real difference and could afford to, and might be motivated to if we were smart enough, would be big business. If we could get them to set up a center in every business site that would contain preventive health care, child care, after-school care, and elder care, then maybe we could begin to reach a lot of people. I don't think we need to use the schools for this, but Ed Zigler at Yale has a model he calls the "School of the 21st Century," in which all these caregiving situations are gathered into school buildings that are not in use and made into centers for families in their communities. In our Touchpoints model, we are recommending that parent centers be established in every community where parents could receive child care, preventive health care, after-school care, and elder care. Parent resource centers, such as Family Support America, could be established for peer resources. Parents could then begin to feel a sense of community around them.

Our Touchpoints model has been developed at Children's Hospital in Boston to train multidisciplinary representatives from communities that are ready for change in an outreach, relational model. We want to improve preventive health care and child care with several goals. At each visit of parents and child, the provider (child care or medical care) identifies the strengths versus the failures of the parent. The child's development is the language between professional and parent. The parent is valued as the expert in the child's development. In this way, the passion of the parent is fostered. The relationship is transactional versus top-down. Each visit becomes an opportunity for sharing the child's new achievements and encouraging the child's development, both physical and psychological. Twenty-five centers have espoused our ideas, and they are changing communities to become parent-friendly. Our goal is to offer preventive outreach for the present 40 percent of underserved. We do know what to do. Can we do it?...

## Relationships in Day Care

It is also important to consider now how these same principles can be applied to other contexts where children may find themselves such as family day care, makeshift baby-sitting arrangements, as well as institutional day care settings and care by relatives. These same standards for the nurturing care of children growing up in families apply to these other settings. In other words, a child in family day care or day care center should spend most of her time in facilitated activities or direct one-to-one interactions. However, in observations of day-care settings we found it rare that there were long interactive sequences between the caregivers and the babies.

Since it is so hard for caregivers to have long, nurturing interactions when caring for four or more babies (standard in most institutional day care), and because of the staff turnover that is characteristic of most institutional day-care settings, as well as the tendency to have staff change each year as children move from the infant room to the toddler room to the preschool room, we believe that in the first two years of life full-time day care is a difficult context in which to provide the ongoing, nurturing care by one or a few caregivers that the child requires. Part-time day care, on the other hand, may be quite helpful in giving mothers and fathers a chance to do other things and may not compromise either the security of ongoing nurturing care or the types of experiences we have described. But 35-plus hours a week for infants and toddlers makes it very difficult to have the consistency of caregiver and the depth of nurturance required, or the amount of facilitating interaction with the environment or direct interaction that we believe is healthy for infants and toddlers.

Because some families will need full-time day care in the early years, we must work to improve its quality. This means lower child/caregiver ratios, better training and salaries and maintaining the same caregiver from birth to roughly age 3. Although there is general agreement on the need to improve day care, improvements in the last 25 years have been modest. As we pointed out earlier, studies of the quality of available day care are not optimistic. We may be trying to rationalize a system that simply isn't providing the essentials of what children need. It may therefore be best to reconsider our assumptions. The best way these assumptions can be reconsidered is by each and every family having good and accurate information. With awareness we believe most will make a wise and enlightened choice.

## Recommendations

In making the recommendations that follow, we are both mindful of the fact that there are many circumstances where nonparental care may be highly desirable or absolutely necessary. Single parents working to put food on the table, even if able to provide high-quality care themselves, may have no choice but to use out-of-home child care for 40-plus hours a week. Here, the goal would be to find the best care available and to work with the child care providers as a team to provide integrated care for that baby or toddler. There may be families where there is emotional stress in individuals or family stress that makes it highly desirable to have 30-plus hours of care provided by others. On balance this will provide a much stronger support system for this particular baby or toddler. Each circumstance has to be weighed individually, and parents have to make wise and enlightened choices regarding their own particular situation.

### Continuous Relationships

- In the first three years, every child needs one or two primary caregivers who remain in a steady, intimate relationship with that child.
- During the infancy, toddler, and preschool years, children should always be in the sight of caregivers. There should be no time, other than when they are sleeping, that they are out of sight of caregivers.
- No more than one-third of infants', toddlers', and preschoolers' time should be spent in fully independent activities. The time that is spent in independent activities should be spent for 10 or 15 minutes here and there rather than a longer period in independent activities.
- The other two-thirds or longer time should be spent between two types of activities: those in which the caregiver facilitates interactions with the environment and direct interaction, such as cuddling, holding, shared pretend play, and funny face games. Infants and toddlers need at least four or more 20-minute or longer periods of direct interactive time. Preschoolers need at least three of these direct, interactive play opportunities. In a two-parent family, both parents should be part of these spontaneous, joyful games.
- During the facilitated time, caregivers are available to comment on, respond to, and help in the child's explorations, though also engaged in other activities, such as cooking or putting clothes in the washing machine. Some of this time a small child could be accompanying parents to the supermarket or being a junior chef. During the school years, when we consider available time, we are considering time minus schooltime, after school activities, and peer playtime. Here, too, we recommend that of the available time two-thirds be spent with the caregiver being available for facilitating or directly interacting. The "facilitating" time could be spent helping a child with homework, hobbies, or other activities. The times of direct involvement, which should include at least two 20-minute periods (each parent should participate where possible) might mean imaginative play, games or other activities in which the child can take the lead.

- We recommend that working parents both be available for at least two-thirds of the evening hours, from 5:30 or 6:00 to 9:00, and that, if possible, in addition, one of the parents be available in the late afternoon when the children are home, often playing with peers or siblings, or involved in after-school activities. Also, the parents should be available enough so that they or the children don't have to be measuring each moment of time and the guidelines outlined above can be taken for granted.

## Parental Leave

We recommend a leave of most of the first year of life for one parent.

## Day Care

- We do not recommend full-time day care, 30 or more hours of care by nonparents, for infants and toddlers *if* the parents are able to provide high-quality care themselves and *if* the parents have reasonable options. We also recommend improving day care considerably by lowering ratios, improving training and wages, and, for children in full-time day care, having the same caregiver remain with the infant she cares for for three to four years. Those families that require day care will then have options for higher-quality day care than is now the case.
- In the first three years, a primary caregiver should be assigned to each child and should remain the same from year to year.
- For the first year there should be no more than three babies to one adult.
- For the second year, there should be no more than four toddlers to one adult.
- For the third and fourth years, there should be no more than five to eight children to one adult.

## Group or Institutional Settings

- Various types of institutional arrangements, including children in group situations, need to follow the same guidelines outlined earlier for the family. Ongoing nurturing care with one or a few constant primary caregivers should include direct or "facilitated" interactions for at least two-thirds of the available time. In-service training, growing financial incentives with experience and training, and support structure to facilitate nurturing attitudes are all important components of satisfying this requirement for ongoing nurturing care in group or institutional settings.

# POSTSCRIPT

## Is Institutional Child Care Beneficial to Children?

The quality of child care appears to be one of the most important issues in the debate over whether or not to send young children to child-care centers. Low adult-child ratios, competent and caring caregivers, and clean and nurturing environments are what contribute to quality child care. Is this type of setting preferable over being at home with a parent who does not want to be there and who does nothing to stimulate a child intellectually or emotionally? Consider another alternative—poor quality child care, with multiple caregivers who have no training and no desire to work with young children in a dirty, nonstimulating environment. Contrast this scenario with a child's being at home with a parent who loves the child and provides educational materials and one-on-one interaction most of the day. These are the extremes to the question of how and where to best care for young children.

Another factor that confounds this argument is how much time and what quality of time parents who use day care spend with their children when they are at home. Mediocre out-of-home care can be mitigated by a stimulating home environment when children and parents are together. On the other hand, a poor, nonnurturing home environment, which could be devastating for a child's development, can be supplemented positively by a quality child-care experience.

An April 2001 release of the results from a longitudinal study by the National Institute of Child Health and Human Development, a federal agency that has been studying children in child-care settings for 10 years, made headlines and caused a furor in the child-care industry. Some conclusions of the study, many say, were taken out of context and sensationalized by the press. It was reported that children who attended day care were found to be more aggressive than their stay-at-home counterparts. In actuality, the level of aggression for day care children was still within the normal range of behavior. These kinds of misinterpretations and partial facts create confusion for parents who are just trying to do the best they can for their children. American society asks parents to work to support their families but then asks them to stay home to take care of their children. This dichotomy of thinking and expectations makes it difficult to feel good about any choice make related to child care.

# ISSUE 2

## Does Maternal Employment Have a Negative Effect on Infant Development?

**YES: Jay Belsky and David Eggebeen**, from "Early and Extensive Maternal Employment and Young Children's Socioemotional Development: Children of the National Longitudinal Survey of Youth," *Journal of Marriage and the Family* (November 1991)

**NO: K. Alison Clarke-Stewart**, from "A Home Is Not a School: The Effects of Child Care on Children's Development," *Journal of Social Issues* (vol. 47, no. 2, 1991)

### ISSUE SUMMARY

**YES:** Jay Belsky and David Eggebeen, both professors in the College of Health and Human Development at Pennsylvania State University, conclude that maternal employment during a child's infancy has detrimental effects on its social and behavioral development.

**NO:** K. Alison Clarke-Stewart, a professor of social ecology, argues that children who attend child-care centers are more socially and intellectually advanced than children who are cared for in the home by their mother or another caregiver.

As more women moved into the workforce in the 1960s, research on maternal employment and its effects on children became a popular topic of study. In the past several decades maternal employment has evolved from being studied as one factor that affects children to a more complex issue. It was once thought to have a direct influence on development; now researchers agree that maternal employment is more than just a question of whether or not the mother works. The issue must be studied within the context of the family system and must simultaneously answer questions such as, What quality of care does the child receive? How does the mother feel about her work? What societal and family support do the mother and child receive?

Researchers are divided on what variables to study, as well as what methods to use in studying maternal employment effects. For example, some combine several social classes to study the interactive effect of working mothers with type of child-care arrangements, whereas others examine only one social class and how it interacts with the mother's personality traits and family environment type.

The effects of maternal employment are determined by many factors, such as a mother's work satisfaction and morale, amount of work, and a mother's perception of quality verses quantity time with children. Depending on which study one reads, how the data were collected, and which combination of variables was studied, different conclusions are reported. For example, some research states that employed mothers spend more quality time with their children, whereas others show exactly the opposite, that nonemployed mothers spend more quality time with their children.

Research on maternal employment has become more sophisticated in recent years, yet the question still remains: Should mothers stay home with their babies? Often women will drop out of the workforce, for at least the first few years, to stay home and care for their children. The concept that an attachment to the mother in the first few years is critical to a child's later development may indeed have validity, according to some researchers. Conversely, other research suggests that quality child-care providers may be able to meet the same needs that mothers previously met.

In the following selections, Jay Belsky and David Eggebeen use the database from the National Longitudinal Survey of Youth to examine maternal employment in children's infancy and its effect on children's later development at four to six years of age. K. Alison Clarke-Stewart studies alternate forms of child care and their effects on child development, but her conclusions relate directly to the effects of maternal employment.

**Jay Belsky and David Eggebeen**

# Early and Extensive Maternal Employment and Young Children's Socioemotional Development

Dramatic changes took place in the United States in the 1980s in the timing of mothers' return to work, with increasing numbers of women returning to paid employment within a year of their infant's birth. The implications of this change for the care and development of children have been hotly debated in recent years. The purpose of the present investigation is to address some, though by no means all, features of what became known as the infant day care controversy (Fox and Fein, 1990).

Upon reviewing studies of maternal employment and of nonparental care involving infants, Belsky (1988, 1990a) concluded that children who experienced 20 or more hours per week of nonparental care in their first year of life of the kind routinely available in the United States (often proxied by extensive maternal employment) are at elevated risk of developing insecure attachments to their mothers (e.g., Belsky and Rovine, 1988; Jacobson and Wille, 1984; Vaughn, Gore, and Egeland, 1980) and of being more disobedient toward adults and aggressive toward peers as three- to eight-year-olds (e.g., Haskins, 1985; Rubenstein and Howes, 1983; Schwarz, Strickland, and Krolick, 1974) than other children. Vandell and Corasaniti (1990) sought to evaluate empirically Belsky's conclusion and extend research by focusing not simply upon the first year of life but on child-care experience *across* the preschool years. They discovered, in the course of analyses designed specifically to address the controversy stimulated by Belsky's (1988) review, that children who had initiated care for 30 or more hours per week in their first year and whose care at this level continued through their preschool years evinced poorer academic and social functioning than did children whose full-time care began sometime later—and that this was true whether one looked at teacher reports, parent reports, peer reports, or the children's own self-reports. Particularly interesting from the standpoint of the current inquiry were their related findings that in the case of many dependent measures of child functioning, children whose full-time care (30 hours per week) began in their second year often functioned just as poorly as those whose care was initiated in their first year.

From Jay Belsky and David Eggebeen, "Early and Extensive Maternal Employment and Young Children's Socioemotional Development: Children of the National Longitudinal Survey of Youth," *Journal of Marriage and the Family,* vol. 53 (November 1991). 

Critics of such findings have highlighted many limitations of the studies reviewed by Belsky (1988, 1990a) and thus of conclusions drawn by him. Especially important for the current investigation is the observation that effects attributed to early and extensive maternal employment and/or child care may be the result of selection factors. Because subjects are not randomly assigned to family and rearing conditions, it may be that certain families that rely upon particular rearing arrangements would, for example, raise insecure, aggressive, and disobedient offspring irrespective of their maternal employment or child-care situation. As a result of this cogent criticism, it is widely recognized that background differences between families need to be examined and, if necessary, controlled before comparisons are made of the development of children with varying child-care and maternal employment histories.

Many studies—and the conclusions that Belsky (1988, 1990a) drew on the basis of them—also have been criticized because they involve small samples of convenience. Thus, it remains unclear how representative the data base is and how generalizable are the findings derived from it. In light of this state of affairs, and the need for extensive background controls, it was judged that the National Longitudinal Survey of Youth represented a unique opportunity to examine the developmental correlates of early and extensive maternal employment/child care. This national sample is larger, more diverse, and more representative than any ever studied with a concern for socioemotional development and early and extensive maternal employment and child care. Moreover, the data base includes a wealth of background information on the child, the mother, and the family.

On the basis of the work summarized and the issues raised, we set out to create three discrete groups of four-, five-, and six-year-olds from the survey data base pertaining to the Children of the National Longitudinal Survey of Youth (Baker and Mott, 1989) so that they could be compared on the available indices of social and emotional functioning once confounding background factors were identified and statistically controlled. One group was to be of children whose mothers were employed, on average, for 30 or more hours per week in their first year and who continued paid employment in their second and third year; a second of children whose mothers did not begin employment on such a full-time basis until their second year and who continued such work through their third year; and the third of children whose mothers were not employed or employed on only a minimal basis (less than 10 hours per week) throughout their child's first three years of life. Thus, we chose to follow Vandell and Corasaniti's (1990) innovative lead by constructing multiyear patterns of maternal employment and child care, rather than focusing upon a single year. Further, we selected 30 hours per week as the marker of full-time maternal employment, not only because this was the cutoff that Vandell and Corasaniti used, but also because Belsky and Rovine (1988) found, in the only study of first-year maternal employment and child care to distinguish between extensive and full-time employment and care, that the rate of insecure infant-mother attachments was greater in households in which mothers worked 35 or more hours per week than in those in which they were employed between 20 and 35 hours per week. Finally, we chose to include a group of children whose mothers began full-time employment in their second year so we could test Vandell and Corasaniti's (1990) findings regarding full-time care initiated in the second year of life. It was anticipated that group differences in measures of adjustment would be most likely to emerge when the two early and extensive employment and care groups (full-time initiated in first or second year) were contrasted with the third group (no employment and minimal employment), though differences between the early and extensive care groups also were examined.

Like much research on maternal employment and child care, the current investigation is not without limitations. Perhaps most noteworthy is the absence of information pertaining to the quality of child care that children experience when the mother is employed. The fact that quality of nonmaternal care influences children's development makes this lacuna all the more serious (for reviews, see Belsky, 1984, 1990b; Phillips et al., 1987). Moreover, in the only study to date to examine *simultaneously* age of entry into full-time care and quality of care, Howes (1990) discovered that the effects of care of limited quality are most pronounced when care is initiated in the first year. This finding suggests that power to discern effects in the present investigation may be limited by the inability to examine timing of entry into care in the context of quality of care.

Although the NLSY data set does not permit examination of interactions between quality of care and timing of mother's return to work, the sample size and its racial and economic diversity do make possible evaluations of other notable interactions. In this inquiry we sought to determine whether the effects of early and extensive maternal employment and child care were moderated either by indices of family socioeconomic status or by child temperament. The focus upon socioeconomic moderators is based upon speculation that developmental costs may be associated with extensive maternal employment and child care in the case of children from economically advantaged families who "lose" time with their well-educated and highly skilled mothers, whereas developmental benefits may accrue to children from economically disadvantaged and/or single-parent families because of the much-needed financial resources that maternal employment brings to the family or to the enriched experiences that nonmaternal care might provide (Bronfenbrenner and Crouter, 1983; Lande, Scarr, and Gunzenhauser, 1989). The focus upon child temperament is based upon Kagan and colleagues' (1978) proposition that temperamentally shy, inhibited, and/or fearful children may find early child care particularly stressful and may be least able to cope with and thus benefit from early maternal employment.

## Data and Method

### The NLSY Sample

The data for this study are drawn from the National Longitudinal Survey of Labor Market Experience of Youth (NLSY). This survey is a national probability sample of 12,686 men and women who were aged 14 to 21 in 1979, and who have been interviewed annually since. Included in this sample is an oversample of black, Hispanic, and economically disadvantaged nonblack, non-Hispanic youths. The annual interviews have generated a wealth of information on employment, educational, and family-related experiences. The retention rate for this panel has been extremely good, with nearly 92% of the original respondents retained as of the 1986 interview and with little variation across subgroups (Baker and Mott, 1989).

As part of the 1986 interview, the 2,918 women in the sample who had become mothers were given supplemental questionnaires to gather information on maternal and child health, the home environment, family relationships, child's behavior and activities, and child-care histories. In addition, 4,971 children of these women (nearly 95% of the eligible children) were assessed. Trained interviewers gathered information on children's cognitive, social, emotional, and physiological development through maternal report, direct observation, and the use of standardized tests administered in the child's home. These data were then integrated with selected information from the eight years of data collected on their mothers to form a child-mother data set (Baker and Mott, 1989).

We have selected to sample from all white and black children from four to six years old ($n = 1{,}248$)....

## Child Outcome Measures

Available for investigation of four-to-six-year-olds in the NLSY were five measures of socioemotional functioning: compliance, inhibition, attachment insecurity, sociability, and behavior problems (see Baker and Mott, 1989, for extensive discussion of scale origins, construction, and psychometric properties)....

## Construction of Maternal Employment and Child Care Groups

Two sets of information pertinent to the timing and extent of maternal employment were available in the longitudinal data set that we planned to use to create discrete maternal employment/child care groups. One involved detailed information on the number of hours and weeks of employment mothers reported for each quarter of each year and the other involved a simple yes-no answer for each year of the child's life to the question of whether the child was "cared for in any regular arrangement such as a babysitter, relative, daycare center, nursery school, play group or some other *regular* arrangement" (emphasis in original).

... [E]mployment patterns... were reduced to three types (and a residual group) to reflect distinct family ecologies that might differ, according to the literature reviewed in the introduction, with respect to their impact on the developing child: (*a*) children whose mothers were classified as not working in each of their first three years of life (and who were presumed not to have received routine nonparental care); (*b*) children whose mothers were not classified as employed full-time in their first year, but who were so classified in their second and third year (and presumed not to have received routine nonmaternal care on a full-time basis in their first year but to have done so thereafter); (*c*) children whose mothers were classified as employed full-time in their first year and extensively thereafter (i.e., at minimum, part-time) (and presumed to have experienced routine nonmaternal care across their first three years); and (*d*) all other children....

## Background Factors

Three sets of background factors, reflecting child, mother, and household characteristics, were selected for consideration.

*Child characteristics.* ... A child's weight at birth was reported by the mother in the first interview after the birth....

*Mother characteristics.* Mother's age at the child's birth was coded into four categories (less than 20; 20–21, 22–23, and 24–26). Years of completed education by the first interview after the child's birth was represented by a three-level variable (less than high school, high school diploma, some college) for the descriptive analysis but was kept as a continuous measure in the multivariate models. Finally, marital status at the first interview after the birth of the child was coded to distinguish mothers who were never married, currently married with spouse present, or "other" (separated, divorced, widowed, spouse absent).

Mother's self-esteem was measured by a summary variable created from Rosenberg's (1965) 10-item self-esteem scale, which was administered to all the mothers in the 1980 NLSY main survey.... Mother's attitudes toward appropriate family roles were measured by responses to the question "Are traditional husband/wife roles best?" Answers were scored on a 4-point scale ranging from "strongly disagree" to "strongly agree." Mother's intellectual ability was measured by her score on the Armed Forces Qualification Test (AFQT), which was taken by all NLSY participants in 1980.... Mother's contribution to the family income was measured by taking mother's total income as a percentage of the total family income.... This was obtained two interview rounds before the birth of the child in order to avoid any confounds caused by reduced employment due to pregnancy and birth.

*Household and family characteristics.* The various indicators of household and family size (presence of grandparents, number of working adults, household size, urban or rural residence) were all obtained from the first interview after the child was born....

The two measures of economic resources (total family income and whether the family was below the poverty line) were obtained from the last interview before the child was born....

# Results

Before examining the relation between maternal employment and children's socioemotional development, it was necessary to determine which of the background maternal and family household factors as well as newborn characteristics varied across employment groups. Thus, in a series of preliminary analyses, the three groups were compared. In a subsequent series of regression analyses, we examined the relation between maternal employment during the first three years of the child's life and child functioning at four, five, or six years of age, after controlling for differences between maternal employment groups that emerged from the preceding analysis of the ecology of maternal employment.

## The Ecology of Early and Extended Maternal Employment

... With respect to child characteristics, no relation was discerned between maternal employment and infant gender, birth weight, and gestational age. Black children, however, were disproportionately likely to have mothers who did not work during their entire first three years of life; and firstborn children were more likely to have mothers who worked full-time in their first or second year of life than were later-born children. In both cases, though, the major differences were between children whose mothers were not employed at all and children whose mothers entered full-time employment in either their first or second year.

... Mothers who were not employed across the first three years of the child's life were most likely to have given birth to the child while teenagers, to have the fewest years of education, to have never been married at the child's birth, to have contributed the least to the family's income, to attend church more frequently, to have low self-esteem, to have scored the lowest on the measure of intelligence, and to have held the most traditional attitudes toward gender roles.

In light of these findings and others reported in the literature (e.g., Eggebeen, 1988), it should not be surprising to discover that the maternal employment groups also differed with respect to household composition and economic resources. As expected, mothers were less likely to be employed across the child's first three years when there were more people living in the household and when more working adults were present in the household. Maternal employment, however, was unrelated to the presence of a grandparent in the household. Finally, children living in rural areas were more likely to have a nonemployed mother.

With respect to economic factors,... children whose mothers were not employed in their first three years of life were disproportionately concentrated in the lowest income groups and significantly more likely to be in poverty, while children of mothers who initiated employment in the first year were more likely to be in the highest income brackets and the least likely to be in poverty.

## Maternal Employment and Socioemotional Development

The preceding analyses, consistent with other research, clearly indicate that maternal employment is not randomly assigned. As a result, selection effects plague virtually all efforts to illuminate the effects of maternal employment and child care upon child development. In order to address this problem, we sought to identify factors that covaried significantly with both maternal employment and the indices of socioemotional development (ADJUST, SHY), so that these could be statistically controlled in subsequent regression analyses. This would permit an assessment of the relation between maternal employment and child development that was relatively unconfounded with ecological and demographic factors.

Four variables were identified that covaried significantly with maternal employment and with at least one of the two socioemotional composite measures: child birth order (firstborn vs. later-born), maternal education (in years at time of child's birth), family poverty status (at time of birth), and maternal intelligence as indexed by the Armed Forces Qualification Test (AFQT).[1] In addition to these factors, child gender, age, and race were also added to the list of control variables so that interactions between these factors and maternal employment could be examined once the main effects of these factors were controlled.[2] . . .

## Discussion

Research during the past decade on early and extensive maternal employment and infant day care led Belsky (1988, 1990a) to call attention to developmental risks associated with more than 20 hours per week of nonparental care (as routinely available in the U.S.) initiated in the first year. This analysis of NLSY data was designed to address two specific criticisms of much previous work and to build upon Vandell and Corasaniti's (1990) empirical test of Belsky's conclusions.

By relying upon the NLSY data base, we sought to study a larger and more representative sample of young children than has been studied to date. Because the sample we subjected to empirical analysis consists of higher percentage of black, uneducated, young, and unmarried women than exists in the national population, however, we must exercise caution against generalizing the results of the study too broadly. Nevertheless, the fact that none of the discerned effects of early and extensive maternal employment were moderated by a host of demographic factors suggests, in this sample at least, that those effects are not restricted to some subset of subjects studied.

The NLSY data set also enabled us to control for a host of background factors that differed across maternal employment groups in an effort to control for selection effects. The fact that the variables we controlled reflect only a subset of all that could be controlled means, of course, that not every conceivable selection effect has been taken into account. This should caution us from concluding that truly causal effects have been discerned in regression analyses of the kind employed in this inquiry. However, when the analyses reported were rerun with controls for every single background variable . . . , the effects of early and extensive maternal employment remained statistically significant.

The design of the study built directly upon Vandell and Corasaniti's (1990) discovery that developmental outcomes that Belsky (1988, 1990a) found to be associated with more than 20 hours per week of nonparental care in the first year of life were often associated with full-time nonparental care that began in the second year. It was because the data reviewed by Belsky did not permit consideration of this timing-of-entry distinction, and because Vandell and Corasaniti (1990) discerned relations between child-care experience *across* the preschool years and the behavioral development of children in elementary school, that we chose to create a quasi-experimental design that identified children whose mothers began working full-time in their first year of life and in their second year of life. Throughout this work it has been our presumption that within the very first years of life, full-time maternal employment and reliance upon extensive nonmaternal care typically co-occur. While it is certainly the case that many four-year-olds in child-care programs for even 20 hours per week have mothers who are not employed, it is just as certainly the exception to find a mother working more than 30 hours per week in the first and second year of life and not relying upon some form of routine nonmaternal care during this time.

The findings of this inquiry provide only mixed support for Belsky's (1988, 1990a) conclusion that more than 20 hours per week of nonparental care in the first year of life is a risk factor for the development of aggression and noncompliance. As suggested by the findings of Vandell and Corasaniti (1990), analyses of the NLSY data indicate that full-time employment initiated in the first or second year is associated with lower levels of adjustment than more limited maternal employment across the child's first three years of life. This broad conclusion is warranted because the results presented remained unchanged when the analyses reported were modified so that the comparison group comprised not simply children whose mothers were not employed or only minimally employed across their first three years ($n$ = 398), but all children whose mothers did not work full-time in the first or second year ($n$ = 661).

The absence of any effects uniquely attributable to full-time employment in the first year may be the direct result of the absence of any information on the quality of nonparental care. This suggestion is based upon Howes's (1990) recent discovery that the effects of full-time nonparental care in the first year are consistently moderated by quality of care, whereas this is far less the case of care initiated thereafter.

Despite this study's failure to reveal any effects specifically attributable to full-time maternal employment initiated in the first year of life, it is noteworthy that, as anticipated—and consistent with Belsky's analysis of the literature—it was the composite dependent measure ADJUST rather than SHY that turned out to be associated with early and extensive maternal employment, once confounding background factors were controlled. Thus, statistical effects of maternal employment emerged not simply on one of the two composite variables subject to analysis, but on the very measure that was hypothesized to be most likely associated with early and extensive maternal employment.

When the composite ADJUST measure was decomposed into its three constituent elements, it was discovered that only for the index of compliance did a reliable association between early and extensive maternal employment and child functioning obtain. The absence of a relation between employment and either the index of behavior problems or of attachment security may reflect the fact that no such associations exist or, alternatively, that the methods used to study these constructs in the NLSY were limited. Certainly, most attachment researchers would question the validity of using a few maternal-report items to measure this developmentally dynamic construct. Questions can be raised also about the maternal-report index of behavior problems, especially since research linking aggression with early and extensive maternal employment and child care has focused upon aggression *toward peers,* with measures based upon actual observations of children's behavior in group settings (e.g., Haskins, 1985) or teacher reports (e.g., Vandell and Corasaniti, 1990). Before embracing the null hypothesis—that is, that early and extensive maternal employment is not related to attachment security and aggression—we must keep issues of measurement in mind.

It is noteworthy that the component analysis of the adjustment composite variable revealed that it was not simply the case that children whose mothers did not work (or who worked only minimally) during their first three years of life were simply excessively compliant in comparison with agemates whose mothers were employed on a full-time basis beginning in their first or second year of life. Recall that it was the latter children who were significantly more likely to score in excess of one standard deviation below the mean on the compliance measure. These findings are consistent with Belsky's (1988) original conclusion that early and extensive child care/maternal employment is a risk factor for the development of noncompliance.

An alternative interpretation is also possible. Rather than providing evidence of noncompliance, which carries with it developmentally negative overtones, the effects discerned may merely reflect the fact that children whose mothers initiate full-time employment during their first or second year of life are more assertive than the children to whom they were compared. Unlike noncompliance, the notion of increased assertiveness does not carry with it such negative overtones. Perhaps consistent with this alternative interpretation of the compliance data is the fact that the evidence... reveals that as children get older they tend to become less compliant (i.e., more assertive?). Thus, it may be argued that early and extensive maternal employment speeds up the developmental process, perhaps making children "precociously independent."

While this is certainly a tenable argument—and one that cannot be resolved with the data at hand—it is worth noting that the noncompliance-equals-assertiveness line of reasoning presumes that psychological and behavioral developments that typically occur later in children's lives are developmentally beneficial when they transpire earlier. Thus, if children tend to become less compliant and more assertive as they grow up, becoming this way at an earlier age is evidence of precocity and thereby, developmental advantage.

The problem with such reasoning becomes apparent when behaviors other than compliance are considered. Just because children are more likely to drink, drive, stay out late, and commit petty acts of delinquency as they get older does not mean that doing these things earlier in life reflects maturity. We know, in fact, that such behavioral precocity is often a harbinger of more serious problems to come. The point here is not to equate the kind of noncompliance measured with the few items available to this study with much more serious risk-taking behavior, but rather to raise questions about the interpretation that earlier is better, that noncompliance reflects assertiveness, and that early and extensive maternal employment fosters precocious independence. Needless to say, this is an issue that should be addressed in future research.

Despite the fact that early and extensive maternal employment was found to predict less adjustment and, more specifically, greater noncompliance, it must be noted that, however statistically significant this effect was, it accounted for very little variance in the dependent measures. In fact, in the final regression model, the main effect of employment and the interaction between employment and shyness explained only 1.56% of the variance in the composite measure ADJUST. . . .

Our work with the NLSY data set—and particularly our analysis of the one-item child-care variable—convinces us that measurement error in survey data such as we analyzed is probably not minimal. While this does not lead us to dismiss the utility of the NLSY data base, it does lead us to be cautious about dismissing statistically significant findings that are consistent with other research and with our predictions. Indeed, from our standpoint, the results of the present inquiry do not indicate that early and extensive maternal employment, as it is routinely experienced in the United States, has a dramatic and devastating effect upon the socioemotional development of young children, but rather that Belsky's (1988, 1990a) risk-factor conclusion remains valid. Still to be determined are the processes by which such early experience becomes related to the developmental outcomes with which we have found them to be associated. After all, the study reveals that an anticipated, statistically significant association of only modest magnitude exists between early and extensive maternal employment and a composite index of adjustment in the NLSY data set. What remains to be explained, now that this predicted relation has been chronicled, are the mechanisms that account for it. There is no shortage of possibilities that merit empirical consideration. Unfortunately, those that concern the quality of nonmaternal care that children experience when their mothers work are beyond the purview of the NLSY.

## Notes

1. Age of mother at birth of the child was related to the pattern of employment over the first three years of a child's life. However, no relationship between age and any of the outcome measures was discerned in these data.
2. Results of these analyses, and other analyses discussed in the text, are available from the authors.

## References

Baker, Paula, and Frank Mott. 1989. NLSY Child Handbook 1989. Columbus: Center for Human Resources Research, Ohio State University.

Belsky, Jay. 1984. "Two waves of day care research: Development effects and conditions of quality." Pp. 1–34 in Ricardo Ainslie (ed.), The Child and the Day Care Setting. New York: Praeger.

Belsky, Jay. 1988. "The 'effects' of infant day care reconsidered." Early Childhood Research Quarterly 3: 235–272.

Belsky, Jay. 1990a. "Developmental risks associated with infant day care: Insecurity, aggression, and noncompliance?" In S. Chehrazi (ed.), Balancing Work and Parenting: Psychological and Developmental Implications of Day Care. New York: American Psychiatric Press.

Belsky, Jay. 1990b. "Parental and nonparental care and children's socioemotional development: A decade in review." Journal of Marriage and the Family 52: 885–903.

Belsky, Jay, and M. Rovine. 1988. "Nonmaternal care in the first year of life and infant-parent attachment security." Child Development 59: 157–176.

Bronfenbrenner, Urie, and Anne Crouter. 1983. "The evolution of environmental models in developmental psychology." Pp. 358–414 in P. Mussen (ed.), Handbook of Child Psychology (Vol. 1). New York: Wiley.

Eggebeen, David J. 1988. "Determinants of maternal employment for white preschool children: 1960–1980. Journal of Marriage and the Family 50: 149–159.

Fox, N., and G. Fein (eds.). 1990. "Infant day care: The current debate." Norwood, NJ: Ablex.

Haskins, Ronald. 1985. "Public school aggression among children with varying day-care experience." Child Development 56: 689–703.

Howes, Carollee, 1990. "Can the age of entry into child care and the quality of child care predict adjustment in kindergarten?" Developmental Psychology 26: 292–303.

Jacobson, Joseph L., and Diane E. Wille. 1984. "Influence of attachment and separation experience on separation distress at 18 months." Child Development 20: 477–484.

Kagan, Jerome, Richard Kearsley, and Phillip Zelazo. 1978. Infancy. Cambridge, MA: Harvard University Press.

Lande, Jeff, Sandra Scarr, and Nina Gunzenhauser (eds.). 1989. Caring for Children. Hillsdale, NJ: Erlbaum.

Phillips, Deborah, K. McCartney, S. Scarr, and C. Howes. 1987. "Selective review of infant day care research: A cause for concern!" Zero to Three 7(2): 18–21.

Rosenberg, Morris. 1965. Society and the Adolescent Self-image. Princeton, NJ: Princeton University Press.

Rubenstein, Judy, and Carollee Howes. 1983. "Adaptation to toddler day care." In S. Kilmer (ed.), Advances in Early Education and Day Care. Greenwich, CT: JAI Press.

Schwarz, J. Conrad, R. C. Strickland, and G. Krolick. 1974. "Infant day care: Behavioral effects at preschool age." Developmental Psychology 10: 502–506.

Vandell, Deborah, and Mary Corasaniti. 1990. "Child care and the family: Complex contributors to child development." In K. McCartney (ed.), Child Care and Maternal Employment: A Social Ecology Approach. San Francisco: Jossey-Bass.

Vaughn, Brian, Fred Gore, and Byron Egeland. 1980. "The relationship between out-of-home care and the quality of infant-mother attachment in an economically disadvantaged population." Child Development 51: 1203–1214.

**K. Alison Clarke-Stewart**

# A Home Is Not a School

Assessments of 150 2–4-year-olds in six different child care arrangements revealed that the social and intellectual development of children in centers (part time or full time) was advanced over that of the children in home care (with mother, sitter, or day care home provider). Previous research was reviewed to account for this finding. It was concluded that the most likely causes of the difference in children's development were educational lessons, opportunities to practice skills and follow rules with a variety of peers and nonparental adults, and encouragement of independence by nonauthoritarian teachers—experiences that are qualitatively different from the experiences most children have in home care environments.

There has been a dramatic shift over the past 15 years in the environments in which young American children spend their time. Whereas 15 years ago fewer than one-third of the preschool-aged children in this country were in any kind of preschool program, now over half attend a nursery school, kindergarten, or day care center (U.S. Bureau of the Census, 1987). An even more striking rise has occurred for infants and toddlers; their participation in such programs has more than doubled in the same period. In addition, over 5 million young children now spend a significant portion of their time in other kinds of nonparental care—with a babysitter, a neighbor, an aunt, or a paid day care home provider. Every year the number of young children in some form of "nontraditional" child care environment increases markedly.

A question that concerns parents, politicians, and psychologists is what effects these alternative forms of child care have on children's development. Until quite recently, however, data about the effects of different kinds of child care were lacking. Although day care had existed in this country since at least 1838, when the first day nursery was opened in Boston (Steinfels, 1973), and for longer than that if informal arrangements between neighbors or with live-in housekeepers are included, the first systematic studies of child care environments and effects did not appear until 1970 (Caldwell, Wright, Honig, & Tannenbaum, 1970; Keister, 1970). Since that time, a sizable number of studies of child care have been undertaken, and now important evidence is beginning to accumulate. The evidence concerning the effects of child care on *infants* has been

From K. Alison Clarke-Stewart, "A Home Is Not a School: The Effects of Child Care on Children's Development," *Journal of Social Issues,* vol. 47, no. 2 (1991), pp. 105–121.  References omitted.

spotlighted lately (e.g., Clarke-Stewart, 1989; Howes, 1990). But there are still unanswered questions about the effects of child care on toddlers and preschoolers. For these children, the major issue is not whether daily separations from mother impair development—the burning question for infants—but rather, what are the relative advantages and disadvantages of different types of child care for children's social and cognitive development? The present paper offers one answer to this question, based upon the results of available research.

## Differences Between Children in Different Child Care Environments

In research conducted in Chicago (Clarke-Stewart, 1984; Clarke-Stewart & Gruber, 1984), 150 children, 2 and 3 years old, were selected for a study of child care. They were in six different child care arrangements: (1) care at home by parents, (2) care by a sitter in the child's home, (3) care in a day care home, (4) care in a center or nursery school part time; (5) care in a center full time, and (6) care in a center part time and with a sitter at home part time. To ensure a wide and representative sampling of the kinds of child care environments available, the study included no more than 4 children from any single child care setting. The children were in their first nonparental child care environments and had been there for less than a year. They were followed over a year-long period, observed six times in their family and child care settings, and their moment-to-moment experiences were recorded. Children also were brought into a laboratory playroom on two occasions for extensive assessments of their social skills, and on one occasion were given standard assessments of social, emotional, and cognitive development at home (see Clarke-Stewart, 1984, for details). The researchers assessing the children's development were not the same ones who had observed them at home or in their day care settings; they were blind to the care arrangements of the children they were assessing. From the data collected in the assessments of the children's development, a set of complex, empirically intercorrelated, and conceptually meaningful variables was created....

Differences between children in the six child care arrangements were estimated by analyzing differences in mean scores on these seven child development variables, covarying out the child's age and family SES. The results of these analyses... were clear and consistent. On all these variables reflecting advanced social and intellectual skills—verbal ability, nonverbal cognition, social cognition, creativity with materials, cooperation with the examiner, cooperation with an unfamiliar peer, and overall social competence—there were no significant differences among the children in different home care environments (with mother, sitter, or day care home provider), nor were there differences among the children in different center environments (part time or full time); but the children in center care (child care arrangements, 4–6) performed at higher levels than the children in home care (child care arrangements 1–3). Only 2 of the 15 analyses did not reveal a significant difference between children in home care and center care, and these two analyses (for creative play with materials and cooperation with the examiner during the first assessment) were in the same direction and approached significance.

The difference between children in home and center environments did not occur, however, for another set of variables that assessed children's social relationships rather than their social or intellectual competence. No differences were found between these settings for children's security of attachment to mother, hostility toward mother, help or comforting of mother, compliance with mother's requests, or positive interaction with a familiar playmate. Marked variability among individual children was observed for these variables, but it was not related to type of child care. This suggests that the observed difference between children in home and center care is specific to the development of social competence and intellectual knowledge rather than occurring for all kinds of behavior or development.

The findings from this study are consistent with the results of other research (reviewed by Clarke-Stewart & Fein, 1983; and more recent studies by Andersson, 1989; Burchinal, Lee, & Ramey, 1989; Robinson & Corley, 1989; Tietze, 1987; Wadsworth, 1986). These studies all suggest that children in day care centers and preschool programs tend to be more socially skilled and intellectually advanced than children at home with their parents, sitters, or in day care homes. Significant differences favoring center attendees have not been found in all studies, in all samples, or on all indices of social or cognitive competence, of course (e.g., Ackerman-Ross & Khanna, 1989; Lamb, Hwang, Broberg, & Bookstein, 1988; Scarr, Lande, & McCartney, 1988). But when differences have been found, they consistently favor children in center care.

In the realm of social competence, there is evidence that children in center care are more self-confident, self-assured and outgoing, less timid and fearful, more assertive, self-sufficient, and independent of parents and teachers, yet more helpful and cooperative with peers, mother, or examiner when the situation requires it. They are more verbally expressive, more knowledgeable about the social world (e.g., they know their own name, address, and birthday earlier), more comfortable in a new or stressful situation, and more competent to manage on their own (Cochran, 1977; Fowler, 1978; Kagan, Kearsley, & Zelazo, 1978; Lally & Honig, 1977; Rubenstein, Howes, & Boyle, 1981; Schwarz, Krolick, & Strickland, 1973). When they get to school, they are better adjusted, more task oriented and goal directed, and show more leadership and persistence (Fowler & Khan, 1974; Howes, 1990; Lally & Honig, 1977). in Sjolund's (1971) international review, only 3 of the available 56 studies failed to find a significant difference favoring the social skills of children in nursery school compared to children without this experience.

In the domain of intellectual ability, of the more than 20 studies of child care that have included some measure of children's intelligence or intellectual development, only 2 have reported significantly higher scores for children reared at home than for children of comparable family backgrounds who were in day care centers (Melhuish, 1990, for vocabulary only; Peaslee, 1976, for language and IQ). Other studies consistently show that children in day care centers do at least as well as those at home with their parents and often they do better, at least for a time (e.g., Cochran, 1977; Fowler, 1978; Golden et al., 1978; Kagan et al., 1978; Ramey, Dorval, & Baker-Ward, 1983; Robinson & Robinson, 1971; Rubenstein & Howes, 1983; Winnett, Fuchs, Moffatt, & Nerviano, 1977).

In Sjolund's (1971) review, 21 of 36 studies assessing children's intellectual development showed advanced development in children attending nursery school compared to those who were not in nursery school; the other 15 showed no significant difference. Comparisons of children in day care homes and day care centers, similarly, have often revealed significant differences between children in these two kinds of day care, favoring the children in centers (e.g., Bruner, 1980; Robinson & Corley, 1989; Winnett et al., 1977).

In the assessments of particular kinds of intellectual abilities, differences favoring center care children have been found in eye–hand coordination (Cochran, 1977; Kagan et al., 1978), creative use of materials (Provost, 1980), memory (Ramey et al., 1983), problem solving and reasoning (Fowler, 1978; Garber & Heber, 1980; Moss, Blicharski, & Strayer, 1987), and knowledge about the physical world (Stukat, 1969). Advanced language abilities have also been observed in children who are in center care (Fowler, 1978; Garber & Heber, 1980; Ramey et al., 1983; Rubenstein & Howes, 1983; Rubenstein et al., 1981; Scarr et al., 1988; Stukat, 1969).

In brief, then, differences favoring children in center care appear across a range of intellectual abilities including both verbal and nonverbal skills. These differences are not permanent, but they have been observed to last for a year or two after "graduation" into elementary school (Haskins, 1989; Larsen & Robinson, 1989; Lee et al., 1989; Tietze, 1987; Wadsworth, 1986). There is some evidence to suggest that they are more likely for children who have been in center care from infancy (Andersson, 1989). There is also evidence to suggest that they are more likely for children from low-income families who are in model child care programs (see Clarke-Stewart & Fein, 1983). But differences also appear for middle-class children in community child care. In our Chicago study, no effort was made to select child care of high quality. The child care settings observed were just the ones that parents had come up with; they were not model programs. They were, however, generally of decent quality (the average adult–child ratio in the centers was 1 to 5, standard deviation = 4).

## Causes of the Difference Between Children in Different Child Care Environments

More than simply documenting the differences between children in different child care environments, research offers some tentative suggestions about what causes these differences. Here, four possible reasons for the differences between children are examined: (1) differences in the *amount* of attention and stimulation in centers and homes, (2) differences in the *kind* of attention and stimulation in centers and homes, (3) differences in the *quality* of attention and stimulation in centers and homes, and (4) preexisting differences in the children themselves and their families.

### Differences in Amount of Attention and Stimulation

One reason that the development of children in center care is advanced might be that center programs simply provide *more* of the same kind of stimulation that predicts advanced development in other care environments. Perhaps centers are just like homes, but more so.

One piece of evidence that could be used to support this hypothesis would be a finding that centers offer children more physical stimulation—more space and materials—of the same kind as found in homes, and that this stimulation predicts advanced child development. The available evidence, however, offers no support for this idea. Although extreme differences in the amount of space per child have indeed been related to children's behavior and development in child care environments (Prescott, 1973; Rohe & Patterson, 1974; Ruopp, Travers, Glantz, & Coelen, 1979; Smith & Connolly, 1980), because homes generally offer more space per child than centers, this relation cannot explain the advanced development of children in centers. There may be more play materials in centers than in homes (e.g., Golden et al., 1978), but probably this is not important in accounting for the difference in children's development either, because studies of the effects of the number of toys in children's environments suggest that toys alone are not a direct promoter of development (Golden et al., 1978; Rubenstein & Howes, 1979).

Another kind of evidence that could support the hypothesis that centers offer children more stimulation would be a finding that care givers in centers interact more with children than do care givers at home. The social and intellectual development of individual children in day care centers has indeed been positively related to the amount of adult attention they receive (Carew, 1980; Clarke-Stewart, 1984; Phillips, McCartney, & Scarr, 1987; Phillips, Scarr, & McCartney, 1987; Ruopp et al., 1979; Whitebook, Howes, & Phillips, 1990). But of the studies comparing the amount of caregiver attention in homes and in centers, the majority show that children at home receive more attention from the care giver than do children in centers (Clarke-Stewart, 1984; Cochran, 1977; Golden et al., 1978; Hayes et al., 1983; Melhuish, 1990; Prescott, 1973; Tizard et al., 1980; Tyler & Dittman, 1980). Once again, the available data do not support the hypothesis that the important difference between center and home environments is simply the amount of stimulation that children receive.

## Differences in Kind of Attention and Stimulation

Perhaps, then, the important difference between homes and centers is not the amount of stimulation the child receives, but the kind. Center environments differ qualitatively from home environments in a number of ways.

*Peers.* Most obviously, perhaps, centers offer children the opportunity to interact with other children their age. It has been observed that playing with a peer raises the complexity and creativity of children's activities with materials (Rubenstein & Howes, 1983; Sylva, Roy, & Painter, 1980), that social play is more advanced with a familiar playmate (Doyle, Connolly, & Rivest, 1980; Rubenstein & Howes, 1979), and that this more complex level of play then generalizes to interaction with unfamiliar peers (Lieberman, 1977). However, interaction with agemates is less likely to have a direct effect on the child's language acquisition. Language development is facilitated by hearing a more advanced language model, not by listening to peer chatter (McCartney, 1984; Sjolund, 1971). It seems unlikely, therefore, that the presence of other children alone would account for the observed difference in intellectual development typically found for children in different child care environments—although it may affect their social development.

Results of studies comparing different types of child care support this suggestion. First, if peers were the critical factor, then all group programs, not just programs in centers should show the effect. But as has already been noted, children in day care homes do not generally show the same level of competence as children in centers—despite the fact that they spend as much time interacting with peers (Clarke-Stewart, 1984; Howes & Rubenstein, 1981). Second, more peer interaction occurs in more "open" or unstructured preschool programs—programs with fewer teacher-directed activities like lessons—but gains in cognitive development and achievement are typically lower in these programs than in more structured programs (Miller & Dyer, 1975). Third, measures of social and intellectual competence in our research in Chicago (Clarke-Stewart, 1984) and in research in Bermuda (McCartney, 1984) were not significantly positively correlated with the amount of peer interaction experienced by individual children.

Children's competence in the Chicago study was, however, correlated with the number of different children interacted with in the care setting. Thus, children may gain from exposure to a wider *variety* of other children. Dunn and Kontos's (1989) observation that when there were more children in day care homes children engaged in higher levels of play would support this suggestion. But the advantage of diversity exists only up to a certain point. When the number of children becomes too large (larger than 11 toddlers or 18 preschoolers in a group), a lower level of play and intellectual development is observed (Ruopp et al., 1979; Smith & Connolly, 1980; Sylva et al., 1980). Altogether, then, there seems to be little evidence to support the hypothesis that the important difference between center care and home care is simply the presence of any other children or the amount of interaction with other children. Contact in centers with a greater diversity of peers, who vary in age, sex, race, and individual qualities, may, however, be a significant contributor. In the Chicago study, children who had the opportunity to interact with older peers in their classes were developmentally advanced (Clarke-Stewart, 1984).

*Care givers.* The variety of different adults with whom the child has an opportunity to interact also may contribute to development. In the study in Chicago, the number of adults that children encountered in centers was, on the average, greater than in homes (see also Howes, 1983), and the number of adults so encountered was positively related to children's competence (Clarke-Stewart, 1984).

The adults encountered in homes and centers are also different in another way that is likely to affect children's development: Center care givers are more likely to have been trained in child development (Clarke-Stewart, 1984; Goelman & Pence, 1987). Care givers with more training are more interactive, helpful, talkative, and didactic (Fosburg et al., 1980; Kinney, 1989; Lazar et al., 1977; Tyler & Dittman, 1980), and the children in their care make more cognitive gains (Clarke-Stewart, 1984; Ruopp et al., 1979). When preschool teachers are trained to use more cognitively demanding strategies in talking to the children, the children's achievement is advanced (Sigel, 1986).

Perhaps because of their training, center care givers compared to home care givers (whether mothers or sitters) are less directive and authoritarian, more likely to help, to explain, to make tasks into games, and to respond to children's initiation of play (Bryant, Harris, & Newton, 1980; Cochran, 1977; Hess, Price, Dickson, & Conroy, 1981; Howes & Rubenstein, 1981; Prescott, 1973; Rubenstein & Howes, 1979; Tyler & Dittman, 1980). Because authoritarian discipline is related to children's lower intellectual and social competence (see Clarke-Stewart & Apfel, 1979), this difference between homes and centers may be another part of the explanation for the observed difference between settings in children's development.

*Physical equipment and materials.* Another possibility is that different kinds of physical equipment and materials are provided in day care centers and homes, and that this contributes to the observed differences in children's development. Within center settings, high-level, cognitively challenging, and constructive activity with materials is more likely with building materials or during teacher-directed art or music activities (Pellegrini, 1984; Sylva et al., 1980)—and these kinds of opportunities are likely to be more frequent in centers than in homes. In homes, the opportunities are greater for tactile exploration with sand, water, dough, and soft objects, for cooking and "messing around" (Cochran, 1977; Prescott, 1973; Rubenstein & Howes, 1979), but academic and construction materials are less common. The physical materials and equipment in centers, then, may encourage more frequent intellectual activities.

But the physical environment alone is unlikely to account for all the differences observed. Simply adding novel materials to preschool classrooms or having more varied materials accessible does not lead to cognitive gains; it is only in combination with teacher behavior that materials are related to children's advanced development (Busse, Ree, Gatride, & Alexander, 1972; Ruopp et al., 1979). Moreover, toys and materials are not likely to account for observed differences in social competence; advanced social behavior involving cooperation, conversation, and complex interaction with peers is more common with dolls, dress-ups, dramatic props, and social toys like checkers and pickup sticks than with puzzles, art, books, or intellectual exercises (e.g., Howes & Rubenstein, 1981; Smith & Connolly, 1980; Quilitch & Risley, 1973; Sylva et al., 1980), and the former materials are more common in homes than in centers (Rubenstein & Howes, 1979). Although physical materials may contribute to children's development, in themselves they cannot account for the differences in competence observed in different child care environments.

*Program and curriculum.* Other qualitative differences between home and center care involve the kind of activities the programs offer. In centers, rules, lessons, and schedules are more likely to be fixed and based on the needs of the group rather than those of the individual child. Thus, children in centers must learn to recognize and adapt to "abstract," arbitrary, general rules and to take in information presented formally, whereas children at home operate in a concrete "hands-on" context, where rules and lessons, as such, are limited. Children who have been in day care center programs for some time have been found to display a more advanced understanding of social rules than newly enrolled children (Siegal & Storey, 1985). It has been suggested (Cole, Gay, Glick, & Sharp, 1971) that "schooling" in this institutional sense facilitates the development of advanced intellectual skills. It is also plausible to expect that it would foster the social, language, and test-taking skills and knowledge in which center children are advanced.

Another difference in program activities is the extent of educational instruction. Most home care providers, whether parents or paid professionals, do not have education as their primary goal. Nor do they follow a set curriculum. There are several hints that this may be an important distinction between home and center care. Children in more educationally oriented programs—ones with more prescribed educational activities such as lessons, guided play sessions, teaching of specific content, and more direct teacher instruction—perform better than those in less educationally oriented programs, for example. They do more constructive and complex play with materials and with peers, and score higher on intelligence and achievement tests (Clarke-Stewart, 1984; Ferri, 1980; Fowler, 1978; Johnson, Ershler, & Bell, 1980; Lazar et al., 1977; McCartney, 1984; Miller & Dyer, 1975; Sylva et al., 1980; Tizard, Philips, & Plewis, 1976; Winnett, Fuchs, Moffatt, & Nerviano, 1977). In correlational analyses, the more direct teaching children receive, the greater is their competence (Clarke-Stewart, 1984; McCartney, 1984). There may even be a match between the particular content taught and the outcomes exhibited (Fowler, 1978; Miller & Dyer, 1975). Most telling, when care in day care homes was enriched by the experimental addition of a structured educational curriculum, the intellectual competence of the children was observed to improve to the level of children in day care centers (Goodman & Andrews, 1981). An educational curriculum, then, seems a likely candidate for contributing to the advanced cognitive development of children in centers.

Qualitative differences between the kinds of teaching that occur in center environments and in home environments may also be involved. In homes, "teaching" is likely to be casual and informal; children have more free time and time alone, and they learn from exploring household objects, helping the care giver, performing real-life tasks, and seeing real live role models—not from explicit lessons (Cochran, 1977; Prescott, 1973; Tyler & Dittman, 1980). Conversations are longer, include more complex utterances, offer children more opportunities to ask questions and express opinions, and are more "inductive" (Cochran, 1977; Fiene, 1973; Prescott, 1973; Tizard et al., 1980; Tyler & Dittman, 1980)—e.g., "What would you like for lunch?" might lead to a long discussion about individuals' food preferences, the time it takes to prepare food, what foods are nutritious, and so on. In centers, conversations are more likely to be "deductive" and convergent, taking the form of teacher questions and child answers (Cochran, 1977; Fiene, 1973; Prescott, 1973; Tyler & Dittman, 1980; Wittmer & Honig, 1989). The parallel question in a center would be "What are we having for lunch today?" and it might lead to a discussion of peas as vegetables, other vegetables the child can name, what colors and sizes they are, and so on. It seems reasonable that the kinds of conversations occurring in centers are the kind that would prepare children to do well on standardized tests of intelligence. They may not be designed to enhance practical problem solving or sensitivity to human needs, but they are directed toward the kinds of school skills that are assessed in tests of intellectual development.

In sum, it appears that differences in the kinds of attention and stimulation in home and center environments account for many of the differences observed in children's competence. In particular, it seems likely that the educational emphasis and nonauthoritarian style of center care givers, combined with the availability of stimulating educational materials, the presence of a variety of adults and other children, and the influence of institutional regulations, create a school-like environment that facilitates the development of social skills and intellectual competence as measured by standardized tests.

## Differences in Quality of Stimulation

It has been suggested recently (e.g., Lamb et al., 1988), however, that observed differences in children's development in centers and homes are the result of differences in the quality of child care rather than the type of child care environment. Lamb and his associates found that the social skills of preschool children in Sweden were related to the observed quality of their experiences in child care rather than to whether the children were in home care or centers. In that study, the day care centers they observed were of lower quality than the homes (more negative events occurred). Similarly, in another study, conducted in England, in which children in centers did not show advanced intellectual development, the centers observed were of generally poor quality (Melhuish, 1990). It makes sense that children would do better in a high-quality home than in a poor quality center. But in the real world of child care in America, or at least in the centers and homes that have been the targets of study, it seems likely that centers, on the average, offer care and stimulation of higher quality than do homes, on the average. Thus, perhaps quality and type of care are confounded. Differences between children in different child care environments are most marked when the centers are of high quality and/or the children come from disadvantaged families (Andersson, 1989; Fowler & Khan, 1974; Robinson & Robinson, 1971; Scarr et al., 1988). Differences are least when the homes are of high quality. For example, in research by Goelman and Pence (1987), although the competence of children in *unregulated* day care homes in Canada was inferior to that of children in centers, the competence of children in *regulated* homes was equivalent.

We do not have a clear answer to the question of whether the differences observed between children in homes and in centers are due to differences in overall quality or to differences in the specific kinds of stimulation each offers. Center environments may confer unique benefits. Certain things may be easier to accomplish in centers. There may be subtle differences between environments that are glossed over by an emphasis on global quality. Or it may be that, although typical practice in centers is often more educational than typical practice in homes, this is not a *necessary* difference between the two environments. Untangling these possibilities remains a task for future research.

## Preexisting Differences in Children and Families

Before concluding that children's competence is solely the result of differences in their child care experiences, however, the contributions of the family and of the child to the advanced competence of children in center care must be examined. Although socioeconomic differences had been statistically controlled in the reported analyses of the Chicago study, there is always the possibility that family variables contribute to the observed pattern of advanced development in center children.

Parents of children in centers may provide more stimulation and education for their children than do parents of children in home care. In well-controlled studies in which center and home care families have been matched (e.g., on SES), there are generally large areas of overlap where no differences between the groups of parents are observed. But when differences are observed, they are in the direction of greater verbal stimulation and play, and less authoritarian discipline for mothers using center care than for mothers using only home care (Garber & Heber, 1980; Clarke-Stewart, 1984; Ramey et al., 1979; Rubenstein et al., 1981)....

The difference is less likely to be the result of changes in the parents' behavior as a result of learning about child development from center staff. Although one study did show that parents whose children were attending a model day care center program, in which they were encouraged to visit and participate, became more child centered and more like the teachers in the program (less likely to ignore, scold, refuse, or coax the child) than a matched sample of parents whose children were not in the program (Edwards, Logue, Loehr, & Roth, 1985), in most centers little communication between parents and teachers occurs spontaneously, and when it does, it does not lead to more agreement (Powell, 1978). Moreover, even when a formal parent education component is part of the day care program, this does not ensure that parents' behavior will change (e.g., Fowler, 1978; Lally & Honig, 1977). It is unlikely, therefore, that parent education at the center is a strong contributor to the difference observed between parents using center care and home care.

There is, however, always the possibility that something in the children themselves who are placed in centers accounts for their advanced development. Perhaps they are selected for center care (by staff or by parents) because they are already more competent. This possibility cannot be ruled out. It is a fact that many centers accept only children who are toilet trained. This would force mothers who must work to use day care homes or babysitters for care of less mature toddlers. But, once the child is toilet trained, center staff would be unlikely to be able to select on the basis of maturity or competence without more screening than is commonly done. Moreover, advanced development in center children has also been observed in studies where children were matched on IQ at the beginning of their child care experience (Fowler, 1978) or in which self-selection was eliminated by randomly assigning children to center or home care (Garber & Heber, 1980; Ramey et al., 1983). While self-selection may magnify the differences in children's development, then, it is unlikely to be the most significant contributor.

## Conclusions and Implications for Future Research

In sum, preschool children who have spent some time in center child care are, on the average, socially and intellectually advanced over their peers who have only been at home. This advanced development is likely to arise from a combination of factors, not a single critical cause. Experiences at home, including those initiated or evoked by the child, may contribute to the advanced development of children whose parents have chosen to put them in centers. Even more important, the advanced development of children in centers is likely to be the result of lessons to foster social and intellectual skills, instructions in recognizing and following rules, opportunities to practice skills and follow rules with a variety of peers and nonparental adults, and encouragement of independence and self-direction by trained and nonauthoritarian teachers. The experiences of children in centers are substantially different from those children are likely to have at home—with parents, babysitters, or day care home providers. Home is where the heart is, but the head is influenced by more than home experiences. A home is not a school. Center environments differ qualitatively from home environments, and the differences in the kinds of experience they offer are likely to have significant effects on the development of children growing up in them.

The test of just how significant these effects are remains for future researchers. In the past, researchers took an overly simple approach to defining and assessing child care, as if "child care" were a single uniform condition rather than an enormous variety of environments, programs, and settings (see Clarke-Stewart & Fein, 1983). They did not study the full range of home and center care for the whole range of children. They did not observe and compare children's experiences in home and center environments. They did not analyze the relations between child care and family factors. They sidestepped the issues of causal direction and extent. They did not allow for the further complicating factor that children often move from one type of child care setting to a different type.

In order to investigate more fully the effects of child care on children's development, researchers must overcome these limitations. They must examine in detail the nature of children's experiences in different kinds of child care environments, paying particular attention to the educational content of those experiences, and attempting to identify intellectually and socially valuable components. They then should probe the implications of their descriptive observations experimentally, by controlling the components of programs in centers and by supplementing the components of experiences in homes. Only by systematically enriching home care with the educationally focused opportunities more typically found in centers, only by unconfounding quality and type of care, will we find out with any degree of certainty whether a home cannot be a school.

# POSTSCRIPT

## Does Maternal Employment Have a Negative Effect on Infant Development?

Although researchers agree that maternal employment studies need to examine the interaction of several variables, such as the quality of child care, they do not agree on which sets of variables combine to give an accurate picture of how a mother's employment affects children. A balanced perspective on maternal employment effects can be found in *Working Women and Their Families* by Jacqueline Lerner (Sage Publications, 1994).

Attitudes toward maternal employment effects have been altered by societal changes such as time-saving appliances (for example, the dishwasher, automatic washer and dryer, self-cleaning oven, and microwave), drive-through food eateries, the women's liberation movement, the election of more women to political office, and the economic necessity for single as well as both parents to work.

If single welfare mothers are required to work, how will their children fare? Does the research tell us enough about the need for mothers to be with their children in their first three years of life? Are child-care centers an appropriate option for the working mother? Or should mothers stay home with their young children and delay entrance into the workforce?

## Suggested Readings


Bogenschneider, K., & Steinberg, L. (1994, January). Maternal employment and adolescents' academic achievement: A developmental analysis. *Sociology of Education, 67*, 60–77.

Goldman, K. W. (1993). *My mother worked and I turned out ok.* New York: Garnet Press.

Greenstein, T. N. (1993, September). Maternal employment and child behavioral outcomes: A household economics analysis. *Journal of Family Issues, 14*, 323–354.

# ISSUE 3

## Should Hospitals Continue Early Discharge Policies for Newborns?

**YES: John R. Britton, Helen L. Britton, and Susan A. Beebe**, from "Early Discharge of the Term Newborn: A Continued Dilemma," *Pediatrics* (September 1994)

**NO: Elizabeth H. Thilo and Susan F. Townsend**, from "What Are the Pitfalls of Early Discharge?" *Contemporary OB/GYN* (January 1997)

### ISSUE SUMMARY


**YES:** John R. Britton, Helen L. Britton, and Susan A. Beebe, all affiliated with the Department of Pediatrics at the University of Utah Medical Center in Salt Lake City, review the available data on the appropriate time to discharge a newborn and summarize some of the studies that promote early discharge.

**NO:** Elizabeth H. Thilo, an associate professor of pediatrics, and Susan F. Townsend, an assistant professor of pediatrics, contend that the recently recommended 48-hour hospital stay for newborns may still not be long enough to catch some of the medical problems that infants can develop.


In 1995 there was an uproar in the medical community, which spread to the public, concerning the common practice of discharging mothers and newborns from hospitals 12 to 24 hours after birth. Many insurance companies would pay for hospital costs only for the first 24 hours after childbirth. Outrage that babies were being released from the hospital before it was considered medically safe by many health care professionals led to legislation in several states and eventually to the U.S. Senate. Laws were passed that required insurance companies to extend their coverage to 48 hours after birth when recommended by the doctor. It was concluded that 48 hours, not 24 hours, was a more reasonable amount of time to ensure the health of the newborn baby. Yet a 48-hour discharge is still considered an "early discharge."

It is becoming more common for insurance companies to cover hospital costs for a 48-hour hospital stay, but is 48 hours long enough to ensure the health and safety of a newborn? Some physicians question the efficacy of discharging newborns only 48 hours after birth, whereas others say that this would not create health problems for healthy newborns. Early discharge saves money and, according to some researchers, is associated with a better outcome than a longer hospital stay is.

The roots of this issue can be traced back to the 1960s and 1970s, when families fought to be released from the hospital sooner than the traditional five to seven days. Many mothers wanted to go home, where they felt more comfortable and could save on costs. This movement snowballed until the 1990s, when 12 to 24 hours became a common hospital stay after childbirth.

The authors of the following selections agree that the decision about when to release a newborn from the hospital should be determined on a case-by-case basis, with the physician and parents considering a variety of factors. Health care professionals seldom mention insurance companies or legislative bodies as partners in the decision of early discharge. Should insurance companies have the power to interfere in a medical decision? If insurance companies do not get involved in health care costs, will insurance premiums go through the roof? Are there long-term effects related to early discharge of newborns, or are potential problems merely short-term?

Early discharge raises questions not only about the health and safety of babies but about society as well. How much health care should a newborn receive? Who should decide? Shortening the hospital stay of newborns and their mothers by one day can save $4 billion per year, according to a 1997 study by Elizabeth H. Thilo and Susan F. Townsend. This is a significant savings for everyone who pays insurance premiums. Is it appropriate to consider a cost savings in this situation? Should insurance companies be a partner in deciding when a newborn should be released from the hospital? Should state legislatures be involved in the decision? How does one juggle health issues and financial concerns with mandates from state legislatures? What are the implications for the later development of children who develop serious illnesses after leaving the hospital too soon?

Studies of the effects of early discharge of newborns have not settled the debate over how long newborns should stay in the hospital after birth. There are concerns over how these studies were conducted and their results. In the following selections, John R. Britton, Helen L. Britton, and Susan A. Beebe present findings of studies that support the practice of early discharge. Thilo and Townsend contend that "the definitive study on the safety of early discharge has not yet been performed." They question the safety of letting a newborn leave the hospital after only 48 hours.

**John R. Britton, Helen L. Britton, and Susan A. Beebe**

# Early Discharge of the Term Newborn: A Continued Dilemma

Although it has recently become common practice to discharge healthy term infants with their mothers at increasingly earlier postnatal ages,[1] current opinion varies widely regarding the desirability of this practice. Proponents of early discharge claim that it is safe and may be advantageous from both a medical and psychosocial standpoint. Opponents, on the other hand, argue that an element of risk may be involved because detection of significant illness may be either missed or delayed outside of the hospital.[2] To further complicate the issue, economic considerations often limit the choice of families and their physicians. Third party payers usually fund only the shortest possible inpatient hospital stays, thus constituting a driving force behind the trend to earlier discharge.[2]

The United States appears to have taken the lead in the practice of early discharge, and it is not uncommon in this country for a term newborn to leave the hospital at 12 to 24 hours postnatally. Recently, 1- to 3-day postnatal stays have also become more popular in other Western countries, such as the United Kingdom, Australia, and Scandinavia, where 6- to 10-day hospitalizations had been customary in the past.[3–7] Medical, social, and economic considerations have presumably influenced such trends, as they have in the United States.

Because of these changes, questions regarding the timing of hospital discharge of term infants are faced almost daily by practicing pediatricians throughout the world. In 1980, the American Academy of Pediatrics recommended criteria to be met by early discharge candidates,[8] and these continue to form the basis for their current guidelines.[9] However, few pediatricians are familiar with the limited information on this subject, which has never been reviewed in the pediatric literature. In this review, available data on early newborn discharge will be presented with particular emphasis upon the safety and benefits of this practice. Since published studies are heterogeneous with respect to methodology and study design, analytical approaches such as meta-analysis are unfortunately not applicable.[10] Moreover, almost all published studies suffer from substantial methodological limitations, and only a few satisfy as many as three of the 11 criteria that have been suggested for adequacy of clinical study design by DerSimonian et al.[11] Accordingly, these methodological concerns will be discussed in a separate section....

## Psychosocial Issues and Early Discharge

Proponents of early discharge often argue that this practice may be associated with a variety of psychosocial benefits, such as facilitation of bonding and attachment, increased breastfeeding, enhanced family interactions, and generally improved patient satisfaction. Although some studies lend support to these beliefs, others are less convincing of a beneficial effect.

In a randomized, controlled study at a tertiary maternity hospital in Vancouver, Carty and Bradley evaluated 131 women and their infants discharged at 12 to 24 hours, 25 to 48 hours, or 4 days postpartum.[12] As determined by a questionnaire, mothers in the two early discharge groups were significantly more satisfied with their care; those hospitalized longer demonstrated less confidence and greater depression as assessed by standardized psychological testing. In a Swedish study, mothers and fathers in an early discharge group were more satisfied with medical care than those undergoing a traditional 6-day postpartum stay.[7] Other reports have shown an association between early discharge and improved maternal postpartum adjustment[5] and increased time spent by fathers with their infants during days 2 to 4 postnatally.[13]

Several reports suggest that early discharge may foster enhanced breastfeeding. In a Swedish study,[14] infants discharged early were breastfed significantly more often on the third and fourth days postnatally than those staying in the hospital, although no difference in incidence of breastfeeding was observed during the subsequent 10 days. Among Canadian mothers, a significant association of early discharge with unsupplemented breastfeeding at 4 to 6 weeks postpartum was noted.[12]

Similar psychosocial benefits of early discharge were not observed in other early discharge reports. A study conducted in 1962 found decreased satisfaction among mothers discharged early from an inner-city hospital in New York.[15] In a randomized trial conducted at a California health maintenance organization,[16] no difference in satisfaction was noted between mothers discharged early and late. Two groups[13,17] observed no differences in the practice of breastfeeding as related to the time of newborn discharge.

One study compared simultaneous discharge of low-income mothers and their infants at 24 to 47 hours postnatally with maternal discharge at a similar time without their infants.[18] Simultaneous discharge was associated with higher maternal attachment scores, fewer concerns, and greater satisfaction than discharge with separation.

## Morbidity and Mortality: Relationship to Time of Discharge

Although the Committee on the Fetus and Newborn of the American Academy of Pediatrics has stated that there is "an element of risk in early discharge",[8] this risk remains poorly defined. Among published series of infants discharged early, mortality rates are low and not significantly different from those of accompanying controls or the general population of infants from which the study groups were drawn.[15,19–21] Most early discharge studies have attempted to compare morbidity, expressed as rates of hospital re-admission, between infants discharged early and late.

The first early discharge program reported from New Orleans, LA, in 1943 suggested the safety of hospital discharge at 2 to 5 days postnatally.[22] In a report from Bradford, England, in 1959,[23] hospital re-admission rates during the first 14 days postnatally were evaluated among infants discharged at approximately 48 hours after birth. Although this practice of "early discharge" was considered a drastic step at the time, only four of 741 infants discharged early required re-admission to the hospital.[23] Subsequent reports from this center confirmed a low rate of re-admission (0.5% to 0.9%), as did those from other British hospitals during the 1960s.[19–21,24,25] Later reports from around the world suggested the medical safety of a 1- to 3-day postnatal stay.[26–28]

With the advent of even shorter hospital stays for newborns in more recent years, concern regarding the safety of this practice again arose, prompting further evaluation. A variety of institutions, ranging from university hospitals to free-standing birthing centers, reported discharge as early as the first day after birth, with re-admission rates ranging from 0% to 11%.[29–40] The few reports that have included a comparison group of infants discharged at a later age suggest similar rates of re-admission for early and late discharge groups.

Only three prospective, randomized controlled studies provide information regarding the medical safety of early discharge.[3,12,16] For these, discharge times varied, infant numbers were small and follow-up periods variable, making comparison difficult. In a study from the Kaiser-Permanente Medical Center in San Francisco, 44 infants discharged at a median age of 26 hours were compared to a control group of 44 infants discharged at a median age of 68 hours.[16] The two groups were similar with respect to ethnicity, socioeconomic status, and parenting characteristics. Almost half of the infants in the early discharge group actually went home prior to 24 hours postnatally. Only two infants in the group discharged early required rehospitalization, compared to four infants in the late discharge group that required a prolonged stay for medical problems. There were no significant differences in morbidity between groups within the first 6 weeks postnatally. A confusing aspect of this study was considerable overlap in discharge times between early and control (late) discharge groups. In a report from a Swedish hospital,[3] expectant mothers were invited to participate in a study in which they were randomized prenatally to either early discharge (24 to 48 hours) with domicilliary visits or a traditional stay (control group, average length, 6 days). There were 50 infants in the early discharge group and 54 controls. One infant from each group was re-admitted to a neonatal unit within the first week because of feeding and/or respiratory problems; no infant required re-admission for jaundice. There were no differences between groups on follow-up through the 6th postnatal week. In Vancouver, Carty and Bradley[12] randomized mothers and their infants prenatally to discharge at 12 to 24 hours (44 infants), 25 to 48 hours (49 infants), and 4 days after birth (38 infants). One infant was re-admitted to the hospital from each of the early discharge groups during the first 6 postnatal weeks; there were no re-admissions from the control group.

Although criteria for re-admission undoubtedly vary widely among centers, reported re-admission diagnoses appear quite similar. Hyperbilirubinemia requiring phototherapy is the most common, accounting for approximately three-fourths of all cases.[3,12,15,16,26–40] Because of the recent increased popularity of home phototherapy, a lower figure might be expected in a more current study. Other commonly reported re-admission diagnoses include infection, apnea, respiratory disorders, and feeding problems.[3,12,15,16,26–40]

Published studies have focused upon morbidity and mortality associated with early discharge, yet possible negative complications of a prolonged hospital stay have not been adequately investigated. In one report, infants remaining in the hospital had a higher rate of admission to a level II nursery than did those discharged early.[41] Increased exposure to nosocomial pathogens and the imposition of artificial schedules by the hospital environment have been suggested as possible detrimental effects of a prolonged stay.[15] Perhaps overly aggressive assessment of normal variations in newborn physiology may be incurred in the hospital, such as frequent bilirubin drawings on mildly jaundiced infants, with a consequent increase in cost and iatrogenic risk. These possibilities deserve further exploration.

## Socioeconomic Factors and Early Discharge

From an economic perspective, financial saving and more optimal utilization of health care resources are often cited as advantages of early discharge, yet published studies vary in their conclusions with respect to these issues. Several short-stay programs were motivated by limitations in numbers of obstetrical beds.[15,21–23] However, McIntosh[42] found that although an early discharge program in Alberta, Canada, was effective in reducing length of hospital stay and costs, it did not actually reduce pressure on bed space in a maternity unit. Yanover and coworkers[16] noted that the costs incurred for infants discharged early with home follow-up were comparable to those of a similar group kept in the hospital. Other reports suggest that substantial financial savings may be achieved by early discharge.[18,29,37,43] The magnitude of such savings may very likely depend upon the relative expense incurred by follow-up and rehospitalization.

Unfortunately, many families for whom early discharge is either financially attractive or mandated by third party payers may also be at risk for inadequate follow-up or recognition of medical problems. In a study of low-income mothers discharged with their infants 24 to 36 hours postpartum, 10% failed to return for a follow-up visit within 48 hours, even though they had signed a contract agreeing to do so.[41] This population had been carefully screened for medical risk factors, yet still had a high rate of hospital re-admission. Possibly, similar low-income groups who are less carefully screened might be at even greater risk for unidentified medical or social problems. Limitations of public health support or resources may further enhance this risk.

It is possible that early discharge may provide a safer and more attractive alternative to home birth for those mothers who are opposed to hospitalization. Unfortunately, this question has not been adequately addressed in the literature.

## Methodological Aspects of Early Discharge Studies

Most published studies on early discharge describe outcomes of specific individual programs, each with its own particular and often unique characteristics. Socioeconomic factors, geography, nationality, ethnicity, birth setting, and other population characteristics vary widely, as do criteria for determining an infant's candidacy for early discharge. Varied methods of risk screening and parental education have been utilized, maternal support systems at home differ widely, and mechanisms of follow-up vary from phone calls to home and office visits. The definition of early discharge differs considerably among studies: infants discharged in the "late" group in one study may actually go home at an earlier postnatal age than the "early" group of another. As a result, it is often difficult to compare data from different reports or to generalize results from one program to other settings.

Most reports state or imply that the infant is well at discharge, but few stipulate requirements for ascertaining health or selection criteria used to establish early discharge candidacy. Often, neither the period of follow-up nor the number of patients lost to follow-up are given, and in some cases the readmission rate is either unstated or difficult to discern.[5,37–40] Only a few of the reports that include a control group have employed randomization in group assignment.[3,12,16] Bias in patient selection thus constitutes a major obstacle in the interpretation of such studies. In some, the decision to discharge early was prompted by bed space limitations[15,18]; in others, mothers chose early discharge. In the few prospective randomized studies, mothers were recruited prenatally to participate in trials in which they might have a chance to leave the hospital earlier than otherwise.[3,12,16] In these cases, evaluation of psychosocial outcomes, such as parental satisfaction, depression, or anxiety, may be biased depending upon the extent of realization of parental expectations. Similarly, recruitment of mothers to participate in early discharge studies may select those with greater parenting capabilities, and mothers that choose early discharge may have enhanced home support mechanisms, more personal resources, and stronger motivation to succeed in the endeavor than women forced to leave the hospital earlier than desired.[39,40,44] Finally, reports of psychosocial outcomes, with only one exception,[18] have assessed the effects of combined early discharge of both mother and infant, closely related factors that are difficult to separate in study design.

A major concern regarding most studies involves the definition of morbidity. Details of individual cases are rarely given, and the age of presentation of medical problems is usually not stated. Criteria for medical concern are likely to vary considerably among practitioners, especially for problems such as jaundice, and it is possible that an infant re-admitted at one center might be followed as an outpatient at another. Moreover, in comparison studies the interpretation of outcome measures manifested beyond the time of discharge of both early and late groups may be difficult because of an inability to determine whether outcomes are related to the duration of initial hospitalization or factors arising during the interim. This is especially true for long observation periods after discharge. For example, the finding in one report that early and late discharge groups had similar rates of re-admission over a 6-week period does not support meaningful conclusions regarding safety of the time of discharge,[45] since medical problems presenting later (in this report, 68% were infections) commonly arise de novo and are often unrelated to events of the immediate newborn period. Conversely, assessing re-admission rates during a period after discharge that is short in comparison to the initial hospitalization may also be misleading: that infants kept in the hospital for greater than 48 hours should have lower rates of re-admission during the first week than those discharged at 24 to 36 hours might be expected,[41] because the portion of that week spent as an outpatient is correspondingly less. As a result, such a finding does not necessarily reflect differences in morbidity between the two discharge groups.

Because rates of re-admission are low, large numbers of infants would be needed in a controlled trial to detect differences in risk of rehospitalization between early and late discharge groups.[46] For example, assuming a minimum incidence of problems requiring re-admission in the population to be 1%, 38 211 infants would be needed in each group to detect a difference in outcome of 25% ( $\alpha = .05$; $\beta = .1$). It is unlikely that a study of this magnitude could be performed at a single center, and a multicenter effort would be needed. Most published reports have included only small groups of infants, and consequently sufficient statistical power is lacking. Because groups are small a single additional re-admission in either early or late discharge groups could, in many cases, affect the overall outcome of the study.

## Conclusion and Recommendations

Available data regarding early discharge of the term newborn is thus fraught with bias and methodological flaws, and consequently guidelines regarding this issue have been difficult to establish. Possible risks of early discharge remain of concern to many physicians, who feel that early signs of disease will be missed out of the hospital. On the other hand, the superiority of a longer hospitalization in facilitating improved outcomes has not been established, and arguments that continued hospitalization poses increased risk are equally tenable. In the absence of definitive medical data, current practices remain based upon clinical judgment, and economic considerations continue to emerge as directive forces behind the trend to discharge early.

Considering the very low incidence of morbidity among term newborns, it would seem that discharge as early as the first day postnatally may be safe if adequate psychosocial support and appropriate follow-up are available. Although as yet unvalidated, the guidelines for early discharge initially recommended by the American Academy of Pediatrics in 1980[8] still seem appropriate today.[9] These criteria include term delivery, appropriate growth for gestational age, normal physical examination, and a minimum of 6, preferably 12 hours of hospitalization, during which thermal homeostasis and successful feeding have occurred. Appropriate screening (cord blood type and coombs) and follow-up at 2 to 3 days postnatally were also recommended. Based upon observations that an uneventful transitional period was predictive of subsequently low neonatal morbidity, we have advocated careful monitoring during this period as a means of ascertaining health prior to discharge.[43] Finally, assessment of the adequacy of social environment and parenting skills should play an important part in the decision-making process. Until more definitive data are available, the decision regarding when to discharge the well term newborn must remain an individual one, made by the practioner based upon the medical, social, and economic aspects of each case.

## References


1. Norr KF, Nacion K. outcomes of postpartum early discharge, 1960–1986. A comparative review. *Birth.* 1987;14:135–141
2. Eidelman AI. Early discharge—early trouble. *J Perinatol.* 1992;12:101–102
3. Waldenstrom U, Sundelin C, Lindmark G. Early and late discharge after hospital birth. Health of mother and infant in the postpartum period. *Uppsala J Med Sci.* 1987;92:301–314
4. Gee A. Transfer home—two aspects of transfer home of mother and baby. *Midwives Chronicle & Nursing Notes.* 1984;97:8–9
5. James ML, Hudson CN, Gebski VJ, et al. An evaluation of planned early postnatal transfer home with nursing support. *Med J Australia.* 1987;127:434–438
6. Verbrugge HP. Youth health care in the Netherlands: a bird's eye view. *Pediatrics.* 1990;66:1044–1047
7. Waldenstrom U. Early discharge with domiciliary visits and hospital care. Parents' experiences of two modes of post-partum care. *Scan J Caring Sci.* 1987;1:51–58
8. Committee on Fetus Newborn, American Academy of Pediatrics. Criteria for early infant discharge and follow-up evaluation. *Pediatrics.* 1980;65:651
9. American Academy of Pediatrics, American College of Obstetricians and Gynecologists. *Guidelines for Perinatal Care,* Third Edition, 1992, pp 108–109
10. Fisher LD, Van Belle G. *Biostatistics: A Methodology for the Health Sciences.* New York: John Wiley Sons, Inc; pp 893–897
11. DerSimonian R, Charette J, McPeek B, Mosteller F. Reporting on methods in clinical trials. *New Eng J Med.* 1982;306:1332–1337
12. Carty EM, Bradley CF. A randomized, controlled evaluation of early postpartum hospital discharge. *Birth.* 1990;17:199–204
13. Waldenstrom U. Early and late discharge after hospital birth: father's involvement in infant care. *Early Human Dev.* 1988;17:19–28
14. Waldenstrom U, Sundelin C, Lindmark G. Early and late discharge after hospital birth: breastfeeding. *Acta Paediatr Scand,* 1987;76:727–732
15. Hellman LM, Kohl SG, Palmer J. Early hospital discharge in obstetrics. Lancet. 1962;1:227–232
16. Yanover MJ, Jones DJ, Miller MD. Perinatal care of low-risk mothers and infants: early discharge with home care. *N Engl J Med.* 1976;294:702–705
17. Arborelius E, Lindell D. Psychological aspects of early and late discharge after hospital delivery. *Scand J Soc Med.* 1989;17:103–107
18. Norr KF, Nacion KW, Abramson R. Early discharge with home follow-up; impacts on low-income mothers and infants. *JOGN Nurs.* 1988;22:133–141
19. Pinker GD, Fraser AC. Early discharge of maternity patients. *Br Med J.* 1964;7:99–100

20. Theobald GW. Weekly antenatal care and home on the second day. *Lancet.* 1962;4:735–737
21. Arthturton MW, Bamford FN. Paediatric aspects of the early discharge of mater nity patients. *Br Med J.* 1976;3:517–520
22. Guerriero WF. A maternal welfare programme for New Orleans. *Am J Obstet Gynecol.* 1943;46:312–313
23. Theobald GW. Home on the second day: The Bradford experiment. *Br Med J.* 1959;2:1364–1367
24. College of General Practitioners, Bradford Group. A survey of 100 early discharge cases. *Lancet.* 1966;1:536–540
25. Craig GA, Muirhead JMB. Obstetric aspects of the early discharge of maternity patients. *Br Med J.* 1967;3:520–522
26. Power DJ, Wolf E, Van Coeverden de Grooot HA. Early discharge from maternity units in Cape Town. *S Afr Med J.* 1980;58:893–895
27. Thurston NE, Dundas JB. Evaluation of an early post partum discharge program. *Can J Public Health.* 1985;76:384–387
28. Jansson P. Early postpartum discharge. *Am J Nursing.* 1985;5:547–550
29. Cottrell DG, Pittala B, Hey D. One day maternity care: a pediatric view. *J Am Osteopath Assoc.* 1986;83:216–221
30. Rollins AJ, Kaplan JA, Ratkay ME, et al. A homestyle delivery program in a university hospital. *J Fam Practice.* 1979;9:407–414
31. Barton JJ, Rovner S, Puls K, Read PA. Alternative birthing center: experience in a teaching obstetric service. *Am J Obstet Gynecol.* 1980;137:377–384
32. Avery MD, Fournier LC, Jones PL, Sopovic CP. An early postpartum hospital discharge program. Implementation and evaluation. *JOGN Nurs.* 1982;11:233–235
33. Scupholme A. Postpartum early discharge: an inner city experience. *J Nurs Mid.* 1981;26:19–22
34. Neuenschwander F, Meier M, Witschi M. Die ambulante Geburt: Erfahrungen und Organisation. *Ther Umsch.* 1981;38:981–984
35. Dudenhausen JW, Stauber M. Erfahrungen mit der sogenannten ambulanten Geburt in der Klinik. *Arch Gynecol.* 1983;235:617–623
36. Berryman GK. An early discharge program. *Mil Med.* 1991;156:583–584
37. Waskerwitz S, Fournier L, Jones P, Meier W. A comparative analysis of newborn outcome in a hospital-based birthing center. *Clin Pediatr.* 1985;24:273–277
38. Mehl LE, Peterson GH, Sokolosky W, Whitt MC. Outcomes of early discharge after normal birth. *Birth and Family J.* 1976;3:101–107
39. Patterson PK. A comparison of postpartum early traditional discharge groups. *Q Rev Bull.* 1987;13:365–371
40. Lemmer CM. Early discharge: outcomes of primiparas and their infants. *JOGN Nurs.* 1987;16:230–236
41. Conrad PD. Wilkening RB, Rosenberg AA. Safety of newborn discharge in less than 36 hours in an indigent population. *Am J Dis Child.* 1989;143:98–101
42. McIntosh ID. Hospital effects of maternity early discharge. *Med Care.* 1984;22:611–619
43. Britton HL, Britton JR. Efficacy of early newborn discharge in a middle-class population. *Am J Dis Child.* 1984;138:1041–1046
44. Waldenstrom U, Lindmark G. Early and late discharge after hospital birth. A comparative study of parental background characteristics. *Scand J Soc Med.* 1987;15:159–167
45. Pittard WB, Geddes KM. Newborn hospitalization: a closer look. *J Pediatr.* 1988;112:257–262
46. Detsky AS, Sackett DL. When was a 'negative' clinical trial big enough? *Arch Intern Med.* 1985;145:709–712

**Elizabeth H. Thilo and**
**Susan F. Townsend**

# What Are the Pitfalls of Early Discharge?

What constitutes the ideal hospital stay for a healthy term infant? Who should decide whether mother and baby are ready for discharge—the mother, the doctor, or the insurer? What follow-up arrangements are needed when babies are discharged early? How early is "early"? And what effect does early discharge have on newborn screening for metabolic disease?

These questions have become increasingly newsworthy in recent months. Reports of bilirubin encephalopathy and severe dehydration in newborns discharged after short hospital stays have attracted public attention, and a number of state legislatures have passed laws requiring third-party-payers to cover longer postpartum stays.

In the 1970s, when early new-born discharge first attracted public attention, it was a parent-driven request: Well-educated parents with good support systems at home wanted to shorten the typical postpartum stay from 4 or more days to 2 or less. More recently, early newborn discharge has evolved into an insurer-driven quest to cut health-care costs. Childbirth is the most common reason for hospitalization in the US. With some 4 million births per year, savings from shortening the hospital stay by 1 day per birth have been estimated at nearly $4 billion a year. But as short stays become standard practice, the question of safety is crucial.

## Developing Standards for Safety

The Committee on the Fetus and Newborn of the American Academy of Pediatrics (AAP) published updated and detailed minimum criteria for early newborn discharge in 1995 (Table 1).[1] The Committee suggests that all criteria be fulfilled before the newborn is discharged, and says this is "unlikely" in a hospital stay of less than 48 hours.

The new guidelines clarify safety standards considerably, but practical problems remain. For example, the guidelines state that "the mother's knowledge, ability, and confidence to provide adequate care for her baby are documented by the fact that she has received training sessions" in feeding and newborn care. Such training could be incorporated into childbirth education classes or prenatal visits, and not postponed until the brief postpartum hospital stay. But what if the mother doesn't feel confident and knowledgeable after such training? Should her continued hospital stay be covered by insurance? What about newborns whose home environment is considered too risky for discharge? Should insurers pay for care until, as the guidelines put it, "a plan to safeguard the infant is in place"? If the answer to questions like these is yes, how can insurers be made to comply?

One approach is to mandate coverage for a minimum length of stay. The states of Massachusetts, New Jersey, and North Carolina now have laws requiring postpartum hospital insurance to cover a minimum 48-hour hospital stay for an uncomplicated vaginal delivery, and 96 hours for a cesarean section. Maryland law permits discharge of a mother and newborn infant if AAP and the American College of Obstetricians and Gynecologists (ACOG) medical stability criteria are met, which is now equivalent to a 48-hour recommendation. Similar laws have been introduced in the US Senate and are pending in 20 states.[2] In a somewhat different approach, insurers in Colorado were persuaded to allow a 48-hour stay in a compromise with legislators so as to avoid specific legislation.

It's too early to tell what effect legislation will have on average length of stay and costs, or to what extent new parents will take advantage of these laws. In addition, both AAP and ACOG endorse collaborative decision-making between physicians and parents in determining the length of hospital stay, not timetables mandated by legislators or insurers.[1,2]

## Research Gives Limited Guidance

Published findings on early discharge of term newborns are limited by methodological variability and flaws in study design. One finding that seems secure is that an uncomplicated transition period (first 6 hours) is important in predicting short-term outcome.[4] In a retrospective study of a middle-class population, one team reported that the majority of newborn illnesses were present in the first 6 hours; a normal transition period predicted continued wellness 98% of the time (99% when jaundice was excluded).[4] Only 1% of infants who were initially well (17 of 1,583) became ill with a problem other than jaundice between 6 hours and 2 weeks of age. However, this study did not address the question of optimal timing of discharge for infants who achieved a successful transition.

The definitive study on the safety of early discharge has not yet been performed, although several authors have recently published comprehensive reviews.[5–7] Some investigators have concluded that the literature supporting the safety and efficacy of early discharge is "fraught with bias," that the studies available are too small to have statistical power, and that guidelines recommended by the AAP in 1980 still seem reasonable.[5] They also note that no evidence supports the notion that longer stays would improve outcome. They calculate that, because readmission rates are low (around 1%), a comparison of early and late discharge outcomes would require more than 38,000 infants in each category to detect a difference of 25%. They recommend a minimum of 12 rather than 6 hours of hospitalization so that feeding can begin to be established, and suggest that decisions about when to discharge a well, term

*Table 1*

## Criteria for Early Newborn Discharge

Uncomplicated antepartum, intrapartum, and postpartum course for baby and mother
Single birth
Vaginal delivery
Term gestation (38–42 wk), with birthweight appropriate for gestational age by appropriate growth curve, with normal exam
Baby shows normal, stable vital signs for 12 hr preceding discharge
- Thermal homeostasis (axillary temperature 36.1 °C–37°C in open crib)
- Respiratory rate < 60/min
- Heart rate 100–160 beats/min

Baby has voided and stooled; if circumcised, no excess bleeding for ≥ 2 hr
Baby has fed at least twice, demonstrating coordinated suck, swallow, and breathing
No significant jaundice in first 24 hr of life
Mother has adequate knowledge to care for her newborn, documented by training in:
- Breastfeeding or bottle feeding—trained staff should assess breastfeeding
- Knowledge of normal urine and stool frequency
- Cord, skin, infant genital care
- Recognition of common signs of infant illness, especially jaundice
- Infant safety issues (car safety seats, sleep positioning)

Support (family members or health-care providers) available to mother and baby for first few days after discharge. Supporters:
- Familiar with newborn care and knowledgeable about lactation
- Able to recognize jaundice and dehydration

Laboratory data obtained and reviewed as normal or negative, including:
- Maternal testing for syphilis and hepatitus B
- Cord/infant blood type, direct Coombs' test if indicated

Newborn screening sample obtained according to state regulations; if sample obtained before 24 hr of milk feedings, follow-up testing is assured
Initial hepatitus B vaccine given or scheduled within first week
Physician-directed source of continuing care identified:
- If discharged at < 48 hr, definite appointment for exam within next 48 hr
- Examiner competent in newborn assessment, reports to physician on day of visit

Family, environmental, and social risk factors assessed, including but not limited to:
- Substance abuse, history of child abuse or neglect, no fixed home, teen mother, lack of social support (especially for single, first-time mother), domestic violence

If risk factors are present, discharge delayed until a plan to safeguard the baby is in place

*Source:* AAP Committee on Fetus and Newborn[1]

newborn be made on an individual basis determined by "the medical, social, and economic aspects of each case."

Another group addressed the shortcomings in the current literature.[6] No adequately designed studies have evaluated early discharge in the absence of additional, routine follow-up services, for example. Also, limited information is available about compliance with follow-up visits. Most studies concluding that early discharge is "safe" were too small to detect significant adverse outcomes, were conducted under restricted conditions, or showed clear bias in how results were interpreted. After analyzing more than 20 studies, the authors stated that "the currently available literature provides little scientific evidence to guide discharge planning for most apparently well newborns and their mothers." In addition, they said that there is "no evidence to support the general safety or advisability of early discharge in the absence of stringent selection criteria and post-discharge nurse home visits." This view reinforces the need to be selective about which infants to discharge early and the need for prompt follow-up in the home.

In another evaluation of the literature, one researcher examined only experimental or quasi-experimental studies.[7] One noted the methodological flaws cited above—small sample size and restrictive protocols that included well-defined follow-up. Interestingly, the definition of "early" discharge in the studies he examined varied from 2 hours to 5 days. He also pointed out that most studies used readmission of the infant or mother as the only measure of health outcome, probably because readmission is the easiest outcome to measure. Other possible outcomes, such as success at breastfeeding, parent satisfaction, and compliance, have not been evaluated.

These reviews indicate that available data are too limited to predict a length of stay that would guarantee safety and optimal outcome for most newborns. However, most clinicians agree on the major safety issues associated with early discharge: avoiding severe jaundice, providing adequate follow-up, and screening accurately for congenital disorders.

## Jaundice Redux

Jaundice is the most common cause for hospital readmission in the first 2 weeks of life. In recent years, a gentler approach to nonhemolytic jaundice in well, term infants has coincided with the trend to shorter newborn hospital stays, resulting in the return of kernicterus.[8–11] The shorter the hospital stay, the higher the readmission rate in the first 2 weeks of life for severe jaundice and dehydration.[12]

At the time of discharge, neonatal jaundice is not apparent; in the absence of hemolysis, it rarely is at 24 hours of age. Intake during the hospital stay may have been inadequate, although the feeding pattern in the first 24 hours is often sluggish and it's difficult to judge whether the infant is getting enough to eat. The infant goes home, often breastfeeding, perhaps with inadequate intake over the next several days that is not recognized by the mother. After 4 to 8 days, the baby returns to the hospital with excessive weight loss, dehydration, and hyperbilirubinemia.

Although not usually life threatening on its own, marked hyperbilirubinemia should not be ignored. It is often the most easily recognized sign of problems with breastfeeding intake.... Specific instructions for the breastfeeding mother may help her recognize problems in the baby. We tell mothers to contact their health provider if they do not see signs of adequate intake, and advise them to supplement breastfeeding with expressed milk or formula if the baby shows signs of dehydration.

## Follow-Up Is Crucial

Clearly, as length of stay decreases, the importance of follow-up increases. The traditional 2-week checkup is too late to pick up serious jaundice, dehydration, and excessive weight loss in a baby who is not breastfeeding well, and the occasional infant with serious congenital heart disease or a metabolic problem that was not apparent at the time of early discharge.

The AAP as part of routine preventive care, recommends a follow-up visit 2 to 4 days after discharge for any newborn who goes home before 48 hours, but there are difficulties in providing this service. Some insurers don't cover an office visit at this time, and some parents have trouble with transportation in the days after birth.[13] For these reasons, home visits by nurses have been widely endorsed, particularly in the lay press. Many insurers who mandate 24-hour discharge include a home nurse visit in their reimbursement package. The problems with home visits are a lack of standardization in the background, training, and experience of the personnel performing these duties, and a lack of consistency in the evaluation of the infant. In the Denver area, the Kaiser Permanente system has solved these problems by employing a group of nurses with experience in perinatal care who do only newborn home visits. If such a specialized group of personnel is not available, home nursing visits can be structured to follow specific guidelines, with explicit instructions to contact the primary care provider for certain indications.

A follow-up visit that conforms to these guidelines will provide consistent assessments and allow the visiting nurse to recognize problems with lactation and jaundice before the baby is compromised. The only specialized equipment needed is a well-calibrated scale. A careful history of intake and elimination should be obtained, and the infant observed while breastfeeding if possible. In our opinion, the visiting nurse should undress the infant completely for the examination and weigh the baby. The nurse should report any heart murmur immediately and arrange for a physician examination without delay. The visiting nurse should have a working knowledge of normal newborn vital signs, normal patterns of weight loss following birth, normal elimination patterns, and common breastfeeding problems, in order to discuss the findings with the physician and make referrals to a lactation specialist when necessary.[14] The nurse should fax a summary of the visit to the primary care provider the same day as the home visit.

For such a program to succeed, both home health nurses and primary care physicians need more instruction in lactation. A 1995 survey of recently trained pediatricians, obstetricians, and family physicians revealed a serious lack of breastfeeding knowledge and training, with fewer than 50% of senior residents and 75% of practicing physicians feeling that their training in breastfeeding issues was adequate.[15] Only 50% to 60% of respondents knew the appropriate interventions for low milk supply or jaundice in the breastfeeding newborn. Clearly, training and continuing education programs for physicians and others who work with new breastfeeding mothers should give more attention to these issues. This is particularly critical because specialized lactation-support services are likely to be early casualties when hospitals cut their budgets.[16]

## What About Screening?

What are the effects of early newborn discharge on newborn screening tests? Should testing be done even when discharge before 12 or 24 hours is anticipated? One group recommends drawing the newborn screen sample before discharge regardless of the baby's age, since this may be the only opportunity to detect a problem, and many of the results will be reliable.[17] Early sampling does not affect the results of hemoglobin electrophoresis, galactosemia testing, and testing for biotinidase deficiency, since these tests rely upon a protein marker (hemoglobin S, for example) or the absence of an enzyme. Tests that depend on the accumulation of a metabolite or rapid changes in hormone levels at birth, however, may be affected. These include screens for hypothyroidism, congenital adrenal hyperplasia, maple syrup urine disease, homocystinuria, and phenylketonuria (PKU). Although the exact effects of the timing of the sample are not known for most of these, research has been done on PKU and hypothyroidism.[17,18]

Phenylaline levels will be reliably elevated by 24 hours of age, even in breastfed infants.[17] Therefore, if the PKU screen is drawn after 24 hours, it will not need to be repeated. However, since laboratories in most states do not do quantitative phenylalanine levels, but rather the less sensitive Guthrie test, a bioassay, a second PKU screen will be required if the first sample is obtained at less than 24 hours of age.[18]

Thyroid screening may need to be repeated, depending on the screening method used in your region. There is normally a surge of TSH at birth, with normal $T_4$ levels. If your screening method relies on TSH testing, samples taken within the first day of life will yield many false positives. Programs that rely on $T_4$ measurements generally also include TSH testing on the lowest 10% of samples, and therefore will also have higher recall rates for early discharge infants with low normal $T_4$ who have a mildly elevated TSH level. The AAP recommends that any infant with a TSH level greater than 40 mU/L be considered hypothyroid until proven otherwise, and to repeat testing in those with mildly elevated TSH levels between 20 and 40 mU/L.[19]

## Where Do We Stand?

Early discharge has led to unforeseen problems in some patients. Experience shows that many infants fare well if discharged at 24 hours or even less, while a few go on to develop problems with feeding, jaundice, or, rarely, infection or cardiac symptoms. To avert these problems, reliable, knowledgeable follow-up within 48 to 72 hours of discharge is imperative. This early follow-up ensures that repeat PKU screening will occur, adequacy of breastfeeding will be assessed, and the infant will be evaluated for jaundice and other medical problems. Efforts to improve prenatal education in breastfeeding and newborn care should also be pursued and could be incorporated into prenatal visits. With a systematic approach to parent and physician education, and appropriately guided early follow-up, the physician and mother can work together to determine the best length of stay for that mother-infant pair.

## References


1. AAP Committee on Fetus and Newborn: Hospital stay for healthy term newborns. Pediatrics 1995;96:788
2. Annas G: Women and children first. N Engl J Med 1995;333:1647
3. Algeo D: Insurers' agreement kills hospital-stay bill. The Denver Post, January 30, 1996
4. Britton HL, Britton JR: Efficacy of early newborn discharge in a middle class population. Am J Dis Child 1984;138:1041
5. Britton JR, Britton HL, Beebe SA: Early discharge of the term newborn: A continued dilemma. Pediatrics 1994;94:291
6. Braveman P, Egerter S, Peral M, et al: Early discharge of newborns and mothers: A critical review of the literature. Pediatrics 1995;96:716
7. Margolis LH: A critical review of studies of newborn discharge timing. Clin Pediatr 1995;34(12):626
8. Newman TB, Maisels MJ: Evaluation and treatment of jaundice in the term newborn: A kinder, gentler approach. Pediatrics 1992;89:809
9. AAP Provisional Committee for Quality Improvement and Subcommittee on Hyperbilirubinemia: Practice parameter: Management of hyperbilirubinemia in the healthy term newborn. Pediatrics 1994;94:558
10. Sola A: Changes in clinical practice and bilirubin encephalopathy in "healthy term newborns." Pediatr Res 1995;37:145A
11. Hansen TWR: Kernicterus in a full-term infant: The need for increased vigilance (Letter). Pediatrics 1995;95:798
12. Lee K-S, Perlman M. Ballantyne M, et al: Association between duration of neonatal hospital stay and readmission rate. J Pediatr 1995;127:758
13. AAP Committee on Practice and Ambulatory Medicine: Recommendations for preventive pediatric health care. Pediatrics 1995;96(2):insert
14. Freed GL, Landers S, Schanier RJ: A practical guide to successful breast-feeding management. Am J Dis Child 1991;145:917
15. Freed GL, Clark SJ, Sorenson J, et al: National assessment of physicians' breastfeeding knowledge, attitudes, training, and experience. JAMA 1995;273:472
16. Eicher D: Breastfeeding program dealt a blow: Cutbacks, changes trim services. The Denver Post, January 29,1996
17. Doherty LB, Rohr FJ, Levy HL: Detection of phenylketonuria in the very early newborn blood specimen. Pediatrics 1991;87:240
18. Early discharge from the newborn nursery: A potential threat to effective newborn screening (editorial). Screening 1994;3:45
19. AAP section on Endocrinology and Committee on Genetics, and American Thyroid Association Committee on Public Health: Newborn screening for congenital hypothyroidism: Recommended guidelines. Pediatrics 1993;91:203

# POSTSCRIPT

## Should Hospitals Continue Early Discharge Policies for Newborns?

Britton, Britton, and Beebe concede that there are methodological flaws in the studies on early discharge, but they maintain that there is evidence that early discharge is safe for the majority of babies. The three physicians wrote their selection before the mandatory 48-hour hospital stay for newborns was instituted, but their summary of the available data on the appropriate time for discharging term newborns provides valuable research on the subject. They report studies that show psychosocial benefits of early discharge. These include a facilitation of bonding, attachment, increased breast-feeding, enhanced family interactions, and overall improved patient satisfaction.

Thilo and Townsend detail the minimum criteria for early newborn discharge, which has been published by the Committee on the Fetus and Newborn of the American Academy of Pediatrics. Although the criteria for discharge seem clear, there are some vague areas that are difficult to measure. Is 48 hours enough time for the doctor to ascertain that the baby will stay healthy? Thilo and Townsend state that there is little evidence to show that all of the criteria can be met within 48 hours.

## Suggested Readings


Braveman, P., Egerter, S., Pearl, M., Marchi, K., & Miller, C. (1995, October). Problems associated with early discharge of newborn infants. Early discharge of newborns and mothers: A critical review. *Pediatrics, 96*(4), 716–726.

Hammonds, K. (1996, January). Newborn babies, bawling moms. *Business Week (Industrial/Technology Edition), 40*(3457).

Kyong-Soon, L., Periman, M., Ballantyne, M., Ailed, I., & To, T. (1995, November). Association between duration of neonatal hospital stay and readmission rate. *Journal of Pediatrics, 127*(5), 758–766.

Margolis, L. (1995, December). A critical review of studies of newborn discharge timing. *Clinical Pediatrics, 34*(12), 626–634.

Oh, W. (1995, October). Hospital stay for healthy term newborns. *Pediatrics, 96*(4), 788–790.

Survival of drive-through babies same as others—study. (1996, September). *American Medical News, 39*(33), 11.

# ISSUE 4

## Does Transracial Adoption Harm a Child's Development?

**YES: Leslie Doty Hollingsworth**, from "Symbolic Interactionism, African American Families, and the Transracial Adoption Controversy," *Social Work* (September 1999)

**NO: Rudolph Alexander, Jr. and Carla M. Curtis**, from "A Review of Empirical Research Involving the Transracial Adoption of African American Children," *Journal of Black Psychology* (May 1996)

### ISSUE SUMMARY


**YES:** Leslie Doty Hollingsworth, assistant professor at the University of Michigan, contends that socialization within an African American family is a unique and distinct experience for children. As a consequence, children not socialized in these families cannot effectively embrace African American definitions of self and family.

**NO:** Rudolph Alexander, Jr. and Carla M. Curtis, both professors at Ohio State University, offer research maintaining that African American children are not psychologically harmed by transracial adoptions.


American society has long embraced the notion that children do much better by being adopted into loving homes rather than being placed in institutions or orphanages. The family unit not only socializes a child but can provide a child with nurturance, a sense of security, and unconditional love. Unfortunately, there are hundreds of thousands of children in U.S. society who, for various reasons, are not with their biological families. They, like all children, are in need of and entitled to loving families, but they cannot get them. These are mostly nonwhite children. The question thus arises: Should these children be adopted, transracially, by white families, especially if the alternative is a succession of foster homes or institutionalization?

Transracial adoption typically refers to a family in which a minority child (e.g. Asian American, Native American, African American, or Latino) or a child with a mixed racial background is adopted by an Anglo-American couple. Transracial adoptions account for about 15 percent of all adoptions in the United States annually. This type of adoption became more commonplace in the United States in the late 1940s. Children with mixed racial backgrounds came from Europe and Asia after World War II, Korean American children came from the Korean War, and refugee Chinese children in Hong Kong were adopted by Anglo-American couples in the United States. Finding adoptive homes for Native American children followed. The movement to place African American children with Anglo-American families is the most recent evolution of transracial adoption.

A common opinion among adoption professionals today is that eligible children should be placed in an adoptive home without delay. However, whenever possible, children should be raised by people of their own culture and heritage. The Multi-Ethnic Placement Act of 1994 forbade using race as the sole factor in deciding whether or not a family can adopt a given child. Race is to be used as one of several factors in the decision. The National Association of Black Social Workers (NABSW) has argued vociferously against transracial adoption. Its position is that the practice is destructive to minority families and communities. The sentiment of the members of this group is so strong that they have even suggested that the placement of African American children with Anglo-American families could be conceived as a form of cultural genocide. Leora Neal, executive director of the National Association of Black Social Workers Child Adoption, Counseling, and Referral Service outlines several problems incurred by transracial adoptees:

- They may feel unaccepted by both the Anglo-American and minority community from which they came.
- In a racist society, children need to learn coping skills. Since white parents have never had to deal with racism, they are often ill equipped to help their children understand and deal with it effectively.
- Children lose contact with the fullness of their culture of origin.
- Adopting family members do not always realize that they are now part of a mixed-race family. As a result, they must acknowledge and accept this fact.

As you read the following two selections, consider the issue from both the adoptive parents' point of view and the child's. What are the critical issues that come to your mind that might cause you to support the point of view of the NABSW? Which issues might cause you to support prospective parents and children who are involved in a transracial adoption?

**Leslie Doty Hollingsworth**

# Symbolic Interactionism, African American Families, and the Transracial Adoption Controversy

## Historical Background

Transracial adoption is the legal adoption of children of one race or ethnic group by a family of a different race or ethnic group. In the United States transracial adoption almost without exception has involved the adoption by white parents of children of racial or ethnic minority groups from the United States or other countries. In cases in which African American children were involved, the practice began to increase during the 1950s (Simon & Alstein, 1977), precipitated by a decrease in healthy white infants available for adoption and an increase in white parents desiring to adopt (McRoy, 1989). Between 1967 and 1972 approximately 10,000 African American children were transracially adopted, with about 2,500 placements occurring in 1971 (McRoy, 1989). Advocacy groups were established to promote and facilitate transracial adoptions (Simon & Alstein, 1992). Standards-setting groups, such as the Child Welfare League of America (1968), reversed their race- and religion-matching standards, and adoption research began to be directed at examining the motivation for transracial adoption (Hollingsworth, 1998).

In November 1972 the National Association of Black Social Workers (NABSW) (cited in McRoy, 1989, and Simon & Alstein, 1977) passed a resolution opposing the transracial adoption of African American children. The resolution read in part:

> Black children should be placed only with Black families, whether in foster care or adoption. Black children belong physically, and psychologically and culturally in black families in order that they receive the total sense of themselves and develop a sound projection of their future. Human beings are products of their environment and develop their sense of values, attitudes, and self-concepts within their own family structure. Black children in white homes are cut off from the healthy development of themselves as black people (cited in Simon & Alstein, 1977, p. 50).

From Leslie Doty Hollingsworth, "Symbolic Interactionism, African American Families, and the Transracial Adoption Controversy," *Social Work*, vol. 44, no. 5 (September 1999). 

Although the wording of the actual resolution became a source of controversy, much of the controversy was about some of the supporting language:

> Our position is based on:
>
> 1. the necessity of self-determination from birth to death of all Black people.
> 2. the need of our young ones to begin at birth to identify with Black people in a Black community.
> 3. the philosophy that we need our own to build a strong nation (p. 50)....

This resolution was not put forward arbitrarily. The experience of African American children in the United States formed the context within which the resolution was introduced. Chestang (1972) was among the first to call social workers' attention to the cultural concerns that transracial adoption presented. He identified three conditions in the United States that characterized the experience of African American people: *societal inconsistency,* which he defined as being put in a position of having to maintain a sense of competence while coping with discrimination and prejudice; *social injustice*—that is, being confronted with inequities in employment, housing, and education on the basis of race; and *personal impotence*—the sense of shame, inadequacy, and diminished self-worth that is associated with being powerless to affect the oppressive situation. Chestang pointed out that African American people are faced with these conditions from birth to death. He called attention to what life under these conditions would be like for African American children who were transracially adopted and for their adoptive families. Finally, he reminded social workers that the situation in which the child welfare system found itself —that is, a large number of African American children in the foster care and institutional systems—was the result of discrimination and other barriers to adoption by African American families and not their unwillingness to adopt....

The rise in opposition to same-race adoption policies, beginning in the early 1980s, has been documented (Hollingsworth, 1998). Opponents were concerned about possible discrimination, about the overresponsibility on the part of children of color for the good of the group, and about the lack of empirical support for same-race policies (Bartholet, 1991). Several highly publicized lawsuits were filed (McRoy, 1989), and transracial adoptions increased once more.

Meanwhile, the NABSW called attention to three circumstances that negatively affected the status of African American children in the child welfare system. First, experience with the child welfare system did not demonstrate a commitment to the preservation of African American families. Children frequently were removed from their families because of neglect. Although neglect has been shown to be associated with poverty, the economic condition of these families that may have given rise to the neglect of children seldom was addressed. In addition, barriers existed that impeded the children's placement with relatives. Second, efforts to reunite children with their biological families were insufficient. The NABSW called attention to the fact that African American children tended to remain in foster care or the institutional system after having been removed from their families and that the child welfare and judicial systems lacked the capacity to reunite these children with their families in a timely manner. Moreover, biological parents frequently did not have the financial resources necessary to correct the circumstances that led to their children's removal. However, substantial resources were directed to foster parents and institutions, leading the NABSW to question whether institutions were retaining children to acquire more funds for their care. Third, the NABSW continued to object to the implication that African Americans do not adopt in large enough numbers to resolve the crisis of African American children in the foster care system. The organization called attention to the fact that the majority of children in the foster care system were hard-to-place white children with special needs and that only 1 percent or fewer white families who were willing to adopt African American children requested those with special needs (special needs typically are defined as being over eight years old, in sibling groups, and with emotional and physical disabilities). Adoption alone was considered insufficient to address the foster care crisis.

The Omnibus Budget Reconciliation Act of 1993 (P.L. 103–66) eventually was passed. This legislation provided funding for the expansion of community-based family support programs and family preservation programs. The NABSW ("Preserving," 1994) subsequently modified its position on transracial adoption. In its current position, it places priority on family preservation and reunification with birth families, alternative care by biological relatives, and adoption by same-race nonrelatives, recognizing the importance of providing permanent homes for all children. Transracial adoption is seen as a last resort. Children should not be removed from their birth families when economic resource limitations or institutional barriers are the sources of the problem ("Preserving," 1994).

The Interethnic Adoption Section of the Small Business Job Protection Act of 1996 (P.L. 104–188) lacked language that had allowed the best interests of the child to be considered in decisions to use race or ethnicity in adoptive placements. Penalties were established for federally funded agencies that delayed or denied placement based on these considerations. The Adoption and Safe Families Act of 1997 (P.L. 105–89) was passed. Although the law is credited with better protecting children from maltreatment, it makes it easier to terminate the rights of biological parents. It occurs in a legislative environment of diminishing economic resources to poor families whose children are at greatest risk of maltreatment. . . .

## Symbolic Interactionist Explanation

. . . [T]he African American community consists of people and institutions similar in their African heritage (Nobles, 1974) and in their experience with racism and oppression (Baldwin, 1981). Thus, the African American community is central in the socialization of African American children.

Symbolic interactionism has framed a number of studies of African American life. These include studies that demonstrate the lower rate of work-family conflicts among African American women who were socialized to balance both roles (Myers, 1989), the appropriateness of group work for intervention with African American youths from low-income families who present school behavior problems (Brown, 1984), the meaning of leisure among older African American women (Chin-Sang & Allen, 1991), and common experiences of African Americans with AIDS (Hudson & Morris, 1994). Baldwin's (1981) African self-consciousness theory derives from assumptions that are consistent with symbolic interactionism. A preference for the adoption and socialization of African American children by same-race parents can be understood from this perspective.

... [T]he objection to transracial adoption may be understood in terms of the meaning that Africans and African Americans attach to children. According to the African scholar Mbiti (1969), it is desirable in traditional African societies to have many children because the dead are believed to remain among the living as long as there is someone who remembers them and can refer to them personally by name. Traditional Africans think of their children as divine gifts (Erny, 1973), as is evident in the Ashanti proverb that "children are the reward of life" (Willis, 1996). It is possible that children also have a special meaning in contemporary African American communities that causes these communities to want to hold on to them. The acceptance of children born outside of marriage (the idea that "there are no illegitimate children") and the active role of grandparents in their care (Flaherty, Facteau, & Garver, 1995) exemplifies this position.

The relationship between meaning and behavior is also apparent in NABSW's definition of its constituency as being the black individual, the black family, and the black community. Its mission is directed toward their welfare and toward a commitment to action for the improvement of social conditions over personal interests. Considered within this framework, that the organization opposes transracial adoption is fully comprehensible....

As a method of survival on arriving in a foreign land, African slaves established plantation communities (James, 1992). The process by which slave children learned to call non-blood-related adults "uncle" and "aunt" is believed to have socialized them into the slave community. The community, then, became the family of the child whose parents had been sold or were required to work and live away from the child. After the Civil War, U.S. officials, preparing to arrange the care of what they believed were thousands of orphaned black children who were freed but whose parents had already been sold, were surprised that the children had already been taken into the families of former friends and neighbors (Gutman, 1976).

In its code of ethics, the National Association of Black Social Workers recognizes the concept of a black extended family, with all black people considered as kin, and with no distinction made between the destiny of other black people and [one's] own destiny. It seems clear, therefore, that the meaning of such concepts as the family is influenced by the interaction of African and African American people in the life of the ethnic group.

"Meanings are handled in and modified through an interpretive process used by the person in dealing with things he or she encounters" (LaRossa & Reitzes, 1994, p. 143). Among Africans and African Americans, adoption traditionally seems to have been interpreted as a natural and informal process arising in response to a need rather than a formal one involving legal ownership and individual rights. Thus, the results of Hill's (1977) survey of the informal adoption patterns of African Americans from 1969 to 1976 showed that 90 percent of children who were born "out-of-wedlock" were kept by the extended family— the majority (57 percent) by grandparents and great-grandparents and the next largest number (26 percent) by aunts and uncles.

As a result of such knowledge development as that provided by Hill (1977), professionals who were involved in adoption services and policy making began to attach a different meaning to the resistance to transracial adoption. Agency policies and practices were modified to reflect an emphasis on same-race adoptions. In some instances separate agencies or programs were established that specialized in the recruitment of same-race adopters. The success of these programs has been described elsewhere (Gant, 1984; Gilles & Kroll, 1991; Hairston & Williams, 1989; Jackson-White, Dozier, Oliver, & Gardner, 1997; McRoy, Oglesby, & Grape, 1997).

A surge has been noted in kinship foster care arrangements, especially among African Americans. Because adoption has been interpreted by African Americans as an informal process, many African Americans are resistant to formally adopting the kin who are in their care (Hollingsworth, 1998). Although these arrangements are often permanent, relatives cite the fact that the children are already family and that they do not want to create dissension with the child's birth parents whom they consider family also (Thornton, 1991). Some associate the practice of paying fees to adopt children with slave trading (Gilles & Kroll, 1991). The differences in interpretation, however, do not change the outcome of the process—that is, that permanent homes and families are provided to children who need them.

... The NABSW (cited in Simon & Alstein, 1977) indicated that African American children could "receive [a] total sense of themselves and develop a sound projection of their future" only in African American families (p. 50). The organization also asserted that because "human beings are products of their environment and develop their sense of values, attitudes, and self-concepts within their own family structure, . . . black children in white homes [would be] cut off from the healthy development of themselves as black people" (p. 50). According to symbolic interactionism, it is through contact with others in the social group that children learn a sense of "I," "my," and "mine," as well as a concept of "we" (LaRossa & Reitzes, 1994). If the individual is to develop an African American self-identity, it is necessary that it be acquired in a family in which African Americans are present.

The African American "self" is considered a collective rather than an individual one. Mbiti (1969) wrote of traditional Africans: "In traditional life, the individual does not and cannot exist alone except corporately. He owes his existence to other people, including those of past generations and his contemporaries. He is simply part of the whole. The community must therefore make, create, or produce the individual; for the individual depends on the corporate group" (p. 108).

According to Mbiti (1969), traditional Africans live according to the tenet, "I am, because we are, and since we are therefore I am" (pp. 108–109). Nobles (1974) also discussed the African extended self, whereby individual identity and purpose evolve from an identification with the collective. The position taken by the NABSW (cited in McRoy, 1989, and Simon & Alstein, 1977) therefore can be considered a lived example of a collective identity and as clarifying the group identity that Africa-descended people require.

"Self-concepts, once developed, provide an important motive for behavior" (p. 144). If the identity of African Americans is a collective one, actions that are perceived as a threat to the survival of the group can be expected to motivate individuals to act to resist the threat. The NABSW concern about genocide (cited in McRoy, 1989, and Simon & Alstein, 1977) or in this case, concern about the elimination of the African American group through the widespread transracial adoption of African American children can be understood within this context. Abdullah (1996) called attention to the original wording of the United Nations' 1948 position on genocide: "Genocide . . . is the committing of certain acts with the intent to destroy—wholly or in part—a national, ethnic, racial or religious group as such, including measures to prevent birth and forcibly transferring children of one group to another" (United Nations, 1991, as cited in Abdullah, 1996, p. 260). . . . Assertions often are found in the public media and in some professional literature that African American children are languishing in the foster care system while potential parents wait to adopt them. The implication is that the alternative to transracial adoption for African American children is life in a foster home or institution. Other realities are seldom mentioned, such as the small number of white families who want to adopt transracially, the willingness of relatives to provide care and of nonrelative African American families to become foster parents and adoptive parents, and the relationship of insufficient economic and social support to child maltreatment in many families (Hollingsworth, 1998). Also, the dual cultural adaptation that is required of African Americans and members of other ethnic groups in the United States (Chestang, 1972; DuBois, 1903; Norton, 1978) may increase the potential for influences from the larger society. . . .

## Implications for Research, Practice, and Policy Advocacy

. . . Based on the symbolic interactionist conceptualization that has been presented here, I make four recommendations. First, social work scholars should continue to examine scientifically the questions that have been set forth regarding transracial adoption (Alexander & Curtis, 1996; Bartholet, 1991). Theory building and empirical falsification continue to be the standards that are used by scholars to examine research questions. This work should be conducted from an African-centered ideological perspective (Allen, 1978). It also should be phenomenological, so that the lived experiences of African American children in families may be examined.

Second, social workers should become familiar with theories that have already been advanced about African American life and culture and with research that has been conducted with regard to questions of racial identity and self-esteem effects of transracial adoption. Baldwin's (1981) theory of African self-consciousness and Nobles' (1978) concept of Africanity are examples, as are studies by Andujo (1988); Hollingsworth (1997); Baker (1992); Black (1985); Feigelman and Silverman (1983); Grow and Shapiro (1974); McRoy and Zurcher (1983); Shireman (1988); Shireman and Johnson (1975; 1980); Johnson, Shireman, and Watson (1987); Simon and Alstein (1977, 1981, 1987, 1992); Simon, Alstein, and Melli (1994); Vroegh (1997), and Womack (1981). Reviews by Alexander and Curtis (1996), Curtis (1996), Hollingsworth (1997), and Silverman (1993) are useful. Many of these can be used to advance the critical analysis and dialogue suggested by Doherty et al. (1994) within the context of African-centered values and culture. However, social work critics should examine the validity and reliability of the studies and the perspectives that have been used in interpreting their results.

Third, social workers should be familiar with the realities faced by African American children and families in the child welfare system. The relationship of poverty and single-female parenthood to child maltreatment has been documented consistently (Johnson, 1997; Pelton, 1978; 1988; Sedlak & Broadhurst, 1996). Child maltreatment and especially child neglect are frequent reasons for the removal of children from their birth families and for their placement in foster care or adoptive homes. African American families are represented disproportionately in the rates of poverty and the statistics of single-female parenthood (Hollingsworth, 1998). It is therefore simplistic to limit examination to the results rather than the causes of the phenomena that bring African American children into the foster care system.

Finally, social workers should advocate for public policies and agency practices that recognize the African American family as a unique cultural group, offering a valuable socialization experience for African American children. Such policies and practices are necessary to ensure that the legitimate identity and the psychosocial health of African Americans are protected.

In conclusion, I have used symbolic interactionism to conceptually frame objections to the transracial adoption of African American children, taking the position that the community of people of African descent (that is, the African diaspora) forms the group within which their children are socialized. Because meaning and development of the self are dependent on the group, African American children necessarily require the African American family for socialization into the group. From a symbolic interactionist perspective, becoming a part of the larger group structure is a natural outcome for its members. Thus, rather than being discriminatory or self-serving, the early objection to transracial adoption by the National Association of Black Social Workers and the expressed support for ethnic consistency in adoption by groups such as the North American Council on Adoptable Children (Gilles & Kroll, 1991) are in the service of the healthy development of African American children. Research, theory development, analysis of existing research and theory, and policy advocacy are important to this process.

## References


Adoption and Safe Families Act of 1997, P.L. 105–89, 111 Stat. 21150.

Abdullah, S. B. (1996). Transracial adoption is not the solution to America's problems of child welfare. *Journal of Black Psychology, 22,* 254-261.

Alexander, R., Jr., & Curtis, C. M. (1996). A review of empirical research involving the transracial adoption of African American children. *Journal of Black Psychology, 22,* 223–35.

Allen, W. (1978). The search for applicable theories of black family life. *Journal of Marriage and the Family, 40,* 117–29.

Andujo, E. (1988). Ethnic identity of transethnically-adopted Hispanic adolescents. *Social Work, 33,* 531–535.

Baker, M. E. (1992). *Psychological adjustment of adopted minority children.* Unpublished master's thesis, University of North Carolina at Chapel Hill.

Baldwin, J. (1981). Notes on an Africentric theory of black personality. *Western Journal of Black Studies, 5,* 172–179.

Bartholet, E. (1991). Where do black children belong? The politics of race matching in adoption. *University of Pennsylvania Law Review, 139,* 1163–1256.

Black, S.E.C. (1985). *The perception of racial identity in transracial and inracial adoptees.* Unpublished master's thesis, University of Houston.

Brown, J. A. (1984). Group work with low-income black youths. *Social Work with Groups, 7,* 111–124.

Chestang, L. (1972). The dilemma of biracial adoption. *Social Work, 17,* 100–105.

Child Welfare League of America. (1968). *Standards for adoption service.* Washington, DC: Author.

Child Welfare League of America. (1973). *Standards for adoption service.* Washington, DC: Author.

Chin-Sang, V., & Allen, K. R. (1991). Leisure and the older black woman. *Journal of Gerontological Nursing, 17,* 30–34.

Curtis, C. M. (1996). The adoption of African American children by whites: A renewed conflict. *Families in Society, 77,* 156–165.

Doherty, W. J., Boss, P. G., LaRossa, R., Schumm, W. R., & Steinmetz, S. K. (1994). Family theories and methods: A contextual approach. In P. G. Boss, W. J. Doherty, R. LaRossa, W. R. Schumm, & S. K. Steinmetz (Eds.), *Sourcebook of family theories and methods: A contextual approach* (pp. 3–30). New York: Plenum Press.

DuBois, W.E.B. (1903). *The souls of black folk.* Chicago: A. C. McClurg.

Erny, P. (1973). *Childhood and cosmos.* New York: Black Orpheus Press.

Feigelman, W., & Silverman, A. (1983). *Chosen children: New patterns of adoptive relationships.* New York: Praeger.

Flaherty, M. J., Sr., Facteau, L., & Garver, P. (1995). Grandmother functions in multigenerational families: An exploratory study of Black adolescent mothers and their infants. In R. Staples (Ed.), *The Black family: Essays and studies* (pp. 195–203). Belmont, CA: Wadsworth.

Foster, H. J. (1983). African patterns in the Afro-American family. *Journal of Black Studies, 14,* 201–232.

Gant, L. M. (1984). *Black adoption programs: Pacesetters in practice.* Ann Arbor, MI: National Child Welfare Training Center.

Gilles, T., & Kroll, J. (1991). *Barriers to same race placement.* St. Paul, MN: North American Council on Adoptable Children.

Goddard, L. L. (1996). Transracial adoption: Unanswered theoretical and conceptual issues. *Journal of Black Psychology, 22,* 273–281.

Grow, L. J., & Shapiro, D. (1974). *Black children—white parents: A study of transracial adoption.* New York: Child Welfare League of America.

Gutman, H. G. (1976). *The black family in slavery and freedom: 1970–1925.* New York: Random House.

Hairston, C. F., & Williams, V. G. (1989). Black adoptive parents: How they view agency adoptive practices. *Social Casework, 70,* 534–538.

Herzog, E., Sudia, C., Harwood, J., & Newcomb, C. (1971). *Families for black children: The search for adoptive parents.* Washington, DC: U.S. Government Printing Office.

Hill, R. D. (1977). *Informal adoption among black families.* Washington, DC: National Urban League.

Hollingsworth, L. D. (1997). Effect of transracial/transethnic adoption on children's racial and ethnic identity and self-esteem: A meta-analytic review. *Marriage & Family Review, 25,* 99–130. Co-published simultaneously in H. E. Gross & M. B. Sussman (Eds.), Families and adoption (pp. 99–130). Binghampton, NY: Haworth Press.

Hollingsworth, L. D. (1998). Promoting same-race adoption for children of color. *Social Work, 43,* 104–116.

Howard, A., Royse, D. D., & Skerl, J. A. (1977). Transracial adoption: The black community perspective. *Social Work, 22,* 184–189.

Hudson, A. L., & Morris, R. I. (1994). Perceptions of social support of African Americans with acquired immunodeficiency syndrome. *Journal of National Black Nurses' Association, 7,* 36–49.

Indian Child Welfare Act of 1978, P.L. 95–608, 92 Stat. 3069.

Jackson-White, G., Dozier, C. D, Oliver, J. T, & Gardner, L. B. (1997). Why African American adoption agencies succeed: A new perspective on self-help. *Child Welfare, 76,* 239–254.

James, C.L.R. (1992). The Atlantic slave trade and slavery: Some interpretations of their significance in the development of the Unites States and the Western World. In F. W. Hayes, II (Ed.), *A turbulent voyage: Readings in African American studies* (pp. 213-236). San Diego: Collegiate Press.

Johnson, P. R., Shireman, J. F., & Watson, K. W. (1987). Transracial adoption and the development of black identity at age eight. *Child Welfare, 66,* 45–55.

Johnson, S. (1997) *Child welfare: Challenges and opportunities* [The 1997 Fedele F. and Iris M. Fauri Lecture]. Ann Arbor: University of Michigan.

LaRossa, R., & Reitzes, D.C. (1994). Symbolic interactionism and family studies. In P. G. Boss, W. J. Doherty, R. LaRossa, W. R. Schumm, & S. K. Steinmetz (Eds.), *Sourcebook of family theories and methods: A contextual approach* (pp. 135–163). New York: Plenum Press.

Mbiti, J. S. (1969). *African religions and philosophy.* New York: Praeger.

McRoy, R. G. (1989). An organizational dilemma: The case of transracial adoptions. *Journal of Applied Behavior Science, 25,* 145–160.

McRoy, R. G., & Zurcher, L. A. (1983). *Transracial and inracial adoptees: The adolescent years.* Springfield, IL: Charles C Thomas.

McRoy, R. G., Oglesby, Z., & Grape, H. (1997). Achieving same-race adoptive placements for African American children: Culturally sensitive practice approaches. *Child Welfare, 76,* 85–104.

Multiethnic Placement Act of 1994, P.L. 103–382, 108 Stat. 4057.

Myers, L. W. (1989). Early gender role socialization among black women: Affective or consequential? *Western Journal of Black Studies, 13,* 173–178.

Nobles, W. W. (1974). Africanity: Its role in black families. *Black Scholar, 5,* 10–17.

Norton, D. G. (1978). *The dual perspective: Inclusion of ethnic minority content in the social work curriculum.* New York: Council on Social Work Education.

Omnibus Budget Reconciliation Act of 1993, P.L. 103–66, 107 Stat. 312.

Pelton, L. H. (1978). Child abuse and neglect: The myth of classlessness. *American Journal of Orthopsychiatry, 48,* 608–617.

Pelton, L. H. (1988). The institution of adoption: Its sources and perpetuation. In D. Valentine (Ed.), *Infertility and adoption* (pp. 87–117). Binghampton, NY: Haworth Press.

Penn, M. L., & Coverdale, C. (1996). Transracial adoption: A human rights perspective. *Journal of Black Psychology, 22,* 240–245.

*Preserving African American families: Position statement.* (1994). Detroit: National Association of Black Social Workers.

Sedlak, A. J., & Broadhurst, M.L.A. (1996). *Executive summary of the third national incidence study of child abuse and neglect.* [Online]. Available: http://www.casanet.org/library/abuse/stabuse/htm.

Shireman, J. F. (1988). *Family life project: A longitudinal adoption study– Growing up adopted: An examination of major issues* (Phase IV). Chicago: Chicago Child Care Society.

Shireman, J. F., & Johnson, P. R. (1975). *Adoption: Three alternatives* (Phase I). Chicago: Chicago Child Care Society.

Shireman, J. F., & Johnson, P. R. (1980). *Adoption: Three alternatives* (Phase II). Chicago: Chicago Child Care Society.

Shireman, J. F., & Johnson, P. R (1986). A longitudinal study of black adoptions: Single parent, transracial, and traditional (Phase III). *Social Work, 31,* 172–177.

Simon, R. J. (1978). Black attitudes toward transracial adoption. *Phylon, 39,* 135–142.

Simon, R. J., & Alstein, H. (1977). *Transracial adoption.* New York: John Wiley & Sons.

Simon, R. J., & Alstein, H. (1981). *Transracial adoption: A follow-up.* Lexington, MA: Praeger.

Simon, R. J., & Alstein, H. (1987). *Transracial adoptees and their families: A study of identity and commitment.* New York: Praeger.

Simon, R. J., & Alstein, H. (1992). *Adoption, race and identity: From infancy through adolescence.* New York: Praeger.

Simon, R. J., Alstein, H., & Melli, M. S. (1994). *The case for transracial adoption.* Washington, DC: American University Press.

Silverman, A. R. (1993). Outcomes of transracial adoption. *Future of Children: Adoption, 3,* 104–118.

Small Business Job Protection Act of 1996, P.L. 104-188, 110 Stat. 17550.

Thornton, J. L. (1991). Permanency planning for children in kinship homes. *Child Welfare, 70,* 593–601.

Vroegh, K. S. (1997). Transracial adoptees: Developmental status after 17 years. *American Journal of Orthopsychiatry, 67,* 568–575.

Willis, M. G. (1996). The real issues in transracial adoption: A response. *Journal of Black Psychology, 22,* 246–253.

Womack, W. M., & Fulton, W. (1981). Transracial adoption and the black preschool child. *Journal of the American Academy of Child Psychiatry, 20,* 712–724.

**Rudolph Alexander, Jr. and**
**Carla M. Curtis**

# NO

# A Review of Empirical Research Involving the Transracial Adoption of African American Children

In 1972, the National Association of Black Social Workers (NABSW) strongly advocated same-race adoption of African American children, thwarting a growing policy of placing African American children with White families (Adamec & Pierce, 1991). The position of NABSW was that the placement of African American children with White families constituted cultural genocide (Adamec & Pierce, 1991; Bartholet, 1991, 1993) and was unnecessary (Aigner, 1986; G. K. Smith, personal communication, September 4, 1992; National Association of Black Social Workers, 1992). Furthermore, some African American professionals contended that these children had been psychologically harmed by these placements (Hermann, 1993). Other mental health professionals speculated that transracial adoption was more stressful to African American children than inracial adoptions involving Whites (Helwig & Ruthven, 1990). For these reasons, a national policy of same-race adoption was pursued for more than a decade, and transracial adoptions dropped precipitously (Hayes, 1993).

However, this policy has been abruptly reversed. First, in recent years social scientists retrieved previous research, pointing to the benefits of transracial adoptions and presenting more recent findings (Silverman, 1993; Simon & Altstein, 1981, 1987, 1992; Simon, Altstein, & Melli, 1994). Second, the courts got involved, repeatedly ruling in favor of White parents wanting to adopt African American children (*McLaughin v. Pernsley,* 1988; *Reisman v. State Dept. of Human Servs.,* 1993). Third, legislators began decrying the perceived crisis in foster care and adoption. Estimates were that 500,000 children were in foster care—where many children wait to be adopted—and African American children constituted the largest group, or 40% (Davis, 1995). In New Jersey, Maryland, and Louisiana, more than 50% of the children in foster care were African American (McRoy, 1995). Concerned about this situation, Senator Howard Metzenbaum introduced legislation in 1994 that forbade discrimination in adoption and foster care placement. This legislation, known as the Multiethnic Placement Act, was passed by the 104th Congress and was signed by President Clinton weeks later.

From Rudolph Alexander, Jr. and Carla M. Curtis, "A Review of Empirical Research Involving the Transracial Adoption of African American Children," *Journal of Black Psychology,* vol. 22, no. 2 (May 1996). 

These recent events in the courts and in Congress seem to dismiss NABSW's position that African American children have been harmed by their adoption in White families. Typically, commentaries about studies that have supported transracial adoptions have universally accepted the findings of these studies without critically evaluating the research methodology (e.g., see Silverman, 1993). A critical evaluation may or may not lead to similar conclusions; however, such scrutiny is needed given the importance of the issue. For this reason, we critically review the empirical literature to discern the impact of parenting by White families upon African American children's mental health....

## Adjustment Studies

### Descriptive Cross-Sectional Studies

In an early study, Grow and Shapiro (1974) studied 125 transracial families to learn the extent to which the families experienced a successful adoption. In effect, adjustment was operationalized to be successful adoption. The researchers chose not to employ a comparison group, conceding that same-race was preferable. Hence this study was descriptive. They administered two personality tests to the children and obtained parents' assessments of their children in several areas. Based on this conceptualization, they concluded that 77% of the children had adjusted successfully following their adoption by White families. In another descriptive study, Johnson, Shireman, and Watson (1987), using the Clark Doll Test [in which children identify a doll as having a "race" similar to their own], found that 73% of African American children adopted by White parents identified themselves as African Americans compared to 80% of African American children adopted by African American parents. These researchers concluded that 73% of the transracial adoptees were doing well, compared to 80% of the inracial adoptees.

The two studies discussed above were descriptive and did not use inferential statistics to test relationships between and among variables. Accordingly, these studies did not provide much information. However, a number of studies employed comparison groups consisting of either White adoptive children or African American children adopted by African American parents. Studies that used comparison groups provide more knowledge about the relationship between the type of family and the extent of adjustment.

### Cross-Sectional Comparison Studies

McRoy, Zurcher, Lauderdale, and Anderson (1982) compared African American children who had been adopted by White and African American families. These researchers, indicating that their study was exploratory, were interested in possible differences in the children's level of self-esteem and extent of racial identity. Using cross-tabulation, they studied 60 families and found no differences in the children's level of self-esteem. However, they found differences in the extent of racial identity. The researchers concluded that White families might be able to provide a loving home for children, but these families may not be able to instill a sense of positiveness about identity. However, they stopped short of recommending against transracial adoption. Instead, they stated that when a transracial adoption was completed, an independent assessment needed to be made of the total ecological environment.

Brenner (1993) studied how transracial adoption affected children's identity formation and other adolescent developmental tasks. In addition, the researcher studied racial identity and the extent to which children engaged in search behaviors (i.e., the practice of looking for birth parents). Of the children, 11 were Asian, 8 were White, and 5 were African American. All the parents were White. Brenner found that African American children did not manage their emotions and frustrations. They also had more uneasiness with their physical appearance than White and Asian adoptees. All the African American children engaged in search behaviors, whereas a majority of White and Asian children did not. Brenner concluded that, all in all, no significant difference existed between transracial and inracial children, and the status of the children was unrelated to issues regarding adjustment and identity formation (Brenner, 1993).

## Multivariate Analysis

Indirectly looking at adjustment, several researchers compared the amount of disruption in White and African American adoptions. They employed a multiple discriminant analysis to learn which of 23 variables predicted a stable or unstable adoption. One of the 23 variables was the extent of matching—whether an African American child was matched with an African American or White family. Six variables were related to the dependent variable: the child's age, the child's sex, the number of problems experienced by children, whether there was a previous adoption placement, whether the adoption was by a foster parent, and the mother's education level. Because matching was not significant, the researchers concluded that transracial adoptions were no more likely to be unstable than inracial adoption (Barth, Berry, Yoshikami, Goodfield, & Carlson, 1988).

Specifically examining the quality of the children's experiences, Rosenthal, Groze, and Curiel (1990) surveyed 1,328 families who adopted transracially and inracially and received 799 returned questionnaires. Of this total, 22% of the families were transracial. Using multiple regression, they found some differences between the two groups of children. Particularly, the transracial group had more history of sexual abuse, group home experience, and psychiatric placement. Controlling for these variables, however, they concluded that as a group, transracial adoptees were doing reasonably well.

In a somewhat related study about the difficulties of African American children adopted by White families, Silverman and Feigelman (1981a) examined questionnaires of 97 White families who adopted African American children and 56 families who adopted White children. They found that African American children exhibited more maladjustment and were more likely to experience hostility in their environments preceding their adoption than White children.

African American children were more likely also to be older than White children at adoption. The researchers concluded that the age of the child at adoption had more of an impact on adjustment than transracial adoption (Silverman & Feigelman, 1981a).

Revealing more of their study, Silverman and Feigelman (1981b) mailed 1,121 surveys and received 713 returned questionnaires. They used factor analysis to create a measure of maladjustment based on parental responses to four questions, which later was reduced to three. The resulting index had a range of 1 to 12 (1 = *no maladjustment,* 12 = *extreme maladjustment*). No child received a score of more than 8. They used cross tabulation and found significant relationships between the extent of maladjustment and the race of the child, the degree of family opposition to the adoption, age of the child at adoption, and age of the child at the time of the study. African American children in particular were found to be more maladjusted. The researchers then put these significant variables into a regression equation and found that only age at adoption and the degree of family opposition predicted the extent of maladjustment among the children (Silverman & Feigelman, 1981b).

The studies discussed above were primarily cross-sectional designs that used surveys. In a cross-sectional design, a researcher examines a phenomenon, such as transracial adoption, at one point in time. It is referred to as a snapshot of a problem. Longitudinal designs, however, allow the examination of a phenomenon over a long period of time and thus permit observations of changes in the phenomenon (Rubin & Babbie, 1993). Some transracial adoption researchers have conducted surveys, but a few researchers have studied the issue of transracial longitudinally.

## Longitudinal Studies

Shireman and Johnson (1986) compared African American children adopted by single parents, White families, and African American families. The children were studied at 4, 8, 12, 16, and 20 years of age. Using the Clark Doll Test, Shireman and Johnson found that African American children in White homes had a more positive racial identity at age 4 than African American children in African American families. By age 8, the two groups were similar. In subsequent years, the children's adjustment was studied. Adjustment was measured by the number and severity of problems as reported by the parents, direct observations using projective testing, and standardized test materials. The researchers concluded that overall adjustment was excellent (Shireman & Johnson, 1986).

In another longitudinal study, Feigelman and Silverman (1984) compared White, Korean, Colombian, and African American children adopted by White families. Their primary measure was the extent of maladjustment and differences among the groups of children. They found, using multiple regression, that African American children had poorer adjustment than the other three groups of adoptees. However, this difference disappeared when age of the children was examined.

Building upon Feigelman and Silverman's work and tying his findings to American studies, Bagley (1993) studied 27 Afro-Caribbean and mixed-race children adopted by White families in Britain. Bagley's measures were the extent of psychoneurosis, depression, free floating anxiety, self-esteem, identity, ego identity, and self-image. Originally, the children were studied in 1979 and 12 years later. Bagley found no differences between the children on any variable.

The most active researchers in transracial adoption have been Simon and Altstein, who have followed a group of African American children for about 20 years. Their research began in 1972 when they received the names of families who had adopted transracially in five Midwest cities. Their primary hypothesis was that the "atypical environment in which children were being reared would affect their responses in such a manner as to mute the typical White preferences and reduce differences in responses about awareness and identity that are attributed to race" (Simon & Altstein, 1992, p. 127). They were initially able to interview 204 families and 366 children. Of the children, 120 were African American and the remainder were White and Native American. The researchers' primary variables of interest were the extent of racial identity, awareness, and attitudes. Over a 20-year period, they have regularly reported that African American children adopted by White families fared no worse than other children (Simon & Altstein, 1992; Simon et al., 1994).

All of the previously discussed studies focused primarily upon adjustment and racial identity, and the consensus of these studies has been that African American children have had adequate adjustment and racial identity. A few researchers, however, have focused on how African American children's intelligence was affected when adopted by White families. The extent of a child's intelligence is tangentially related to mental health because teachers have been found to respond more favorably to perceived high-intelligent children than perceived low-intelligent children. The effect of this differential treatment is that perceived low-intelligent children are led to feel inferior (Winston, 1987).

## Transracial Adoption and Intelligence

Weinberg, Scarr, and Waldman (1992) studied school achievement and the intelligence quotient (IQ) of 101 transracially adopted children. This was the second study of a longitudinal research project that was conducted 10 years earlier. In the first study, the purpose was to examine the relationship between cross-fostering and IQ performance of African American and biracial (i.e., one African American and one White parent) children (Scarr & Weinberg, 1976). These researchers hypothesized that social environment played a critical role in IQ development. They found that their subsequent data supported their earlier study. Particularly, they originally hypothesized that African American children adopted by White families would perform well on IQ tests because these children were being socialized within the culture (e.g., home and school) that produced the test. That is to say, Whites developed IQ tests based on their culture. So children, regardless of race, reared in the White culture would perform better on IQ tests than children not reared in that culture (Weinberg et al., 1992).

Also, Moore (1986), reporting the validity and reliability of all measures, compared African American and biracial children who had been adopted by White and African American families. All children were placed by two adoption agencies. Twenty-three children were placed with African American parents, and of this number, six were biracial. Likewise, 23 children were placed with White families, and 14 of their children were biracial. The adoption worker indicated that African American families had expressed an interest in children who had African American biological parents. This preference was the reason that fewer biracial children were placed with African American families. All the children were placed with the families before the age of 2, and all the families were classified as middle class. The researcher administered the IQ test to children between the ages of 7 and 10 and found that the children adopted by White families scored higher on the IQ tests. Also, children adopted by White parents were found to be more assertive. The researcher concluded that the ethnicity of the rearing environment was more important than social class or the mother's educational level (Moore, 1986).

## Methodological Issues

A neglected aspect of most social research is that researchers favor statistical significance. They also are interested in whether a majority or minority of a group of research participants is better or worse on some social or psychological measure. As an example, one researcher reported that about 75% of transracially adopted children were doing well. Unstated was that 25% of transracially adopted children were not doing well in their White families. At first glance, the 25% may cause some African American professionals to become alarmed and conclude that transracial adoptions are harmful. However, a more thoughtful examination would force professionals to look at the percentage of inracially adopted families that were assessed to be doing well. This percentage was 80%. So, 20% of these families were not doing well. Race could not be used to explain this situation. Further, only a 5% difference existed between the transracial and inracial groups.

Although the tendency to overlook the lesser percentage in social and psychological research is regrettable when children are involved, lessons may be drawn from medical research. In medical research, a newly developed medication may be shown to help 75% of patients with a serious illness. This discovery would be considered to be significant, and this new medication likely would receive quick approval to be used. Then, the goal of the medical researcher would be to find out why the other 25% did not receive the same benefits and what medications may be needed for them. Social research has not followed medical research in this respect. So, statistical significance and percentages continue to be highlighted.

These shortcomings aside, certainly, the weight of the research evidence favors proponents of transracial adoption, albeit all the evidence was not produced by the strongest research methodology. For instance, a random probability sample of *all* families who have adopted transracially was not conducted. Although researchers used samples that were available, they failed to note the limitations and weaknesses of their sampling methods. Instead, they confidently extrapolated their findings to the entire country.

The most active researchers in this area were Simon and Altstein, who published several books on their study and whose work has been cited by several courts. Methodologically, a number of research limitations are apparent in their work that they did not acknowledge. These limitations should have caused them to temper their conclusions. For instance, Simon and Altstein's primary data analysis methods were descriptive statistics and cross-tabulations. Firm conclusions from correlational studies cannot be made because these studies tend to have low internal validity and rival hypotheses always exist. Typically, researchers control for these alternative explanations by use of control and comparison groups. When these cannot be utilized, multivariate analysis, which provides statistical control, is employed. Either experimental studies or multivariate analyses lend themselves to stronger conclusions based on the findings. Other methods, such as use of correlation and cross-tabulation, should force researchers to temper their conclusions.

Another issue is the sampling method used by Simon and Altstein, who conducted longitudinal research on families in the Midwest who were members of two organizations. Little was written about whether these two organizations were representative of White families who have adopted African American children. Further, in subsequent studies based on their original sample, they lost a significant number of their families. Because their final sample was significantly smaller, they failed to state that their ultimate findings might be suspect because they did not know how the families they could not find might differ. These unresearched families might have had significantly adverse problems that skewed Simon and Altstein's ultimately favorable conclusions. Their failure to acknowledge this possibility and temper their conclusions is a substantial weakness in their methodology.

Related to the issue of sampling is the external validity of their findings. According to Rubin and Babbie (1993), a study may have sound internal validity but lack external validity. External validity refers to the extent to which a study's conditions, setting, and population may be generalized to other locations. Although a study does not have to be representative of all characteristics of a community to have good external validity, it should address the extent to which the study's findings may be generalized. Simon and Altstein suggested that their study has strong external validity and supported a national policy of transracial adoption. Although these issues were apparent in Simon and Altstein's work, as well as in many researchers' works, their studies provided little support for them to make definitive conclusions about transracial adoption.

On the other hand, opponents of transracial adoption, such as NABSW and other African American professionals, had no empirical support for their positions. They stated that African Americans encountered significant mental health problems by their placement in White families, but could not produce any empirical studies supporting their position. In sum, African American professionals have failed to research transracial adoptions to support their contention of psychological damage to African American children. Because no empirical research existed to support this contention, courts have been forced to accept the findings of proponents of transracial adoptions.

## Conclusion

The foremost criticism is aimed at African American professionals and researchers who allowed this area to go virtually unresearched. Obviously, African American researchers could have sought grants to study this issue themselves. If they believed that psychological harm had been and was being done to African American children, their research studies should support the conclusion. If the measures used to operationalize psychological variables are inadequate or biased, African American researchers bear the responsibility of creating unbiased instruments. African American faculty can do some of this research themselves. They can also encourage African American graduate students to develop culturally sensitive scales for their theses and dissertations. A research project can have as its end the development of a valid and reliable scale. Of course, the research that produces these scales and subsequent studies that assert that African American children are psychologically harmed by transracial adoption must be scrutinized as other research is scrutinized.

Undoubtedly, the weight of empirical evidence supports the placement of African American children with White families for both foster care and adoption. No empirical evidence exists to demonstrate that such placements are harmful to the mental health of African American children. However, the conclusion drawn from the literature that African American children are not harmed by transracial adoption should not convey that African American children should be placed with White families as a first choice. Most professionals and legislators have acknowledged that same-race adoptions are desirable and preferable for children. Race may be a factor, as the Multiethnic Placement Act permits, but cannot be the sole factor. This acknowledgment provides options for the African American community.

African American professionals—such as members from NABSW and other organizations—who oppose transracial adoption can further enhance efforts to work with adoption and child protection agencies to recruit more African American families as potential adoptive parents. Throughout the United States, many child welfare agencies have initiated special programs and projects. They have encouraged the support of African American churches, civic organizations, and fraternal societies to recruit more African American adoptive parents.

Once prospective adoptive parents are identified, they must be evaluated to determine if placement is appropriate. The African American community can monitor this process to ensure that African American families are not indiscriminately denied the opportunity to adopt based on family assessments (Day, 1979; Hill, 1977; Howard, 1984). In some locations, African American social workers are working hard to see that African American families are not discriminated against when they seek to adopt. For instance, an African American social worker, who ironically refused to join NABSW because of its racial views, zealously enforced Massachusetts state policy that allowed any African

American family that passed a criminal history check to be eligible to adopt (Rabin, 1995).

For localities that prefer a more formal assessment, a different standard should be used in assessing African American families. One such model is the Afrocentric model for family assessment and child development. This model is empirically based and standardized and helps to identify qualified African American parents (T. Oliver, personal communication, September 6, 1994).

Another option is for the African American community to work to alleviate the stresses that influence family disruption and dissolution. This effort would reduce the need for foster placement, and in many cases, the relinquishment of parental rights. Effectively addressing such problems as drugs, crime, poverty, and teen pregnancy prevents the breakdown of the family unit that makes placement and adoption necessary. In sum, effectively addressing some of the social problems in the African American community would lead to fewer African American children needing homes. But when the need to place an African American child in a foster or adoptive home exists, an African American family could be easily found. Then, there would be no need to declare without scientifically accepted evidence that African American children's mental health is harmed by transracial adoption.

## References

Adamec, C., & Pierce, W. L. (1991). *The encyclopedia of adoption.* New York: Facts on File.

Aigner, H. (1986). *Adoption in America coming of age.* Greenbrae, CA: Paradigm.

Bagley, C. (1993). Transracial adoption in Britain; A follow-up study with policy consideration. *Child Welfare, 72,* 285–299.

Barth, R. P., Berry, M., Yoshikami, R., Goodfield, R. K., & Carlson, M. L. (1988). Predicting adoption disruption. *Social Work, 33,* 227–233.

Bartholet, E. (1991). Where do Black children belong? The politics of race matching in adoption. *University of Pennsylvania Law Review, 139,* 1163–1256.

Bartholet, E. (1993). *Family bonds: Adoption and the politics of parenting.* Boston: Houghton Mifflin.

Brenner, E. M. (1993). Identity formation in the transracially-adopted adolescent (Ph.D. dissertation, California School of Professional Psychology). *Dissertation Abstracts International, 15,* 3871.

Davis, R. (1995, April 13). Suits back interracial adoptions: Minority kids wait longer, groups say. *USA Today,* p. 3A.

Day, D. (1979). *The adoption of Black children.* Lexington, MA: Lexington Books.

Feigelman, W., & Silverman, A. R. (1984). The long-term effects of transracial adoption. *Social Service Review, 58,* 589–602.

Grow, L. J., & Shapiro, D. (1974). *Black children. White parents: A study of transracial adoption.* New York: Child Welfare League of America.

Hayes, P. (1993). Transracial adoption: Politics and ideology. *Child Welfare, 72,* 301–310.

Helwig, A. A., & Ruthven, D. H. (1990). Psychological ramifications of adoption and implications for counseling. *Journal of Mental Health Counseling, 12,* 24–37.

Hermann, V. P. (1993). Transracial adoption: Child-saving or child snatching. *National Black Law Journal, 13,* 147–164.

Hill, R. B. (1977). *Informal adoption among Black families.* Washington, DC: National Urban League.

Howard, M. (1984). Transracial adoption: Analysis of the best interests standard. *Notre Dame Law Review, 59,* 503–555.

Johnson, P., Shireman, J., & Watson, K. (1987). Transracial adoption and the development of Black identity at age eight. *Child Welfare, 66,* 45–56.

McLaughin v. Pernsley, 693 F. Supp. 318 (E.D. Pa. 1988).

McRoy, R. G. (1995, June 5). Questions: Should Congress facilitate transracial adoptions; No: Lower barriers to Black adoptive families. *Washington Times,* p. 19.

McRoy, R. G., Zurcher, L. A., Lauderdale, M. L., & Anderson, R. N. (1982). Self-esteem and racial identity in transracial adoption. *Social Work, 27,* 522–526.

Moore, E. G. J. (1986). Family socialization and the IQ test performance of traditionally and transracially adopted Black children. *Developmental Psychology, 22,* 317–326.

National Association of Black Social Workers (NABSW). (1992, Fall). *National Association of Black Social Workers* [Newsletter]. Detroit, MI.

Rabin, R. (1995, July 10). Can Black children raised by White parents develop a positive sense of self and a strong racial identity? *Newsday,* p. B04.

Reisman v. State Dept. of Human Servs., 843 F. Supp. 356 (W. D. Tenn., 1993).

Rosenthal, J. A., Groze, V., & Curiel, H. (1990). Race, social class, and special needs adoption. *Social Work, 35,* 532–539.

Rubin, A., & Babbie, E. (1993). *Research methods for social work* (2nd ed.). Pacific Grove, CA: Brooks/Cole.

Scarr, S., & Weinberg, R. A. (1976). IQ test performance of Black children adopted by White families. *American Psychology, 31,* 726–739.

Shireman, J. F., & Johnson, P. R. (1986). A longitudinal study of Black adoptions: Single parent, transracial, and traditional. *Social Work, 31,* 172–176.

Silverman, A. R. (1993). Outcomes of transracial adoption. *The Future of Children, 3,* 104–118.

Silverman, A. R., & Feigelman, W. (1981a). *The adjustment of Black children adopted by White families.* Paper presented at the Annual Meeting of the American Sociological Association. Toronto, Ontario.

Silverman, A. R., & Feigelman, W. (1981b). The adjustment of Black children adopted by White families. *Social Casework, 62,* 529–536.

Simon, R. J., & Altstein, H. (1981). *Transracial adoption: A follow-up.* Lexington, MA: D. C. Heath.

Simon, R. J., & Altstein, H. (1987). *Transracial adoptees and their families: A study of identity and commitment.* New York: Praeger.

Simon, R. J., & Altstein, H. (1992). *Adoption, race, and identity: From infancy through adolescence.* New York: Praeger.

Simon, R. J., Altstein, H., & Melli, M. S. (1994). *The case for transracial adoption.* Washington, DC: American University Press.

Weinberg, R. A., Scarr, S., & Waldman, I. D. (1992). The Minnesota transracial adoption study: A follow-up IQ test performance at adolescence. *Intelligence, 16,* 117–135.

Winston, J. A. (1987). Fulfilling Brown's promise: The second generation fight for educational opportunity. *Lawyers' Committee for Civil Rights Under Law Committee Report, 1*(3)1, 18–19.

# POSTSCRIPT

## Does Transracial Adoption Harm a Child's Development?

There are many more minority children in need of adoptive homes than can be accommodated intraracially. Is there a place for transracial adoption, which can be effective for children yet satisfy the concerns of those opposed to it? Perhaps if the prospective family was screened to ascertain sensitivity to some of the problems enumerated in the Introduction to this issue and outlined by Hollingsworth and Alexander and Curtis, the family could experience some success in maximizing the child's ethnic and psychological development.

From the parental perspective, consider the plight of suitable white adoptive parents. Many of them feel that the system is unjust in that they might wait years for a child, regardless of race, while suitable black adoptive parents, for example, rarely wait as long. Is this not a form of discrimination? Often these frustrated white parents look toward foreign adoptions. This does nothing to help address the problem of the need for adoptive parents for American children waiting to be adopted. How could this be a benefit to society?

Transracial adoption continues to be intensely debated. However, there may be some common ground upon which those on both sides of the issue can agree: (1) There could be increased efforts in the area of family planning, which would help diminish the growing numbers of children in need of adoption; (2) American society must be creative in developing interventions that strengthen all types of families in order to reduce the number of children who might be removed from their families of origin.

### Suggested Readings


Hayes, Peter. (1993) Transracial adoption: Politics and ideology. *Child Welfare, 72,* 301–310.

National Association of Black Social Workers (April, 1994). Position Statement: Preserving African-American Families. Detroit, MI: National Association of Black Social Workers.

Silverman, A. R. (1993). Outcomes of transracial adoption. *The Future of Children*, 3, 104–118.

Simon, R. J., Alstein, H., & Melli, M. S. (1994). *The Case for Transracial Adoption.* Washington, DC: American University Press.

`http://www.transracialadoption.com` provides a wealth of statistics and information in support of parents who adopt transracially.

# On the Internet . . .

## Kids Count

This Kids Count section of the Annie E. Casey Foundation Web site posts data on national and state indicators of child well-being, referred to as state report cards. The Annie E. Casey Foundation is an organization that is dedicated to building a better future for disadvantaged children in the United States.

http://www.aecf.org/kidscount/

## Children's Defense Fund

The Children's Defense Fund site includes data from every state on issues related to child care.

http://www.cdfactioncouncil.org

## National Network for Child Care (NNCC)

This site from the National Network for Child Care (NNCC) provides resources for raising children. Included are additional Web sites designed especially for children, as well as Web sites that offer activities for children, nutrition information, and information on parent involvement issues.

http://www.nncc.org

## Educational Resources Information Center (ERIC)

This Educational Resources Information Center (ERIC) Web site, sponsored by the U.S. Department of Education, leads to numerous documents related to elementary and early childhood education as well as to other curriculum topics and issues.

http://www.ed.gov

## Child Welfare Review

Child Welfare Review is a forum for inquiry into issues related to the welfare of children. It contains conflicting and contrasting viewpoints.

http://www.childwelfare.com/kids/news.htm

## Children Now

Children Now focuses on improving conditions for children who are poor or at risk. Articles offer information on education, the influence of media, health, and security.

http://www.childrennow.org

# PART 2

## Early Childhood

*The period of early childhood is sometimes referred to as the preschool years. It generally encompasses ages two or three through four or five. This is a time when children become much more adept at taking part in physical activities, satisfying curiosities, and learning from experience. Preschoolers play more frequently with other children, become increasingly skilled in daily tasks, and are much more responsive to people and things in their environment. Many children begin school during their preschool years, an experience that gives them their first extended contacts with a social institution other than the family. Changing attitudes about discipline, family size, divorce, and the mass media all have implications for a child's development. This section examines some of the choices families make in rearing their preschool children.*

# ISSUE 5

## Is Spanking Detrimental to Children?

**YES: Murray A. Straus**, from "Spanking and the Making of a Violent Society," *Pediatrics* (October 1996)

**NO: Robert E. Larzelere**, from "A Review of the Outcomes of Parental Use of Nonabusive or Customary Physical Punishment," *Pediatrics* (October 1996)

### ISSUE SUMMARY

**YES:** Murray A. Straus, codirector of the Family Research Laboratory at the University of New Hampshire, argues that spanking with any frequency teaches children aggressiveness and is associated with subsequent violent behavior.

**NO:** Robert E. Larzelere, director of Residential Research at Boys Town, Nebraska, agrees that no professional believes that abusive physical punishment of children is acceptable but contends that spankings, or nonabusive physical punishment, which have been used by parents for years, should not be considered detrimental to children.

The topic of spanking (also known as corporal punishment) provokes highly emotional responses from family practitioners, parents, and researchers. There seems to be no one who is neutral about the subject. Were you spanked when you were a child? What was used to spank you? bare hand? hairbrush? ruler? switch? Do you think the spankings negatively affected you, or did they teach you how to act appropriately? Parents and children often quote the following to support the ritual of spanking: "Spare the rod and spoil the child; I was spanked and I turned out OK; spankings teach children how to act; kids need spankings to know who's boss."

If you were not spanked, what was used to correct your misbehavior? Was the misbehavior explained? Were your good deeds rewarded as your bad deeds were punished? Perhaps verbal abuse or a slap in the face was used to correct your behavior, or maybe you were ignored altogether. These techniques are similar to spanking and, in fact, are often considered the same as spanking in research studies. What about children who were not spanked or corrected in any way? Are these children considered spoiled or out of control?

A public opinion poll commissioned by the National Committee for the Prevention of Child Abuse in 1994 asked parents how they disciplined their children during the previous year. Parents responded by naming more than one method. Denying privileges was used by 79 percent of the parents; confining in room was used by 59 percent; 49 percent spanked or hit their child; and 45 percent used insults or swearing. What was most notable about the statistics was that for the first time a majority of parents (51 percent) reported that they did not spank their children.

Although spanking is a popular form of guidance in the United States, five countries have outlawed spanking: Austria, Norway, Denmark, Sweden, and Finland have banned physical punishment of children. Proponents of spanking are quick to point out that some of these countries' child abuse rates have not declined as a result of the spanking ban.

Spanking has been associated with violence, which is receiving overwhelming attention in the media. Violence is perceived as a social ill that has infiltrated schools, post offices, medical facilities, and restaurants (all of which have been the sites of mass shooting sprees). Do spankings in childhood lead to increased violent behavior in the teen and adult years?

As children are spanked, hit, or physically punished, do they see spanking as an acceptable problem-solving option? They do something wrong and get hit for it; that's how parents solve the problem of misbehavior. When parents spank their children, are they guiding them or controlling them? If parents do not spank, how do they teach their children right from wrong? Does any kind of punishment, such as yelling or taking away privileges, help shape appropriate behavior? What message are parents sending? What is the best way to help children become responsible, moral adults?

Murray A. Straus has made a career out of linking all kinds of negative outcomes to spanking or corporal punishment. In the following selection, he argues that when children are spanked, they see it as a way of dealing with problems. Straus sees spanking as modeling violence for children and detrimental to society as a whole. In the second selection, Robert E. Larzelere identifies what he considers fallacies of numerous research studies on spanking. He distinguishes between beatings, which he feels are not acceptable, and spankings, which he contends can be useful as a guidance tool.

**Murray A. Straus**

**YES**

# Spanking and the Making of a Violent Society

Most of the world's societies are violent in the sense that they have high rates of physical assault, homicide, and war. The United States (US) is the most violent of the advanced industrial societies. The current US homicide rate of 8.5 per 100 000 is three times the Canadian rate of 2.3 per 100 000, and about eight times the rate of Western European countries. Nevertheless, many societies are even more violent. The Mexican homicide rate of 19.4 is more than double that of the US, and the rate for the cities of Colombia (110.4 per 100 000) is more than ten times higher.

Most of the world's societies also bring up children violently through the use of corporal punishment. Perhaps the correspondence between the preponderance of violence and that of corporal punishment is just a coincidence. Obviously, corporal punishment and assaults and murders differ in severity, and also in the cultural definition that makes one legitimate and the other criminal. However, there is also a correspondence between the behavior involved in corporal punishment and the behavior involved in criminal assaults and homicides that is seldom perceived. Everyone understands that corporal punishment is carried out to correct or control misbehavior. What is not understood is that almost all assaults by adults and about two thirds of homicides are also carried out to correct what the offender perceives as misbehavior. Typical examples include a confrontation between two men over a loan of $50 that is to be paid back in 1 week. Now it is 3 months later. They get into a fight, and one ends up dead. Fights between adults almost always occur over what the aggressor thinks are moral transgressions, such as welshing on a promise to pay back a loan; an insult, or making a pass at another person's girlfriend or boyfriend. Thus, both corporal punishment and criminal violence occur in response to what the parent who spanks or the man who throws a punch consider outrageous or persistent misbehavior. Moreover, corporal punishment, like most assaults and homicides, is usually impulsive, done in anger, and often regretted. In an as yet unpublished study of a random sample 1003 mothers in two Minnesota cities, I asked about the circumstances connected to the times they had used corporal punishment in the last 6 months. I found that 44% said that, in half or more of

From Murray A. Straus, "Spanking and the Making of a Violent Society," *Pediatrics,* vol. 98, no. 4 (October 1996), pp. 837-842. 

the times they used corporal punishment, it was because they had "lost it" and 54% said that spanking was the wrong thing to have done in half or more of the instances. Durant's study of a Canadian sample[1] revealed similar misgivings about spanking.

Although corporal punishment may share key elements with criminal assaults, that is hardly evidence that corporal punishment is one of the factors making our society so violent. This [selection] examines that issue more systematically by reviewing evidence from research that has investigated the links between corporal punishment and societal violence. Two types of research will be examined: studies that compare the level of violence in societies characterized by differences in use of corporal punishment; and studies that compare the level of violence during adulthood of individuals who have been exposed to different levels of corporal punishment.

## Comparison of Societies

### Anthropological Studies

*Societal case studies.* More than 50 years ago, the anthropologist Ashley Montague argued that "Spanking the baby may be the psychological seed of war" (*Boston Sunday Globe,* January 5, 1941). He later invited eight anthropologists who had studied one of the relatively few nonviolent societies to contribute chapters to a book called *Learning Non-Aggression: The Experience of Non-Literate Societies.*[2] Although those eight societies differed tremendously, they had in common nonviolent child rearing, ie, they did not spank children.

Montague did not argue that nonspanking alone will produce a nonviolent society. On the contrary, the eight societies described in his book show that a great deal more is required, especially a high level of attention to a child's needs and safety, and positive rather than punitive modes of dealing with misbehavior. If spanking is a risk factor for societal violence, it is only one of many risk and protective factors. Consequently, rather than a one-to-one relationship between spanking and societal violence, the cross-cultural evidence suggests only that corporal punishment is associated with an increased *probability* of societal violence. A probabilistic relationship is typical of most disease vectors. Heavy smoking, for example, does not guarantee lung cancer. Rather, it increases the risk of death from smoking-related diseases to about one out of three.[3] This is a large risk, but it also means that two thirds of heavy smokers do *not* die of these diseases. Just as most heavy smokers will not die of a smoking-related disease, most people who have been exposed to corporal punishment will *not* be violent adults.

*Human Relations Area Files data.* Although in depth analyses of child rearing in nonviolent societies are highly informative, they do not provide statistical evidence. One approach to obtaining a statistical test of the idea that corporal punishment is associated with societal violence is through use of the Human Relations Area Files (HRAF). The HRAF is an archive of anthropological data on over 300 societies. Levinson[4] found that corporal punishment is used in about three quarters of the world's societies, and that the frequency of use varies greatly. Levinson also coded the data on violence between adults and found a correlation of .32 between the extent to which corporal punishment is used and the extent of wife-beating. Although this is a strong association, and one that persists when a number of other variables have been statistically controlled, it is the only aspect of societal violence that Levinson found to be strongly associated with corporal punishment. Thus, analyses of the HRAF data provide only limited evidence for a link between corporal punishment and societal violence.

### Attitudes Favoring Corporal Punishment in Ten Nations

Nancy Burns and I[5,6] used data from Edfeld[7] on the degree to which parents and teachers in ten European countries approved of corporal punishment to examine the relationship between corporal punishment and societal level violence. We found that the greater the degree of approval of corporal punishment, the higher the overall homicide rate and also the homicide rate for infants. When multiple regression was used to control for variables such as the gross national product, and educational and military expenditures, the relationship between endorsement of corporal punishment by teachers and the infant homicide rate remained significant, but not the overall homicide rate. Although the results are somewhat equivocal, they are consistent with findings from many other cross-cultural studies which have found that all types of violence tend to be related to each other (summarized in Levinson 1989).[4]

### State-to-State Difference in Corporal Punishment in Schools

There is considerable variation among the states in the extent to which corporal punishment is permitted in schools. At the time the data to be reported were gathered by Hyman and Wise,[8] some states permitted only the principal to hit children, others permitted both the principal and teachers. At the extreme were states that permitted any school employee to hit a child. Florida even prevented school districts from forbidding corporal punishment. This information was used to create a corporal punishment Permission Index score for each state.[6] I found that the more use of corporal punishment is authorized in a state, the higher the rate of violence by students and the higher the homicide rate. Although the murders could have been committed by persons who were physically punished in school a decade or more earlier, it is more likely that the findings reflect the often found tendency for one type of violence to be related to other types of violence.[4] Because this linkage crosses the boundaries between "legitimate violence" (such as corporal punishment) and "criminal violence," it illustrates what I have called the "cultural spillover" principle.[9]

## Individual-Level Evidence

If corporal punishment is one of the factors that tends to increase the level of violence in a society, that relationship should also be observable in the individual life histories of members of a society. This section summarizes the research my colleagues and I have carried out to investigate the links between corporal punishment and criminal behavior by adolescents and adults. I omitted studies of children, partly because that type of research is well-documented elsewhere, starting with the classic study by Sears, Maccoby, and Levin,[10] and continuing with a spate of recent studies such as Strassberg, Dodge, Pettit, and Bates,[11] but mainly because the focus of this [selection] is on societal violence. Most people take "societal violence" to mean violence by adolescents and adults. That is unfortunate because the implicit discounting of nonlethal violence by children, and the resulting toleration or discounting of violence by children, including sibling violence, contributes to adult violence. Even the most dismissed type of childhood violence, sibling violence, has serious harmful side effects on child victims.[12]

*Direct linkages.* The top three arrows in Fig 1 summarizes findings from studies which show that the more corporal punishment experienced in middle childhood or early adolescence, the greater the probability of crime and violence. The data on delinquency in the top row were obtained by interviewing parents of a nationally representative sample of children. We found that the more corporal punishment these parents used, the greater the probability of the child being delinquent.

The next row of Fig 1 refers to a 33-year longitudinal study of high-risk boys.[13] The crime data is from a search of court records of convictions when the boys in the sample were middle-aged. Figure 2 shows that, even after controlling for the criminal record of the father, corporal punishment is associated with a doubling of the percent sons who were convicted of a serious crime.

The data on non-family assaults in the third row of Fig 1 were obtained by interviewing adults and asking about corporal punishment they experienced at about age 13 and 14. They were also asked whether, during the previous 12 months, they had ever gotten so angry at an adult who was not part of their family that they hit that person.

The studies in the first three rows therefore show that corporal punishment of school-age children and early adolescents is associated with adult violence and other crime. Obviously, these data cannot tell us about corporal punishment of toddlers. However, the findings apply to the majority of American children because the National Family Violence Surveys and other studies show that over half of children age 13 and 14 are still being hit at that age.[14]

*Linking processes.* As important as are the relationships between corporal punishment and adult crime summarized by the top three rows of Fig 1, those studies did not provide information on the processes that could bring about the link between corporal punishment and violence as an adult. The remainder of Fig 1 summarizes findings from the studies that my colleagues and I have carried out to test theories about linking processes.

The first of the theories diagramed in Fig 1 identifies anger as an intervening process. This theory was suggested by a study Ellen Cohn and I did of 270 college students. We gave these students a list of possible reactions to corporal

*Figure 1*

Links Between Corporal Punishment and Adult Violence

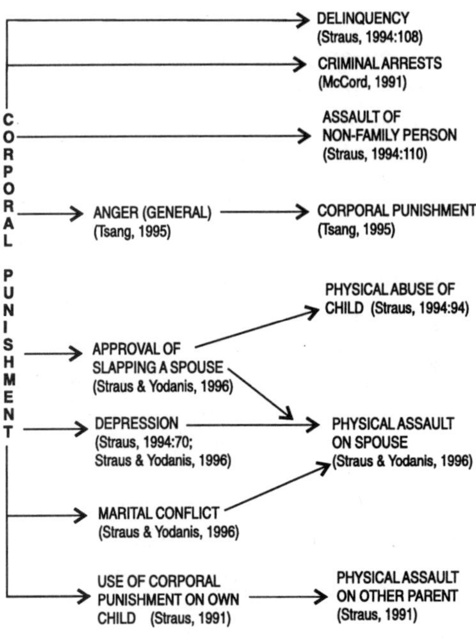


punishment and asked them to check their reactions to the first time they could remember being hit by their parents and the most recent occasion. For both the first and most recent instances, 42% checked "hated them." Because their hatred was for something that goes on for an average of about 14 years, it led us to the hypothesis that anger at parents could be generalized to anger at humanity, ie, that corporal punishment increases the risk of becoming a generally angry person. That hypothesis was tested by Tsang[15] on a sample of 1002 mothers in Minnesota. Tsang found that the more corporal punishment the mothers had experienced, the more likely they were to have high scores on a scale measuring their current level of anger, and that the higher the score on the anger scale, the greater the use of corporal punishment on their own children.

The next intervening process diagrammed in Fig 1 involves elements of social learning theory. Respondents in the 1985 National Family Violence Survey were asked this question: "Are there situations that you can imagine in which you would approve of a wife slapping her husband's face?" and a parallel question about a husband slapping a wife's face. Twenty-two percent approved of a wife slapping a husband and 14% approved of a husband slapping a wife.[16] Carrie Yodanis and I found that the more corporal punishment a person expe-

*Figure 2*

**Criminality of Sons, by Father's Use of Corporal Punishment, Controlling for Father's Criminality**

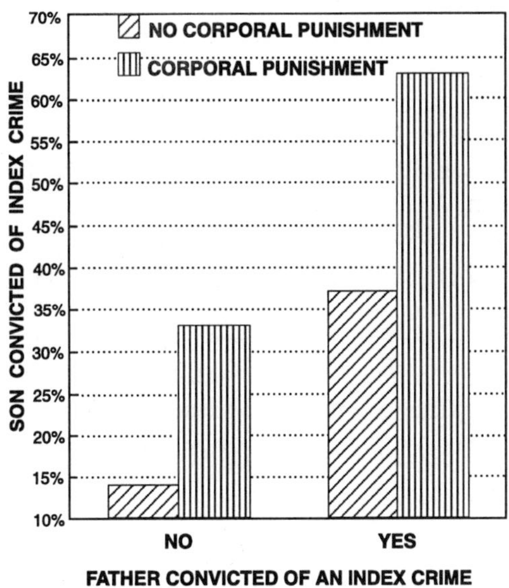


Ambridge-Somerville Youth Study: 133 2-parent families (McCord, 1991) 33 year longitudinal study of high risk youth.

rienced, the more likely they were to agree when asked these two questions. We also found, not surprisingly, that those who agreed were more likely to have actually hit their partner in the previous 12 months. We interpret this as showing that corporal punishment provides a model for what to do when someone misbehaves and persists in the misbehavior. Unfortunately, sooner or later, almost all spouses misbehave, at least as their partner sees it, and they often persist in the misbehavior. Thus, the "Johnny I've told you ten times" principle applied to children can also apply to spouses, and that is what we found. Specifically, the more corporal punishment, the greater the probability of believing that there are occasions when it is okay to slap a partner, and in turn, those who believe that are more likely to actually hit their partner.[17]

The line running from approval of slapping a spouse to physical abuse of child in Fig 1 indicates that the same process that helps explain why corporal punishment is related to assaults on a spouse also helps explain why the amount of corporal punishment a parent experienced is also associated with the probability of severely assaulting a child.

One of the most important findings from our research on the links between corporal punishment and adult psychosocial problems is that corporal punishment is associated with a greater probability of being depressed.[18] This is a serious enough problem by itself. In addition, we found that depression is associated with an increased probability of physically assaulting a partner. This is consistent with research showing that depression is not just an attack on the self, but also tends to be externalized in the form of aggression.[19]

Another process that may explain the link between corporal punishment and assaulting a spouse is shown by the entry in Fig I for marital conflict. We found that the more corporal punishment, the higher the probability of the marriage being characterized by long-standing and unresolved conflicts. Our guess is that corporal punishment is related to unresolved marital conflicts because the more parents use corporal punishment to deal with a child, the less opportunity the child has to observe and participate in nonviolent modes of conflict resolution. A high level of marital conflict, in turn, is linked to a higher probability of violence against a spouse.

The last row of Fig 1 refers to the possible effects of spanking on the parents themselves. I found that the more parents used corporal punishment on their children, the more likely they were to also hit their spouse. This could indicate a "role practice" effect. That is, each time a father or mother spanks a child for misbehaving, they are practicing the idea that people who misbehave should be hit, and a certain proportion of parents then apply this principle to their partner.

## Why We Don't Perceive the Connection

The evidence summarized above clearly shows that corporal punishment is associated with adult violence and other crime. Some of this evidence has been available for many years. However, it has mostly been ignored. A current example is the violence prevention programs in a large proportion of American schools. I examined four of these programs. All four seemed to be well-designed. None of the four, however, addressed the most frequent type of violence encountered by teenagers—being hit by a parent. Remember that more than half of all 13 and 14 year olds are hit by their parents each year, and that among teens who are hit by parents, it happens an average of about eight times per year.[6] None of the four programs even mention the inconsistency between what they are trying to teach and the example set by most of the parents. It may be beyond the power of a school-based program to get parents to stop hitting their children, but they can at least explain that it is also wrong for parents to correct misbehavior by hitting. Until that is done, it is unrealistic to expect teenagers to accept the idea that hitting is not the way to deal with a friend who insults him/her or makes a pass at his girlfriend or boyfriend.

Another example of the neglect of corporal punishment was revealed by a content analysis of textbooks on child development.[20] These books devote an average of only half a page to corporal punishment, despite the fact that it is a part of the socialization experience of over 90% of American children. Additional documentation of the extent to which the findings of research on corporal punishment has been ignored may be found in the preface and chapters 1 and 11 of *Beating The Devil Out Of Them: Corporal Punishment in American Families.*[17]

The recent pamphlet *Raising Children to Resist Violence: What You Can Do*[21] could be a sign that the head-in-the-sand era of American child psychology is ending. This pamphlet says that "Hitting, slapping, or spanking children as punishment shows them that it's okay to hit others to solve problems and can train them to punish others in the same way they were punished."

However, there are also signs in the opposite direction. Legislation to restore corporal punishment in the schools, for example, was introduced in several state legislatures in 1995. So it is important to understand why the link between corporal punishment and societal violence is so rarely perceived.

## Problems With the Evidence

The evidence summarized in this [selection] is dependable in the sense that similar findings occur over and over, and in the sense that most of the statistical analyses controlled for a number of potentially confounding variables, such as the age of the parent and the child, socioeconomic status, whether there was violence between the parents, and ethnic group. Nevertheless, it is a large leap from the correlations described in this [selection] to concluding that corporal punishment causes societal violence.

One of the most important problems is the possibility that the link between corporal punishment and violence as an adult occurs because parents use corporal punishment to respond to aggressive and violent children. To the extent that it is the child's aggression that causes the parents to use corporal punishment, it should not be surprising to find that 20 years later, as adults, the same tendency toward aggression shows up in the form of higher rates of wife-beating and other violence. The most that such research can show is that corporal punishment was not effective in suppressing aggression. To go beyond that requires longitudinal evidence. A longitudinal study could take into account the aggressiveness of the child at the time corporal punishment was used. That would permit finding out if spanking a child who hits another child reduces the chance that, as an adult, this person will hit others, as is widely believed, or as I believe, increases the risk of hitting others when an adult.

Unfortunately, there is as yet no published research linking corporal punishment to adult violence that can answer the question of whether corporal punishment makes things better or worse by taking into account the fact that parents hit children because they are aggressive. However, a forthcoming study does.[22] This is a study of three large cohorts of children. As shown in Fig 3, we found that, after holding constant the level of antisocial behavior at the start of the study (and also other variables such as emotional support and cognitive stimulation), the more corporal punishment parents used to correct that misbehavior, the worse the child's behavior was 2 years later.

Although there have been legitimate scientific bases for skepticism regarding the evidence on the links between corporal punishment and violence, I

*Figure 3*

**Antisocial Behavior in 1988 by Corporal Punishment of Children 3 to 6 in 1986, Controlling for 1986 Antisocial Behavior**

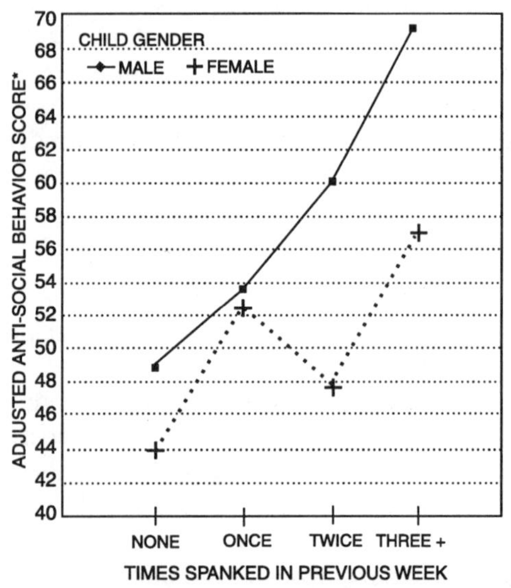


*Mean adjusted for T1 anti-social behavior, T1 cognitive stimulation, T1 parental emotional support, race, and SES.

think the fundamental reasons lie elsewhere. The following sections identify some of these extra-scientific reasons.

## Corporal Punishment and Personal Experience

A major obstacle to accepting the evidence that corporal punishment is linked to violence occurs because that evidence seems to contradict personal experience. The seeming contradiction occurs because, as was pointed out earlier, most people who were spanked, like most heavy smokers, will *not* suffer a harmful side effect. They can say, and almost everyone does say, "I was spanked and I'm okay."

Another reason findings from research on the harmful effects of corporal punishment are likely to be ignored is that it requires admitting that one's parents did something seriously wrong, and the even greater difficulty in acknowledging having brought up one's own children in a way that unnecessarily exposed them to risk of serious harm.

Perhaps the most important reason the evidence linking corporal punishment to violence has been ignored is the lack of direct, observable evidence. The harmful side effects do not occur right away, often not for years. When they do occur, for example in the form of depression, almost no one even considers the possibility that this depression might be the result of the disciplinary efforts of loving parents.

The delayed effects and the small proportion seriously hurt are the same reasons the harmful effects of smoking were not perceived for centuries. As noted previously, epidemiologic research shows that one third of very heavy smokers die of lung cancer or some other smoking-induced disease. That, of course, means that two thirds of heavy smokers do *not* die of these diseases.[3] So most heavy smokers can say "I've smoked more than a pack-a-day for 30 years and I'm okay." Similarly, most people who were spanked can say "My parents spanked me, and I'm not a child abuser."

### Other Obstacles to Perceiving the Effects of Corporal Punishment

Much of the opposition to steps to end corporal punishment is based on one or the other of the ten cultural myths about corporal punishment described in chapter 10 of *Beating The Devil Out Of Them: Corporal Punishment in American Families.*[17] There are also other and even more deeply embedded obstacles described in the concluding chapter of that book. Space limitations prevent more than mentioning these problems, but they reflect deep-seated aspects of American culture and the American psyche. Among these are the cultural norms supporting use of violence for socially desirable ends, extreme individualism, fear of government intervention in the family, and the opposition of Protestant fundamentalists.

## Conclusions and Implications

There are a number of other methodological problems and limitations in addition to those just discussed. Consequently, none of the studies reviewed can show that spanking causes violence. Neither, however, can this evidence be dismissed. One reason is that although the limitations of the studies prevent concluding unequivocally that corporal punishment causes violence, each of the studies could have falsified the hypothesized link between corporal punishment and violence, whereas all but a few have shown that corporal punishment is associated with violence or other crime.

Another reason the evidence summarized in this [selection] is important, despite the limitations of each of the studies, is that the weak point of one study may be dealt with in another study. Of course, that other study, in turn, will have its own limitations. But when so many different studies, using such a variety of methods, almost always show that corporal punishment is related to violence and other antisocial behavior, it is truly remarkable. That remarkable situation is similar to the relationship between smoking and lung cancer at the time of the first surgeon general's report. The report concluded that, while a definitive study did not exist, the cumulative weight of the evidence led to the conclusion that smoking does cause lung cancer. That conclusion is still denied by the tobacco industry, but is otherwise almost universally accepted.

It may not be many years before we also conclude that, despite the limitations of individual studies, corporal punishment is dangerous to the health of children and to society and all birth certificates will have a warning notice to that effect. Of course, corporal punishment is only one of many causes of violence. Consequently, even if all parents stopped hitting their children, it would not mean the end of violence. But, it is not unreasonable to think that it might result in at least a 10% reduction in violence and other crime. That would be a profound change for the 10% who are spared these problems. However, there are also indirect victims. A much larger percentage will be spared the pain of being victimized by crime. An even larger number will be spared the trauma of having a family member victimized. A still greater number will be spared some of the economic costs of crime and prisons and mental health treatment. Although it is currently impossible to know the percentages, and to be sure that some new evil will not replace hitting children, the research reviewed suggests that, in addition to many other benefits,[17] a society in which parents never spank will be a society with less violence and other crime.

## References

1. Durant JE. Public attitudes toward corporal punishment in Canada. In: *Internaional Symposium on Violence in Childhood and Adolescence.* Bielefeld, Germany: University of Bielefeld; 1994
2. Montague, A, ed. *Learning Non-Aggression: The Experience of Non-Literate Societies.* New York: Oxford University Press; 1978
3. Mattson, ME, Pollack ES, Cullen JW. What are the odds that smoking will kill you? *Am J Public Health.* 1987;77:425–431
4. Levinson D. *Family Violence in Cross-Cultural Perspective.* Newbury Park, CA: Sage Publications; 1989
5. Burns NM, Straus MA. *Cross-National Differences in Corporal Punishment, Infant Homicide, and Socioeconomic Factors.* Durham, NH: University of New Hampshire; 1987
6. Straus MA, Donnelly D. Violence and crime. In: Straus MA, ed. *Beating the Devil Out of Them: Corporal Punishment in American Families.* San Francisco, CA: Lexington/Jossey-Bass; 1994:99–120.
7. Edfeldt AW. *Violence Towards Children: An International Formulative Study.* Stockholm, Sweden: Akademilitteratur; 1979
8. Hyman IA, Wise KH. *Corporal Punishment in American Education.* Philadelphia: Temple University Press; 1979
9. Baron L, Straus MA. *Four Theories of Rape in American Society: A State-Level Analysis.* New Haven, CT: Yale University Press; 1988
10. Sears RR, Maccoby EC, Leven H. *Patterns of Child Rearing.* Evanston, IL: Row, Peterson and Company; 1957
11. Strassberg Z, Dodge KA, Petit GS, Bates JE. Spanking in the home and children's subsequent aggression toward kindergarten peers. *Develop Psychopathology.* 1994;6:445–461
12. Kessier R, Magee WJ. Childhood family violence and adult recurrent depression. *J Health Soc Beh.* 1994;35:13–27
13. McCord J. Questioning the value of punishment. *Soc Prob.* 1991;38:167–179
14. Straus MA. Hitting adolescents. In: Straus M, ed. *Beating the Devil Out of Them: Corporal Punishment in American Families.* San Francisco, CA: Lexington/Jossey-Bass; 1994:35–48

15. Tsang R. *Social Stress, Social Learning, and Anger as Risk Factors for Corporal Punishment.* Durham, NH: Family Research Laboratory, University of New Hampshire; 1995
16. Straus MA, Kaufman Kantor G, Moore D. Change in cultural norms approving marital violence from 1968 to 1992. In: Annual meeting of the American Sociological Association; 1994; Los Angeles, CA
17. Straus MA. *Beating the Devil Out of Them: Corporal Punishment in American Families.* San Francisco, CA: Jossey-Bass/Lexington Books; 1994
18. Straus MA, Yodanis CL. Corporal punishment in adolescence and physical assaults on spouses in later life: what accounts for the link: *J Marriage Fam.* In press
19. Berkowitz L. *Aggression: Its Causes, Consequences, and Control.* Philadelphia, PA: Temple University Press; 1993
20. Straus MA. The conspiracy of silence. In: Straus MA, ed. *Beating the Devil Out of Them: Corporal Punishment in American Families.* San Francisco, CA: Lexington/Jossey-Bass; 1994
21. American Psychological Association and the American Academy of Pediatrics. *Raising Children to Resist Violence: What You Can Do.* Elk Grove Village, IL: American Academy of Pediatrics Division of Publications; 1995
22. Sugarman DB, Straus MA, Giles-Sims J. Corporal punishment and anti-social behavior: a longitudinal analysis. *Arch Pediatr Adolesc Med.* In press

**Robert E. Larzelere** 

# A Review of the Outcomes of Parental Use of Nonabusive or Customary Physical Punishment

Some physicians and social scientists recently have suggested that "reducing or banning parental use of nonabusive physical punishment (ie, spanking) would reduce violence and other societal problems. Much of the research used to justify such a position, however, has been cross-sectional or has included the use of unreasonably harsh or abusive measures of physical punishment. Although all professionals oppose abusive physical punishment, nonabusive physical punishment is more controversial. The purpose of this [selection] to review empirical studies from peer-reviewed journals that have investigated child outcomes associated with nonabusive physical punishment by parents.

## Method

Several means were used to locate published articles for this review. A recent review[1] identified all relevant journal articles from 1984 to 1993 on physical punishment in the home, using a computer search of PsychLit and Medline, a search of the relevant references in the articles found in the computer search, and an author search for all authors with more than one relevant article. First, to expand on their work, a search of Social Sciences Citation Index was done for 1984 to 1994 for journal articles citing classic references on parental discipline by Baumrind, Becker, Bell, Chamberlin, Clifford, Grinder, Hoffman, Johannesson, Lefkowitz, Lepper, Lytton, Maccoby, Parke, Patterson, Perry, Sears, and Straus and for articles citing major references on punishment by Aronfreed, Axelrod, Azrin, LaVoie, and Walters. Second, any article published from 1974 to 1995 that was cited as investigating an association between parental physical punishment and a child outcome was considered. Studies prior to 1974 had to be cited as a prospective longitudinal study, a sequential analysis, or a clinical treatment study, or they had to be cited in Steinmetz's 1979 review.[2] Third, *Current Contents: Social and Behavioral Sciences* was searched during 1995 to identify recent articles with "punishment" or "spanking" in their titles. Finally, participants of the 1996 conference on the *Short-and Long-Term Consequences of*

From Robert E. Larzelere, "A Review of the Outcomes of Parental Use of Nonabusive or Customary Physical Punishment," *Pediatrics,* vol. 98, no. 4 (October 1996), pp. 824-828. 

*Corporal Punishment* were asked to identify any relevant journal articles that these search procedures had missed.

The first selection criterion for inclusion in this review was publication in a peer-reviewed journal. Second, a study had to include at least one measure of nonabusive or customary physical punishment by parents. This excluded findings about punitiveness broadly defined and measures of physical punishment dominated by severity or abusiveness (eg, ratings of the severity of physical punishment) or by nonspanking tactics (eg, washing a child's mouth out with soap). Third, the referent period for the parental discipline measure had to clearly precede the time period for the child outcome measure in the data collection.

A finding was counted as a beneficial outcome if nonabusive or customary physical punishment significantly ($P < .05$) predicted a desirable outcome in the child (eg, improved compliance). A finding was counted as a detrimental outcome if physical punishment significantly predicted a detrimental outcome in the child (eg, lower self-esteem or more delinquency). A study was summarized as finding predominantly beneficial or predominantly detrimental outcomes if (a) its only relevant statistical analysis was significantly in the specified direction, (b) one of its two or three relevant analyses was significantly in the specified direction, or (c) at least two of its relevant analyses were significantly in the specified direction. Otherwise a study was summarized as showing a neutral outcome.

## Results

Of 166 potentially relevant empirical articles, 35 met the inclusion criteria. Six of those were clinical treatment studies (including 4 randomized field studies), 2 were sequential analyses, 10 were prospective longitudinal studies, and 17 were retrospective studies. The Table summarizes all of these except the retrospective studies, which could not be included due to space limitations.[3–19] The results and conclusions, however, incorporate all 35 studies. Altogether, 9 articles (26%) found predominantly beneficial child outcomes associated with nonabusive or customary physical punishment, 12 articles (34%) found predominantly detrimental outcomes, and the other 14 articles (40%) found neutral outcomes, ie, neither beneficial nor detrimental outcomes.

The research design, the age of the child, and whether the study focused explicitly on nonabusive physical punishment each tended to differentiate studies with beneficial versus detrimental outcomes. First, the studies with stronger internal validity tended to find beneficial outcomes. All six (100%) of the clinical treatment studies (including four randomized field studies) and both (100%) of the sequential studies showed predominantly beneficial outcomes associated with customary or nonabusive physical punishment. Three (30%) of the 10 prospective longitudinal studies found predominantly detrimental outcomes, whereas the other 7 (70%) prospective studies found neutral outcomes. Nine (53%) of the 17 retrospective studies found predominantly detrimental outcomes, 7 (41%) found predominantly neutral outcomes, and 1 (6%) found predominantly beneficial outcomes.

*Table*

## Methodologically Strongest Studies of Child Outcomes of Nonabusive or Customary Physical Punishment by Parents

| Study | Age and Gender[a] | N | Type of Sample | Measure of Physical Punishment[b] | Other Discipline Responses | Types of Child Outcomes | Outcome of Physical Punishment[c] |
|---|---|---|---|---|---|---|---|
| Randomized clinical field trials | | | | | | | |
| Bean and Roberts (1981)[21] | 2–6 B, G | 24 | Clinic-referred | 2-slap spank backup for time out (TO) | Child release, non-time-out control | Compliance with parent commands | + |
| Percent compliance improved more with spank than in either of other two conditions. Fewer TOs than Child Release group. | | | | | | | |
| Day and Roberts (1983)[22] | 2–5 B, G | 16 | Clinic-referred | 2-slap spank backup | Room time out (barrier) | Compliance with parent commands | + |
| Switching from chair to room time out just as effective in increasing compliance as chair time out with spank back-up. | | | | | | | |
| Roberts (1988)[24] | 2–5 B, G | 18 | Clinic-referred | 2-slap spank backup | Brief room time out (isolation) | Compliance to parent commands, escapes from time out chair, TO verbalizations | + |
| Back-ups equally effective in reducing escapes from time out and in increasing compliance. Room-time-out back-up had fewer verbalizations in 1st chair time out. | | | | | | | |
| Roberts and Powers (1990)[25] | 2–6 B, G | 36 | Clinic-referred | 2-slap spank backup | Room TO, child release, hold | Compliance, TO escapes, number of chair TOs needed | + |
| Spank and room TO yielded fewer escapes from TO and fewer TOs than Hold or Child Release back-ups. Fifteen children needed alternative back-up (switch to spank in 12 cases), which increased compliance. | | | | | | | |
| Other treatment studies | | | | | | | |
| Bernal et al (1968)[26] | 8 B | 1 | Clinic-referred | Good, hard whack on rear | Ignore | Compliance, aggression | + |
| Increased compliance, decreased aggression, increased liking for son. | | | | | | | |
| Roberts (1982)[23] | 2–6 B, G | 32 | Clinic-referred | 2-slap spank back-up | None | Escapes from time out | + |
| Reduced mean number of escapes from time out from 1st to 2nd time out attempt. | | | | | | | |

| Study | Age and Gender[a] | N | Type of Sample | Measure of Physical Punishment[b] | Other Discipline Responses | Types of Child Outcomes | Outcome of Physical Punishment[c] |
|---|---|---|---|---|---|---|---|
| Sequential analyses with statistical controls | | | | | | | |
| Larzelere and Merenda (1994)[29] | 2–3 B, G | 38 | Volunteers in response to newspaper article | Slap hand, spank as defined by mothers | Reason, nonphysical punishment, combinations of above, and other | Delay until next recurrence of disobedience or fighting | + |
| Punishment without reasoning delayed the next disobedience recurrence the most at high levels of child distress. Reasoning delayed disobedience recurrences the most at intermediate levels of child distress. Either type of punishment with reasoning at intermediate child distress was the best at delaying disobedience recurrences overall. | | | | | | | |
| Larzelere et al (1996)[30] | 2–3 B, G | 38 | Volunteers | Slap hand, spank as defined by mothers | Reason, nonphysical punishment, combinations of above, and other | Delay until next recurrence of disobedience or fighting | + |
| The combination of either type of punishment with reasoning was associated with a longer delay until the next misbehavior recurrence than following reasoning alone, punishment alone, or other discipline responses. | | | | | | | |
| Prospective longitudinal studies | | | | | | | |
| Crowne et al (1969)[32] | 5 (TI), 18 (T2) B, G | 83 | Kindergarten | Frequency of spanking by each parent, extent of physical punishment | Deprivation of privileges, withdrawal of love | Realistic aspirations (vs overcautious or unrealistic), unusual shifts in aspirations | 0 |
| Mothers' spanking frequency associated with realistic aspirations more than with unrealistic aspirations (females). Mothers' spanking freq + r with number of unusual shifts in aspirations. Love withdrawal + r with overly cautious aspirations (males). | | | | | | | |
| Deater-Deckard et al (in press)[20] | 4 (TI), 4.5–7.5 (T2) B, G | 566 | Kindergarten | Mother's spontaneous report of PP as part of responses to 5 misbehavior vignettes | None | Externalizing problems (teacher report) and aggression and conflict with teacher (peer nominations) | –/0 |
| Physical punishment + r with all 3 measures of acting out for European-Americans, PP – r with all 3 measures for African-Americans, but non-significantly so. | | | | | | | |

| Study | Age and Gender[a] | N | Type of Sample | Measure of Physical Punishment[b] | Other Discipline Responses | Types of Child Outcomes | Outcome of Physical Punishment[c] |
|---|---|---|---|---|---|---|---|
| Grinder (1962)[33] | 5(T1) 11-12(T2) B, G | 140 | Kindergarten | Extent of physical punishment | Isolation, love withdrawal, privileges deprivation | Resistance to temptation to cheat for prize in lab game | 0 |
| Physical punishment unrelated to resistance to temptation as were other discipline responses. | | | | | | | |
| McClelland and Pilon (1983)[34] | 5(T1) 31-32(T2) B, G | 78 | Kindergarten | Extent of physical punishment | Deprivation of privileges | Need for Achievement (n Ach), need for affiliation, need for power | 0 |
| Physical punishment – r with n power for males only; Deprivation of privileges unrelated to all adult needs. | | | | | | | |
| McCord (1988)[27] | 5–18 (T1), adult (T2) B | 130 | From at-risk neighborhoods | Parents used physical punishment, but not explosive or high on marital conflict | None | Criminality, "egocentrism" | 0 |
| Those whose parents used PP were higher on egocentrism, but egocentrism was the extent to which they looked back on their lives with pride and a sense of achievement or refused a $20 payment. PP group not different from non-PP group on criminality. | | | | | | | |
| McCord (1991)[37] | 8–16 (T1), adult (T2)B | 130 | From at-risk neighborhoods | Fathers' or both parents' use or non-use of phys punishment | None | Criminality | –/0 |
| Fathers' PP + r with index crime convictions, significantly so for non-criminal fathers. Parental affection eliminated this association of PP with adult criminality. | | | | | | | |
| Sears (1961)[35] | 5(T1) 12(T2) B, G | 160 | Kindergarten | Extent of physical punishment | Deprivation of privileges, love withdrawal | Anti- and pro-social, projected, and self-aggression, and aggression anxiety | 0 |
| Of 10 correlations with later aggression, physical punishment + r only with prosocial aggression in girls. The other discipline responses also had one more + r than – r. | | | | | | | |
| Sears (1970)[36] | 5(T1) 12(T2) B, G | 160 | Kindergarten | Extent of physical punishment | None | Self-esteem | 0 |
| Physical punishment not associated with subsequent self-esteem. | | | | | | | |

| Study | Age and Gender[a] | N | Type of Sample | Measure of Physical Punishment[b] | Other Discipline Responses | Types of Child Outcomes | Outcome of Physical Punishment[c] |
|---|---|---|---|---|---|---|---|
| Simons et al (1994)[31] | 12 –14 (T1), 15 (T2) B, G | 332 | 7th-grade students in 8 Iowa counties | How often spanked or hit with object (combined with youth and parent reports) | None | Delinquency, aggressiveness, psychological well-being | 0/+ |
| Physical punishment unrelated to outcomes after controlling for positive parental involvement except that mother's physical punish predicted lower delinquency in girls. | | | | | | | |
| Strass-berg et al (1994)[28] | 4 (T1) 4.5 (T2) B, G | 273 | Kindergarten | Spanking frequency during past year, including spanking with object | Parental violence | Observed bullying and reactive, instrumental, and total aggression at school | |
| Spanked children higher than the 11 nonspanked/non-abused children on total aggression & reactive aggression, though not on bullying or instrumental aggression. Spanking frequency not related to any aggression measures. | | | | | | | |

*[a] B = boys, G = Girls. T1 = First data collection period (Time 1). T2 = Subsequent data collection period (Time 2).*
*[b] TO = time out. PP = physical punishment. + r = positively associated (i.e., correlated). –r = negatively associated. freq = frequency.*
*[c] + = predominantly beneficial subsequent outcomes for children. – = predominantly detrimental subsequent outcomes for children. 0 = generally neutral subsequent outcomes for children. 0/+ = generally neutral outcomes, but one more directional outcome was beneficial than was detrimental.*

Second, the age of the child when physically punished accounted for differing patterns in the findings. Eighteen studies investigated physical punishment prior to age 13. Eight (44%) of those 18 studies found predominantly beneficial outcomes, 7 (39%) found predominantly neutral outcomes, and only 3 (17%) found predominantly detrimental outcomes. Thirteen other studies measured physical punishment during years both before and after age 13. Five (38%) of those 13 studies found predominantly detrimental outcomes, 7 (54%) found predominantly neutral outcomes, and 1 (8%) found predominantly beneficial outcomes. All 4 studies (100%) that explicitly measured spanking of teenagers found predominantly detrimental outcomes.

Those studies that excluded abuse from their measures of physical punishment were more likely to find predominantly beneficial outcomes. Of 11 studies with such exclusions, 6 (55%) had beneficial outcomes, 4 (36%) showed neutral outcomes, and only 1 (9%) had detrimental outcomes. The remaining 24 studies measured customary physical punishment without excluding abusive or physically violent parents from their measure of physical punishment. Only three (13%) of those 24 studies found beneficial outcomes, 10 (42%) had neutral outcomes, and 11 (46%) showed detrimental outcomes.

The pattern of findings in these studies are also related to other methodological and substantive distinctions. These will be summarized briefly, followed by findings comparing physical punishment with alternative discipline responses. Certain methodological characteristics tended to be more common in the studies with beneficial outcomes compared with those with detrimental outcomes. Studies showing beneficial outcomes tended to control for preexisting differences on child outcome variables, for parenting characteristics, and for general differences between families. They were more likely to use behavioral observations or timely reports of behaviors and to be prospective rather than retrospective. Studies that specified a two-spank procedure to the buttocks invariably found beneficial outcomes. Studies that did not rely solely on one interview for both the physical punishment measure and the child outcome measure were more likely to find beneficial outcomes. Finally, the only study of ethnic minorities found that physical punishment was associated (nonsignificantly) with beneficial outcomes for African Americans, almost directly opposite of the detrimental outcomes found for European Americans in the same study.[20]

The following characteristics of physical punishment were associated with beneficial or neutral outcomes, compared with detrimental outcomes: Used less than weekly (as recalled by adults)[8,13] or, with a teenager, fewer than 10 times annually;[17] used at nonabusive levels of severity;[4,5,9,20–28] used by parents who were not physically violent against family members;[27] used without a potentially damaging instrument;[5,9] used during ages 2 to 6[21–25,29,30] and possibly between ages 7 and 12;[9,12,14,27] used privately;[9] used with reasoning,[30] preferably with an intermediate level of child distress;[29] and used primarily as a back-up for less aversive discipline responses.[21–25,29,30] Parents who obtained better outcomes associated with physical punishment were positively involved with their child,[6,10,31] had child-oriented motivations for using spanking rather than parent-oriented motivations,[12] did not increase their children's fear of parental discipline,[9] followed through with their warnings,[9] and cooperated with each other in discipline responsibilities.[9] They did not use verbal putdowns,[10,11] and they changed their main discipline method to grounding when their children got older.[5]

All 6 treatment studies, both sequential studies, 3 of the 10 prospective studies, and 7 of the 17 retrospective studies compared the outcomes of physical punishment with the outcomes of one or more alternative discipline responses. Grounding (for older children) was the only alternative discipline response that had more beneficial outcomes than did physical punishment.[5,11] Nine alternative discipline responses were found to have less beneficial outcomes than did physical punishment: physical restraint and a child-determined release from time out with 2- to 6-year-olds;[25] reasoning without punishment, punishment without reasoning, and discipline responses other than punishment or reasoning with 2- and 3-year-olds;[30] ignoring with an 8-year-old;[26] love withdrawal with 5-year-olds;[32] and nonphysical punishment,[19] and verbal putdowns[10] in older children.

## Conclusions

The most important finding of the review is that there are not enough quality studies that document detrimental outcomes of nonabusive physical punishment to support advice or policies against this age-old parental practice. Only 30 relevant journal articles were found from 1974 through 1995, an average of less than 1 1/2 per year. Next, many of the studies had methodological weaknesses, and the stronger ones were more likely to find beneficial outcomes of physical punishment. A particularly pervasive weakness was that no prospective or retrospective study controlled for the original frequency or severity of child problem behavior, which would be like studying cancer recurrences following radiation treatment without taking into account the severity or existence of the original cancer. More quality research is needed on nonabusive physical punishment. Public and private agencies should make quality research on the broader topic of parental discipline a top priority.

*How* parents use discipline tactics may be more important than which ones they consider off limits. Effects of physical punishment, as well as nonphysical punishment, probably depend on when and how parents implement it, its role in their overall approach to parental discipline, and the overall parent-child relationship. Other aspects of parental discipline may be more important indicators of dysfunctional parenting than whether parents spank or not.

## References

1. Lyons JS, Anderson RL, Larson DB. *The Use and Effects of Physical Punishment in the Home: A Systematic Review.* Paper presented at the meeting of the American Academy of Pediatrics: November 1993; Washington, DC
2. Steinmetz SK. Disciplinary techniques and their relationship to aggressiveness, dependency, and conscience. In: Burr WR, Hill R, Nye FI, Reiss IL, eds. *Contemporary Theories about the Family, I.* New York, NY: Free Press; 1979;405-438
3. Bithoney WG, Snyder J, Michalek J, Newberger EH. Childhood ingestions as symptoms of family distress. *AJDC.* 1985;139:456–459
4. Bryan JW, Freed FW. Corporal punishment: normative data and sociological and psychological correlates in a community college population. *J Youth Adolesc.* 1982;11:77–87
5. Caesar P. Exposure to violence in the families-of-origin among wife-abusers and maritally nonviolent men. *Violence Vict.* 1988;3:49–63
6. Carroll JC. The intergenerational transmission of family violence: the long term effects of aggressive behavior. *Aggressive Behav.* 1977;3:289–299
7. Gelles RJ, Straus MA. Violence in the American family. *J Soc Iss.* 1979; 34:15–30
8. Hemenway P, Solnick S, Carter J. Child rearing violence. *Child Abuse Negl.* 1994;18:1011–1020
9. Holmes SJ, Robins LN. The role of parental disciplinary practices in the development of depression and alcoholism. *Psychiatry.* 1988;51;24–36
10. Joubert CE. Self-esteem and social desirability in relation to college students retrospective perceptions of parental fairness and disciplinary practice. *Psychol Rep.* 1991;69:115–120
11. Joubert CE. Antecedents of narcissism and psychological reactance as indicated by college students; retrospective reports of their parents' behaviors. *Psychol Rep.* 1992;70:1111–1115
12. Larzelere RE, Klein M, Schumm WR, Alibrando SA, Jr. Relations of spanking and other parenting characteristics to self-esteem and perceived fairness of parental discipline. *Psychol Rep.* 1989;64:1140–1142
13. Lieh-Mak F, Chung SY, Liv YW. Characteristics of child battering in Hong Kong: a controlled study. *Br J Psychiatry.* 1983;142;89–94
14. MacIntyre DI, Cantrell PJ. Punishment history and adult attitudes towards violence and aggression in men and women. *Soc Behav Pers.* 1995;23:23–28

15. Rhue JW, Lynn SJ. Fantasy proneness: developmental antecedents. *J Pers.* 1987;55;121–137
16. Straus MA. Family patterns and child abuse in a nationally representative American sample. *Child Abuse Negl.* 1979;3:213–225
17. Straus MA. Discipline and deviance: physical punishment of children and violence and other crime in adulthood. *Soc Prob.* 1991;38:133–154
18. Straus MA, Kaufman Kantor G. Corporal punishment of adolescents by parents: a risk factor in the epidemiology of depression, suicide, alcohol abuse, child abuse, and wife beating. *Adolescence.* 1994;29:543–561
19. Tennant FS, Jr., Detels R, Clark V. Some childhood antecedents of drug and alcohol abuse. *Am J Epidemiol.* 1975;102:377–385
20. Deater-Deckard K, Dodge KA, Bates JE, Pettit GS. Physical discipline among African-American and European-American mothers: links to children's externalizing behaviors. *Dev Psychol.* In press
21. Bean AW, Roberts MW. The effect of time-out release contingencies on changes in child noncompliance. *J. Abnorm Child Psychol.* 1981;9:95–105
22. Day DE, Roberts MW. An analysis of the physical punishment component of a parent training program. *J Abnorm Child Psychol.* 1983;11:141–152
23. Roberts MW. Resistance to timeout: some normative data. *Behav Assess.* 1982;4:239–248
24. Roberts MW. Enforcing chair timeouts with room timeouts. *Behav Modif.* 1988;12:353–370
25. Roberts MW, Powers SW. Adjusting chair timeout enforcement procedures for oppositional children. *Behav Ther.* 1990;21:257–271
26. Bernal ME, Duryee JS, Pruett HL, Burns BJ. Behavioral modification and the brat syndrome. *J Consult Clin Psychol.* 1968;32:447–455
27. McCord J. Parental behavior in the cycle of aggression. *Psychiatry.* 1988;51:14–23
28. Strassberg Z, Dodge KA, Pettit GW, Bates JE. Spanking in the home and children's subsequent aggression toward kindergarten peers. *Dev Psychopathol.* 1994;6:455–461
29. Larzelere RE, Merenda JA. The effectiveness of parental discipline for toddler misbehavior at different levels of child distress. *Fam Rel.* 1994;43:480–488
30. Larzelere RE, Schneider WN, Larson DB, Pike PL. The effects of discipline responses in delaying toddler misbehavior recurrences. *Child Family Behav Ther.* 1996;18:35–57
31. Simons RL, Johnson C, Conger RD. Harsh corporal punishment versus quality of parental involvement as an explanation of adolescent maladjustment. *J Marriage Fam.* 1994;56:591–607
32. Crowne DP, Conn LK, Marlowe E, Edwards CN. Some developmental antecedents of level of aspiration. *J Pers.* 1969;37:73–92
33. Grider RE. parental childrearing practices, conscience, and resistance to temptation of sixth grade children. *Child Dev.* 1962;33:803–820
34. McClelland DC, Pilon DA. Sources of adult motives in patterns of parent behavior in early childhood. *J Pers Soc Psychol.* 1983;44:564–574
35. Sears RR. Relation of early socialization experiences to aggression in middle childhood. *J Abnorm Soc Psychol.* 1961;63:466–492
36. Sears RR. Relation of early socialization experiences to self-concepts and gender role in middle childhood. *Child Dev.* 1970;41:267–289
37. McCord J. Questioning the value of punishment. *Soc Prob.* 1991;38:169–179

# POSTSCRIPT

## Is Spanking Detrimental to Children?

Spanking is a popular child-rearing technique in America. If one believes that spanking is effective in guiding children, are the possible long-term effects of anxiety, depression, and aggression worth the trade-off? If spanking leads to increased violence in children and adults, what form of guidance can parents use? After all, who wants a generation of uncontrollable, self-centered individuals leading the country?

Some child-development experts agree that reasoning, talking, and listening to children works well in teaching right from wrong as well as in preserving the child's self-concept. They admit that this child-rearing approach takes more time, but they maintain that the benefits outweigh the costs. Other child-rearing authorities feel that spankings, when correctly administered within the context of a loving home, are effective in positively shaping a child's behavior.

A variety of resources on spanking such as Web sites and telephone hot lines are available. Parents who feel that they are in danger of hurting their children can get help by calling a toll-free hot line, Child Help USA, at 1-800-442-4453.

## Suggested Readings


Baumrind, D. (1996). The discipline controversy revisited. *Family Relations, 45,* 405–414.

Colvard, K. (1996). Spanking and triage. *Pediatrics, 98*(4), 807–808.

Ellison, C., & Sherkat, D. (1993, February). Conservative Protestantism and support for corporal punishment. *American Sociological Review, 58,* 131–144.

Giles-Sims, J., Strauss, M., & Sugarman, D. (1995, April). Child, maternal, and family characteristics associated with spanking. *Family Relations, 44,* 170–176.

Rosemond, J. (1994). *To spank or not to spank: A parents' handbook.* Kansas City: Andrews & McMeel Publishers.

Samalin, N., & Whitney, C. (1998). Why spanking doesn't work. *Parents' Magazine, 73*(8), 67–71.

Straus, M. (1994). *Beating the devil out of them: Corporal punishment in American families and its effects on children.* Boston: Lexington Books/Macmillan.

Survey says some mothers still believe that spanking is good discipline. (1995, January). *Jet, 87,* 14–18.

# ISSUE 6

## Are Fathers Really Necessary?

**YES: W. J. Doherty, Edward F. Kouneski, and Martha F. Erickson**, from "Responsible Fathering: An Overview and Conceptual Framework," *Journal of Marriage and the Family* (May 1998)

**NO: Alexis J. Walker and Lori A. McGraw**, from "Who Is Responsible for Responsible Fathering?" *Journal of Marriage and the Family* (May 2000)

ISSUE SUMMARY

**YES:** Professor of family social science W. J. Doherty, psychologist Edward F. Kouneski, and Martha F. Erickson, director of the University of Minnesota's Children, Youth and Family Consortium, explore the contextual influences on fathering and conclude that a quality marriage in the optimal context promotes responsible fathering.

**NO:** Professor of human development and family sciences Alexis J. Walker and Lori A. McGraw, 4-H program coordinator at Oregon State University, contend that there is no empirical evidence that children need active fathers in their lives.

There has been a dramatic rise in single-parent homes headed by men. Since the 1990 census, households headed by single fathers have risen from about 1.3 million homes in 1990 to over 2.1 million in 2000. As a consequence of this increase, an issue that has confronted researchers revolves around the necessity of two-parent families. One specific issue that has been hotly debated is whether or not fathers are necessary in raising children. Children need nurturing, guidance, and economic security, but must they receive these things from *both* father and mother? Some scholars argue that children need active, involved fathers throughout their childhood and adolescence. If this does not occur, the children may be more prone to involvement in crime, premature sexuality, out-of-wedlock childbirth, lower educational achievements, depression, substance abuse, and poverty.

Other scientists question whether or not the ability to meet children's needs is gender-specific. While few would argue that it is more challenging to raise a child in a single-parent home, well-socialized and successful children have come from single-parent homes. The vast majority of these homes are female-headed. In fact, there are over 7.5 million single mothers raising children in the United States today. Another consideration is that there has been an increase in adoption by gay and lesbian parents in two-parent homes. While these children may face challenges in dealing with the prejudice associated with being raised in such households, one might ask why children would be permitted to be adopted into these homes if there was evidence that children needed both a male and a female parent. Many scientists argue that there is little, if any scientific evidence that suggests children must be raised by both a male and a female.

As you read the following selections, consider the type of family in which you were raised. Was your upbringing an optimal situation? Did the role that your father played have a positive or a negative effect on your life? W. J. Doherty, Edward F. Kouneski, and Martha F. Erickson contend that children need and deserve fathers who are actively involved with their children throughout childhood and adolescence. To achieve this, they promote responsible fathering as a way to help meet the needs of children. Alexis J. Walker and Lori A. McGraw believe that while there may be an ideological basis for the assumption that children need and deserve active and involved fathers, empirical support for this ideal is lacking.

**W. J. Doherty, Edward F. Kouneski, and Martha F. Erickson**

# Responsible Fathering: An Overview and Conceptual Framework

## Responsible Fathering

The use of the term "responsible fathering," which was the original language used by the U.S. Department of Health and Human Services in commissioning our work, reflects a recent shift by academics and professionals away from value-free language and toward a more explicit value-advocacy approach. "Responsible" suggests an "ought," a set of desired norms for evaluating fathers' behavior. The term also conveys a moral meaning (right and wrong) because it suggests that some fathering could be judged "irresponsible." The willingness to use explicitly moral terms reflects a change in the social climate among academics, professionals, and policymakers, who until recently embraced the traditional notion that social science, social policy, and social programs could be value free. In the late twentieth century, there is more appreciation of the inevitability of value-laden and moral positions being part of social science and social interventions and a greater willingness to be explicit about values so that they can be debated openly and their influence on social science and policy can be made clear, rather than being covert (Doherty, 1995a; Doherty et al., 1993; Wolfe, 1989). Indeed, there has always been a strong but implicit undercurrent of value advocacy in fathering research, much of it conducted by men and women interested in promoting more committed and nurturing involvement by men in their children's lives. Similarly, there has always been a moral undertone to the focus on fathers' deficits that has characterized much of the literature on absent, "deadbeat," and emotionally uninvolved fathers (Doherty, 1990). The term "responsible fathering," as we use it, applies to fathers across all social classes and racial groups, not narrowly to men in lower social classes

From W. J. Doherty, Edward F. Kouneski, and Martha F. Erickson, "Responsible Fathering: An Overview and Conceptual Framework," *Journal of Marriage and the Family*, vol. 60 (May 1998). 

or minority groups. Now that value advocacy has become more explicit in the fathering area (Dollahite, Hawkins, & Brotherson, 1997), responsible fathering needs to be clearly defined. James Levine and Edward Pitt (1995) have made an important start in their delineation of responsible fathering. They write:

> A man who behaves responsibly towards his child does the following:
>
> - He waits to make a baby until he is prepared emotionally and financially to support his child.
> - He establishes his legal paternity if and when he does make a baby.
> - He actively shares with the child's mother in the continuing emotional and physical care of their child, from pregnancy onwards.
> - He shares with the child's mother in the continuing financial support of their child, from pregnancy onwards. (pp. 5–6)

Levine and Pitt's elements of responsible fathering have the advantage of referring to both resident and nonresident fathers, a reflection of the diversity of fathers' situations. The authors also assert that commitment to this ethic of responsible fatherhood extends beyond the father to the mother, to professionals who work with families, and to social institutions entrusted with the support of families. We employ Levine and Pitt's definition in this [selection], but we narrow our scope to men who are already fathers; we do not address the issue of postponing fatherhood.

The developmental backdrop for the discussion of fathering reflects children's needs for predictability, nurturance, and appropriate limit setting from fathers and mothers, as well as for economic security and a cooperative, preferably loving relationship between their parents (Hetherington & Parke, 1993). Furthermore, the specific needs of children vary by their developmental stage. Parents are required to provide higher levels of physical caregiving when their children are infants and greater levels of conflict management when their children become adolescents. Although we do not review the literature on the effects of active fathering on children, an assumption behind this [selection] —and our value stance—is that children need and deserve active, involved fathers throughout their childhood and adolescence. The prime justification for promoting responsible fathering is the needs of children. . . .

## Influences on Fathering: A Conceptual Model

The fathering literature has been long on empirical studies and short on theory. Researchers mostly have adapted concepts from social sciences to fit their particular area, but work is beginning on overarching conceptual frameworks to guide research and program development. In his review of theory in fathering research, Marsiglio (1995) mentions life course theory (which emphasizes how men's experience of fatherhood changes with life transitions), social scripting theory (which emphasizes the cultural messages that fathers internalize about their role), and social identity theory (which focuses on how men take on the identity of a father in relation to their other social roles). Hawkins, Christiansen, Sargent, and Hill (1995), Hawkins and Dollahite (1997), and Snarey

(1993) have used Erik Erikson's developmental theory in their work on how fathering can promote generativity among adult men. Other scholars have explored the utility of economic theories to understand fathers' decisions to invest in, or withdraw from, their children (Becker, 1991).

The most specific conceptual model frequently used in the fatherhood literature is Lamb's and Pleck's four-factor model of father involvement, which is not explicitly grounded in a broader theory such as Erikson's theory or social identity theory. (See Lamb et al., 1985.) Lamb and Pleck proposed that father involvement is determined by motivation, skills and self-confidence, social support, and institutional practices. These factors may be viewed as additive, building on one another, and as interactive, with some factors being necessary prior to others. For example, motivation may be necessary for the development of skills. Ihinger-Tallman, Pasley, and Buehler (1995) proposed an eight-factor model of mediators between father identity and actual involvement after divorce: mother's preferences and beliefs, father's perception of mother's parenting, father's emotional stability, mother's emotional stability, sex of child, coparental relationship, father's economic well-being, father's economic security, and encouragement from others. Recently, Park (1996) articulated a systems model of residential father involvement that includes individual, family, extrafamilial, and cultural influences.

Based on the research literature, prior theoretical work on fathering, and the systemic ecological orientation described earlier, we present a conceptual model of influences on responsible fathering. (See Figure 1.) Unlike prior work, the model is intended to include fathering inside or outside marriage and regardless of coresidence with the child. The focus is on the factors that help create and maintain a father-child bond. The model attempts to transcend the dyadic focus of much traditional child development theory by emphasizing first the child-father-mother triad and then larger systems' influences.

The model highlights individual factors of the father, mother, and child; mother-father relationship factors; and larger contextual factors in the environment. Within each of these domains, the model outlines a number of specific factors that can be supported by the research literature. The center of the model is the interacting unit of child, father, and mother, each formulating meanings and enacting behaviors that influence the others. The three are embedded in a broader social context that affects them as individuals and affects the quality of their relationships.

We are particularly interested in highlighting factors that pertain to fathers because one of the goals of this [selection] is to guide father-specific research, program development, and public policy. All of the factors in the model affect the mother-child relationship, as well, because they are generic to parenting (see Belsky, 1984), but many of them have particular twists for fathers. Because theory and research on parenting so often have been derived from work on mothers, it seems particularly important to illuminate the distinctive influences on fathering. The arrows point to the father-child relationship, in particular to the four domains of responsible fathering covered in this review—paternity, presence, economic support, and involvement. Although the model can depict fathers' indirect influence on their children through their support for

*Figure 1*

Influences on Responsible Fathering: A Conceptual Model

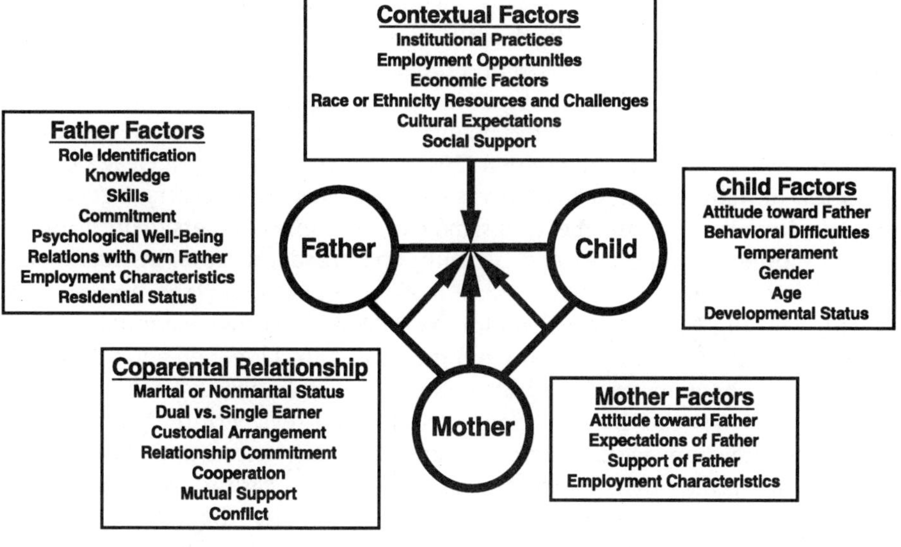


the mother, the focus here is on direct father-child interaction. And although the influences depicted in the model also can be viewed as influencing the father directly, we prefer to focus on the effects on father-child relations because enhancing those relations and, therefore, the well-being of children is the ultimate goal of programs for fathers.

The research reviewed for this [selection] supports the notion that father-child relations are more strongly influenced than mother-child relations by three of the dimensions of the model: the coparental relationship, factors in the other parent, and larger contextual factors.

## Coparental Relationship

A number of studies have shown that the quality of father-child relations both inside and outside marriage is more highly correlated with the quality of the coparental relationship than is true for the mother-child relationship (Belsky & Volling, 1987; Cox, Owen, Lewis, & Henderson, 1989; Feldman, Nash, & Aschenbrenner, 1983; Levy-Shiff & Israelashvili, 1988). Fathers appear to withdraw from their child when they are not getting along with the mother, whereas mothers do not show a similar level of withdrawal. This is one way to understand the tendency of fathers to remove themselves from their children's lives after a breakup with the mother, especially if they have a negative relationship with the mother (Ahrons & Miller, 1993). As Furstenberg and Cherlin (1991) have asserted, for many men, marriage and parenthood are a "package deal." Or one might say that in American culture, a woman is a mother all of her life, but a man is a father if he has a wife. Furthermore, if he has a wife but does not get along with her, he may be present as a father, but the quality of his relationship with his children is apt to suffer.

One reason that fathering is particularly sensitive to the marital or coparental relationship is that standards and expectations for fathering appear to be more variable than those for mothering. There is more negotiation in families over what fathers will do than over what mothers will do and hence more dependence among fathers on the quality and outcome of those negotiations (Backett, 1987). As Lewis and O'Brien (1987) state, men have a less clear "job description" as fathers than women do as mothers. Therefore, fathers' behavior is strongly influenced by the meanings and expectations of fathers themselves, as well as mothers, children, extended family, and broader cultural institutions.

One of the most sensitive areas of research on fathering is the importance of fathers being married to the children's mothers. Because many fathers are not married to the mother, it can seem prejudicial to these men and their children—and perhaps to single-parent mothers—to emphasize the importance of marriage. On the other hand, an implication of our review of the research and our conceptual framework is that, for most American heterosexual fathers, the family environment most supportive of fathering is a caring, committed, and collaborative marriage. This kind of marriage means that the father lives with his children and has a good partnership with their mother. These are the two principal intrafamilial determinants of responsible fathering.

Some of the controversy over the role of marriage in responsible fathering can be circumvented by specifying the quality of the marriage, as we have done. It is the quality of the marital process, rather than the legal or coresidential status, that most affects fathering. One might argue, then, that being married is not important because cohabiting couples could have the same qualities of relationship. Although, in principle, this is true, the best national research on cohabitation indicates that cohabitation is a temporary arrangement for most heterosexual couples; they eventually either marry or break up (Bumpass et al., 1991). We conclude that, in practice, the kind of mother-father relationship most conducive to responsible fathering in contemporary U.S. society is a caring, committed, collaborative marriage. Outside of this arrangement, substantial barriers stand in the way of active, involved fathering.

## Mother Factors

Among external influences on fathering, the role of the mother has particular salience because mothers serve as partners and sometimes as gatekeepers in the father-child relationship, both inside and outside marriage (De Luccie, 1995). Mother factors in the conceptual model, of course, interact with the coparental relationship because the mother's personal feelings about the father influence the coparental relationship. But there is also evidence that, even within satisfactory marital relationships, a father's involvement with his children, especially young children, is often contingent on the mother's attitudes toward, expectations of, and support for the father, as well as the extent of her involvement in the labor force (De Luccie, 1995; Simons, Whitbeck, Conger, & Melby, 1990). Marsiglio (1991), using the National Survey of Families and Households data set, found that mothers' characteristics were more strongly correlated with fathers' involvement than fathers' own characteristics were. Indeed, studies have shown that many mothers, both inside and outside marriage, are ambivalent about the fathers' active involvement with their children (Baruch & Barnett, 1986; Cowan & Cowan, 1987). Given the powerful cultural forces that expect absorption by women in their mothering role, it is not surprising that active paternal involvement would threaten some women's identity and sense of control over this central domain of their lives. The evolution of a social consensus on responsible fathering, therefore, will necessarily involve a consensus that responsible mothering means supporting the father-child bond.

## Contextual Factors

Research demonstrates the particular vulnerability of fathering to contextual and institutional practices—from the establishment of legal paternity to the greater impact of unemployment on fathering than on mothering. Lack of income and poor occupational opportunities appear to have a particularly negative effect on fathering (Thomson, Hanson, & McLanahan, 1994). The prevalence of the abandonment of economic and psychological responsibilities among poor, unemployed men and among other men who undergo financial and employment crises is partly a function of the unique vulnerability of fathering to perceived success in the external environment (Jones, 1991; McLoyd, 1989). This analysis suggests that fathering is especially sensitive to changes in economic forces in the work force and marketplace and to shifts in public policy. It also suggests that fathering suffers disproportionately from negative social forces, such as racism, that inhibit opportunities in the environment. McLoyd (1990), in a review and conceptual analysis of economic hardship in African American families, describes how poverty and racism combine to create psychological distress, which is, in turn, associated with more negative parenting styles and more difficulty in the coparental relationship.

Our conceptual model also depicts the positive contribution of ethnic and cultural factors to fathering. One aspect of responsible fathering, that of economic support, is nearly universally expected of fathers by their cultures (Lamb, 1987b). LaRossa (1997), in his historical analysis, has demonstrated how changing cultural expectations in the first part of the twentieth century led to more nurturing father involvement in the U.S. Allen and Connor (1997) have examined how role flexibility and concern for children in the African American community create opportunities for men to become involved in surrogate father relationships with children who lack day-to-day contact with their biological fathers. Unfortunately, there has not been much empirical research that examines fathering in its cultural context, using representative samples of fathers to explore how cultural meanings and practices influence fathers' beliefs and behaviors.

The final contextual factor in the model is social support, which Belsky (1984) emphasized in his theoretical model of parenting and which McLoyd (1990) documented as a crucial factor in diminishing the negative effects of poverty on parenting behavior. However, most of the research on social support specifically for fathers has focused on mothers as sources of social support. Pleck (1997) reviewed the limited research on extrafamilial social support for fathering and found the studies skimpy and inconsistent, except for the pattern that highly involved fathers tend to encounter negative attitudes from acquaintances, relatives, and fellow workers. Clearly, there is a need for studies that examine the sources and influences of social support on fathering, particularly the role of other fathers.

From the perspective of both the contextual factors and the mother factors discussed thus far, fathering can be conceptualized as a more contextually sensitive process than mothering is. Not that mothering is not also contextually sensitive, but the cultural norms are stricter on the centrality and endurance of the mother-child dyad, regardless of what is happening outside that relationship. Father-child relations, on the other hand, are culturally defined as less dyadic and more multilateral, requiring a threshold of support from inside the family and from the larger environment. Undermining from the mother or from a social institution or system may induce many fathers to retreat from responsible fathering unless their own individual level of commitment to fathering is quite strong.

This point about the ecological sensitivity of fathering is a principal conclusion of this [selection]. It suggests that fathering programs and policy initiatives that focus only on fathers will benefit mainly fathers who already have a supportive social and economic environment. Fathers whose context is less supportive—for example, fathers who do not live with their children, who have strained relationships with the mother, or who are experiencing economic stress —will need more extensive and multilateral efforts to support their fathering.

## Child Factors

Individual child factors are included in the model for completeness, but the child factors studied in the research literature do not appear to be as important as the other dimensions in influencing fathering. Fathers do appear to find it easier to be more involved with their sons, especially older sons, presumably because they identify with them and are more comfortable communicating with them (Marsiglio, 1991). Most of the other child factors, such as age, appear to influence mothers as much as fathers, although Larson (1993) and Larson and Richards (1994) have documented how fathers withdraw more from parent-adolescent conflict than mothers do. More research is needed on the influence of the child's temperament and developmental status on relations with nonresidential fathers. Similarly, research is needed on how the child's beliefs about father involvement influence fathers' and mothers' expectations and behavior.

## Mother-Child Relationship Factors

We include this domain for theoretical completeness, but we could find no research directly examining how the father-child relationship is affected by the mother-child relationship. Such effects may be tapped indirectly through other dimensions in the model, such as the mother's attitudes toward the father's involvement with the child. For example, a close mother-child bond, combined with an ambivalent maternal attitude toward paternal involvement, might lead to less closeness of the father than a situation in which a mother had the same attitude but, herself, was less close to the child.

## Father Factors

Fathers' role identification, skills, and commitment are important influences on fathering (Baruch & Barnett, 1986; Ihinger-Tallman et al., 1995; Pleck, 1997). These three appear to fluctuate from low to high levels along with a number of interpersonal and contextual factors, such as the mother's expectations and the father's residential status with his children (Marsiglio, 1995; Ihinger-Tallman et al., 1995). In American culture, fathers are given more latitude for commitment to, identification with, and competence in their parental role. This latitude brings with it the price of confusion for many fathers about how to exercise their roles (Daly, 1995).

The variability of the individual father factors suggests two important implications of our conceptual model: that the positive support from mothers and the larger context can move men in the direction of more responsible parenting even in the face of modest personal investment, and that strong father commitment, knowledge, and skills are likely to be necessary to overcome negative maternal, coparental, and contextual influences. This latter point is similar to Lamb's (1987a) hypothesis that high levels of father motivation can override institutional barriers and the lack of social support.

As for the father's experience in his own family of origin, some research suggests that the father's relationship with his own father may be a factor—either through identifying with his father or compensating for his father's lapses—in contributing to his own role identification, sense of commitment, and self-efficacy (Cowan & Cowan, 1987; Daly, 1995). Snarey (1993), in a longitudinal study, documented the role of multigenerational connections between fathers.

The final father factors, psychological well-being and employment characteristics, have been studied extensively. Research examining psychological adjustment and parenting quality consistently shows a positive relationship between fathers' (and mothers') psychological well-being and their parenting attitudes and skills (Cox et al., 1989; Levy-Shiff & Israelashvili, 1988; Pleck, 1997). The research on job loss and economic distress generally has examined declines in psychological well-being as mediating factors leading to poorer fathering (Elder et al., 1984; Elder et al., 1985; Jones, 1991). And fathers' work situations have been shown to have mixed relationships with involvement with children. Specific work schedules are not strongly related to involvement, but greater flex time and other profamily practices are associated with more father involvement (Pleck, 1997). Indeed, consistent with other research on fathering, mothers' employment characteristics are more strongly associated with fathers' involvement than fathers' employment characteristics. When mothers are employed, fathers' proportionate share of parenting is greater, although studies are inconsistent about the absolute level of father involvement (Pleck, 1997).

## Conceptual Overview

The conceptual model outlines multiple factors that influence fathering, from individual and relational to contextual. The factors can be viewed as additive. For example, low identification with the parental role, combined with low expectations from the mother, would be strongly associated with low involvement of the father in both residential and nonresidential contexts. High identification with the parental role, combined with high expectations from the mother, would lead to greater father involvement in any residential context.

The factors in the model also can be viewed as interactive. For example, high role identification and good employment and income might be sufficient to offset low expectations from the mother. Similarly, not living with the child could be offset by the father's strong commitment to his children and the support of the mother. And strong institutional support through public policies could mitigate unmarried fathers' and mothers' reluctance to declare paternity.

Although the conceptual framework is intended to apply to the four domains of responsible fathering (paternity, presence, economic support, and involvement), most of the research has focused on one or another of these areas. Indeed, the bulk of the empirical research has been on father involvement. Researchers have tended to assume that economic factors uniquely influence economic support and that father factors uniquely influence father involvement. Putting a range of factors into one model challenges researchers to examine how all the factors might influence all the domains of responsible fathering. We acknowledge that some components of the model are likely to influence some aspects of fathering more than others.

Finally, the model should be seen as depicting a dynamic set of processes, rather than a set of linear, deterministic influences. Systemic, ecological models run the risk of reducing the target behavior—in this case, responsible fathering—to a contextually determined phenomenon stripped of individual initiative and self-determination. We want to emphasize the pivotal role of fathers, themselves, in appropriating or discarding cultural and contextual messages, in formulating a fathering identity and developing fathering skills with their own children, in working out their feelings about their own fathers, and in dealing collaboratively with their children's mother. The social construction of fatherhood is an evolving creation of all stakeholders in the lives of children, and contemporary fathers have a central role in this creation. The active construction of fathering by fathers, themselves, is not a prominent theme in the research literature, although it is crucial to programs that work with fathers. More qualitative research is needed to explore the kinds of identity development and social negotiation that constitute the experience of fathering.

## Conclusion

This [selection] delineates a conceptual model of influences on fathering that can serve as a stimulus for future research, programming, and policy development. The main premise, supported by a variety of studies, is that fathering is uniquely sensitive to contextual influences, both interpersonal and environmental. Fathering is a multilateral relationship, in addition to a one-to-one relationship. A range of influences–including mothers' expectations and behaviors, the quality of the coparental relationship, economic factors, institutional practices, and employment opportunities–all have potentially powerful effects on fathering. These contextual factors shape the major domains of responsible fathering discussed here: acknowledgment of paternity, willingness to be present and provide economic support, and level of involvement with one's children. When these influences are not supportive of the father-child bond, a man may need a high level identification with the father role, strong commitment, and good parenting skills to remain a responsible father to his children, especially if he does not live with them.

This review and conceptual model deal with factors that promote active, involved fathering, not with the effects of that kind of fathering on children. (See review by Pleck, 1997.) Nor do we take a position on whether there are essential characteristics of fathering versus mothering or whether having parents of two genders is necessary for the well-being of children. The growing literature on gay and lesbian parenting suggests that these kinds of questions are more complex than many scholars assumed in the past (Patterson, 1992; Patterson & Chan, 1997). However, it is not necessary to resolve these issues in order to address the factors that enhance and inhibit the parenting of men in the role of father in the late twentieth century.

A potentially controversial conclusion of this [selection] is that a high quality marriage is the optimal context for promoting responsible fatherhood. This position moves opposite the trend in contemporary family studies to disaggregate marriage and parenting. We do not suggest that men cannot parent adequately outside this context or that children must be raised in a married household in order to grow up well adjusted. However, we believe that the research strongly indicates that substantial barriers exist for most men's fathering outside a caring, committed, collaborative marriage and that the promotion of these kinds of enduring marital partnerships may be the most important contribution to responsible fathering in our society.

An encouraging implication of this systemic, ecological analysis is that there are many pathways to enhancing the quality of father-child relationships. Fathering can be enhanced through programs and policies that help fathers relate to their coparent, that foster employment and economic opportunities if needed, that change institutional expectations and practices to better support fathers, and that encourage fathers' personal commitment to their children.

## References

Ahrons, C. R., & Miller, R. B. (1993). The effect of the postdivorce relationship on paternal involvement: A longitudinal analysis. *American Journal of Orthopsychiatry, 63,* 441–450.

Allen, W. D., & Connor, M. (1997). An African American perspective on generative fathering. In A. J. Hawkins & D. C. Dollahite (Eds.), *Generative fathering: Beyond deficit perspectives.* Newbury Park, CA: Sage.

Backett, K. (1987). The negotiation of fatherhood. In C. Lewis & M. O'Brien (Eds.), *Reassessing fatherhood: New observations on fathers and the modern family.* Newbury Park, CA: Sage.

Baruch, G. K., & Barnett, R. C. (1986). Consequences of fathers' participation in family work: Parent's role strain and well-being. *Journal of Personality and Social Psychology, 51,* 983–992.

Becker, G. S. (1991). *A treatise on the family.* Cambridge, MA: Harvard University Press.

Belsky, J. (1984). The determinants of parenting: A process model. *Child Development, 55,* 83–96.

Belsky, J., & Volling, B. L. (1987). Mothering, fathering, and marital interaction in the family triad during infancy. In P. W. Berman & F. A. Pedersen (Eds.), *Men's transitions to parenthood: Longitudinal studies of early family experience* (pp. 37–63). Hillsdale, NJ: Erlbaum.

Bumpass, L. L., Sweet, J. A., & Cherlin, A. (1991). The role of cohabitation in declining rates of marriage. *Journal of Marriage and the Family, 53,* 913–927.

Cowan, C. P., & Cowan, P. A. (1987). Men's involvement in parenthood: Identifying the antecedents and understanding the barriers. In P. W. Berman & F. A. Pedersen (Eds.), *Men's transitions to parenthood: Longitudinal studies of early family experience* (pp. 145–174). Hillsdale, NJ: Erlbaum.

Cox, M. J., Owen, M. T., Lewis, J. M., & Henderson, V. K. (1989). Marriage, adult adjustment, and early parenting. *Child Development, 60,* 1015–1024.

Daly, K. J. (1995). Reshaping fatherhood: Finding the models. In W. Marsiglio (Ed.), *Fatherhood: Contemporary theory, research, and social policy* (pp. 21–40). Thousand Oaks, CA: Sage.

De Luccie, M. F. (1995). Mothers as gatekeepers: A model of maternal mediators of father involvement. *The Journal of Genetic Psychology, 156,* 115–131.

Doherty, W. J. (1990). Beyond reactivity and the deficit model of manhood: A commentary on articles by Napier, Pittman, and Gottman. *Journal of Marital and Family Therapy, 17,* 29–32.

Doherty, W. J. (1995a). *Soul searching: Why psychotherapy must promote moral responsibility.* New York: Basic Books.

Doherty, W. J., Boss, P. G., LaRossa, R., Schumm, W. R., & Steinmetz, S. K. (1993). Family theories and methods: A contextual approach. In P. G. Boss, W. J. Doherty, R. LaRossa, W. R. Schumm, & S. K. Steinmetz (Eds.), *Family theories and methods: A contextual approach.* New York: Plenum Press.

Dollahite, D. C., Hawkins, A. J., & Brotherson, S. E. (1997). Fatherwork: A conceptual ethic of fathering as generative work. In A. J. Hawkins & D. C. Dollahite (Eds.), *Generative fathering: Beyond deficit perspective.* Newbury Park, CA: Sage.

Elder, G., Liker, J., & Cross, C. (1984). Parent-child behavior in the Great Depression: Life course and intergenerational influences. In P. Baltes & O. Brim (Eds.), *Life span development and behavior* (Vol. 6, pp. 109–158). Orlando, FL: Academic Press.

Elder, G., Van Nguyen, T., & Caspi, A. (1985). Linking family hardship to children's lives. *Child Development, 56,* 1628–1636.

Feldman, S. S., Nash, S. C., & Aschenbrenner, B. G. (1983). Antecedents of fathering. *Child Development, 54,* 1628–1636.

Furstenberg, F. S., & Cherlin, A. J. (1991). *Divided families: What happens to children when parents part.* Cambridge, MA: Harvard University Press.

Hawkins, A. J., Christiansen, S. L., Sargent, K. P., & Hill, E. J. (1995). Rethinking fathers' involvement in child care. In W. Marsiglio (Ed.), *Fatherhood: Contemporary theory, research, and social policy* (pp. 41–56). Thousand Oaks, CA: Sage.

Hawkins, A. J., & Dollahite, D. C. (1997). Generative fathering: Beyond deficit perspectives. Thousand Oaks, CA: Sage.

Hetherington, E. M., & Parke, R. D. (1993). *Child psychology: A contemporary view.* New York: McGraw-Hill.

Ihinger-Tallman, M., Pasley, K., & Buehler, C. (1995). Developing a middle-range theory of father involvement postdivorce. In W. Marsiglio (Ed.), *Fatherhood: Contemporary theory, research, and social policy* (pp. 57–77). Thousand Oaks, CA: Sage.

Jones, L. (1991). Unemployed fathers and their children: Implications for policy and practice. *Child and Adolescent Social Work Journal, 8,* 101–116.

Lamb, M. E. (1987a). Introduction: The emergent American father. In M. E. Lamb (Ed.), *The father's role: Cross-cultural perspectives* (pp. 3–25). Hillsdale, NJ: Erlbaum.

Lamb, M. E. (Ed.). (1987b). *The father's role: Cross-cultural perspectives.* Hillsdale: NJ: Erlbaum.

Lamb, M. E., Pleck, J., Charnov, E. L., & Levine, J. A. (1985). Paternal behavior in humans. *American Zoologist, 25,* 883–894.

LaRossa, R. (1997). *The modernization of fatherhood: A social and political history.* Chicago: University of Chicago Press.

Larson, R. W. (1993). Finding time for fatherhood: The emotional ecology of adolescent-father interactions. In S. Shulman & W. A. Collins (Eds.), *Father-adolescent relationships* (pp. 7–25). San Francisco: Jossey-Bass.

Larson, R. W., & Richards, M. H. (1994). *Divergent realities: The emotional lives of mothers, fathers, and adolescents.* New York: Basic Books.

Levine, J. A., & Pitt, E. W. (1995). *New expectations: Community strategies for responsible fatherhood.* New York: Families and Work Institute.

Levy-Shiff, R., & Israelashvili, R. (1988). Antecedents of fathering: Some further exploration. *Developmental Psychology, 24,* 434–440.

Lewis, C., & O'Brien, M. (1987). Constraints on fathers: Research, theory and clinical practice. In C. Lewis, & M. O'Brien (Eds.), *Reassessing fatherhood: New observations on fathers and the modern family* (pp. 1–19). Newbury Park, CA: Sage.

Marsiglio, W. (1991). Paternal engagement activities with minor children. *Journal of Marriage and the Family, 53,* 973–986.

Marsiglio, W. (1995). Fathers' diverse life course patterns and roles: Theory and social interventions. In W. Marsiglio (Ed.), *Fatherhood: Contemporary theory, research, and social policy* (pp. 78–101). Thousand Oaks, CA: Sage.

McLoyd, V. C. (1989). Socialization and development in a changing economy: The effects of paternal job loss and income loss on children. *American Psychologist, 44,* 293–302.

McLoyd, V. C. (1990). The impact of economic hardship on Black families and children: Psychological distress, parenting, and socioemotional development. *Child Development, 61,* 311–346.

Park, R. D. (1996). *Fatherhood.* Cambridge, MA: Harvard University Press.

Patterson, C. J. (1992). Children of lesbian and gay parents. *Child Development, 63,* 1025–1042.

Patterson, C. J., & Chan, R. W. (1997). Gay fathers. In M. E. Lamb (Ed.), *The role of the father in child development* (3rd ed.). New York: Wiley.

Pleck, J. H. (1997). Paternal involvement: Levels, sources, and consequences. In M. E. Lamb (Ed.), *The role of the father in child development* (3rd ed.). New York: Wiley.

Simons, R., Whitbeck, L., Conger, R., & Melby, J. (1990). Husband and wife differences in determinants of parenting: A social learning and exchange model of parental behavior. *Journal of Marriage and the Family, 52,* 375–392.

Snarey, J. (1993). *How fathers care for the next generation: A four-decade study.* Cambridge, MA: Harvard University Press.

Thomson, E., Hanson, T., & McLanahan, S. S. (1994). Family structure and child well-being: Economic resources versus parent socialization. *Social Forces, 73,* 221–242.

U.S. Department of Health and Human Services (1995). *Report to Congress on out-of-wedlock childbearing* (Pub. No. PHS 95-1257-1). Washington, DC: U.S. Government Printing Office.

Wolfe, A. (1989). *Whose keeper? Social science and moral obligation.* Berkeley: University of California Press.

Alexis J. Walker and Lori A. McGraw

# Who Is Responsible for Responsible Fathering?

William Doherty, Edward Kouneski, and Martha Erickson proposed a conceptual framework on "Responsible Fathering." For both empirical and theoretical reasons, we found their essay to be problematic. The proposed model excludes key features of fatherhood and of motherhood, and researchers who attempt to operationalize it or practitioners who attempt to develop programs from it are destined to be misguided.

We are not concerned that the authors wrote from a position of advocacy. We agree that the new research on fatherhood primarily reflects a position valuing involved fathers and that discussions about absent fathers sometimes have a moral overtone. This is particularly evident in policy arenas. Congress, in fact, titled a 1998 child support bill, The Deadbeat Parents Punishment Act. As demonstrated by the plethora of empirical studies blaming mothers for their children's behavioral, psychological, and social problems (Caplan & Hall-McCorquodale, 1985), discussions about motherhood have moral overtones as well. Arguments grounded solely in ideology are inherent in the nature of public discourse. What is important for researchers who advocate a specific policy position in our journals is to adhere to principles and practices agreed upon within a scientific community, regardless of ideology (Furstenberg, 1999).

We appreciate the authors' willingness to make their underlying assumptions explicit. We draw attention to the empirical literature the authors neglected, however, and raise questions about their explicit and implicit reasoning. We take issue with their assumptions and their conclusions, and we critique their model by highlighting the sociohistorical context of fatherhood, childhood, and motherhood.

## What Do Children Need?

A key, explicit assumption of the authors is "that children *need* [italics added] and deserve active, involved fathers throughout their childhood and adolescence" (p. 279). Although there might be an ideological basis for this assumption, it lacks empirical support. Members of the scientific community may

From Alexis J. Walker and Lori A. McGraw, "Who Is Responsible for Responsible Fathering?" *Journal of Marriage and the Family*, vol. 62 (May 2000). 

agree on what children need—broadly defined—for biological, physical, emotional, psychological, and social well-being. There is not agreement, however, that these needs must be met by a parent of a certain gender. In their study of children from single-parent households, Downey, Ainsworth-Darnell, and Dufur (1998) asked: "Do women and men play unique roles in shaping children's well-being?" (p. 878). They concluded that "the challenge for family researchers is to distinguish between familial characteristics that are necessarily important for creating positive family environments for children and those, such as sex of parent, that are not" (p. 892). We have no objection to children having actively involved fathers, but research has demonstrated that children's needs can be met within the full range of fathers' involvement, from no involvement to fathers raising children on their own (Acock & Demo, 1994; Risman, 1987).

## Which Fathers Matter?

Doherty et al. focused on heterosexual, biological fathers "to delimit the review" (p. 279). Except for marital status, nothing in the authors' conceptual model accounts for their emphasis on biological fathers. Furthermore, there is no empirical evidence that biology predisposes fathers to be responsible and involved (Cooksey & Fondell, 1996). The authors deliberately excluded adoptive, gay, step, fictive kin, and other father surrogates, many of whom are involved, responsible fathers. They suggested that nonbiological and gay fathers deserve empirical and programmatic focus, but they saw such focus as beyond the scope of their paper. Given the authors' concerns about children's needs and the variety of ways through which men function as fathers in contemporary society (e.g., Hawkins & Eggebeen, 1991), we are at a loss to understand their decision. Because there are involved and engaged fathers who are meeting their children's needs in all of the excluded groups, a contextual model of responsible fathers would and should include them.

## Mothers' "Gatekeeping," Fathers' Resistance

Doherty et al. exaggerated the problematic behavior of mothers and minimized the role fathers play in their own involvement with their children. They found three studies, two of them focused on young fathers, providing evidence that mothers and grandmothers act as gatekeepers between their husbands and their children. They also cited larger scale studies (e.g., Marsiglio, 1991), demonstrating that father involvement is tied more closely to mothers' than to fathers' characteristics. They relied on this research to argue that mothers control fathers' involvement. The authors concluded that "*many* [emphasis added] mothers are ambivalent about fathers' active involvement with their children" (p. 287). Because their essay was published, an additional study of mothers' gatekeeping has been reported (Allen & Hawkins, 1999).

Gatekeeping by mothers is an idea that has emerged to explain the relatively low levels of involvement of fathers with their children. It has been conceptualized in a variety of ways, most recently as a mother's cognitive schema that includes (a) high standards for housework and child care and enjoying control over family work; (b) an identity that is dependent on others' views of how well-groomed one's children are and how clean one's home is; and (c) a conventional attitude that women enjoy housework and find it easier to do housework and child care than men do (Allen & Hawkins, 1999). Note that interaction with children, other than through housework or child care, was neither part of this conceptualization nor measured as an outcome of gatekeeping. Allen and Hawkins did not include in gatekeeping the idea that fathers may play a direct or indirect role in setting standards for housework and childcare or in influencing the division of labor in other ways. Although they attempted to include mothers' sense of responsibility for family work (these items were eliminated because of poor measurement properties), they did not consider fathers' sense of responsibility. Furthermore, neither mothers' desires nor their deliberate attempts to exclude fathers from interacting with their children were included. Even accepting this limited conceptualization, however, only one fifth of their sample of married mothers could be described as "gatekeepers."

In contrast to the idea that mothers keep fathers from their children, evidence suggests that women generally value and actively promote relationships between children and fathers (e.g., Haavind, 1984; Marsiglio, 1991; Pleck, 1985; Thompson, 1991). Even stepmothers function in this way. Consider recent evidence from the wives of remarried men over 60 in the Normative Study of Aging. Vinick and Lanspery (1998) described stepmothers as "'carpenters' of damaged family relationships" (p. 4) who worked to establish friendly contact with adult children who were hostile toward their fathers. Stepmothers encouraged their husbands to keep in touch with their children, reminding them to make phone calls, issuing invitations, or communicating with the stepchildren themselves. In separate interviews, their husbands spontaneously supported these findings. Vinick and Lanspery concluded:

> Stepmothers often fulfilled pivotal roles in stepfamilies as rebuilders and nurturers of associations with the younger generation. Relationships with stepchildren, as well as husbands' relations with their own biological children, had frequently improved due, in large measure, to women's efforts, acting on their own behalf, and that of their husbands and their stepchildren. (p. 5)

To emphasize women who are ambivalent about or act as gatekeepers of fathers' involvement does a disservice to mothers. We do not deny that some mothers make it difficult for fathers to connect with their children, but any instance of gatekeeping must be viewed in the larger context of mothers' facilitation and of men's authority in families. This empirical question has yet to be addressed: To what extent are mothers able to limit coresidential fathers' involvement when fathers have a strong interest in building connections with their children?

Doherty et al. wrote about mothers' gatekeeping but not about men's resistance. Fathers play a role in their limited involvement with children by resisting mothers' attempts to facilitate interaction. Arendell (1992, 1995) described how fathers' resistance to cooperating with mothers may become stronger after divorce. As husbands and fathers, men have legitimate control and authority in families. They expect, desire, and believe they have certain "rights to their parenthood" (1992, p. 569), and they see these rights as challenged after divorce. Similarly, Bertoia and Drakich (1993) demonstrated that, rather than involvement with and responsibility for children after divorce, noncustodial fathers felt they "deserved" access, information, and decision-making authority equal to that of custodial mothers. A focus on legitimacy and authority works against fathers' involvement with their children. As Arendell (1992) concluded, uninvolved nonresidential fathers do not see fathering "as an array of activities, interactional processes, and particular kinds of social relations" (p. 582). Instead, they focus on fatherhood as a status concomitant with certain rights. In part, then, men's conceptualization of fatherhood forecasts their involvement with their children.

## Fathers and Financial Support

Doherty et al.'s model and discussion of responsible fathering minimized children's dependence on fathers' financial resources. There is ample and compelling empirical support that the most important activity fathers can do for their children's well-being is to support them financially (e.g., Crockett, Eggebeen, & Hawkins, 1993; King, 1994; McLanahan & Sandefur, 1994). Regardless of family structure, fathers who provide economic resources improve their children's developmental outcomes (Acock & Demo, 1994). In our society, men have greater access to resources than women do, and men are defined, in part, through their ability to be good providers (Bernard, 1981). Doherty et al. pay insufficient attention to this aspect of father involvement.

We intend neither to reduce men to their ability to provide money, nor to minimize the role mothers increasingly play in generating income for family members. Instead, we take issue with Doherty et al.'s decision to ignore the social context in which men's participation as fathers is grounded. There is simply no getting around the fact that men's financial contributions matter for both residential and nonresidential children, and that currently, these contributions have a greater impact on children than any other aspect of fathers' involvement.

That the social context creates differing financial imperatives and opportunities for women and men also makes it problematic to compare nonresidential mothers to nonresidential fathers. Doherty et al. minimized problems with noncustodial fathers' financial support by comparing it to that of noncustodial mothers. The causes and consequences of noncustodial motherhood are not the same as those for noncustodial fatherhood (e.g., Arditti & Madden-Derdich, 1993; Cancun & Meyer, 1998). At a minimum, being a noncustodial mother is far more nonnormative than being a noncustodial father. Furthermore, the reasons for noncustodial mothers' noncompliance with child support have yet to be determined. One cannot conclude, as Doherty et al. did, that "there is something in the structure of nonresidential parenting, rather than in the culture of fatherhood, that is the principal inhibitor of economic support for children outside of marriage" (p. 282).

The authors attributed fathers' noncompliance, in part, to mothers' role in "misusing the funds and . . . withholding the children from the father" (Doherty et al., p. 282). What fathers describe as misusing funds, mothers describe as meeting children's needs. What fathers see as withholding children from them, mothers see as a strategy to gain fathers' compliance with child support orders. Stephens (1996) reported county data from Texas in which 14,000 complaints were registered for noncompliance compared with 700 complaints regarding visitation. Most noncustodial fathers were satisfied with the frequency and duration of their visits with children, and fathers' complaints were unrelated to compliance (Stephens). Again, Arendell's (1992, 1995) research is relevant here. Some noncustodial fathers view child support payments as a loss of control over their income rather than as a way to enhance and support their children. This is lamentable because the problems caused by noncompliance are significant, particularly given the effect of such support on children's well-being.

## Marriage and Father Involvement

The authors identified marriage as the best context for involved fathers. To support their position, they noted the problems fathers have interacting with and relating to their children, highlighting these problems for never-married and divorced fathers and minimizing the same problems for married fathers. For example, they cited research by Zill, Morrison, and Coiro (1993) showing that 65% of children aged 18 to 22 whose parents divorced reported poor relationships with their fathers. This same study found that nearly 1 in 3 (29%) children in the same age group with *married* parents also reported poor relationships with their fathers. Although the proportion is higher for divorced fathers, the proportion in stable families is alarmingly high. In contrast, mothers' relationships with their children, both inside and outside of marriage, are generally positive (Aquilino, 1994; Rossi & Rossi, 1990; Silverstein & Bengtson, 1997).

Doherty et al. also overstated the role of marriage in father involvement in other ways. For example, they exaggerated fathers' involvement when wives are employed. They reported that fathers with employed wives perform a greater proportion of parenting activities than do fathers with nonemployed wives. They did not explain that the proportion is greater primarily because employed wives do less than nonemployed wives. They stated that "fathers are a significant source of primary care when mothers work" (p. 284). Careful attention to this literature demonstrates that fathers serve as primary care providers in response to their wives' paid work schedules (e.g., Brayfield, 1995; Presser, 1988). Caregiving fathers of younger children typically work for pay during daytime hours, and their wives typically work for pay during evening and nighttime hours. Most of the time during which fathers are responsible for young children is when their children are asleep. In contrast, fathers provide daytime, after-school care for older children who have less demanding needs for care.

By not attending to the context in which fathers are fully responsible for their children, Doherty and his colleagues risk exaggerating fathers' involvement, as well as fathers' interest in being involved. We agree that fathers are capable of caring involvement with their children. It is not necessary to exaggerate what fathers do to support this view. That some serve as primary child care givers provides hope that fathers indeed may be more involved in the future.

Doherty and his colleagues argued that "a caring, committed, collaborative marriage" (p. 290) fosters responsible fatherhood. Unstated is the fact that husbands' behavior is a major contributor to this type of marriage (e.g. Gottman, 1998). Husbands who are responsive to and appreciative of their wives and who facilitate their wives' sense of partnership and equality have better quality marriages (Hochschild, 1989; Schwartz, 1994; Thompson, 1991). Coltrane (1989) found that fathers who participate in child care from infancy also have more egalitarian partnerships with their wives. The connection between a collaborative marriage and an involved father may reflect something other than marital quality. The type of man who helps to develop a cooperative marriage may be the type of man who will be an involved father.

Collaborative marriages are not inevitable. Furthermore, prescribing marriage as a solution to the lack of father involvement is not without risk. Marriages characterized by conflict have a negative influence on children (e.g., Buehler et al., 1998; Gottman, 1998). An emphasis on marriage or other aspects of family structure absent of consideration of family process is misguided (e.g., Cooksey & Fondell, 1996; King, 1994; Miller, Forehand, & Kotchick, 1999). Indeed, Demo (1992) concluded that family structure has far less influence on child outcomes than is assumed. Data on fathering demonstrate that marriage is neither a sufficient nor a necessary context for responsible fathering. In considering her findings and those of others, King concluded that relationship quality, an important precursor to marital stability, is not changed easily by intervention or by social policy.

Toward the end of their article, Doherty et al. stated that "a high quality marriage is the optimal context for promoting responsible fatherhood" (p. 290), suggesting that "the promotion of these kinds of enduring marital partnerships may be the most important contribution to responsible fathering in our society." They were concerned that their conclusion would be "potentially controversial" because it is opposite of a "trend in contemporary family studies to disaggregate marriage and parenting" (p. 290). It is inappropriate and unfair to take practitioners of the discipline to task in this way. The disaggregation of marriage and parenting is not a trend in the study of families. It is, instead, a trend in the lived experience of individuals in the United States and in other industrialized nations that is well documented by researchers in the field (e.g., Adler, 1997).

## Father Involvement

The literature in family science has attended increasingly to fathers, highlighting their importance to their children, and arguing that their contributions have been minimized. Although the authors reviewed a chapter by Pleck ( 1997) concluding that heterosexual, married, biological fathers are significantly more involved now than they were 20 years ago, empirical evidence suggests otherwise (e.g., Perkins & DeMeis, 1996; Press & Townsley, 1998; Sanchez & Thomson,

1997). In 1988, Ralph LaRossa highlighted the disjunction between the culture and the conduct of fatherhood. All evidence suggests that this disjunction continues to exist. Doherty et al. stated their intention to avoid between-gender comparisons but pointed out that fathers' involvement remains well below that of mothers. Our point is that fathers' involvement is well below that of the cultural standard for fathers.

Studies using nationally representative data sets show little change in residential and nonresidential father involvement over time, and no influence or weak influence on child outcomes when fathers are involved (e.g., Cooksey & Fondell, 1996; Harris, Furstenberg, & Mariner, 1998; Stephens, 1996). For example, despite public and scholarly discourse to the contrary, except during the 1990–1991 economic recession, there was virtually no change from the mid-1960s to 1993 in the proportion of preschoolers cared for by fathers when mothers are employed (Casper & O'Connell, 1998). King's (1994) research is illustrative of the literature on the involvement of nonresidential fathers. Using the National Longitudinal Survey of Youth, she reported "that there is only limited evidence to support the hypothesis that nonresident father involvement has positive benefits for children" (p. 970). Other researchers (Mott, Kowaleski-Jones, & Menaghan, 1997) have found no significant long-term effects of father absence on children's behavior. (See also Argys, Peters, Brooks-Gunn, & Smith, 1998.) This does not mean that all fathers are uninvolved with their children or that fathers who are highly involved have no influence. It does mean that, on average, the level of fathers' involvement continues to be minimal and that there is insufficient variance in father involvement for it to have strong and significant associations with child outcomes.

One consistent and key predictor of father involvement is education (e.g., Amato & Booth, 1997; Cooksey & Craig, 1998; Cooney, Pedersen, Indelicato, & Palkovitz, 1993; King, 1994; Stephens, 1996). Highly educated men appear to have adopted a cultural standard for fathers that is at odds with fatherhood as practiced by the vast majority of men, most of whom have far less education. Given that education is so important in predicting fathers' involvement, policies and programs should stress greater access to and support for education for all men so as to encourage responsible fatherhood.

## Fatherhood, Motherhood, and Social Location

Doherty and his colleagues suggested that, in comparison with mothers, fathers suffer disproportionately from negative social forces, such as racism, that inhibit them from being involved with their children. Fathers of color do suffer from racism, but so do mothers and children (e.g., Hill Collins, 1992). Oppression based on social location is a system of interacting influences: racism, classism, sexism, heterosexism, and ageism. Some individuals are affected by more of these influences than are others.

Additionally, fathers have greater access to economic resources than mothers do, and this fact shapes both fathering and mothering (Gerson, 1993; LaRossa, 1988). There are fewer deterrents to fathers' than to mothers' participation in paid labor, a highly valued activity, and fathers have greater discretion than mothers to participate in child care, a less valued activity. Fathers lose status when they participate in labor defined as "women's work" (Gerson, 1993; Hochschild, 1989). Thus, not all fathers choose to be involved. For fathers to become more responsible for child care and more involved with their children would require a restructuring of paid and unpaid work. This restructuring would necessitate fathers giving up paternal privilege (Goode, 1982).

## Who Is Responsible for Responsible Fathers?

We do not agree that Doherty et al.'s model is a contextual, social constructionist one. Any such model would attend to a number of features absent from their analysis. We note, for example, their failure to attend to a key feature of the needs of children: that they are socially constructed. Children's "needs" have evolved over time to shape and control the behaviors of mothers as much as they have been about promoting children's development (Ambert, 1994; Ehrenreich & English, 1978; Gerson, 1985). Fatherhood, motherhood, and childhood are *all* social constructions. A fully contextual model cannot ignore this key fact, nor the patriarchal context in which this social construction occurs.

Another context the authors ignored is the gendered nature of mothering and fathering in the United States. Their model disproportionately placed responsibility for fathers' involvement with their children on women. Instead of identifying things mothers can do to "move men in the direction of more responsible fathering" (p. 288)—activities destined to be described as nagging—we ask what responsibility *men* have for being responsible fathers?

We share the authors' inclusive and flexible definition of who can nurture, discipline, and provide for children. In an ideal world, parenting—the activities of nurturing, disciplining, and providing for children—would be work taken up by women *and* by men according to their individual proclivities and within a climate of economic justice and an ethic of care at all levels of society (Okin, 1989). We do not live in such a society, however. In our society, women and men do not have access to the same level of economic resources, nor are they held equally accountable for the undervalued activity of caring for dependent people. Any definition of responsible fathering must reflect the real world, even if it aims for a better world in the future.

## References

Acock, A. C., & Demo, D. H. (1994). *Family diversity and well-being.* Newbury Park, CA: Sage.

Adler, M. A. (1997). Social change and declines in marriage and fertility in Eastern Germany. *Journal of Marriage and the Family, 59,* 37–49.

Allen, S. M., & Hawkins, A. J. (1999). Maternal gatekeeping: Mothers' beliefs and behaviors that inhibit greater father involvement in family work. *Journal of Marriage and the Family, 61,* 199–212.

Amato, P R., & Booth, A. ( 1997). *A generation at risk: Growing up in an era of family upheaval.* Cambridge, MA: Harvard University Press.

Ambert, A. (1994). An international perspective on parenting: Social change and social constructs. *Journal of Marriage and the Family, 56,* 529–543.

Aquilino, W S. (1994). Impact of childhood family disruption on young adults' relationships with parents. *Journal of Marriage and the Family, 56,* 295 313.

Arditti, J. A., & Madden-Derdich, D. A. (1993). Noncustodial mothers: Developing strategies of support. *Family Relations, 42,* 305-314.

Arendell, T (1992). After divorce: Investigations into father absence. *Gender & Society, 6,* 562-586.

Arendell, T (1995). *Fathers and divorce.* Thousand Oaks, CA: Sage.

Argys, L. M., Peters, H. E., Brooks-Gunn, J., & Smith, J. (1998). The impact of child support on cognitive outcomes of young children. *Demography, 35,* 159-173.

Bernard, J. (1981). The good provider role: Its rise and fall. *American Psychologist, 36,* 1-12.

Bertoia, C., & Drakich, J. (1993). The fathers' rights movement: Contradictions in rhetoric and practice. *Journal of Family Issues, 14,* 592-615.

Brayfield, A. (1995). Juggling jobs and kids: The impact of employment schedules on fathers' caring for children. *Journal of Marriage and the Family, 57,* 321-332.

Buehler, C., Krishnakumar, A., Stone, G., Anthony, C., Pemberton, S., Gerard, J., & Barber, B. K. (1998). Interparental conflict styles and youth problem behaviors: A two-sample replication study. *Journal of Marriage and the Family, 60,* 119-132.

Cancun, M., & Meyer, D. R. (1998). Who gets custody? *Demography, 35,* 147-157.

Caplan, P J., & Hall-McCorquodale, I. (1985). The scapegoating of mothers: A call for change. *American Journal of Orthopsychiatry, 55,* 610-613.

Casper, L. M., & O'Connell, M. (1998). Work, income, the economy, and married fathers as child-care providers. *Demography, 35,* 243-250.

Coltrane, S. (1989). Household labor and the routine production of gender. *Social Problems, 36,* 473-490.

Cooksey, E. C., & Fondell, M. M. ( 1996). Spending time with his kids: Effects of family structure on fathers' and children's lives. *Journal of Marriage and the Family, 58,* 693-707.

Cooksey, E. C., & Craig, P H. ( 1998). Parenting from a distance: The effects of paternal characteristics on contact between nonresidential fathers and their children. *Demography, 35,* 187-200.

Cooney, T M., Pedersen, E A., Indelicato, S., & Palkovitz, R. (1993). Timing of fatherhood: Is "on-time" optimal? *Journal of Marriage and the Family, 55,* 205-215.

Crockett, L. J., Eggebeen, D. J., & Hawkins, A. J. (1993). Father presence and young children's behavioral and cognitive adjustment. *Journal of Family Issues, 14,* 355-377.

Demo, D. H. ( 1992). Parent-child relations: Assessing recent changes. *Journal of Marriage and the Family, 54,* 104-117.

Doherty, W. J., Kouneski, E. E, & Erickson, M. F. (1998). Responsible fathering: An overview and conceptual framework. *Journal of Marriage and the Family, 60,* 277-292.

Downey, D. B., Ainsworth-Darnell, J. W., & Dufur, M. J. (1998). Sex of parent and children's well-being in single-parent households. *Journal of Marriage and the Family, 60,* 878-893.

Ehrenreich, B., & English, D. (1978). *For her own good: 50 years of the experts' advice to women.* Garden City, NY: Anchor Press.

Furstenberg, E E, Jr. (1999). Children and family change: Discourse between social scientists and the media. *Contemporary Sociology: A Journal of Reviews, 28,* 10-17.

Gerson, K. (1993). *No man's land: Men's changing commitments to family and work.* New York: Basic Books.

Gerson, K. (1985). *Hard choices: How women decide about work, career, and motherhood.* Berkeley, CA: University of California Press.

Goode, W. J. ( 1982). Why men resist. In B. Thorne & M. Yalom (Eds.), *Rethinking the family: Some feminist questions* (pp. 131-147). New York: Longman.

Gottman, J. M. (1998). Toward a process model of men in marriages and families. In A. Booth & A. C. Crouter (Eds.), *Men in families: When do they get involved? What difference does it make?* (pp. 149–192): Mahwah, NJ: Erlbaum.

Haavind, H. (1984). Love and power in marriage. In H. Holter (Ed.), *Patriarchy in a welfare state* (pp. 136–167). Oslo, Sweden: Universitetsforlaget.

Harris, K. M., Furstenberg, F. F., Jr., & Marmer, J. K. (1998). Paternal involvement with adolescents in intact families: The influence of fathers over the life course. *Demography, 35,* 201–216.

Hawkins, A. J., & Eggebeen, D. J. ( 1991 ). Are fathers fungible? Patterns of coresident adult men in maritally disrupted families and young children's well-being. *Journal of Marriage and the Family, 53,* 958–972.

Hill Collins, P. (1992). Black women and motherhood. In B. Thorne & M. Yalom (Eds.), *Rethinking the family: Some feminist questions* (2nd ed., pp. 215–245). Boston: Northeastern University Press.

Hochschild, A., with Machung, A. (1989). *The second shift: Working parents and the revolution at home.* New York: Viking.

King, V. (1994). Variation in the consequence of nonresident father involvement for children's well-being. *Journal of Marriage and the Family, 56,* 963–972.

LaRossa, R. ( 1988). Fatherhood and social change. *Family Relations, 37,* 451–457.

Marsiglio, A. (1991). Paternal engagement activities with minor children. *Journal of Marriage and the Family, 53,* 973–986.

McLanahan, S., & Sandefur, G. (1994). *Growing up with a single parent: What hurts, what helps.* Cambridge, MA: Harvard University Press.

Miller, K. S., Forehand, R., & Kotchick, B. A. (1999). Adolescent sexual behavior in two ethnic minority samples: The role of family variables. *Journal of Marriage and the Family, 61,* 85–98.

Mott, E. L., Kowaleski-Jones, L., & Menaghan, E. G. (1997). Paternal absence and child behavior: Does a child's gender make a difference? *Journal of Marriage and the Family, 59,* 103–118.

Okin, S. M. (1989). *Justice, gender, and the family.* New York: Basic Books.

Perkins, H. W., & DeMeis, D. K. (1996). Gender and family effects on the "second-shift" domestic activity of college-educated young adults. *Gender & Society, 10,* 78–93.

Pleck, J. H. (1985). *Working wives/working husbands.* Beverly Hills, CA: Sage.

Pleck, J. H. (1997). Paternal involvement: Levels, sources, and consequences. In M. E. Lamb (Ed.), *The role of the father in child development* (3rd ed., pp. 66–103). New York: Wiley.

Press, J. E., & Townsley, E. (1998). Wives' and husbands' housework reporting: Gender, class, and social desirability. *Gender and Society, 12,* 188–218.

Presser, H. B. (1988). Shift work and child care among young dual-earner American parents. *Journal of Marriage and the Family, 50,* 133–148.

Risman, B. J. (1987). Intimate relationships from a microstructural perspective: Men who mother. *Gender and Society, 1,* 6–32.

Rossi, A. S., & Rossi, P H. ( 1990). *Of human bonding: Parent-child relations across the life course.* New York: Aldine de Gruyter.

Sanchez, L., & Thompson, E. (1997). Becoming mothers and fathers: Parenthood, gender, and the division of labor. *Gender and Society, 11,* 747–772.

Schwartz, P. (1994). *Peer marriage: How love between equals really works.* New York: Free Press.

Silverstein, M., & Bengtson, V. L. (1997). Intergenerational solidarity and the structure of adult child-parent relationships in American families. *American Journal of Sociology, 103,* 429–460.

Stephens, L. S. (1996). Will Johnny see Daddy this week? An empirical test of three theoretical perspectives of postdivorce contact. *Journal of Family Issues, 17,* 466–494.

Thompson, L. (1991). Women's sense of fairness. *Journal of Family Issues, 12,* 181–196.

Vinick, B. H., & Lanspery, S. (1998, March). *Cinderella's sequel: Stepmothers' long-term relationships with adult stepchildren.* Paper presented at the annual meeting of the American Society on Aging, San Francisco.

Zill, N., Morrison, D. R., & Coiro, M. J. (1993). Long-term effects of parental divorce on parent-child relationships, adjustment, and achievement in young adulthood. *Journal of Family Psychology, 7,* 91–103.

# POSTSCRIPT

## Are Fathers Really Necessary?

What role does a father play in the development of a child? Is it the role of dad and what society says he "should" be that becomes important to the child rather than how he treats his child? Or, is it that is important? If the former is true, then anyone, regardless of how they treat the child, will be important to the child. We often see evidence of this phenomenon in dealing with abused children. No matter what the abuse, most children in this situation want to stay at home with abusive fathers rather than be placed in foster care. When confronted with "telling on" their fathers, children often will not say what abuse has occurred for fear of losing their father's love and being separated from them.

If the latter is true, the quality of interaction and events that children share with their fathers becomes key to their development. Then why couldn't women play that role? Women can interact with children in nearly all of the same ways that men can. Women can just as easily accompany children to baseball games, act as the soccer coach, or go to the school play as can men. Thus the question might not be "are fathers really necessary?" but might be "are men really necessary for the positive development of children?" To many, this would not only mean an assault on the role of fatherhood but also would constitute an attack on men in general.

As with most issues, extremes on either side make less sense than the middle ground. Child development experts would probably agree that the more adults, both male and female, involved in a child's life, the better. Having a variety of people in one's life brings a variety of experiences and an extensive social support network that can benefit children throughout their lives.

Significant research on fathering is becoming more prolific. Perhaps within the next few years scientists will be able to make more definitive statements with regard to the roles for both mother and father in a child's life. One could conclude that we are all responsible for fathering and mothering. This is especially true for families who do not have the choice of raising children in a two-parent system due to divorce or death of a spouse. We must continue to strive to find ways to support all families so that children will experience optimal need gratification as they grow and develop.

## Suggested Readings


Amneus, D. (1995). The father's role in society; `http://www.vix.com`.

Coley, R. L. (1990). Children's socialization experiences and functioning in single-mother households: The importance of fathers and other men. *Child Development, 69*, 219–230.

Popenoe, D. (2000). Life without father; http://ww.themenscenter.com.

Sanchez, L., & Thompson, E. (1997). Becoming mothers and fathers: Parenthood, gender, and the division of labor. *Gender and Society, 11*, 747–772.

Stapleton, M. (2000). The unnecessary tragedy of fatherless children. *Policy and Practice of Public Human Services, 58*, 43–48.

Stephens, L. S. (1996). Will Johnny see Daddy this week? An empirical test of three theoretical perspectives of post-divorce contact. *Journal of Family Issues, 17*, 466–494.

# ISSUE 7

## Does Divorce Create Long-Term Negative Effects for Children?

**YES: Karl Zinsmeister**, from "Divorce's Toll on Children," *The American Enterprise* (May/June 1996)

**NO: David Gately and Andrew I. Schwebel**, from "Favorable Outcomes in Children After Parental Divorce," *Journal of Divorce and Remarriage* (vol. 18, nos. 3–4, 1992)

### ISSUE SUMMARY

**YES:** Karl Zinsmeister, editor in chief of the *American Enterprise*, argues that divorce causes damage from which children never recover and that the conflict within a marriage will not cause the same amount of problems for children that the breakup of a marriage creates.

**NO:** Educators David Gately and Andrew I. Schwebel contend that children of divorce are not doomed to failure; they often display positive characteristics, such as enhanced levels of maturity, self-esteem, empathy, and adaptability.

According to some reports, children from divorced homes are more likely to become divorced themselves. Conversely, other studies indicate that the quality of the postdivorce home is more responsible for subsequent development in children than the divorce itself. Is society setting children up for failed marriages by condoning divorce? Or is divorce simply a way to solve the problem of choosing the wrong marriage partner, giving individuals and families a way to correct that mistake? Does the event of divorce spell disaster for children as they grow into adulthood, or are there other explanations for the problems that children from divorced homes exhibit?

The 1990s saw a movement to do away with no-fault divorce, which has spawned a renewed interest in divorce's effects on children. As the divorce debate evolved from the 1960s to the 1980s, many professionals began viewing divorce as an acceptable alternative to living in an unhappy home. Now family scientists, therapists, and researchers are questioning the belief that children can eventually adjust to the effects of divorce and that it is better for children to live in a divorced home than in an unhappy, intact home.

How does divorce affect children? Do children perceive it as positive or negative? How would their lives differ if their parents work out their problems and stay together? How do the children from divorced families compare with those who grow up in an unhappy, intact family? Do both groups have similar characteristics, or are they different? These are some of the questions related to the study of divorce's effects on children.

There are many studies of divorce's effects on children. Some of these studies show that children benefit from a family's divorce, whereas others show it as the worst thing that ever happens to children. On the positive side, children from divorced families can reap benefits as a consequence of their divorce experience, particularly if the parents model responsible coping skills. Some children do better in a home without the constant tension and fighting that an unhappy, intact home exhibits. These children appear more mature, are more realistic about life, and are more flexible.

On the other hand, problems for children in divorced families are well documented. These children are caught in a situation that they cannot control. Their parents split legally but not emotionally. Such families might ride an emotional roller coaster for years after the initial divorce decree. One parent pitted against the other with the children in the middle is not uncommon. This family turmoil may result in children doing poorly in school, beginning to have sex at an early age, and displaying delinquent behavior. Children are not consulted in the decision to divorce but must live through the instability and confusion that the breakup causes.

In the following selections, arguments are made about the negative and positive effects of divorce on children. Karl Zinsmeister uses studies of children and divorce to argue against the contention made by many parents that it is better to divorce than to rear children in a marriage with conflict. He maintains that children's sense of stability and family structure supersedes parental needs. David Gately and Andrew I. Schwebel analyze a different set of studies of divorce and children; their interpretations of the results and methods of those studies are quite different from those of Zinsmeister.

**Karl Zinsmeister**

# Divorce's Toll on Children

Originally, notes family historian John Sommerville, marriage arose to create "security for the children to be expected from the union." Yet nowadays "the child's interest in the permanence of marriage is almost ignored." During the divorce boom that began in the mid-1960s, divorces affecting children went up even faster than divorces generally, and today *most* crack-ups involve kids. Since 1972, more than a million youngsters have been involved in a divorce *each year.*

The result is that at some time before reaching adulthood, around half of today's children will go through a marital rupture. Most of these youngsters will live in a single-parent home for at least five years. A small majority of those who experience a divorce eventually end up in a step-family, but well over a third of them will endure the extra trauma of seeing that second marriage break up.

The typical divorce brings what researcher Frank Furstenberg describes as "either a complete cessation of contact between the non-residential parent and child, or a relationship that is tantamount to a ritual form of parenthood." In nine cases out of ten the custodial parent is the mother, and fully half of all divorce-children living with their mom have had no contact with their father for at least a full year. Only one child in 10 sees his non-custodial parent as often as once a week. Overall, only about one youngster in five is able to maintain a close relationship with both parents.

Joint child custody receives a lot of publicity (it is now allowed in about half the states), but it remains unusual. In California, where it is much more common than anywhere else, only 18 percent of divorced couples have joint physical custody. Most divorced children still live solely with their mothers.

"For most men," sociologist Andrew Cherlin notes, "children and marriage are part of a package deal. Their ties to their children depend on their ties to their wives." Studies show that remarriage makes fathers particularly likely to reduce involvement with the children from their previous marriage.

Even when divorced parents do maintain regular contact with their children, truly cooperative child rearing is very rare. Most often, research shows, the estranged parents have no communication or mutual reinforcement. As a

From Karl Zinsmeister, "Divorce's Toll on Children," *The American Enterprise,* vol. 7, no. 3 (May/June 1996), pp. 39–44. 

result, mother and father frequently undercut each other, intentionally or not, and parent-child relations are often unhealthy.

A series of interviews with children of divorce conducted by author/photographer Jill Krementz illustrates this phenomenon. "My relationship with my parents has changed because now my mother does all the disciplining," says 14-year-old Meredith, "and sometimes she resents it—especially when we tell her how much fun we have with Dad. It's as if it's all fun and games with him because we're with him so little." Ari, also 14, confides, "I really look forward to the weekends because it's kind of like a break—it's like going to Disneyland because there's no set schedule, no 'Be home by 5:30' kind of stuff. It's open. It's free. And my father is always buying me presents." Zach, age 13, reports "whenever I want to see my other parent I can, and if I have a fight with one of them, instead of having to take off... I can just go eat at my Mom's house or my Dad's."

Other youngsters feel torn in two after a divorce, particularly in cases of joint custody where they must physically bounce back and forth between two houses. "It's hello, goodbye, hello, goodbye all the time," says one father. Gary Skoloff, chairman of the American Bar Association's family law section, explains that "joint custody was going to be a great panacea, the ultimate solution.... But it turned out to be the world's worst situation." The lack of a stable home has proved so harmful to children that several states, including California where the practice was pioneered, have recently revoked statutes favoring joint custody.

## Fear and Loathing of Divorce Among the Young

Children's view of divorce is unambiguous: it's a disaster. In 1988, professor Jeanne Dise-Lewis surveyed almost 700 junior high school students, asking them to rate a number of life events in terms of stressfulness. The only thing students ranked as more stressful than parental divorce was death of a parent or close family member. Parental divorce received a higher rating than the death of a friend, being "physically hit" by a parent, feeling that no one liked them or being seriously injured.

The "fairy tale" believed by adults, says University of Michigan psychologist and divorce expert Neil Kalter, is that if they simply present new family set-ups to their children in a calm, firm way, the children will accept them. Actually, he says, that "is seen by the kids as a lot of baloney." Among the hundreds of children he's worked with in setting up coping-with-divorce programs for schools, "there are very few who have anything good to say about divorce." "Children are generally more traditional than adults," agrees Judith Wallerstein. "Children want both parents. They want family." If children had the vote, she says, there would be no such thing as divorce.

Indeed, Gallup youth surveys in the early 1990s show that three out of four teenagers age 13 to 17 think "it is too easy for people in this country to get divorced." Go into a typical high school today and ask some students what their most important wish for the future is and a surprising number will answer "that there wouldn't be so many divorces." Young Arizonan Cynthia Coan has lots of company when she says, "as a child of divorce, I cannot help but hope that the next generation of children will be spared what mine went through."

You'll sometimes hear the claim that divorce doesn't hurt children as much as conflict in a marriage. This is not supported by the evidence. "For kids," reports Kalter, "the misery in an unhappy marriage is usually less significant than the changes" after a divorce. "They'd rather their parents keep fighting and not get divorced." Even five years later, few of the youngsters in Wallerstein's study agreed with their parents' decision to separate. Only ten percent were more content after the split than before.

Contrary to popular perceptions, the alternative to most divorces is not life in a war zone. Though more than 50 percent of all marriages currently end in divorce, experts tell us that only about 15 percent of all unions involve high levels of conflict. In the vast number of divorces, then, there is no gross strife or violence that could warp a youngster's childhood. The majority of marital break-ups are driven by a quest for greener grass—and in these cases the children will almost always be worse off.

Many mothers and fathers badly underestimate how damaging household dissolution will be to their children. A 1985 British study that quizzed both parents and children found that the children reported being far more seriously upset by their parents' separation than the parents assumed. Despite the common perception that the best thing parents can do for their children is to make themselves happy, the truth is that children have their own needs that exist quite apart from those of their parents. One may argue that a parent should be allowed to rank his own needs above those of his children (though this is not the traditional understanding of how families should work). But one ought not cloak that decision with the false justification that one is thereby serving the children's best interests.

Wade Horn, former commissioner of the U.S. Administration for Children, Youth, and Families, illustrates how parents can be deluded in this way:

> Families used to come to me when I was practicing psychology, seeking advice about how to divorce. They would say, "We want a divorce because we really don't get along very well any more, and we understand that our child will be better off after we divorce than if we stay together." Rarely, if ever, did I hear a family say, "We're having conflict, but we have decided to work as hard as we can at solving our problems because we know that children of divorce are more disturbed than children of intact families."

A major reason parents are making this mistake is because that is what some authorities and many ideologues in the cause of family "liberation" have been telling them. "For years experts said, 'Once the initial trauma wears off, kids make adjustments,' " complains psychologist John Guidubaldi, past president of the National Association of School Psychologists. While it's true that kids make adjustments, Guidubaldi notes in the *Washington Post*, "so do people in prisons and mental institutions. The pertinent question is: Are those adjustments healthy? And the weight of the evidence has become overwhelming on the side that they aren't."

## Short- and Long-Term Effects of Divorce on Children

The longer-term effects of divorce on children are something we've learned a lot about over the last decade. Guidubaldi, who orchestrated one of the large studies documenting these effects, concludes from his work that "the old argument of staying together for the sake of the kids is still the best argument.... People simply aren't putting enough effort into saving their marriages." Family scholar Nicholas Zill points out that "if you looked at the kind of long-term risk factors that divorce creates for kids and translated them to, say, heart disease, people would be startled."

In the early months after divorce, young children are often less imaginative and more repetitive. Many become passive watchers. They tend to be more dependent, demanding, unaffectionate, and disobedient than their counterparts from intact families. They are more afraid of abandonment, loss of love, and bodily harm. A significant number—in some studies a quarter—say they blame themselves for their parents' smash-up.

A small study conducted some years ago by University of Hawaii psychiatrist John McDermott sorted pre-schoolers who had been involved in a divorce a few months earlier into three categories. Three out of 16 children were judged to have weathered the initial storm essentially unchanged. Two of 16 became what he called "severely disorganized" and developed gross behavior problems. The rest, more than two-thirds, he categorized as "the sad, angry children." They displayed resentment, depression, and grief, were restless, noisy, possessive and physically aggressive.

In Judith Wallerstein's landmark study, almost half of the pre-schoolers still displayed heightened anxiety and aggression a full year after their parents' divorce. Forty-four percent "were found to be in significantly deteriorated psychological condition." All of the two- and three-year-olds showed acute regression in toilet training. They displayed unusual hunger for attention from strangers. Older pre-schoolers had become more whiny, irritable, and aggressive, and had problems with play.

Wallerstein's study also returned to its subjects five and 10 years later, and the collected results were quite staggering. In overview they look like this: initially, two-thirds of all the children showed symptoms of stress, and half thought their life had been destroyed by the divorce. Five years down the road, over a third were still seriously disturbed (even more disturbed than they had been initially, in fact), and another third were having psychological difficulties. A surprisingly large number remained angry at their parents.

After a decade, 45 percent of the children were doing well, 14 percent were succeeding in some areas but failing in others, and 41 percent were still doing quite poorly. This last group "were entering adulthood as worried, underachieving, self-deprecating, and sometimes angry young men and women." In addition to their emotional problems and depression, many felt sorrow over their childhoods and fear about their own marriage and childrearing prospects. About a third of the group had little or no ambition at the 10-year mark. Many expressed a sense of powerlessness, neediness, and vulnerability. Most of the ones who had reached adult age regarded their parents' divorce as a continuing major influence in their lives.

It should be noted that the 131 children in the study experienced divorce in what Wallerstein and associates call the "best of circumstances." Most of their parents were college educated, and at the beginning these children were achievers in school. None of the participants was initially being treated for psychiatric disorder. Most of the families were white and middle class; half regularly attended church or synagogue.

Even in families with all these advantages, divorce wreaks havoc among the young. Summarizing her findings on the offspring of broken marriages, Wallerstein has written that "it would be hard to find any other group of children—except, perhaps, the victims of a natural disaster—who suffered such a rate of sudden serious psychological problems." Other long-term studies teach similar conclusions. "Divorce," says psychiatrist McDermott, "is now the single largest cause of childhood depression." Marital disruption, quite clearly, can wound children for years.

## A Catalogue of Behavioral Changes

Let's look more specifically at some of the changes in behavior that affect children of divorce. John Guidubaldi and Joseph Perry found in their survey of 700 youngsters that children of divorced parents performed worse than children of intact families on 9 of 30 mental health measures, showing, among other things, more withdrawal, dependency, inattention, and unhappiness, plus less work effort. Divorced students were more likely to abuse drugs, to commit violent acts, to take their own life, and to bear children out of wedlock.

A University of Pittsburgh study in the late 1980s found that there were 30 percent more duodenal ulcers and 70 percent more suicide attempts—both symptoms of serious psychological stress—among children who had lost a parent. In Wallerstein's middle-class sample, one-third of the girls with divorced parents became pregnant out of wedlock, and 8 percent had at least two abortions. Two-thirds of the girls had a history of delinquency, and almost 30 percent of the boys had been arrested more than once.

The National Survey of Children showed that more than 30 percent of the individuals whose parents separated or divorced before they were eight years old had received therapy by the time they were teenagers. Divorce-children are two to four times as numerous in psychiatric care populations as they are in society at large. In fact, more than 80 percent of the adolescents in mental hospitals, and 60 percent of the children in psychiatric clinics, have been through a divorce. And what is being treated in most cases is much more than just a short-term reaction: the average treatment takes place five years after their parents' marital breakup. At the fully adult age of 23, middle-class women whose mother and father had divorced were three times likelier to have a psychological problem than counterparts from intact families, according to a massive multi-year British study.

Schooling is another problem area. Children exposed to divorce are twice as likely to repeat a grade, and five times likelier to be expelled or suspended.

(Fully 15 percent of all teenagers living with divorced mothers have been booted from school at least temporarily, according to the National Survey of Children.) Even in Wallerstein's middle-class sample, 13 percent of the youngsters had dropped out of school altogether. Barely half of Wallerstein's subjects went on to college, far less than the 85 percent average for students in their high schools. Wallerstein concludes that 60 percent of the divorce-children in her study will fail to match the educational achievements of their fathers.

Children of divorce also frequently have problems with sexual identity. In most studies, boys seem to be harder hit than girls. Pre-school boys tend to be unpopular with male peers, to have difficulty gaining access to play groups, to spend more time with younger compatriots and females, and to engage in more activities traditionally considered to be feminine. Young boys tend to be more vehemently opposed to the divorce, to long more for their father, to feel rejected by him, and to feel uncertain about their masculinity. They are more likely than girls to become depressed and angry. Many later have problems developing intimacy, and build lifestyles of solitary interests and habits.

For girls there is a "sleeper effect"—beginning at adolescence, seemingly well-adjusted individuals often develop serious problems with sexuality, self-control, and intimacy. Kalter found higher rates of substance abuse, running away, and sexual activity among girls who had been through divorce, particularly when the father had departed early on. Wallerstein found that a "significant minority" of girls expressed insecurity, anger, or lack of self-respect in promiscuity, some gravitating to older men or a series of aimless sexual relationships. "I'm prepared for anything. I don't expect a lot," said one 20-year-old. "Love is a strange idea to me. Life is a chess game. I've always been a pawn."

Mavis Hetherington of the University of Virginia has found that girls have special problems when their divorced mothers remarry. She has also shown that the pattern of low self-respect and sexual precocity among girls with a divorced mother does *not* hold true among girls living with a solo mother due to death of the father—apparently it is active alienation from the father, more than his simple absence, that causes the disturbance. This fits well with psychologist Erik Erikson's view that it is less deprivation *per se* that is psychologically destructive than deprivation without redeeming significance.

Wallerstein points out that teenage girls often view their absent fathers with a combination of idealization and distrust.

> The idealized father that the young adolescent girl imagines is the exact opposite of the image that later becomes prominent in her mind as she grows older—namely, the father as betrayer.... Because daughters of divorce often have a hard time finding out what their fathers are really like, they often experience great difficulty in establishing a realistic view of men in general, in developing realistic expectations, and in exercising good judgment in their choice of partner.

Researcher Conrad Schwarz has hypothesized that children who are allied only with their same-sex parent (as a girl growing up with a divorced mother would be) tend to hold a chauvinistic and alienated view of the opposite sex.

Conversely, he suggests, children growing up with only opposite-sex parents (like boys living with divorced mothers) tend to have problems with gender identity and self-esteem. One study that fits this hypothesis found that college-age women who had experienced divorce in childhood were more prone to see men as unfeeling and weak than counterparts from intact families.

Female children of divorced parents are more likely to choose "inadequate husbands" and to have marital problems of their own. They are substantially likelier to have extensive premarital sexual experience and twice as likely to cohabit before marriage. They are more frequently pregnant at their weddings.

And both male and female children of divorce see their own marriages dissolve at significantly higher rates than counterparts who grew up in intact families. Partly this is attitudinal: One eight-year study of 1,300 men and women found that people who had watched their own parents divorce were much more tolerant of the idea of divorce, and that this tolerance translated into increased marital breakup.

The other thing that childhood divorce encourages, of course, is the avoidance of marriage. "My mom got remarried and divorced again, so I've gone through two divorces so far. And my father's also gotten remarried—to someone I don't get along with all that well. It's all made me feel that people shouldn't get married," 14-year-old Ari explained to Jill Krementz.

Divorces involving children thus set a whole train of losses into motion, transporting unhappy effects not only over the years but even across generations. And not even children fortunate enough to live in stable homes are wholly insulated from the turmoil. As writer Susan Cohen observes:

> Although I am not divorced and live in a conventional nuclear family with a husband and two children . . . divorce has been part of my daughter Sarah's life since she was two or three. Divorce is in her books, on her television programs, in her lessons at school, in her conversations with her friends, and in her questions to me.

Indeed, divorce is in the very air our children breathe—with lasting significance for their later views of love, families, and life.

# NO 

**David Gately and Andrew I. Schwebel**

# Favorable Outcomes in Children After Parental Divorce

**SUMMARY.** The present paper is based on a review of the literature that considers the short- and long-term effects parental divorce has on children. Most studies in this literature have identified unfavorable outcomes that develop in many areas of children's lives as they struggle to cope with their changed family situations. However, as children adjust to the challenges they face before, during, and after parental divorce, neutral and favorable outcomes are also possible in one or more areas of their lives. In fact, the literature review indicated that many investigators have identified certain strengths in children who had experienced parental divorce. In particular they have observed that following the divorce of their parents some children, in comparison to peers or their own pre-divorce development, have shown enhanced levels of functioning in four areas: maturity, self-esteem, empathy, and androgyny.

Over ten million divorces were granted in the United States during the 1980s (U.S. Bureau of the Census, 1990). The great number of people affected by divorce in the second half of the 20th century stimulated scholarly interest in this area. One topic that received considerable attention is the effects of parental divorce on children, a group affected at a rate of about one million per year since the mid 1970s (U.S. Bureau of Census, 1990).

Findings consistently show that children experience distress during the process of parental separation and divorce and that it is associated with a variety of short- and long-term negative outcomes (see reviews by Anthony, 1974; Fry & Addington, 1985; Kelly, 1988; Kurdek, 1981; Long & Forehand, 1987; Lopez, 1987; Santrock, 1987). Wallerstein and Blackeslee (1989) stated, "Almost all children of divorce regard their childhood and adolescence as having taken place in the shadow of divorce.... Almost half of the children entered adulthood as worried, underachieving, self-deprecating, and sometimes angry young men and women" (pp. 298–299).

In fact, studies indicate that children may experience difficulties in interpersonal relationships, school behavior, academic achievement, self-esteem, in

From David Gately and Andrew I. Schwebel, "Favorable Outcomes in Children After Parental Divorce," *Journal of Divorce and Remarriage,* vol. 18, nos. 3–4 (1992), pp. 57–63, 66–78. 

future life outlook, etc. Besides delineating the wide range of unfavorable outcomes that can develop in children before, during, and after the divorce, the literature also identifies factors that can moderate and exacerbate the problems children face.

Although much of the literature discusses children's struggle to cope with parental divorce and the unfavorable outcomes they may experience in one or more aspects of their lives, some children in adjusting to their changed circumstances before, during, and after parental divorce may also become strengthened in one or more areas. These individuals develop competencies or grow psychologically because of what they learn while undertaking the divorce-related challenges they face and/or because of the changes they experience in self-view as a result of successfully meeting the challenges.

Decades ago Bernstein and Robey (1962) suggested that successful coping with the demands presented by parental divorce can spur emotional and personality growth in children. Since then a number of investigators have found these favorable outcomes in youngsters relative either to their pre-divorce status or to matched peers from intact family backgrounds. (These include: Grossman, Shea, & Adams, 1980; Hetherington, 1989; Kelly & Wallerstein, 1976; Kurdek & Siesky, 1979, 1980a, 1980b, 1980c; MacKinnon, Stoneman & Brody, 1984; Reinhard, 1977; Richmond-Abbott, 1984; Rosen, 1977; Santrock & Warshak, 1979; Slater, Stewart, & Linn, 1983; Springer & Wallerstein, 1983; Wallerstein, 1984, 1985a, 1987; Wallerstein & Kelly, 1974, 1976, 1980b; Warshak & Santrock, 1983; Weiss, 1979.)

The present paper is based on a comprehensive review of the literature that investigated post-divorce outcomes in children. The review included literature generated from computer searches of the Psychological Abstracts and Family Resources and Educational Resources Information Center data bases. Manual searches of the Psychological Abstracts, The Inventory of Marriage and Family Literature, and the Social Sciences Index bases were conducted to supplement the computer searches. Finally, empirical and theoretical contributions published in books, chapters, and Dissertation Abstracts were reviewed. Following a brief assessment of this body of literature, the present paper focuses on those studies that reported favorable outcomes in children following parental divorce.

Most of the earliest investigations used a pathogenic model that viewed the divorced family as a deviation from the traditional 2-parent family, and attempted to link this "inferior" family structure to negative effects on children's adjustment and psychosocial development (Levitin, 1979). The picture of the effects of parental divorce on children were further colored in a negative way because these projects typically employed clinical samples and studied the crisis period immediately following divorce (Bernstein & Robey, 1962; Kalter, 1977; McDermott, 1968; Westman, 1972).

Later studies employing non-clinical samples showed that, although divorce is associated with an initial crisis reaction in most children, long-term consequences are variable (Hetherington, Cox, & Cox, 1982; Hetherington, 1989). While longitudinal studies demonstrated that parental divorce may have long-term negative effects on the social, emotional, and cognitive functioning of children (Guidubaldi & Cleminshaw, 1985; Hetherington, Cox, & Cox, 1985), they also showed that children may escape long-term negative outcomes if the crisis of divorce is not compounded by multiple stressors and continued adversity (Hetherington, 1979, 1989; Hetherington et al., 1982, 1985).

The finding that divorce does not necessarily result in long-term dysfunction led to a search for individual, family, and environmental factors that moderate children's adjustment. Researchers found the quality of adjustment related to: the child's gender and age at the time of separation/divorce (Guidubaldi & Perry, 1985; Hetherington et al., 1982, 1985; Kalter & Rembar, 1981; Wallerstein & Kelly, 1980a); the child's temperament, locus of control, interpersonal knowledge, and level of coping resources (Ankerbrandt, 1986; Hetherington, 1989; Kurdek & Berg, 1983; Kurdek, Blisk, & Siesky, 1981; Kurdek & Siesky, 1980a); the amount of interparental conflict prior to, during, and following separation/divorce (Emery, 1982; Hetherington et al., 1982; Jacobson, 1978; Wallerstein & Kelly, 1980b); the quality of parent-child relationships (Hess & Camara, 1979; Hetherington, Cox, & Cox, 1982; Wallerstein & Kelly, 1980a); the parents' mental and physical health (Guidubaldi & Cleminshaw, 1985; Guidubaldi & Perry, 1985); the type of custody arrangement (Ambert, 1984; Lowery & Settle, 1985; Santrock & Warshak, 1979; Santrock, Warshak, & Elliot, 1982; Warshak & Santrock, 1983; Wolchik, Braver, & Sandler, 1985); parental remarriage (Clingempeel & Segal, 1986; Hetherington et al., 1982; Santrock, Warshak, Lindbergh & Meadows, 1982); the number of major life changes experienced following divorce (Hetherington et al., 1985; Stolberg, Camplair, Currier, & Wells, 1987), including the amount of financial decline experienced by the post-divorce family (Desimone-Luis, O'Mahoney, & Hunt, 1979); and the social support available to both the parents and children (Isaacs & Leon, 1986).

Drawing upon the concept of stress, Wallerstein (1983a) and Peterson, Leigh, & Day (1984) developed models that could account for the absence of negative outcomes in children. For example, Wallerstein conceived of divorce as an acute social stressor that had consequences and made unique demands on children (differing from those associated with stressors like the death of a parent). Although families experiencing divorce and the loss of a parent pass through similar transitional stages (Schwebel, Fine, Moreland, & Prindle, 1988), studies comparing the short- and long-term effects on children of separation/divorce and death of a parent support Wallerstein's contention (Boyd & Parish, 1983; Felner, Stolberg, & Cowen, 1975; Hetherington, 1972; Mueller & Cooper, 1986; Rozendal, 1983).

Wallerstein (1983a, 1983b) described the sequence of adjustments a child must make: (1) acknowledge the marital disruption, (2) regain a sense of direction and freedom to pursue customary activities, (3) deal with loss and feelings of rejection, (4) forgive the parents, (5) accept the permanence of divorce and relinquish longings for the restoration of the pre-divorce family, and (6) come to feel comfortable and confident in relationships. The successful completion of these tasks, which allows the child to stay on course developmentally, depends on the child's coping resources and the degree of support available to help in dealing with the stressors. Of course, the divorce process also may include pre-separation distress, family conflict, and compromised parenting which both place children at risk and call for them to make adjustments well before the time when the legal divorce is granted (Block, Block, & Gjerde, 1986).

Reports describing protective factors that could mitigate negative outcomes for children following parental divorce complemented findings being described in stress research. More specifically, several authors (Garmezy, 1981; Rutter, 1987; Werner, 1989; Werner & Smith, 1982) found that some children, although exposed to multiple stressors that put them at risk, did not experience negative outcomes. Protective factors diminished the impact of these stressors. Although these investigators studied different stressors, their findings were remarkably similar and suggested that the factors which produce "resilience" in children-at-risk fit into three categories: (1) positive personality dispositions (e.g., active, affectionate, socially responsive, autonomous, flexible, intelligent; possessing self-esteem, an internal locus of control, self-control, and a positive mood); (2) a supportive family environment that encourages coping efforts; and (3) a supportive social environment that reinforces coping efforts and provides positive role models (Garmezy, 1981).

These protective factors reduce the likelihood of negative outcomes by means such as: decreasing exposure to or involvement with risk factors; opening of opportunities for successful task accomplishment and growth; and promoting self-esteem and self-efficacy through secure, supportive personal relationships (Rutter, 1987). Besides helping children avoid short-term harm, these resiliency-building factors strengthen children so they will cope more effectively with and master the stressful life events they will encounter in the future. This "steeling" effect is a favorable outcome that develops after an exposure to stressors of a type and degree that is manageable in the context of the child's capacities and social situation (Rutter, 1987).

The number of studies that identify favorable outcomes of any type of children following parental divorce is small in contrast to the number of studies that have reported unfavorable outcomes. To state the obvious, this difference in the volume of research reports primarily reflects the reality of what children face before, during, and after their parents' divorce. However, a small yet significant part of the difference may be due to the way science has addressed the question of children's outcomes. Specifically, the content of the literature has certainly been shaped, in part, by the fact that neither the pathological nor the stress models heuristically guide researchers to search for favorable outcomes (Kanoy & Cunningham, 1984; McKenry & Price, 1984, 1988; Scanzoni, Polonko, Teachman, & Thompson, 1988) and the fact that the research methods which have been typically employed are more likely to detect negative consequences than positive ones (Blechman, 1982; Kanoy & Cunningham, 1984). For instance, the wide use of measures that identify weaknesses (Blechman, 1982; Kanoy & Cunningham, 1984) and of subjects drawn from clinical samples, who are more maladjusted than their peers (Isaacs, Leon, & Donohue, 1987), makes the likelihood of detecting favorable outcomes unlikely (Kanoy & Cunningham, 1984).

A similar issue is presented by the tendency among researchers to neglect children as a source of data while, at the same time electing to use informants (eg., parents, teachers, clinicians) aware of children's family status (Kanoy &

Cunningham, 1984). Although parents' ratings of their elementary school children's adjustment is not related to the children's assessment of the emotional support they are receiving, the children's self-ratings of their adjustment are significant (Cowen, Pedro-Carroll & Alpert-Gillis, 1990). Teachers hold more negative expectations for children from divorced families than for their counterparts from intact families (Ball, Newman, & Scheuren, 1984) while parents and clinicians, in contrast to the children, tend to overestimate the negative effects of the divorce (Forehand, Brody, Long, Slotkin, & Fauber, 1986; Wolchik, Sandler, Braver, & Fogas, 1985). In fact, correlations between children's ratings of their own post-divorce adjustment and their parent's ratings are typically low (Kurdek & Siesky, 1980b), a finding consistent with correlations found between children's self-ratings and the ratings of adult informants in other areas of the literature (Achenbach, McConaughy, & Howell, 1987)....

The review of... the divorce-adjustment literature suggested four areas, in particular, in which children may experience favorable outcomes following their parents' divorce: in maturity, self-esteem, empathy, and androgyny. Each is discussed below.

## Maturity

Intact families have an "echelon structure" in which parents form the executive unit. In the single-parent home this structure is replaced by a parent-child partnership that encourages children to assume more self and family responsibility and to participate more fully in important family decisions (Weiss, 1979). Such involvement fosters maturity which is evidenced by increased levels of responsibility, independence, and awareness of adult values and concerns.

Studies employing nonclinical samples have supported Weiss's conclusions. Kurdek and Siesky (1980a) reported that about 80% of the 132 5–19 year-old children they sampled (four years post-separation) believed they had assumed increased responsibilities after the divorce and learned to rely on themselves more. Their parents agreed, with about 75% of the 74 parents sampled rating their children as more mature and independent (Kurdek & Siesky, 1980b). Similar findings were reported by Rosen (1977), who assessed children 6–10 years after parental divorce, and by Reinhard (1977), who surveyed 46 adolescents three years post-divorce.

Children from single-parent families spend more time working in the home and taking care of siblings (Amato, 1987; Bohannon & Erikson, 1978; Hetherington, 1989; Zakariya, 1982). These chores can foster maturity in children, if they are age-appropriate and if the children receive adequate support. The maturity may exhibit itself in the form of an increased level of independence, realism, or identity development (Grossman et al., 1980). Single-parents further foster maturity when they (1) involve children in appropriate decision making and in a healthy range of other responsibilities in the post-divorce family (Bohannon & Erickson, 1978; Devall, Stoneman, & Brody, 1986; Hetherington, 1989; Kurdek & Siesky, 1979, 1980a; Reinhard, 1977; Wallerstein, 1985a; Weiss, 1979; Zakariya, 1982), and (2) allow children appropriate access to feelings that they, the adult caretakers, have as vulnerable individuals who may not always be able to meet the children's needs (Springer & Wallerstein, 1983; Wallerstein & Kelly, 1974).

Finally, a distinction is needed between pseudomaturity, a precocious adoption of adult roles and responsibilities, and maturity, an adaptive development that helps individuals cope more effectively. Pseudomaturity is seen in females from divorced families who display flirtatious and attention-seeking behavior with male interviewers (Hetherington, 1972), who engage in earlier and more frequent sexual activity (Boss, 1987; Hetherington, 1972; Kinnaird & Gerard, 1986) and who possess a greater likelihood of premarital pregnancy (Boss, 1987) than counterparts from intact families. Pseudomaturity is also found in both males and females from divorced families who engage in earlier and more frequent dating activity (Booth, Brinkerhoff, & White, 1984; Hetherington, 1972) and marry earlier (Boss, 1987; Glenn & Kramer, 1987) than peers from intact families.

## Self-Esteem

Children may experience increased self-esteem in the aftermath of parental divorce because they cope effectively with changed circumstances, are asked to assume new responsibilities, successfully perform new duties, and so forth. Santrock and Warshak (1979) studied 6–11 year-old children, three years after their parents' divorce, and matched youngsters from intact, mother-custody and father-custody families. Father-custody boys demonstrated higher levels of self-esteem and lower levels of anxiety than intact family boys, while the opposite was true for girls. Slater et al. (1983) studied matched adolescents and found that boys from divorced family backgrounds possessed significantly higher levels of self-esteem than boys from intact and girls from both intact and divorced family backgrounds. Girls from divorced family backgrounds had lower levels of self-esteem than their counterparts from intact families. These results are consistent with Wallerstein and Kelly's (1980a).

One circumstance that appears to foster boys' increased self-esteem in post-divorce families is that they may be more heavily relied upon by custodial parents (most of whom are women) than girls, and as a result may gain a new position of increased responsibility and status. A study of children raised during the Great Depression indicated that older children were strengthened by assuming domestic responsibilities and part-time work (Elder, 1974).

Besides developing as a result of an individual's accomplishments, feelings of self-efficacy may also evolve from vicarious experience, verbal persuasion, and a reduction in the level of fear associated with performing particular behaviors (Bandura, Adams, & Beyer, 1977). Concretely, this suggests that divorcing parents benefit their children by modeling adaptive coping behavior (Kaslow & Hyatt, 1982) and by persuading children to be less fearful and to cope more effectively. Children are most likely to develop hardiness in facing post-divorce challenges if the demands upon them are moderate, if their parents support their efforts to perform new responsibilities, and if family members hold a positive view of divorce-related changes (Maddi & Kobasa, 1984).

## Empathy

Some children in divorced and single-parent families show increased concern for the welfare of family members (Kurdek & Siesky, 1980b; Reinhard, 1977; Weiss, 1979). For example, Hetherington (1989) found older girls in divorced families, in contrast to peers, are more often involved in supportive and nurturing teaching, play, and caretaking activities with younger sisters and tend to help and share more frequently. Likewise, about 25% of Rosen's (1977) South African children sample reported they had gained a greater understanding of human emotions as a result of their parent's divorce 6 to 10 years earlier.

Although Wallerstein (1985b) suggested that children's increase in empathy does not extend beyond the parent-child relationship, Hetherington (1989) believes the increased empathy and sensitivity may reflect a more general orientation. The conditions prevalent during children's adjustment may determine the extent to which empathy develops and generalizes. If children are encouraged to provide age-appropriate emotional and practical support to family members, they may be able to extend themselves, gaining an understanding of others' feelings and, in this way, practice and refine their role- and perspective-taking skills. Hetherington and Parke (1979) suggested that more advanced role-taking skills are related to increased altruism, prosocial behavior, communication skills, moral standards, and empathetic understanding.

## Androgyny

Necessity, encouragement from others, and the observation of models are among the factors that can lead children to shift away from stereotypical sex-role thinking and behavior and toward androgyny. This shift, in turn, can result in increased cognitive and behavioral flexibility (Bem, 1975; Bem & Lenney, 1976; Bem, Martyna, & Watson, 1976).

MacKinnon et al. (1984) investigated the effects of marital status and maternal employment on sex-role orientations in matched groups of mothers and children between 3 and 6 years old. While employment influenced mother's sex-role views, divorce appeared related to children's sex-role views. These authors suggested that the more androgynous sex-role views of the children in the post-divorce homes may stem from the mothers modeling more generalized sex-role behavior, or from the children assuming more nontraditional responsibilities.

Kurdek & Siesky (1980c) investigated the sex-role self-concepts of divorced single parents and their 10 to 19 year-old children, approximately four years post-separation. They found that custodial and noncustodial parents and their children possessed higher levels of self-reported androgyny, when compared to published norms, and that the boys and girls possessed more androgynous sex-role self-concepts than a comparison group of children from intact family backgrounds.

Richmond-Abbott (1984) found that the sex-role attitudes of children, ages 8 to 14, tended to reflect the liberal ones of their divorced, single-parent mothers. However, although the mothers stated that they wanted their children to behave in nontraditional ways, children were encouraged to pursue and tended to prefer sex-stereotyped chores and activities. This fits with the failure of others to find an effect of divorce on preadolescent female's sex-role orientation (Kalter, Riemer, Brickman, & Chen, 1985; Hetherington, 1972). Another finding, that the girls in the sample did foresee themselves engaging in nontraditional behaviors and occupations in the future, supports a conclusion that clear post-divorce increases in androgynous attitudes and behaviors may not emerge until children cope with adolescent identity issues.

Stevenson and Black (1988) conducted a meta-analysis of 67 studies that compared the sex-role development of children in father-present and father-absent homes. The applicability of their findings to the present issue is limited, however, by the fact that father absence because of divorce was not treated separately from father absence because of death or other reasons. Nonetheless, some conclusions they drew fit well with points made above. Specifically, father-absent female adolescents and young adults were slightly but consistently less feminine than their father-present peers in measures of traditionally feminine characteristics such as nurturance and expressiveness. Similarly, father-absent preschool boys, compared to their father-present peers, made fewer stereotypically sex-typed choices in picking toys and activities. However, older father-absent boys were more stereotypical than their father-present peers in their overt behavior, particularly in the expression of aggression. This latter difference could be reflecting the fact that in a mother-headed household an older boy may be asked to assume "man-of-the-house" duties.

In conclusion, the literature suggests that increased androgyny in children may develop following divorce if parents model nontraditional attitudes and behaviors or if children, by necessity and/or with parental encouragement, engage in nontraditional activities following divorce. While children in adolescence may struggle with androgynous thoughts, feelings, and behaviors, by their late teens and early twenties many will have worked through the issues. For example, two studies used by Stevenson and Black (1988) showed that college men who had experienced father absence reported fewer stereotypical vocational preferences. Finally, methodology has affected findings: While data collected from parents and teachers suggest that father-absent boys' behavior is more stereotypical than father-present boys', self-report measures indicate the opposite. In this connection, teachers' assessments have differed depending on whether they thought they were rating a child from a divorced or an intact home (Ball et al., 1984; Santrock & Tracy, 1978).

## Research and Treatment Implications

Research is needed to identify a full list of favorable outcomes that can emerge following children's adjustment to parental divorce. Longitudinal studies would be desirable, especially those using matched comparison groups of intact family children while controlling for possible confounding variables, including parental conflict and family SES.

Hurley, Vincent, Ingram, and Riley (1984) categorize interventions designed to cope with unfavorable consequences in children following parental divorce as either therapeutic or preventative. The therapeutic approaches, which include psychodynamic and family systems interventions, focus on treating psychopathology, while the preventative approaches help healthy children avoid significant dysfunction by coping effectively with the normal post-divorce crisis reaction. Preventative interventions take the form of school-based support groups for children (Cantor, 1977; Gwynn & Brantley, 1987; Moore & Sumner, 1985; Pedro-Carroll & Cowen, 1985) or school and community-based support groups for parents (Davidoff & Schiller, 1983; Omizo & Omizo, 1987) and families (Magid, 1977; Stolberg & Cullen, 1983). Outcome studies show that parents, children, and group leaders believe support groups decrease distress and dysfunction in children (Cantor, 1977; Freeman, 1984; Gwynn & Brantly, 1987; Magid, 1977; Omizo & Omizo, 1987; Pedro-Carroll & Cowen, 1985). At this point, mental health workers could draw from the literature and design a third type of intervention: ones aimed at promoting favorable outcomes in children who must adjust to their parents' divorce.

## References


Achenbach, T. M., McConaughy, S. H., & Howell, C. T. (1987). Child/adolescent behavioral and emotional problems: Implications of cross-informant correlations for situational specificity. *Psychological Bulletin, 101,* 213–232.

Amato, P. R. (1987). Family processes in one-parent, stepparent, and intact families: The child's point of view. *Journal of Marriage and the Family, 49,* 327–337.

Ambert, A. M. (1984). Longitudinal changes in children's behavior toward custodial parents. *Journal of Marriage and the Family,* (May), 463–467.

Ankenbrandt, M. J. (1986). Learned resourcefulness and other cognitive variables related to divorce adjustment in children. *Dissertation Abstracts International, 47* B, DA8628750, 5045.

Anthony, E. J. (1974). Children at risk from divorce: A review. In E. J. Anthony & C. Koupernik (Eds.), *The child in his family: Children at psychiatric risk* (Vol. 3), 461–478. N.Y.: John Wiley & Sons.

Ball, D. W., Newman, J. M., Scheuren, W. J. (1984). Teachers' generalized expectations of children of divorce. *Psychological Reports, 54,* 347–352.

Bandura, A., Adams, N. E., & Beyer, J. (1977). Cognitive processes mediating behavioral changes. *Journal of Personality and Social Psychology, 35,* 125–139.

Bem, S. L. (1975). Sex-role adaptability: One consequence of psychological androgyny. *Journal of Personality and Social Psychology, 31,* 634–643.

Bem, S. L. & Lenney, E. (1976). Sex typing and the avoidance cross-sex behavior. *Journal of Personality and Social Psychology, 33,* 48–54.

Bem, S. L., Martyna, W., & Watson, C. (1976). Sex typing and androgyny: Further explorations of the expressive domain. *Journal of Personality and Social Psychology, 34,* 1016–1023.

Bernstein, N. & Robey, J. (1962). The detection and management of pediatric difficulties created by divorce. *Pediatrics, 16,* 950–956.

Blechman, E. A. (1982). Are children with one parent at psychiatric risk? A methodological review. *Journal of Marriage and the Family, 44,* 179–195.

Block, J. H., Block, J., & Gjerde, P. F. (1986). The personality of children prior to divorce: A prospective study. *Child Development, 57,* 827–840.

Bohannon, P. & Erickson, R. (1978, Jan.) Stepping in. *Psychology Today, 11,* 53–59.

Booth, A., Brinkerhoff, D. B., White, L. K. (1984). The impact of parental divorce on courtship. *Journal of Marriage and the Family, 46,* 85–94.

Boss, E. R. (1987). The demographic characteristics of children of divorce. *Dissertation Abstracts International, 48 1026A, DA8714900.*

Boyd, D. A. & Parish, T. (1983). An investigation of father loss and college students' androgyny scores. *The Journal of Genetic Psychology, 145,* 279–280.

Cantor, D. W. (1977). School based groups for children of divorce. *Journal of Divorce, 1,* 183–187.

Clingempeel, W. G. & Segal, S. (1986). Stepparent-stepchild relationships and the psychological adjustment of children in stepmother and stepfather families. *Child Development, 57,* 474–484.

Cowen, E., Pedro-Carroll, J., & Alpert-Gillis, L. (1990). Relationships between support and adjustment among children of divorce. *Journal of Child Psychology and Psychiatry, 31,* 727–735.

Davidoff, I. F. & Schiller, M. S. (1983). The divorce workshop as crisis intervention: A practical model. *Journal of Divorce, 6,* 25–35.

Desimone-Luis, J., O'Mahoney, K., & Hunt, D. (1979). Children of separation and divorce: Factors influencing adjustment. *Journal of Divorce, 3,* 37–41.

Devall, E., Stoneman, Z., & Brody, G. (1986). The impact of divorce and maternal employment on pre-adolescent children. *Family Relations, 35,* 153–159.

Elder, G. H. (1974). *Children of the great depression.* Chicago: University of Chicago Press.

Emery, R. E. (1982). Interparental conflict and the children of discord and divorce. *Psychological Bulletin, 92,* 310–330.

Felner, R. D., Stolberg, A., & Cowen, E. L. (1975). Crisis events and school mental health referral patterns of young children. *Journal of Consulting and Clinical Psychology, 3,* 305–310.

Forehand, R., Brody, G., Long, N., Slotkin, J., & Fauber, R. (1986). Divorce/divorce potential and interparental conflict: The relationship to early adolescent social and cognitive functioning. *Journal of Adolescent Research, 1,* 389–397.

Freeman, R. (1984). Children in families experiencing separation and divorce: An investigation of the effects of brief intervention. Family Service Association of Metropolitan Toronto (Ontario).

Fry, P. S. & Addington, J. (1985). Perceptions of parent and child adjustment in divorced families. *Clinical Psychology Review, 5,* 141–157.

Garmezy, N. (1981). Children under stress: Perspective on antecedents and correlates of vulnerability and resistance to psychopathology. In A. I. Rabin, J. Arnoff, A. N. Barclay, & R. A. Zucker (Eds.), *Further explorations in personality* (pp. 196–269). N.Y.: Wiley.

Glenn, N. D. & Kramer, K. B. (1987). The marriage and divorce of children of divorce. *Journal of Marriage and the Family, 49,* 811–825.

Grossman, S. M., Shea, J. A., & Adams, G. R. (1980). Effects of parental divorce during early childhood on the ego development and identity formation of college students. *Journal of Divorce, 3,* 263–271.

Guidubaldi, J. & Cleminshaw, H. (1985). Divorce, family health, and child adjustment. *Family Relations, 34,* 35–41.

Guidubaldi, J. & Perry, J. D. (1985). Divorce and mental health sequelae for children: A two-year follow-up of a nationwide sample. *Journal of American Academy of Child Psychiatry, 24* (5), 531–537.

Gwynn, C. A. & Brantley, H. T. (1987). Effects of a divorce group intervention for elementary school children. *Psychology in the Schools, 24,* 161–164.

Hess, R. D. & Camara, K. A. (1979). Post-divorce family relationships as mediating factors in the consequences of divorce for children. *Journal of Social Issues, 35* (4), 79–95.

Hetherington, E. M. (1972). Effects of father absence on personality development in adolescent daughters. *Developmental Psychology, 7,* 313–326.

Hetherington, E. M. (1979). Divorce a child's perspective. *American Psychologist, 34,* 851–858.

Hetherington, E. M. (1989). Coping with family transitions: Winners, losers, and survivors. *Child Development, 60,* 1–14.

Hetherington, E. M., Cox, M., & Cox, R. (1982). Effects of divorce on parents and children. In M. Lamb (Ed.), *Nontraditional families: Parenting and child development* (233–288). Hillsdale, N.J.: Erlbaum.

Hetherington, E. M., Cox, M., & Cox, R. (1985). The long-term effects of divorce and remarriage on the adjustment of children. *Journal of the American Academy of Child Psychiatry, 24* (5), 518–530.

Hetherington, E. M. & Parke, R. D. (1979). *Child psychology: A contemporary viewpoint.* New York: McGraw-Hill Inc.

Hurley, E. C., Vincent, L. T., Ingram, T. L., & Riley, M. T. (1984). Therapeutic interventions for children of divorce. *Family Therapy, 9,* 261–268.

Isaacs, M. B. & Leon, G. (1986). Social networks, divorce, and adjustment: A tale of three generations. *Journal of Divorce, 9,* 1–16.

Isaacs, M. B., Leon, G., & Donohue, A. M. (1987). Who are the "normal" children of divorce? On the need to specify population. *Journal of Divorce, 10,* 107–119.

Jacobson, D. S. (1978). The impact of marital separation/divorce on children: II. Interparental hostility and child adjustment. *Journal of Divorce 2*(1), 3–19.

Kalter, N. (1977). Children of divorce in an outpatient psychiatric population. *American Journal of Orthopsychiatry, 47,* 40–51.

Kalter, N. & Rembar, J. (1981). The significance of a child's age at the time of divorce. *American Journal of Orthopsychiatry, 51,* 85–100.

Kalter, N., Riemer, B., Brickman, A., & Chen, J. W. (1985). Implications of parental divorce for female development. *Journal of the American Academy of Child Psychiatry, 24,* 538–544.

Kanoy, K. W. & Cunningham, J. L. (1984). Consensus or confusion in research on children and divorce: Conceptual and methodological issues. *Journal of Divorce, 74,* 45–71.

Kaslow, F. & Hyatt, R. (1982). Divorce: A potential growth experience for the extended family. *Journal of Divorce, 6,* 115–126.

Kelly, J. B. (1988). Longer-term adjustment in children of divorce: Converging findings and implications for practice. *Journal of Family Psychology, 2,* 119–140.

Kelly, J. B. & Wallerstein, J. S. (1976). The effects of parental divorce: Experiences of the child in early latency. *American Journal of Orthopsychiatry, 46,* 20–32.

Kinnaird, K. L. & Gerrard, M. (1986). Premarital sexual behavior and attitudes toward marriage and divorce among young women as a function of their mothers' marital status. *Journal of Marriage and the Family, 48,* 757–765.

Kurdek, L. A. (1981). An integrative perspective on children's divorce adjustment. *American Psychologist, 36,* 856–866.

Kurdek, L. A. & Berg, B. (1983). Correlates of children's adjustment to their parents' divorce. In L. A. Kurdek (Ed.). *Children and Divorce* (pp. 47–60). San Francisco: Jossey-Bass Inc., Publishers.

Kurdek, L. A., Blisk, D., & Siesky, A. E. (1981). Correlates of children's long-term adjustment to their parents' divorce. *Developmental Psychology, 17,* 565–579.

Kurdek, L. A. & Sieksy, A. E. (1979). An interview study of parents' perceptions of their children's reactions and adjustment to divorce. *Journal of Divorce, 3,* 5–17.

Kurdek, L. A. & Siesky, A. E. (1980a). Children's perceptions of their parents' divorce. *Journal of Divorce, 3,* 339–379.

Kurdek, L. A. & Siesky, A. E. (1980b). Effects of divorce on children: The relationship between parent and child perspectives. *Journal of Divorce, 4,* 85–99.

Kurdek, L. A. & Siesky, A. E. (1980c). Sex-role self-concepts of single divorced parents and their children. *Journal of Divorce, 3,* 249–261.

Levitin, T. E. (1979). Children of divorce. *Journal of Social Issues, 35,* 1–25.

Long, N. & Forehand, R. (1987). The effects of parental divorce and parental conflict on children: An overview. *Developmental and Behavioral Pediatrics, 8,* 292–296.

Lopez, F. G. (1987). The impact of parental divorce on college student development. *Journal of Counseling and Development, 65,* 484–486.

Lowery, C. R. & Settle, S. A. (1985). Effects of divorce on children: Differential impact of custody and visitation patterns. *Family Relations, 34,* 455–463.

MacKinnon, C. E., Stoneman, Z., & Brody, G. H. (1984). The impact of maternal employment and family form on children's sex-role stereotypes and mothers' traditional attitudes. *Journal of Divorce, 8,* 51–60.

Maddi, S. R. & Kobasa, S. C. (1984). *The hardy executive: Health under stress.* Chicago: Dorsey Professional Books.

Magid, K. M. (1977). Children facing divorce: A treatment program. *Personnel and Guidance Journal, 55,* 534–536.

McDermott, J. F. (1968). Parental divorce in early childhood. *American Journal of Psychiatry, 124,* 1424–1432.

McKenry, P. C. & Price, S. J. (1984). The present state of family relations research. *Home Economics Journal, 12,* 381–402.

McKenry, P. C. & Price, S. J. (1988). Research bias in family science: Sentiment over reason. *Family Science Review, 1,* 224–233.

Moore, N. E. & Sumner, M. G. (1985). *Support group for children of divorce: A family life enrichment group model.* Paper presented at Annual Meeting of the National Association of Social Workers, New Orleans.

Mueller, D. & Cooper, P. W. (1986). Children of single parent families: How they fare as young adults. *Family Relations, 35,* 169–176.

Omizo, M. M. & Omizo, S. A. (1987). Effects of parents' divorce group participation on child-rearing attitudes and children's self-concepts. *Journal of Humanistic Education and Development, 25,* 171–179.

Pedro-Carroll, J. L. & Cowen, E. L. (1985). The children of divorce intervention program: An investigation of the efficacy of a school based prevention program. *Journal of Consulting and Clinical Psychology, 53,* 603–611.

Peterson, G., Leigh, G. K., & Day, R. D. (1984). Family stress theory and the impact of divorce on children. *Journal of Divorce, 7,* 1–20.

Reinhard, D. (1977). The reaction of adolescent boys and girls to the divorce of their parents. *Journal of Clinical Child Psychology, 6,* 21–23.

Richmond-Abbott, M. (1984). Sex-role attitudes of mothers and children in divorced, single-parent families. *Journal of Divorce, 8,* 61.

Rosen, R. (1977). Children of divorce: What they feel about access and other aspects of the divorce experience. *Journal of Clinical Child Psychology, 6,* 24–27.

Rozendal, F. G. (1983). Halos vs. stigmas: Long-term effects of parent's death or divorce on college students' concepts of the family. *Adolescence, 18,* 948–955.

Rutter, M. (1987). Psychosocial resilience and protective mechanisms. *American Journal of Orthopsychiatry, 57,* 316–331.

Santrock, J. W. (1987). The effects of divorce on adolescence: Needed research perspectives. *Family Therapy, 14,* 147–159.

Santrock, J. W. & Tracy, R. L. (1978). Effects of children's family structure status on the development of stereotypes by teachers. *Journal of Educational Psychology, 70,* 754–757.

Santrock, J. W. & Warshak, R. A. (1979). Father custody and social development in boys and girls. *Journal of Social Issues, 35,* 112–125.

Santrock, J. W., Warshak, R. A., & Elliot, G. L. (1982). Social development and parent child interactions in father-custody and stepmother families. In M. Lamb (Ed.), *Nontraditional families: Parenting and child development.* Hillsdale, N.J.: Erlbaum, 289–314.

Santrock, J. W., Warshak, R. A., Lindbergh, C., & Meadows, L. (1982). Children's and parents' observed social behavior in stepfather families. *Child Development, 53,* 472–480.

Scanzoni, J., Polonko, K., Teachman, J. T., & Thompson, L. (1988). *The sexual bond: Rethinking families and close relationships.* Newbury Park, CA: Sage Publications Inc.

Schwebel, A. I., Fine, M., Moreland, J. R., & Prindle, P. (1988). Clinical work with divorced and widowed fathers: The adjusting family model. In P. Bronstein & C. Cowen (Eds.), *Fatherhood today: Men's changing role in the family.* New York: Wiley, 299–319.

Slater, E. J., Stewart, K., & Linn, M. (1983). The effects of family disruption on adolescent males and females. *Adolescence, 18,* 933.

Springer, C. & Wallerstein, J. S. (1983). Young adolescents' responses to their parents' divorce. In L. A. Kurdek (Ed.), *Children and divorce.* San Francisco: Jossey-Bass, 15–27.

Stevenson, M. R. & Black, K. N. (1988). Paternal absence and sex-role development: A meta-analysis. *Child Development, 59,* 795–814.

Stolberg, A., Camplair, C., Currier, K., & Wells, M. (1987). Individual, familial, and environmental determinants of children's post-divorce adjustment and maladjustment. *Journal of Divorce, 11,* 51–70.

Stolberg, A. L. & Cullen, P. M. (1983). Preventive interventions for families of divorce: The divorce adjustment project. *New Directions for Child Development, 19,* 71–81.

U.S. Bureau of the Census (1990). *Statistical abstract of the U.S.: 1990.* Washington, D.C.

Wallerstein, J. (1983a). Children of divorce: Stress and developmental tasks. In N. Garmezy and M. Rutter (Eds.), *Stress, coping, and development.* New York: McGraw-Hill Inc., 265–302.

Wallerstein, J. (1983b). Children of divorce: The psychological tasks of the child. *American Journal of Orthopsychiatry, 53,* 230–243.

Wallerstein, J. (1984). Children of divorce: Preliminary report of a ten-year follow-up of young children. *American Journal of Orthopsychiatry, 54*(3), 444–458.

Wallerstein, J. (1985a). Children of divorce: Preliminary report of a ten-year follow-up of older children and adolescents. *Journal of American Academy of Child Psychiatry, 24*(5), 545–553.

Wallerstein, J. (1985b). The overburdened child: Some long-term consequences of divorce. *Social Work, 30*(2), 116–123.

Wallerstein, J. (1987). Children of divorce: Report of a ten-year follow-up of early latency-age children. *American Journal of Orthopsychiatry, 57,* 199–211.

Wallerstein, J. & Blackeslee, S. (1989). *Second chances.* New York: Ticknor & Fields.

Wallerstein, J. & Kelly, J. (1974). The effects of divorce: The adolescent experience. In J. Anthony & C. Koupernik (Eds.), *The child in his family: Children at psychiatric risk* (Vol. 3). N.Y.: Wiley.

Wallerstein, J. & Kelly, J. (1976). The effects of divorce: Experiences of the child in later latency. *American Journal of Orthopsychiatry, 46*(2), 256–269.

Wallerstein, J. & Kelly, J. (1980a). *Surviving the Breakup.* New York: Basic Books Inc.

Wallerstein, J. & Kelly, J. (1980b, Jan.) California's children of divorce. *Psychology Today,* 67–76.

Warshak, R. & Santrock, J. W. (1983). The impact of divorce in father-custody and mother-custody homes: The child's perspective. In L. Kurdek (Ed.), *Children and divorce,* San Francisco: Jossey-Bass Inc., Publishers, 29–45.

Weiss, R. (1979). Growing up a little faster: The experience of growing up in a single-parent household. *Journal of Social Issues, 35*(4), 97–111.

Werner, E. E. (1989). High-risk children in young adulthood: A longitudinal study from birth to 32 years. *American Journal of Orthopsychiatry, 59,* 72–81.

Werner, E. E. & Smith, B. S. (1982). *Vulnerable but invincible: A study of resilient children.* New York: McGraw-Hill Inc.

Westman, J. C. (1972). Effect of divorce on child's personality development. *Medical Aspects of Human Sexuality, 6,* 38–55.

Wolchik, S. & A., Braver, S., & Sandler, I. (1985). Maternal versus joint custody: Children's postseparation experiences and adjustment. *Journal of Clinical Child Psychology, 14,* 5–10.

Wolchik, S. A., Sandler, I., Braver, S., & Fogas, B. (1985). Events of parental divorce: Stressfulness ratings by children, parents, and clinicians. *American Journal of Community Psychology, 14,* 59–74.

Zakariya, S. B. (1982, Sept.). Another look at the children of divorce: Summary report of school needs of one-parent children. *Principal, 62,* 34–38.

# POSTSCRIPT

## Does Divorce Create Long-Term Negative Effects for Children?

Zinsmeister proposes that parents stay together for the sake of the children. According to some studies, children rate divorce second only to the death of a parent as the most stressful event in their lives, and most of them end up not having a close relationship with one of their parents.

Although the number of studies that show negative divorce effects outweighs the number of studies with positive results, Gately and Schwebel use them to illustrate children's resilience. These children developed traits such as a positive personality, self-control, self-reliance, and empathy for others, probably as a result of the divorce.

Is it divorce that creates problems for children, or is it the poverty, family disorganization, and unmet needs accompanying most divorces that cause long-term problems? A common complaint of children of divorce is that there is no adult in whom they can confide.

## Suggested Readings


Amato, P. R. (1994, Spring). Life span adjustment of children to their parents' divorce. *The future of children* (143–164). Los Altos, CA: Center for the Future of Children.

Cherlin, A. (1993, Winter). Nostalgia as family policy (emotional and economic effects of divorce on children). *The Public Interest, 110*, 77–85.

Ehrenreich, B. (1996, April 8). In defense of splitting up. *Time, 147*, 80.

Gill, R. (1992, Spring). For the sake of the children (effects of divorce on children). *The Public Interest, 108*, 81–97.

Jones, S. (1993, May). The two-parent heresy (divorce and single parent families can adversely affect children). *Christianity Today, 37*, 20–22.

Lehrman, K. (1993, May). Growing up with divorce. *Vogue, 193*, 182–186.

Robinson, K. (1994, May/June). Which side are you on? *Networker, 18*, 19–23, 26–30.

Roe, C. (1994, Summer). The pros and cons of divorce. *Single Parent, 37*, 26–28.

# ISSUE 8

## Is Television Violence Viewing Harmful for Children?

**YES: Merrilyn O. Johnson**, from "Television Violence and Its Effect on Children," *Journal of Pediatric Nursing* (April 1996)

**NO: Jib Fowles**, from "The Whipping Boy: The Hidden Conflicts Underlying the Campaign Against Violent TV," *Reason* (March 2001)


### ISSUE SUMMARY

**YES:** Merrilyn O. Johnson, MSN, RN, is from the nursing Ph.D. collaborative program at the Medical University of South Carolina and the University of South Carolina, Columbia. She argues that the negative impact of television viewing is so great that it should be included in health professionals' assessments of children and families.

**NO:** Jib Fowles, a professor of communication at the University of Houston, asserts that although television violence has increased steadily, the violent crime rate has in fact decreased.


The debate over television violence rages on. When asked about violence in contemporary society, many people would respond, "Violence is at epidemic proportions. There is a lot more violence out on the streets now than when I was a kid. It's just not safe to be out anymore. We live in such violent times." There are seemingly endless anecdotes and lots of remorse about more peaceful times. The unison in which society decries the rise in violence begins to disintegrate, however, when one attempts to discern causes for the increases in crimes like murder, rape, robbery, and assault.

One segment of society that is regularly targeted as a contributing cause to the rise in violence is the media, particularly television programming. A common argument is that television is much too violent, especially in children's programming. It has been suggested, for example, that a child will witness in excess of 100,000 acts of simulated violence depicted on television before graduating from elementary school! Children in a lower socioeconomic class may view even more hours of television. Many researchers suggest that this television violence is at least in part responsible for the climbing rates of violent crime, since children tend to imitate what they observe in life.

On the other side, critics argue that it is not what is on television that bears responsibility for the surge in violence. They believe that programming is merely reflective of the level of violence in contemporary society. The argument is that while television watching may be associated with violence, that does not mean that it causes violence. As an example, the critics suggest that we have known for some time that aggressive children tend to watch more aggressive television programming. However, does the aggression predispose an interest in aggressive programming, or does the programming cause the aggression? This is a question that sparks hotly contested debates.

Those who believe television viewing is at least partly responsible for aggressive behavior in children want the United States Congress to more closely regulate the ratings, viewing times, and amount of violence that can be shown on American television. Those on the other side of the issue point to the infringement on First Amendment rights of freedom of expression should such intense regulation be imposed on the media.

The following selections are typical of the debate centered around how violence and television affects children. Merrilyn O. Johnson cites studies to support her claim that children watch too much violent TV, to the extent that their health and well-being are negatively affected. Jib Fowles believes that television is used as a "whipping boy," blamed for the ills of society, including the perceived rise in violent acts. Although there are no champions that rise to television's defense, Fowles contends that the attack on television as the source of societal violence is a big lie and is used to cover up society's real problems.

Merrilyn O. Johnson

# Television Violence and Its Effect on Children

*For **some** children under **some** conditions **some** television is harmful.*

*For **other** children under **other** conditions it may be beneficial.*

*For **most** children under **most** conditions **most** TV is probably neither particularly harmful nor particularly beneficial.*

— Schramm, Lyle, and Parker (1961)

Although written 33 years ago, the above quote on television (TV) viewing and children is as relevant today as it was then. Does watching violence on TV increase or alter the antisocial or aggressive activity of children? The possibility that widespread watching of violent TV programs by children and youth is increasing the level of violence in American society continues to be the most controversial and emotionally arousing issue related to the TV medium. This is because the concentration of violence portrayed on TV has the potential of generating aggressive behavior, both immediately and in the long term (Joy, Kimball, & Zabrack, 1986, cited in Williams, 1986). *Aggression* in this instance refers to physical aggression with the potential to injure as well as verbal abuse, including threats.

TV may affect its viewers in two possible ways: by displacing other activities and through its content (Williams, 1986). American TV contains the most violence of TV in any Western country (Dietz & Strasburger, 1991). Violent content has not changed appreciably in the past decade despite increasing public awareness and concern. Unfortunately cartoon shows and prime-time programming glorify the use of guns and violence as acceptable, justifiable solutions to complex problems (Dietz & Strasburger, 1991).

Ninety-nine percent of American households contain at least one TV, with two thirds containing two or more sets (A. C. Nielson Company, 1988). Children and adolescents comprise between 10% and 20% of the prime-time viewing audience, and they spend more time watching TV (15,000 h) than they do in school (11,000 h). During this time they witness 180,000 murders, rapes, armed robberies, and assaults.

From Merrilyn O. Johnson, "Television Violence and Its Effect on Children," *Journal of Pediatric Nursing,* vol. 11, no. 2 (April 1996).  References omitted.

In 1989, the average child in the United States spent more time watching TV than performing any other activity except sleeping. The Nielson Report on Television (1989) commented that children age 2 to 5 years viewed approximately 27 hours of TV/wk, children age 6 to 11 years viewed more than 23 hours of TV/wk, and adolescents age 12 to 17 years viewed 22 hours of TV/wk. By the time today's children reach 70 years of age, they will have spent 7 years of their lives watching TV (Dietz & Strasburger, 1991). TV therefore represents an influential force in the lives of children and adolescents.

Many variables are involved in the relationship between viewing violence on TV and actual aggressive behavior. Significant developmental and gender variables, family background and attitudes, the viewing context, and the quality and nature of the child's other experiences, as well as his or her perception of TV portrayal, are all important factors that influence TV's impact. Other factors that affect the likelihood of an individual actually performing an aggressive act are characteristics of the viewer, state of arousal, whether the behavior is reinforced, nature of the TV stimuli, and the environment, including the perceived similarity between the observed environment and the viewer's actual environment (Comstock, 1976).

## Background Literature

Parents and social critics express concern regarding the possible negative effects that TV viewing has on children. TV influences children, but in what ways and to what extent is the subject of much debate. The research in this area has focused on the relationship between viewing violence on TV and subsequent aggressive behavior. Numerous researchers have examined media violence in many countries using different methods, providing a degree of consistency of results. A small but genuine association appears to exist between media violence and aggression (Heath, Bresolin, & Rinaldi, 1989).

Children are great imitators. Infants as young as 14 months have shown significant and deferred imitation of televised models (Meltzoff, 1988). Bandura postulated that children can learn aggressive behavior from watching characters on TV. His social learning theory suggests that humans learn ways of behaving, as well as appropriateness and effects of behavior, directly from observing real life as well as indirectly through the mass media. Bandura's contention is that the most effective way to teach children desired behavior is to demonstrate the behavior and have the children model it. Thus, in his classic 1963 "Bobo doll" experiments (Bandura, Ross, & Ross, 1963), young children were exposed to televised films in which an adult behaved aggressively toward inflated dolls (Bobo dolls). Children who had viewed this film played more aggressively with a Bobo doll than did children who had not seen the adult model.

The conclusions of the Bobo doll experiment were further validated by Steur, Applefield, and Smith (1971) who found that nursery school children who watched violent TV programs during their breaks displayed more aggression on the playground than children who viewed nonviolent programs. College students also showed more aggressive behavior when exposed to a segment of violent film as opposed to not viewing a film or viewing a neutral film

(Berkowitz & Rawlings, 1963). These experiments support the notion that a relationship indeed exists between viewing aggressive behavior and acting aggressively, particularly if the TV aggressor is rewarded for the act.

However, some research reviewers have drawn different conclusions from early research findings, suggesting that no significant effect was found between violence on TV and aggression (Hearold, 1986). Feshbach & Singer (1971) even suggest that exposure to aggressive TV content reduces aggressive behavior in some types of children. Commenting on this latter study, Singer (1989) pointed out that the study was marred by procedural flaws that biased and invalidated the findings. Cook, Kendzienski, and Thomas (1983) argue that there is less consistency of results regarding TV violence and aggression than claimed and that biases may have inflated past estimates. They contend that TV's role is probably small compared with other socialization factors.

Several studies have produced evidence that the introduction of TV increases the level of aggression in the community. Centerwall (1992) compared homicide rates in the United States, Canada, and South Africa and was able to show that homicide rates increased predictably after the introduction of TV to a community. This effect was maximal 10 to 15 years later. Earlier studies in Canadian towns with varying exposure to TV showed that a cohort of first- and second-grade students had an increased rate of aggression in the 2 years after introduction of TV compared with two control groups (Joy, Kimball, & Zabrack, 1986). Singer, Singer, and Rapaczynski (1984) studied elementary school children for 5 years and found on parent report that TV viewing was a major predictor of physical aggression.

A longer-term study shows even more disturbing information. Findings of a study of 875 boys from a semirural US community followed up for 22 years strongly indicated that violence viewing at age 8 years significantly predicted a link between exposure to TV violence at age 8 and antisocial behavior 22 years later (Huesmann, Eron, Lefkowitz, & Walder, 1984).

Reviewing the literature in 1989, Heath, Bresolin, and Rinaldi examined studies for behavioral and attitudinal effects of media violence. They looked at laboratory and field research and concluded that the relationship between exposure to media violence and aggressive behavior appeared to be fairly consistent across studies, but methodological weaknesses introduced bias in favor of this conclusion. The researchers emphasized the importance of the "perceived reality of the message" and discussed the lack of realistic consequences for violence shown on TV. They commented on the difference in viewer response where there was a match between personal experience and the media depiction of violence, as this may reinforce violent behavior patterns. They reviewed intervention programs and found that efforts at training parents and children had not been helpful.

This article provoked a letter from Gadow and Sprafkin (1990) who believed that the correlation between aggression in the media and viewer aggressive behavior had little support. Earlier, Gadow and Sprafkin (1989) had examined 20 field experiments to determine the short-term effects on children's behavior of viewing aggression-laden TV shows. Careful analysis, taking full account of design patterns of these studies, showed that more antisocial behavior occurred after viewing aggressive content on TV. However, there was a significant increase in antisocial behavior after viewing low-aggression or nonaggressive TV as well. They discussed this as a nonspecific arousal response to the medium, concluding that watching wholesome TV may not ameliorate conduct problems. The researchers commented that "television's ability to produce increased levels of social activity (both appropriate and negative) is controversial" (p. 404).

Comstock and Strasburger (1990) recommend further research of the scripting of TV programs and of interventions that may assist children in coping with them. In closing they say that

> competition among media ensures that the amount of violence in television, as well as in films, will not be lower in the future. In fact, it may become even greater in graphicness and ferocity. Intervention and remedy therefore, fall to parents, the school, and the community" (p. 42).

In the 4 years since this article was written, we indeed have seen an increase in the phenomena of violence such as Schwarzenegger's "Terminator" movies, "Power Rangers," and the "Ninja Turtles" movies and TV shows. Testimony to Senate hearings in 1993 indicates that many members of the public have concerns about the increasing violence depicted on TV. (Testimony of Judith Myers-Walls and Ken Auletta, 1993). The community has responded by requiring warnings before violent programs on TV; however, at present no data are available to show any effect of these warnings.

The recent growth of cable TV and video movie rentals has increased the number of potential sources of positive and negative programming that may be viewed by children. Competition for a share of the audience appears to have led to greater exploitation of sex and violence in shows on TV. However, there is continued debate as to whether exposure to such programs is universally damaging to children. After analyzing the public debate, court decisions, and scientific consideration of cause and effect, Lande (1993) warns that the role of the viewer is pivotal and that the focus of research should shift to identifying and describing the vulnerable viewer. This concern about features that make an adaptive response to violence difficult is also evident in an article on real violence by Groves, Zuckerman, Marans, and Cohen (1993), and the ensuing correspondence (Butler, 1993; Kosta, 1993).

One group that can be considered to be at intensified risk are the individuals suffering from major psychiatric illnesses. In a forensic hospital the elimination of Music Television (MTV) cable programs from units led to a significant decrease in the frequency of overt aggressive behavior (Waite, Hilbrand, & Foster, 1992). It was postulated that the removal of MTV withdrew a source of cues and arousal for aggressive behavior. These dynamics, observed in adults, are consistent with the experiments of the Bobo dolls in children, and this study may be reasonably projected to the pediatric viewing group because they lack the internal capacity to modify their responses to the stimulus of programs like MTV. The "Beavis and Butthead" controversy also arose because MTV claimed that the satirical quality of the writing could not be recognized by the children and the blurring of the distinction between real and imaginary was claimed to have produced some negative behaviors in children viewing the program. It must be noted that although many concerns are voiced and anecdotal incidents cited, no research has been done on the effect of "Beavis and Butthead" on young children.

The group of children who have little parental input and are "amoral quick learners out there eager to act out any new TV excitement" represent a group who are at high risk for viewing related violence because "Their teacher is a television set" (Coleman, 1993). Modification of their viewing habits and responses to programs will require specific targeted approaches that need to be further developed. Collaboration of educators, psychiatrists, sociologists, pediatricians, nurses, and other health professionals is desirable in this circumstance, and because health care professionals and teachers are consistent "parental-like" figures and are dispersed in the community, this is an acceptable teaching role for nurses.

As evidenced by the review of literature, there are much conflicting data on the influences of media and TV violence. However, it seems to be in the best interest of the child to restrict access and exposure to media violence. Despite many efforts of public and professional groups this is difficult to achieve, particularly within the political system of the United States (Anonymous, 1994). If exposure cannot be restricted, then careful adult supervision with interpretation of the meaning of violence is imperative.

## Strategies for Anticipatory Guidance Related to TV

Because TV is woven into the fabric of today's family life, children's best interests would be served by limiting TV's use and function within the family rather than hoping to rid society of it altogether (Cohen, 1993). If, as mentioned above, TV has its effect by its content and by displacing other activities, then efforts to contain its negative effects must address both these aspects. The nursing profession is uniquely positioned to offer assistance with this effort. Pediatric and community health nurses interact with many families in different roles and settings. Their advice is heeded well, be it offered in the more affluent private pediatric practice or in the clinics of less prosperous neighborhoods, where the nurse is often the most positive, nonthreatening professional the family meets. It is helpful to include the issue of TV violence in anticipatory guidance given to families whatever the environment.

Based on assessment of individual family style, parents' cognition, and social resources available to the family, some useful nursing strategies to assist in creating a balance between TV watching and other activities for children and adults, include the following: (a) educate parents (at an appropriate learning level) about normal child development with emphasis given to the effect that visual media, especially TV, can have on early child development (presentations at Parent-Teacher Association meetings and information sharing in parent newsletters and flyers sent home from schools and daycare centers); (b) encourage parents to spend time with their children; (c) support parents in exercising control over the use of TV in the homes; (d) encourage parents to be role models for their children by participating in activities other than TV viewing and by changing their own TV viewing habits; (e) encourage children to engage in physical activities and exercise; (f) introduce children to games such as Candyland, Monopoly, cards, and other board games; (g) encourage reading as an alternate form of entertainment; (h) counsel parents in the provision of structured bedtime rituals that include reading and talking and less TV; (i) discourage the acquisition of a second TV set or cable TV in households with unsupervised young children; and (j) advise parents against the use of TV as a babysitter or as a reward or punishment.

Family styles are so diverse today that these strategies may not be suitable in every case. However, health care providers need to present options and encourage families to choose the most appropriate ones to best meet the needs of the children.

Strategies to mediate the impact of the content of TV programs on children would include the following: (a) parents watch TV with children to determine the suitability of programs and explain what is being viewed; (b) while watching TV with children, parents provoke discussion and ask questions regarding program accuracy and content; (c) parents block or do not subscribe to cable channels that are considered undesirable for children's viewing; (d) parents foster other creative activities such as active play or production of theatrical, musical, dance, or visual arts activities where children participate in the imaginative experience.

## Recommendations for Community Action

The mounting evidence of effects to some children of watching violence on TV is enough to alarm parents, nurses, teachers, and legislators, but the media industry has been slow to respond. It is gratifying to see that cable TV has instituted a violence rating system and that time-control locks for TV receivers are available. Advocacy organizations for positive children's programming include Action for Children's Television and the American Academy of Pediatrics. TV exists to sell audiences to advertisers, so economic pressure on advertisers creates change.

It is essential for health care professionals to play a role in educating the public regarding optimal TV viewing habits. As part of a standard health care package, information for parents on developmentally appropriate TV for children and how it educates and influences them should be readily available. Nurses can be involved in the development and testing of such interventions. Parents can become involved with helping their children to develop critical viewing skills while limiting viewing time and providing TV substitutes (eg. reading, sports, hobbies). Being a fitting role model for children is the responsibility of every adult.

Another critical area requiring the involvement of health care professionals is that of policymaking and legislative initiatives to ensure that high-quality children's TV programming is required for TV station license renewal. Building coalitions with other groups to monitor and improve TV for children would be most beneficial. Professionals in health care roles can also conduct more research to further define the link between TV violence and childhood aggression. In the past this has been undertaken by psychologists, sociologists and media specialists, with less research documented by educators and those in the business of caring for children's general health and well-being. It is essential that future research be interdisciplinary in nature to address the issue of TV violence from a holistic perspective and to raise the understanding of the effect of repeated exposure to TV violence on the behavior of impressionable infants and children. Nursing has much to offer teams that develop and promote scientifically developed interventions to prevent childhood violence.

## Summary

The literature points to the negative impact on children of viewing violence on TV. It is essential that nurses concerned with the health and well-being of children include TV violence as a major issue in their work with individual clients and in their community activities. This would include interventions with families to affect family TV viewing habits and involvement in political action by petitioning Congress and the Federal Communications Commission to regulate violence on TV. As professionals, nurses can assist in the investigation and testing of the effectiveness of these interventions.

Finally, we must remember, in the words of Dorothy Singer (1989),

> Professionals and parents must be aware of all sources of input for their children, not only peers, textbooks, teachers, and relatives but also from the subtle "stranger" in the living room who talks to children daily with complex messages of fear, violence, materialism, and, only infrequently, with messages of sharing, friendship, and concern for others (p. 446).

**Jib Fowles**

# The Whipping Boy

Although television violence has never been shown to cause hostile behavior, its sinister reputation lives on. This is because the issue masks a variety of other struggles. Many of these conflicts are suppressed because they may pose a threat to social order or are considered unseemly topics for public discussion. Hence, we hear only the polite versions of the conflicts between races, genders, and generations, although these struggles roil national life. Because they are denied full expression, such conflicts are transferred into other debates, including and perhaps especially the issue of television violence.

Television violence is a whipping boy, a stand-in for other clashes, real or imagined. As one astute observer put it a few years back during a previous cycle of panic, "The debate about children and media violence is really a debate about other things, many of which have very little to do with the media."

There are several reasons why television violence has become such an exemplary whipping boy. First, it is a large target, present in one form or another in virtually every household in America. Second, if one puts on blinders, there might seem to be some correspondence between the mayhem on the television screen and real-life aggression; both televised entertainment and the real world deal in hostilities. Third and most important, television violence attracts no champions; the very idea of defending it seems silly to most people. Even industry representatives rarely get beyond conciliatory statements when they are compelled to address the matter. In one survey, 78 percent of entertainment industry executives expressed concern about the content of the action dramas they helped produce. In 1993 Ted Turner, perhaps the most conspicuous industry leader at the time, said in congressional testimony that television was "the single most important factor causing violence in America." The object of derision simply stands still and takes all the abuse that can be heaped on it.

What are the real conflicts that are being displaced? Most entail the stronger overwhelming the weaker, but in some conflicts the weaker retaliate through moral exertion. Here is a brief examination of the most important conflicts.

From Jib Fowles, "The Whipping Boy: The Hidden Conflicts Underlying the Campaign Against Violent TV," *Reason* (March 2001). Adapted from *The Case for Television Violence* (Sage Publications, 1999). Reprinted by permission of Sage Publications, Inc.

## High vs. Low

The attack on television violence is, at least in part, an attack by the upper classes and their partisans on popular culture. In this interpretation, which has been broached repeatedly for a quarter-century, the push to reform television is simply the latest manifestation of the struggle between the high and the low, the dominant and the dominated.

The United States is often regarded as a virtually classless society. Indeed, the overwhelming majority of Americans identify themselves as members of a "middle" class. Everyday experience, however, points in a different direction. Americans constantly make class judgments about one another. They quickly note outward appearances and speech patterns. When necessary, one person learns about the other's occupation and education, where he lives and what car he drives, and locates that person socially. Notions of class rank notoriously crop up in courtship and marriage. Characters in films and television programs radiate class information about themselves to audience members who know precisely how to read such clues.

Perhaps the preeminent living theorist and researcher into matters of class and culture is Pierre Bourdieu. He is best known for his work on the segmentation of society according to preferences in aesthetic taste (for instance, going or not going to art museums). At the center of Bourdieu's work is the concept of *habitus,* an idea similar to that of the English word, *habit.* Habitus is the system of predispositions ingrained in a particular group or social class. It manifests itself in similar thoughts, behaviors, expressions, and leisure pursuits. The shared habitus unites and defines the social entity. Habitus, however, does not shackle individuals; in Bourdieu's scheme, there is ample room for idiosyncratic action.

Another concept special to Bourdieu is *capital,* approximately equivalent to social power. In addition to conventional economic wealth, there are several other kinds of capital in Bourdieu's system. Cultural capital (preferences gained primarily through education), symbolic capital (prestige and honors), and social capital (whom one knows) work together with financial capital to define a person's location in the overall social structure. Social action then becomes a function of class habitus and personal capitals. A final term from Bourdieu's work is *reproduction,* which is the manner by which social classes reproduce themselves and, in doing so, preserve status differences. For Bourdieu, the reproduction of habitus is the key work of a social class.

Although Bourdieu does not discuss television in his magisterial work, *Distinctions* (1984), it does not take much imagination to extend his analysis. He writes in his opening pages that taste (cultural capital) functions as a marker of social class; therefore, different preferences (such as watching television violence or not) can be used to situate a person hierarchically. According to this system, an attack on the most popular medium, on television and especially its violent content, would also be an attack by the dominant class on the habitus of the dominated. To reconfirm social distinctions and maintain exclusivity, members of the dominant class need only profess an opposition to television violence. (Ironically, Bourdieu, mustering all the trappings of a French intellectual, himself attacked television in a series of lectures published in English in 1998, calling the medium "a threat to political life and to democracy itself.")

In the derisive vocabulary of this dominant class, violent content is delivered via the "mass media." This term is used so much that it seems unremarkable, but repetition has concealed its derogatory nature. Programming is not received by an undifferentiated horde; it is received by individuals. In fact, there is no mass, there are no masses. As the cultural critic Raymond Williams wrote in 1958, "The masses are always the others, whom we don't know, and can't know. . . .Masses are other people. There are in fact no masses; there are only ways of seeing people as masses." When dominant Americans chastise the nonexistent phenomena of the "masses" and their "mass medium" of television, with its evil content, what they are really endeavoring is to disparage and suppress the culture of dominated Americans.

The class nature of this conflict is evident in the string of congressional hearings that have addressed television violence. Consider the five such congressional hearings held between 1988 and 1995. Of the 36 non-industry witnesses who testified against television violence, only seven were women. None was black or Hispanic. The 29 white males were identified as presidents, professors, directors, representatives, senators, senior scientists, and other distinguished titles that suggested they were well advanced in their careers. It is this patrician sector of society that for reasons of its own leads the attack on rowdy television violence.

The means by which one enters into society's dominant segment, and in doing so learns to affect reproachful views on television violence, is the academy. The general veneration that greets the academy is a sign of its near-sacred station and of the importance of its role in, as Bourdieu would view it, the reproduction of the dominant class and its habitus. Although the rewards of academics are middling in terms of financial capital, the cultural capital they accrue cannot be surpassed. To have a college degree—only about one-quarter of American adults do—is to have the credential of the dominant; not to have a college degree is to remain forever among the dominated.

Academics strive to regard television with condescension or an affected indifference. "A studied, conspicuous ignorance about television," communication professor Ellen Seiter wrote in 1996, "is a mark of distinction (like all distinctions, it is valued because it is so difficult to maintain)." Professors' general attitude toward television becomes more pointed when the topic of television violence is discussed; they are quick to assert piously that television is dangerously violent. Among college communication teachers, two-thirds of a 1991 sample of 486 instructors agreed that television "increased aggressive behavior." Of 68 scholars who had published papers or reports specifically on television's effects, 80 percent concurred that television violence produced aggressiveness.

Professors researching television's effects, therefore, seem to occupy a doubly honored position. Not only are they, like their colleagues, performing the crucial service of reproducing the dominant classes, but they also are breathing life into a key issue in the struggle between the dominant and the dominated. They may devote their entire careers to demonstrating the dangers of television violence and are bound to receive approbation from the dominant class as a result. No wonder the position of television effects researcher has proven so attractive.

Yet when a given skirmish over violence has exhausted itself and a lull sets in, members of the dominant class revert to their un-self-conscious viewing of televised mayhem. Even college professors watch TV. During one lull in the violence debate, a 1982 study found that media professors did not restrict their children's viewing any more than the rest of the population did.

## Us vs. Them

Perhaps the most striking conflict concealed in the debate over television violence involves the fabrication and control of "the Other." The best-known treatment of the concept of the Other is Edward Said's *Orientalism* (1978). The Orient, argued Said, was one of Europe's "deepest and most recurring images of the Other." It was "almost a European invention" that served as "a Western style for dominating, restructuring, and having authority over the Orient." Superiority over the Other was one motive for this phenomenon; another was self-definition. "The Orient," Said wrote, "has helped to define Europe (or the West) as its contrasting image, idea, personality, experience."

Thus the Other, the "not-us," is a fabrication used both to regulate those classified as the Other and to distinguish the culture of those doing the classifying. It is also a mechanism for emphasizing differences and disregarding similarities in order to maintain group solidarity. The Other differs conceptually from the mass in that the mass can be a part of "us," even if a discredited part, whereas the Other remains outside.

In the United States, the Other is often primarily a Dark Other—blacks and, to a lesser extent, Hispanics. The Dark Other is the recipient of an undeniable assault that plays out in racially charged terms. One form of the assault on the Dark Other is the War on Drugs. This "war" promotes definitions of legal and illegal drugs that have favored whites at the expense of the Dark Other; alcohol and prescription tranquilizers (both of whose records of extensive abuse and human damage are well documented) enjoy legal protection, whereas drugs associated with black culture, such as marijuana and cocaine (the health effects of which, on examination of the data, appear to be negligible), are proscribed. Of course, there is nothing inherent in these drugs that allocates them to the legal or illegal categories. These allocations are socially determined.

The anti–television violence crusades are part of this same assault. People do not worry about their own viewing of violent shows, and in fact they are so at peace with it that they are less likely to acknowledge the violence at all. They worry extensively, however, about what the Dark Other is watching. As British media scholar David Buckingham noted in 1997, "Debates about the negative effects of the media are almost always debates about other people."

"People like us" project a scenario onto the Dark Other in which viewing entertainment violence leads to real-life criminal behavior. This scenario is false in every detail—there exists no uniform Dark Other, and symbolic violence does not produce aggression—but it is upheld due to the emotional conviction behind it and the handy availability of rationalizing "scientific proof." Fears of the Dark Other—fears of difference, of being preyed on, of having one's culture overturned, of invalidating one's identity—are denied expression elsewhere but are allowed to sneak into the attack on television violence. In this way, the Dark Other, his culture, his viewing habits, and his behaviors are disparaged.

There is a curious twist to all this, however—a complexity revealing much about the intricacies of social life. Whereas whites push off the Dark Other with vigor, at the same time they subtly beckon him back. Cultural theorists Peter Stallybrass and Allon White observe that whatever is excluded and displaced to the Other then becomes an object of fascination and is summoned back. The desire for cultural homogeneity produces instead a heterogeneous mix. Thus whites are fascinated by the music, dance, clothing styles, and behavior of blacks. Whites study black athletes, seeking to learn about the prowess of the Other. Whites welcome black entertainers, even when (or especially when) black actors are involved in violent scenarios.

## Old vs. Young

Adults who enlist in the anti-television crusade always insist that it is "impressionable youths" whom they wish to protect. In the guise of shielding youths, however, adults are trying to contain and control them.

This generational conflict emerges in contemporary polls: A 1997 survey by Steve Farkas and Jean Johnson of 2,000 randomly selected American adults found them ill disposed toward both younger children and adolescents. The majority of respondents used harsh terms to characterize 5-to-12-year- olds, such as "lacking discipline," "rude," and "spoiled." Two-thirds of the respondents were very critical of teenagers, calling them "irresponsible" and "wild." According to the report, "Most Americans look at today's teenagers with misgiving and trepidation, viewing them as undisciplined, disrespectful, and unfriendly." Six hundred teenagers were also surveyed, however; they viewed things differently. Most felt happy in their lives and in their relationships with adults. These discrepant attitudes indicate much about the essential nature of generational strife —of who deprecates whom.

Antagonism toward the young can be especially strong in an adult population configured like that of the United States—one that is aging rapidly due to the baby boom phenomenon. As subculture researcher Dick Hebdige observes, in the consciousness of adult society, "Youth is present only when its presence is a problem, or is regarded as a problem." Overall, adults feel threatened by the next generation.

Social scientist Charles Acland has argued that "youth's complex relationship with popular culture as a live and expressive domain is menacing because the uses of culture cannot be policed completely." With adults able only partially to supervise the "menace" of popular culture, children and adolescents turn to their television shows, their movies, their computer games, and their music as an escape from adult restraint. Passing through a difficult stage in life, indeed perhaps the most strenuous one of all, youths turn to television violence for the vicarious release it can offer.

The consumption of symbolic violent content correlates negatively with age. According to a 1993 study commissioned by the Times Mirror Center for People and the Press, age is the single most significant factor in the viewing of television violence: Younger viewers watch much more than do older viewers. Cultural critic James Twitchell suggests that "if you study the eager consumers of vulgarities, you will soon see that this audience is characterized not so much by class (as we tend to assume, due in part to Marxist interpretations of the culture industry) as by maturity."

Youths do not think it probable that there could be any transfer from television's violence to aggression in the real world; of all age groups, they are the least likely to believe there is a connection. Elizabeth Kolbert, a *New York Times* reporter, interviewed three teenage felons on the subject in 1994 and noted, "The three teenagers . . . all scoffed at the notion that what young people see on the screen bore any relation to the crimes they committed."

## Weaker vs. Stronger

There are at least two cases where the anti-television crusade allows a weaker group to mount an attack against a stronger target. The first relates to the struggle between masculinity and femininity. As the male expresses dominion and the female resists it, everything in culture becomes gendered, or has reference to gender. This pervasive rivalry would be expected to find its way into the anti-television campaign as another camouflaged conflict between the dominant and the dominated, but in this instance the thrust is completely reversed. That is, when the struggle between genders enters into the debate over television violence, it does so as an act of resistance by the female against the male—as a small counterstrike.

The power of males is most pointedly realized in the violence some of them direct toward women. Alert to the chance of male animosity, women are prone to feeling wary of violence even in its flattened, symbolic form on the television screen. The figment may draw too close to the real thing, whether experienced or imagined, to permit the degree of unimpeded pleasure that male viewers might enjoy. In surveys females are more likely than males to report there is "too much violence in television entertainment" and have been so since the general question was first asked in 1972. When queried about the amount of violence on specific action programs, women viewers will perceive more of it than will men, presumably because of their awareness of and uneasiness about the vicious content.

The recurring moral crusade against television violence affords women a choice opportunity for retribution. Seemingly untainted by any overt hostility on its own part, the movement to purify televised entertainment, one that all agree is to be rhetorical only, seems to be shielded from any possibility of retaliatory strikes. How much contention against males is bound up in the 1994 assertion of Barbara Hattemer, president of the National Family Foundation, that "as media violence is absorbed into a person's thoughts, it activates related aggressive ideas and emotions that eventually lead to aggressive behavior"? How much gender strife is exposed in the hyperbolic 1996 statement of

Carole Lieberman, chairperson of the National Coalition Against Television, that "more lives are damaged or destroyed by the effects of on-screen violence than by any other medical problem"? She has forgotten heart disease, cancer, and other maladies, and she has done so for a particular reason.

The second case of a counterstrike against a stronger group involves religion. Many of the groups organized in opposition to television violence have religious ties. Here, neither the contestants nor their motives are camouflaged. The partisans on the attacking side are explicit and vociferous; they stand for religiosity, conservative beliefs, and "family values," and they are against licentiousness, media excesses, and symbolic violence. Those under attack—the entertainment industries and, by extension, all sorts of permissive people—respond first with incomprehension and then with annoyance, wishing the conservative and fundamentalist contingent would disappear. It would be easy for the political left to ignore the religious right if the latter did not comprise a well-defined and adamant voting bloc.

This cultural axis could hardly be more different from class antagonism. Social classes are stacked from bottom to top. Here, the axis and its poles can be understood as horizontal, stretching from the most conservative to the most free-thinking. Those gathered at the conservative and evangelical pole come from a wide range of social strata, although they are frequently depicted by their opponents as occupying lower-status positions exclusively. Seeking certainty in the literal word of the Bible, often believing in creationism and patriarchal traditions, and adhering to longstanding customs and attitudes, those clustered at this pole are often moved to take issue with the novelties of social transitions and the uncertainties of modern life.

Fundamentalists rail against the expanding, heaving tableau of television violence, and in organized fashion they strike out against it. The American Family Association (AFA), headed by the Rev. Donald Wildmon, has objected strenuously to video carnage. In 1993 Randall Murphree, editor of the association's *AFA Journal,* wrote: "Violence on the small screen continues to invade America's homes as television offers more graphic murders, bloodier assaults, and general mayhem. And all the while, the dramatic effects on society grow more and more alarming." In 1997 the AFA announced that, by its count, violent incidents in prime time network programs had increased 31 percent from the previous year—an increase far in excess of those measured by other monitors. As an example of the AFA's activities, in August 1997 its "Action Alert" roused its members to contact CBS and "express your concerns about their dangerous agenda of expanding the limits of violence on television through [the cop drama] *Brooklyn South.*"

The issue of television violence affords groups such as the AFA the sanctioned opportunity to carry out a cultural attack—to have at their opponents, to condemn immoral depictions and the entertainment industry that produces and distributes them. Doing so, fundamentalism affirms its presence to others through an issue that is allowed to capture media attention and affirms its role to itself as a guardian of traditional mores. Television violence allows conservative forces the opportunity to carry their standard forward.

As religious conservatives react negatively to social changes of greater and lesser profundity, they may be performing an important service for American civilization. American culture is venturing into areas rarely if ever visited before, and never on such a large scale (for example, in matters of widespread individuality or of social inclusiveness). Some sort of conservative movement may prove useful, much like a sea anchor during turbulence, for steadying the vessel of culture.

## The Big Lie

The widely held belief that television fantasy violence stimulates aggression in the real world and should be censured is what propaganda experts might call "a big lie"—a grotesque fabrication to which all unreflectingly subscribe. What makes this particular big lie different from the propagandists' is that it is not bestowed on an acquiescent population by some cabal; rather, this is one that we all repeatedly tell one another, duping ourselves as we dupe others. We do this for reasons of convenience: By repeating this uncontroverted big lie with ever-increasing volume, we can easily vent some of our own hostilities regarding other, truly confounding social conflicts.

While censure is generally directed by the stronger party toward the weaker, in some instances it flows in the opposite direction. Within the gender wars, and in the invectives of the religious right, condemnations are directed by weaker parties toward stronger targets. But whether the chastising energy flows from the stronger toward the weaker or from the weaker toward the stronger has nothing to do with the actualities of television violence.

Whatever its immediate source, the energy that breathes life into the whipping boy of television violence has its ultimate origins in fear— fear of disorder that, in the extreme, could overturn society. As Charles Acland has written, "A society is always concerned with normalization, with the organization of its order, to assure the continuation of its structures and distribution of power." Although social order is a perpetual preoccupation, at this point in history it would seem to be an obsessive one; witness the outsized emphasis on the containment of crime at a time when crime is on the decline and the reckless hysteria of the War on Drugs. Sociologist Graham Murdock refers to the "fear about the precarious balance between anarchy and order in the modern age." Exactly why this fearful fixation on social order should be occurring now is open to question. Its existence, however, should not be doubted. Indeed, the need to strengthen social controls has a correlate in Americans' increasing imposition of self-controls: Per capita alcohol consumption and cigarette smoking have been on the decline and health club memberships on the rise for most of the past 30 years.

Television is new enough that it is not embraced without reservations, and it has not yet accumulated the social equity that would allow it to be shielded by nostalgia. In addition to its relative novelty, it is enormous, filling up the day (television viewing trails only work and sleep in terms of expended time), and can be menacing on this count. Because everyone has access to television, its use cannot be regulated, and thus for those who want to control it, the medium is believed to be out of control and threatening. The rise of television, observes media scholar Richard Sparks, "has been taken to signify the drift of history beyond willed control or direction. The censure of television bears witness to the fear of the future."

General apprehension about the course of history is in several senses the opposite of video violence—the passivity of fear vs. the frenzy of aggression, the amorphous vs. the detailed, and the actual vs. the symbolic. The two find each other as if magnetized, whereupon the flaying of the whipping boy begins.

# POSTSCRIPT

## Is Television Violence Viewing Harmful for Children?

Almost everyone has access to television if they so choose. There is hardly any other medium so pervasive in American society as television. What is the relationship of television viewing to violent acts? Those who believe that television viewing is the root of all evil support unplugging the "boob tube" and going back to the good old days of reading, listening to the radio, and swapping stories while sitting by the fireplace. At the other end of the continuum, those that argue that television is merely the next evolution of communication technology would promote "going with the flow," grinning and bearing television –for it is surely here to stay–and stop worrying about it. After all, they say, television is ultimately harmless; it cannot make you do anything you do not want to do.

What should be done to effectively address this problem? Is it realistic to revert back to the days prior to the television era? Or should we just relax and stop worrying about the effects of television? After all, many say, children are resilient; they will eventually come to terms with TV's impact on their lives. How much truth lies in Johnson's contention that children's television viewing of violent behavior is associated with antisocial behavior later on in life? Is it more a matter of parental involvement with their children while they are watching television than *what* children watch? Would it be an overreaction to more closely censor television programming? Would programming quality then be forfeited? How should we respond to Fowles's contention that television is being used as the simple explanation for societal violence when the reason is much more complex?

School-aged children are the most targeted when it comes to television advertising. There are more commercial breaks per hour for this type of programming than for others. Additionally, with the widespread access to cable television, children have ever-increasing access to adult programming, many times in unsupervised homes. Some research suggests that although children who spend excessive amounts of time watching television tend to do poorly in school, others who spend a moderate amount of time in front of the set perform better scholastically than those who watch no television at all. Logically, there must be middle-ground solutions to the issue of children, television viewing, and violence.

Perhaps if parents could accept the inevitable, that television is not only here to stay but viewing choices are expanding almost daily, then society could move past this dichotomy of thinking of television as simply good or bad. Television viewing could be thought of as an active endeavor rather than a passive one. Parents could become more involved with their children as they watch television. Through modeling, parents could teach children to be skeptical about television advertisements, point out the differences between fantasy and reality, and explain that the moral values being portrayed on the tube are different from values that are important to the parents.

On the other hand, it is true that television viewing can be overdone. Children who watch TV excessively versus play actively are more likely to be overweight. If children are watching TV to excess, they are not communicating with adults in the family; they are not learning family values but values portrayed on TV. Studies that provide information on violence and its causes can lend additional insight into the role that a variety of societal factors play in perpetuating violence.

# On the Internet . . .

## Council of Chief State School Officers

Officials who head the departments of elementary and secondary education in the United States develop policy and consensus on major education issues, which the Council of Chief State School Officers advocates before the president and Congress. Resources on the council's involvement in a number of issues, from bilingual education to improvement in science and math opportunities, are provided at this site.

http://www.ccsso.org

## National Institute on Out-of-School Time

Directed by the Wellesley College Center for Research on Women, this National Institute on Out-of-School Time project aims to improve the quality and quantity of school-age child care nationally.

http://www.wellesley.edu/WCW/CRW/SAC/

## Family: Single Parenting

This Single Parenting page of ParentsPage.com focuses on issues concerning single parents and their children. Although the articles cover issues concerning single parents of children from infancy through adolescence, most of the articles deal with middle childhood.

http://www.parentsplace.com/family/singleparent/

## National Black Child Development Institute

At this site, the National Black Child Development Institute provides resources for improving the quality of life for African American children through public education programs.

http://www.nbcdi.org

## Common Sense Parenting

This Common Sense Parenting Web site offers parenting tips, answers questions, and lists books and videos that can be ordered through Boys Town, USA. A free parenting booklet, available in both English and Spanish, can also be ordered online.

http://www.parenting.org

# PART 3

## Middle Childhood

*Middle childhood, or school age, is the period from ages five through twelve. The rate of a child's growth generally declines until the later part of this stage of development. Perhaps the most important experience during middle childhood is schooling. As a child progresses through this stage, new significant others outside the family emerge in the child's life. Children gain a broader understanding of the similarities and differences among them. The peer group (especially same-sex peers), teachers, and media personalities take on increased importance for the child. This section examines issues related to schooling, language development, and self-care.*

# ISSUE 9

## Are Boys Better in Math Than Girls?

**YES: Carol J. Mills, Karen E. Ablard, and Heinrich Stumpf**, from "Gender Differences in Academically Talented Young Students' Mathematical Reasoning: Patterns Across Age and Subskills," *Journal of Educational Psychology* (vol. 85, no. 2, 1993)

**NO: American Association of University Women**, from *How Schools Shortchange Girls: A Study of Major Findings on Girls and Education* (American Association of University Women, 1992)

### ISSUE SUMMARY

**YES:** Carol J. Mills, Karen E. Ablard, and Heinrich Stumpf, associates of the Center for Talented Youth Research at Johns Hopkins University, argue that boys perform better than girls on tests for math reasoning ability.

**NO:** A report developed by the Center for Research on Women at Wellesley College for the American Association of University Women concludes that the differences in math achievement between boys and girls are not significant and are narrowing.

You may have heard the common assertion that "boys are better in math and girls are better in verbal skills." Does being born male automatically predispose a child to greater mathematical acuity? Are girls fated to go through life with perpetual math anxiety? Research results are divided on the question of gender and math ability. There are a number of studies that report that boys outperform girls in math. Other reports, based on analyses of over 100 studies, conclude that girls and boys perform equally on math tests.

Some of the reasons for the conflicting conclusions are due to the sample populations studied and the math skills that were tested. Some researchers argue that because boys are more likely to drop out of school than girls, the pool of boys and girls tested may be unequal. The boys left in school might be more likely to be above-average students than the girls. A boy's prior knowledge is also considered to be advantageous. For example, if boys are placed in more accelerated math courses than girls, they will probably perform better on standard math tests.

On the other hand, some researchers contend that there are no real differences in boys' and girls' ability or achievement in math. Math acuity could be more of a self-fulfilling prophecy issue. Boys are expected to be better in math and girls are not. So discrepancies in mathematical performance might simply be the result of children living up to expectations.

In the following selections you will read conflicting conclusions based on similar research studies. Carol J. Mills, Karen E. Ablard, and Heinrich Stumpf conclude that there are clear and distinct differences in boys' and girls' math ability. The report of the American Association of University Women draws the opposite conclusion, that there are no gender differences when it comes to mathematics.

**Carol J. Mills, Karen E. Ablard, and Heinrich Stumpf**

# Gender Differences in Academically Talented Young Students' Mathematical Reasoning: Patterns Across Age and Subskills

When a sample of academically talented students in Grades 2–6 was given a test of mathematical reasoning ability, boys performed better overall than girls. The gender differences for mathematical ability appeared as early as 2nd grade in samples tested over a 7-year period but varied somewhat according to mathematical subskills. There were no substantial gender-related differences on tasks requiring students to identify whether enough information was provided to solve a task; however, boys performed better than girls on tasks requiring application of algebraic rules or algorithms, as well as on tasks in which the understanding of mathematical concepts and number relationships was required.

Speculation and research efforts concerning gender differences in cognitive abilities appear to be a "national preoccupation" (Jacklin, 1989). This is particularly true for differences in mathematical and spatial ability, whereas few consistent gender-related differences have been found for verbal ability.

One of the reasons for the tenacious interest in gender differences in mathematical ability is the possible relationship between mathematics performance and academic or career opportunities and performance (e.g., Sells, 1980). Research results suggest that gender differences in mathematical ability may be related to mathematics attitudes (Armstrong, 1985), self-confidence (Eccles et al., 1985; Fox, Brody, & Tobin, 1985), course choices (Benbow & Stanley, 1983), persistence in a mathematics discipline (Casserly & Rock, 1985), and career choices (Subotnik, Duschl, & Selmon, 1991). It has also been suggested that gender differences in ability combined with gender differences on a variety of other variables (including interests, values, and cognitive style) may represent a particularly persistent constraint on equal representation of men and women across a variety of disciplines (Lubinski & Benbow, 1992; Mills, 1992).

General statements on gender differences in mathematical reasoning ability, however, are likely to be misleading because they mask the complexity of the issue. For example, the age at which gender differences first appear and the direction of such differences differ from one study or review article to another.

In general, small but reliable gender differences in favor of boys/men in mathematical reasoning ability have been consistently noted from adolescence onward (Hyde, Fennema, & Lamon, 1990; Maccoby & Jacklin, 1974; Weiner & Robinson, 1986). Some reviewers have concluded that the differences emerge only in the last 2 or 3 years of high school (Hyde et al., 1990; Meece, Parsons, Kaczala, Goff, & Futterman, 1982; Stage, Kreinberg, Eccles, & Becker, 1985).

Studies reporting gender differences at an earlier age (elementary school) have been based primarily on findings from achievement or knowledge tests as opposed to ability tests (Dossey, Mullis, Lindquist, & Chambers, 1988; Marshall & Smith, 1987). Some of these studies with younger students also have reported girls scoring higher than boys (Hilton & Berglund, 1971; Marshall & Smith, 1987). Overall, the point at which gender differences first appear and the direction they take seem to depend on the content and cognitive demands of the items used.

The appearance and nature of gender differences may also depend on the particular characteristics of the population studied. For example, gender-related differences in favor of boys/men appear to be even more pronounced in academically talented populations. In very select but large samples tested over the past 11 years, boys have consistently scored higher as a group than girls on the mathematics section of the Scholastic Aptitude Test (SAT) as early as the seventh grade (Benbow, 1988; Benbow & Stanley, 1980; Durden, Mills, & Barnett, 1990).

Such differences in mathematical reasoning ability have not been clearly established, however, in academically talented samples at an earlier age. One of the obstacles in the past to such an endeavor has been the belief that the existing mathematical reasoning tests were inappropriate for assessing the ability in younger children (Benbow, 1988). The School and College Ability Test (SCAT), however, has been successfully used for a number of years in above-grade-level testing to identify academic talent in students of elementary school age (Durden, Mills, & Barnett, 1990). Because academically talented students, such as those tested in our study, have been shown to exhibit abstract reasoning ability and formal operational thinking at an earlier age than typically found in a general population of students (Ablard, Tissot, & Mills, 1992; Keating, 1975), gender differences may emerge earlier for these students than previous research has suggested. The nature of gender differences in mathematical reasoning ability in an elementary school population of academically talented students was, therefore, a major focus of the present study.

Another important issue surrounding gender differences in mathematical ability is the identification of subskills and the degree to which the performance of male and female students may differ on specific item types. Researchers such as Hyde et al. (1990), Marshall and Smith (1987), and Stage et al. (1985) have found that mathematical ability consists of several subskills, such as computation and problem solving, that differ in their degree of gender sensitivity.

Tests that predominantly measure computational skills are generally found to favor girls/women or show no gender-related differences at all, whereas tests involving the use of mathematical concepts or mathematical problem solving generally favor boys/men (Hyde et al., 1990). In a study of young adults, Klieme (1989) also found that tasks requiring the application of known mathematical algorithms did not show gender differences as large as did tasks requiring mathematical problem solving. These findings emphasize the need to differentiate between achievement or knowledge tests and tests of ability or aptitude. As Marshall and Smith (1987) have pointed out, it is equally important to examine gender patterns in performance on subcategories of items within a given test. This was also a focus of the present study.

The generalizability of all these findings, however, is challenged by the observation of some authors that gender-related differences in cognitive variables, such as mathematical and spatial ability, have declined during recent years (Emanuelsson & Svensson, 1986; Feingold, 1988; Hilton, 1985; Hyde et al., 1990; Linn, 1991; Rosenthal & Rubin, 1982; Stumpf & Klieme, 1989). Other recent studies (e.g., Cleary, 1991; Oosthuizen, 1991; Stanley, Benbow, Brody, Dauber, & Lupowski, 1991), however, have continued to find substantial differences between male and female students in these domains of cognitive functioning, so this matter is not as yet resolved.

In view of the research findings, three major questions were asked in the present study: (a) In a sample of academically talented elementary school children, do boys and girls differ in mathematical reasoning ability? (b) If a gender difference exists, does it differ by age or grade level? and (c) If gender differences are found for overall mathematical ability, does the pattern of results differ by subskills identified in the test of mathematical reasoning ability?

## Method

### Participants

The participants in our study were 2,586 students between 7 and 11 years of age. These students participated in eligibility testing (between 1985 and 1991) for special course work offered to elementary school children by the Center for Talented Youth at the Johns Hopkins University as part of a program introduced in 1985. Information on the racial, ethnic, and socioeconomic background of students attending the courses is obtained on a voluntary basis. Because such information is incomplete, analyses across subsamples are not reported in this article.[1]

All students had scored at or above the 97th percentile for either verbal or mathematical ability or achievement on a nationally normed test (such as the California Achievement Test) administered in their schools. Although all students could be considered academically talented, not all were talented specifically in mathematics. Therefore, we were able to obtain a sample with a relatively wide range of mathematical ability. Indeed, SCAT scores in the sample ranged across virtually all possible standard scores.

## Procedure

Students identified as academically talented by their scores on a nationally normed mathematical or verbal aptitude test took the SCAT to apply for eligibility for advanced-level course work. Because the students had already shown high academic performance on a grade-appropriate test, a more challenging level of the SCAT (a level designed for students at least two grades above the participants' actual grade level) was administered to prevent ceiling effects and to make finer ability distinctions among these talented students. Testing took place in group sessions.

Two equivalent forms (X and Y) and three difficulty levels (elementary, intermediate, or advanced) of the SCAT were administered to accommodate the various age levels[2] and testing dates (Form X for fall administrations and Form Y for spring administrations). To make the scores on these forms and levels comparable, the raw scores were converted to standard scores as specified in the SCAT manual. The results reported here are predominantly based on the standard scores.

## School and College Ability Test

The SCAT is a nationally normed standardized test developed by the Educational Testing Service; the SCAT Series III (Educational Testing Service, 1980) was used in this study. The test has two parts (subtests), verbal and quantitative, each of which consists of 50 items. Although students took both sections of the SCAT, only the results from the quantitative section were of interest for this article.

The quantitative subtest includes tasks covering a variety of content, such as estimation, fractions, proportions, and geometry. All items are quantitative comparison tasks: The student must decide which of two quantities is greater than the other, whether they are the same, or whether there is not enough information available to make a decision.

The questions on the SCAT III place minimum emphasis on reading and require more resourcefulness and insight than traditional computation items. Although some knowledge of arithmetic operations is necessary to answer the items correctly, no actual computations are required on the test. In fact, students who take the time to do the computations typically do less well and often do not complete the test within the time allowed. Because an "out-of-level" version (i.e., above the student's grade level) of the SCAT was administered to this group of students, thereby ensuring that most of them had not been formally exposed to many of the operations and concepts dealt with in the test, it seems reasonable to consider it a measure of high-level reasoning and problem-solving ability for this sample. Three sample items from the test are presented in the Appendix [at the end of this selection].

The SCAT Series III used in this study represents revisions of the SCAT Series II tests. It has been widely used since 1980 to assess the verbal and quantitative aptitude of 3rd- through 12th-grade students in both public and private schools (Educational Testing Service, 1980). In addition, a number of school districts currently use the SCAT to identify academically talented students for special programs.

The SCAT has been shown to predict scores on the SAT reasonably well (Educational Testing Service, 1980). In addition, the SCAT has successfully predicted how students progressed in advanced-level mathematics and humanities courses offered by the Center for Talented Youth over the past 7 years (Durden et al., 1990; Mills & Ablard, 1992). For more detailed psychometric evaluations of the SCAT, the reader is referred to Ahmann (1985) and Passow (1985).

## Results

Score differences for gender, grade level, and year of testing were examined for statistical significance with analyses of variance (ANOVAs). The regression approach within the Statistical Package for the Social Sciences (Norusis, 1988) was used for the ANOVAs. In this approach, all effects are assessed simultaneously, and each effect is adjusted for all other effects in the model. Given the occasionally observed difference in variance for male and female students, a test for homogeneity of variance (Cochran's test) was conducted. The results of this test indicated that the two variances were not significantly different ($C = .55$, $p > .001$). Because the sample was very large, a conservative criterion ($p < .001$) for classifying a difference as significant was adopted for all statistical tests.

In addition to the significance tests, the formula for unequal variances (Cohen, 1977, p. 44) was used to obtain effect-size estimates (*d* coefficients) for the differences between various groups. These estimates were useful for comparisons among group differences within the present study, as well as for comparisons with findings reported in the literature.

### Grade Level

A 2 (gender) × 5 (grade level) ANOVA conducted for the quantitative subtest revealed significant main effects for gender and grade level, $F(1, 2576) = 99.10$, $p < .001$, and $F(4, 2576) = 448.62$, $p < .001$, respectively. The Scheffé test revealed that boys performed better than girls across all grade levels and that performance increased with grade level for both boys and girls. The interaction effect for gender and grade level on mathematical reasoning performance, however, was not significant, $F(4, 2576) = 0.76$, $p > .05$, indicating that the gender effect did not vary across grade level.

The largest gender difference (for the fifth graders) was about one half of a standard deviation. Even among the youngest students, the second graders, the scores of the boys were higher than those for girls, as documented by means that differ by more than one third of a standard deviation. In view of the previous studies with young subjects (as summarized by Hyde et al., 1990), this finding suggests that gender differences in mathematics ability, at least in a population of highly able students, appear much earlier than thought and are relatively consistent across age levels.

### Mathematical Subskills

Previous research has shown that the concept of mathematical reasoning ability can be broken down into concepts of more specific subskills required to solve mathematical problems. These subskills have been found to vary in the amount of gender-related differences they show (e.g., Hyde et al., 1990; Klieme, 1989). Higher level problem solving and understanding of mathematical concepts are believed to be more gender sensitive than computational skills, for which there is no difference at all or a slight superiority for females (Hyde et al., 1990). Factors underlying students' performance on the SCAT were examined, as well as the extent to which boys differed from girls on these factors....

Before the scores on the three factors were compared across gender (*t* tests), the factor structures for boys and girls (separately) were compared. Three factors were obtained for both sexes and rotated independently to an orthogonal simple structure. Coefficients of congruence (Harman, 1976, p. 344) were computed for each pair of factors from the two subgroups. These coefficients were .95, .94, and .92 for Factors 1, 2, and 3, respectively, thus indicating that the factor structures are basically the same and that it is meaningful to assume a common factor structure.

Factor 1 was characterized by high loadings of items that required the decision that not enough information was available to solve the task (seven of eight items). Although the items vary in format and content, their common element is that students must evaluate the sufficiency of the available information to solve the tasks. A sample item for this factor is provided in the Appendix as Item 1.

Factor 2 was dominated by tasks requiring the understanding of algebraic operations or handling expressions with an unknown quantity, especially when fractions and decimals were involved. A sample item for this factor is given as Item 2 in the Appendix.

Factor 3 was marked by tasks requiring the understanding of mathematical concepts (e.g., the concepts of whole numbers and even numbers) and relationships among numbers, especially when units, proportions (e.g., percentages), or simple statistics (e.g., the arithmetic mean) were to be evaluated. A sample item for this factor is given as Item 3 in the Appendix.

... [B]oys had higher scores than girls on all three factors, but only the differences on Factors 2, $t(685) = 4.18$, $p < .001$, and 3, $t(685) = 4.76$, $p < .001$, were significant; for Factor 1, $t(685) = 2.50$, $p > .01$. In terms of Cohen's (1977) classification, the differences on Factors 2 and 3 represent small effect sizes.

Although the difference of scores on Factor 1 was not significant, the "not enough information" response (Response D) was itself of interest in terms of differential responding by boys and girls. To determine whether boys and girls differed with respect to deciding whether enough information was available for solving a task, we examined gender differences for hits and false alarms.[3] ...

[B]oys had a slightly higher average of hits and a slightly smaller average of false alarms than did girls. Neither difference was statistically significant. As far as the discrimination score is concerned, however, the mean score for boys was significantly higher than that for girls, $t(685) = 3.53$, $p < .001$. Thus, boys were more accurate overall in deciding whether enough information was given to solve a problem. This male advantage for accurately choosing the not enough information response is obviously related to the slight (but nonsignificant) male advantage on Factor 1.

A final analysis was conducted to investigate a recent suggestion that gender-related differences on tests with time-limits may be related to gender differences in test-taking habits and confidence levels (Goldstein, Haldane, & Mitchell, 1990). Goldstein et al. suggested comparing conventional scores with ratio scores (number of items correctly answered divided by number of items attempted, multiplied by 100).

Using the largest subsample in our study, the students who had taken the intermediate level of SCAT Form X, we computed both the conventional and ratio scores and compared them for boys and girls. On the conventional number-correct scores, boys had a raw score mean of 28.12 ($SD = 8.19$) and girls had a mean of 24.19 ($SD = 7.86$), yielding a $d$ coefficient of .49 for the gender-related difference. On the ratio scores, boys had a mean of 61.76 ($SD = 15.76$) and girls had a mean of 54.56 ($SD = 16.03$), which corresponds to a $d$ value of .45. An examination of the d values reveals that the gender differences in this subsample of students are very similar according to either conventional or ratio scores, and they are consistent with the differences reported for all grade levels. Thus, only a small fraction of the gender differences found in the present study can be explained by the factors mentioned earlier and operationalized by the ratio score.

## Discussion

In contrast to studies that have reported a convergence in mental test scores of male and female students in recent years (Hyde et al., 1990; Linn, 1991), we found gender differences in mathematical ability.[4] We are not alone in our findings, because other recent studies have reported gender differences in mathematical ability (Cleary, 1991; Stanley et al., 1991).

The major purpose of this study, however, was not merely to revisit the gender difference issue but to help clarify and further understand such differences. Although an overall gender difference was found in our study, the more important findings are that (a) this difference was discovered as early as second grade in an academically talented population, (b) the magnitude of the gender difference was approximately the same across five grade levels, and (c) mathematical reasoning ability can be meaningfully broken down into several subsets of skills that differ somewhat in their gender sensitivity.

A unique contribution of our study is the finding of gender differences in mathematical reasoning ability in children at a much younger age than has previously been reported. This result was accompanied by the finding that the differences did not change appreciably across age or grade level.

To understand our findings, it is important to consider several related facts. First, we tested reasoning ability, which is rarely done with young elementary school students. Generally, standardized tests before seventh grade focus on specific knowledge and computational skills (achievement tests). Second, we used equivalent forms of the same test across all age levels, which meant that the type of ability tested did not change. Studies reporting changes in gender differences across age are often plagued by changes in test content, format, or focus when testing different age groups (e.g., Hyde et al., 1990; Marshall & Smith, 1987).

It is also important to consider the advanced cognitive development of the subjects in our study. Gender differences appear to be greatest for tasks involving problem solving and understanding of mathematical concepts that require higher level thinking (Hyde et al., 1990). Such differences generally first appear around the age of 12 years, when most children begin to develop formal operational thinking. Because academically talented students have been shown to exhibit performance indicative of formal operations well before 12 years of age (Ablard et al., 1992; Keating, 1975), it is not surprising that we found gender differences in mathematical reasoning at a younger age than has typically been found.

A side benefit of studying the development of reasoning and problem-solving ability in students who are cognitively advanced may be a resulting better understanding of general developmental patterns of such abilities. With the national push for reform in mathematics instruction to include more of an emphasis on problem solving and higher level reasoning in elementary school, an understanding of when and how gender differences in such skills develop takes on immediate importance.

The results of the factor analysis indicate, once again, that mathematical reasoning is not monolithic but can be broken down into several subskills. Our classification of subskills of mathematical reasoning ability, however, is purely post hoc. It is a description of the demands of various tasks, not an identification of cognitive processes involved in these tasks. More research is needed to arrive at a delineation of the basic cognitive processes underlying the specific subskills that make up mathematical reasoning ability, as well as how boys/men and girls/women may or may not differ in their development and use of such processes.

Although we found gender differences in favor of boys on two of the factors identified in the SCAT, on one factor significant differences did not emerge. This factor (Factor 1) contained mainly items requiring subjects to determine whether sufficient information was present to solve the task. However, in an analysis focusing on the discrimination between hits and false alarms on all not enough information responses given by students in our study, boys were more accurate.

Clearly, an understanding of the pattern of gender differences across subskills within what is called "mathematical reasoning ability" is still incomplete. Examining differences across subskills, however, may ultimately prove to be more useful than considering overall scores for understanding the cognitive development of males and females. A similar approach (Linn & Petersen, 1985) in the area of spatial ability proved to be useful in explaining inconsistencies in the literature. In addition, as Marshall and Smith (1987) suggested, an understanding of possible gender differences in the development of different skills may lead to useful educational recommendations for the teaching of mathematics.

Finally, it has been suggested that differences in test-taking styles and attitudes may be responsible for gender differences on tests exhibiting gender sensitivity (Goldstein et al., 1990). Specifically, researchers have hypothesized that female test takers are at a disadvantage on tests, such as the SCAT, that have time limits. A comparison of conventional and ratio scores, however, revealed that only a small fraction of the gender-related differences observed in this study could be explained by such factors.

One should, of course, never generalize from a select sample such as ours to the general population. One caution discussed recently by Feingold (1992) centers around the frequent finding over the years that the scores of male students on a large number of general ability tests have a larger variance than those of female students. Gender differences in the scores of a group selected from the right tail of the distribution may, therefore, show differences in the means even when the overall means are equal, for the simple reason that more high-scoring male students are likely to be selected than high-scoring female students. This may be one of the reasons why studies with select samples (Benbow, 1988; Benbow & Stanley, 1980, 1983; Hyde et al., 1990; Stanley et al., 1991) generally have found larger gender differences than have been found in a population with a full range of ability levels.

Even when such a generalization is explicitly avoided, however, a gender-related difference among highly talented students in the area of mathematical reasoning ability is a finding that needs to be described and explained in its own right. Although such gender differences in academically talented samples are usually small to moderate in magnitude and are not consistently found for all aspects of mathematical reasoning ability, they are consistently found for overall mathematical reasoning ability. In addition, these differences appear at a relatively young age (i.e., early elementary school), and they seem to be stable across age level and year of testing within a population from which future mathematicians and scientists are most likely to come.

## Notes

1. Most students are from a White or Asian background. African Americans and other minorities constitute a small percentage of the sample. The socioeconomic status of most families is middle class, although scholarships are available for students with financial need.
2. The elementary level of the SCAT (designed for mid-3rd-grade through mid-6th-grade students) was given to 2nd-, 3rd-, and 4th-grade students; the intermediate level (designed for mid-6th-grade through mid-9th-grade students) was given to 4th- and 5th-grade students; and the advanced level (designed for mid-9th-grade through 12th-grade students) was given to 6th-grade students.
3. A hit was defined as correctly responding that not enough information was available to solve the problem, whereas a false alarm was defined as indicating that not enough information was available when, in fact, there was. Both scores were standardized to a mean of 0 and a standard deviation of 1.
4. A trend analysis across years was considered because the data in this study were collected over a 7-year span. Most of the data, however, were collected during the last 5 years, a span considered to be too short for such an analysis.

## References


Ablard, K. E., Tissot, S. L., & Mills, C. J. (1992). *Academically talented students' precocious cognitive development and its predictors.* Unpublished manuscript, Johns Hopkins University, Baltimore.

Ahmann, J. S. (1985). Review of School and College Ability Tests, Series III. In J. V. Mitchell (Ed.), *The ninth mental measurements yearbook* (pp. 1315–1316). Lincoln: University of Nebraska Press.

Armstrong, J. M. (1985). A national assessment of participation and achievement of women in mathematics. In S. F. Chipman, L. R. Brush, & D. M. Wilson (Eds.), *Women and mathematics: Balancing the equation* (pp. 59–94). Hillsdale, NJ: Erlbaum.

Benbow, C. P. (1988). Sex differences in mathematical reasoning ability in intellectually talented preadolescents: Their nature, effects, and possible causes. *Behavioral and Brain Science, 11,* 169–183.

Benbow, C. P., & Stanley, J. C. (1980). Sex differences in mathematical reasoning ability: Fact or artifact? *Science, 210,* 1262–1264.

Benbow, C. P., & Stanley, J. C. (1983). Sex differences in mathematical reasoning ability: More facts. *Science, 222,* 1029–1031.

Casserly, P. L., & Rock, D. (1985). Factors related to young women's persistence and achievement in advanced placement mathematics. In S. F. Chipman, L. R. Brush, & D. M. Wilson (Eds.), *Women and mathematics: Balancing the equation* (pp. 225–247). Hillsdale, NJ: Erlbaum.

Cleary, T. A. (1991, October). *Sex differences in testing.* Paper presented at the invitational conference sponsored by the Educational Testing Service, New York.

Cohen, J. (1977). *Statistical power analysis for the behavioral sciences* (Rev. ed.). San Diego, CA: Academic Press.

Dossey, J. A., Mullis, I. V., Lindquist, M. M., & Chambers, D. L. (1988). *The mathematics report card.* Princeton, NJ: Educational Testing Service.

Durden, W. G., Mills, C. J., & Barnett, L. B. (1990). Aspects of gender differentiation in the Johns Hopkins University Center for Talented Youth. In W. Wieczerkowski & T. M. Prado (Eds.), *Highly talented young women* (pp. 166–185). Bad Honnef, Germany: K. H. Bock.

Eccles, J., Adler, T. F., Futterman, R., Goff, S. B., Kaczala, C. M., Meece, J. L., & Midgely, C. (1985). Self-perception, socializing influences, and the decision to enroll in mathematics. In S. F. Chipman, L. R. Brush, & D. M. Wilson (Eds.), *Women and mathematics: Balancing the equation* (pp. 95–121). Hillsdale, NJ: Erlbaum.

Educational Testing Service. (1979). *School and College Ability Tests: Intermediate Level Form X.* Monterey, CA: CTB/McGraw-Hill.

Educational Testing Service. (1980). *School and College Ability Tests (SCAT III): Manual and technical report.* Princeton, NJ: Author.

Emanuelsson, I., & Svensson, A. (1986). Does the level of intelligence decrease? A comparison between thirteen-year-olds tested in 1960, 1966, and 1980. *Scandinavian Journal of Educational Research, 30,* 25–37.

Feingold, A. (1988). Cognitive gender differences are disappearing. *American Psychologist, 43,* 95–103.

Feingold, A. (1992). Sex differences in variability in intellectual abilities: A new look at an old controversy. *Review of Educational Research, 62,* 61–84.

Fox, L. H., Brody, L., & Tobin, D. (1985). The impact of early intervention programs upon course-taking and attitudes in high school. In S. F. Chipman, L. R. Brush, & D. M. Wilson (Eds.), *Women and mathematics: Balancing the equation* (pp. 249–274). Hillsdale, NJ: Erlbaum.

Goldstein, G., Haldane, D., & Mitchell, C. (1990). Sex differences in visual-spatial ability: The role of performance factors. *Memory & Cognition, 18,* 546–550.

Harman, H. H. (1976). *Modern factor analysis.* Chicago: University of Chicago Press.

Hilton, T. L. (1985). *National changes in spatial-visual ability from 1960 to 1980* (Report No. RR-85-27). Princeton, NJ: Educational Testing Service.

Hilton, T. L., & Berglund, G. W. (1971). *Sex differences in mathematics achievement.* Princeton, NJ: Educational Testing Service.

Hyde, J. S., Fennema, E. F., & Lamon, S. J. (1990). Gender differences in mathematics performance: A meta-analysis. *Psychological Bulletin, 107,* 139–155.

Jacklin, C. N. (1989). Female and male: Issues of gender. *American Psychologist, 44,* 127–133.

Keating, D. P. (1975). Precocious cognitive development at the level of formal operations. *Child Development, 46,* 276–280.

Klieme, E. (1989). *Mathematisches Problemloesen als Testleistung* [Mathematical problem solving as test performance]. Frankfurt: Lang.

Linn, M. C. (1991, October). *Sex differences in educational achievement.* Paper presented at the invitational conference sponsored by the Educational Testing Service, New York.

Linn, M. C., & Petersen, A. C. (1985). Emergence and characterization of sex differences in spatial ability: A meta-analysis. *Child Development, 56,* 1479–1498.

Lubinski, D., & Benbow, C. P. (1992). Gender differences in abilities and preferences among the gifted: Implications for the math-science pipeline. *Current Directions in Psychological Science, 1*(2), 61–65.

Maccoby, E. E., & Jacklin, C. N. (1974). *The psychology of sex differences.* Stanford, CA: Stanford University Press.

Marshall, S. P., & Smith, J. D. (1987). Sex differences in learning mathematics: A longitudinal study with item and error analyses. *Journal of Educational Psychology, 79,* 372–383.

Meece, J. L., Parsons, J., Kaczala, C. M., Goff, S. B., & Futterman, R. (1982). Sex differences in math achievement: Toward a model of academic choice. *Psychological Bulletin, 91,* 324–348.

Mills, C. J. (1992, March). *Gender, personality, and academic ability.* Paper presented at the 15th annual meeting of the Eastern Educational Researchers Association, Hilton Head, SC.

Mills, C. J., & Ablard, K. E. (1992). *Academically talented young students' achievement in an individually-paced mathematics program.* Unpublished manuscript, Johns Hopkins University.

Norusis, M. (1988). *SPSS/PC+ V2.0 Base manual.* Chicago: SPSS.

Oosthuizen, S. (1991). Sex-related differences in spatial ability in a group of South African students. *Perceptual and Motor Skills, 73,* 51–54.

Passow, A. H. (1985). Review of School and College Ability Tests, Series III. In J. V. Mitchell (Ed.), *The ninth mental measurements yearbook* (pp. 1317–1318). Lincoln: University of Nebraska Press.

Rosenthal, R., & Rubin, D. B. (1982). Further meta-analytic procedures for assessing cognitive gender differences. *Journal of Educational Psychology, 74,* 708–712.

Sells, L. (1980). The mathematics filter and the education of women and minorities. In L. Fox, L. Brody, & D. Tobin (Eds.), *Women and the mathematical mystique* (pp. 66–75). Baltimore, MD: Johns Hopkins University Press.

Stage, E. K., Kreinberg, N., Eccles, J. R., & Becker, B. J. (1985). Increasing the participation and achievement of girls and women in mathematics, science, and engineering. In S. S. Klein (Ed.), *Handbook for achieving sex equity through education* (pp. 237–269). Baltimore, MD: Johns Hopkins University Press.

Stanley, J. C., Benbow, C. P., Brody, L. E., Dauber, S., & Lupowski, A. E. (1991). Gender differences on eighty-six nationally standardized aptitude and achievement tests. In N. Colangelo, S. G. Assouline, & D. Ambroson (Eds.), *National Research Symposium on Talent Development* (pp. 42–65). Iowa City: University of Iowa Press.

Stumpf, H., & Klieme, E. (1989). Sex-related differences in spatial ability: More evidence for convergence. *Perceptual and Motor Skills, 69,* 915–921.

Subotnik, R. F., Duschl, R. A., & Selmon, E. H. (1991, April). *Retention and attrition of science talent: A longitudinal study of Westinghouse science talent search winners.* Paper presented at the biennial meeting of the Society for Research in Child Development, Seattle, WA.

Weiner, N. C., & Robinson, S. E. (1986). Cognitive abilities, personality and gender differences in math achievement of gifted adolescents. *Gifted Child Quarterly, 30,* 83–47.

## Appendix: Sample Items From the School and College Ability Test, Intermediate Level

(Instructions and items were taken verbatim from the test; Educational Testing Service, 1979, pp. 6–8.)

Each of the following questions has two parts. One part is Column A. The other part is Column B.

You must find out if one part is greater than the other, or if the parts are equal, or if not enough information is given for you to decide. Then, find the row of spaces on your answer sheet which has the same number as the question. In this row mark:

A if the part in Column A is greater,

B if the part in Column B is greater,

C if the two parts are equal,

D if not enough information is given for you to decide.

Column A

1. The number p if $p + q = 1$
2. A number, if one-half of it is 4
3. 0.11

Column B

1. The number q if $p + q = 1$
2. 5
3. $^{10}/_{11}$

American Association of University Women

# Achievement and Participation: What Do the Data Show?

There is considerable evidence that girls earn higher grades than boys throughout their school careers. Test scores, however, because they measure all students on exactly the same material and are available nationally, are the measures most often used to discuss sex differences in achievement. The latest work on achievement differences presents a rather different picture than much of what has been reported and accepted in the past. The traditional wisdom that girls are better in verbal areas while boys excel in quantitative skills is less true today. Data indicate a narrowing of sex differences in tested achievement on a variety of measures. However, a narrowing of differences is not an absence of differences. Important insights can be gained by looking carefully at the continuing gender gaps in educational achievement and participation. Furthermore, research that looks at sex, race, ethnicity, and socioeconomic status reveals critical vulnerabilities among various groups of girls.

## Verbal Skills: Language Arts and Reading

Research does not entirely support the still-common assumption that girls do better in verbal areas than do boys. Almost twenty years ago Eleanor Maccoby and Carol Jacklin challenged the prevailing view that girls performed better than boys on verbal measures in their early years. However, researchers continued to document that girls outscored boys on tests of verbal ability starting at grade five or six. Recent work indicates that sex differences in verbal abilities have decreased markedly. Researchers completing a meta-analysis comparing earlier studies of verbal abilities with more recent research conclude: "There are not gender differences in verbal ability at least at this time, in American culture, in the standard ways that verbal ability has been measured."

Some researchers argue that girls do have certain verbal advantages but that these are not adequately measured by most tests. Furthermore, although boys have outscored girls on the verbal section of the Scholastic Achievement Test (SAT) since 1972, some suggest this may merely reflect the inclusion of more scientifically oriented items on which boys often perform better than do

From American Association of University Women, *How Schools Shortchange Girls: A Study of Major Findings on Girls and Education* (American Association of University Women, 1992).  Notes omitted.

girls. An additional difficulty with the SAT is that test-takers are not a nationally representative sample; they are a self-selected group.

## Reading

A review of three representative surveys of reading skills indicates a mixed picture. In two major surveys—the National Assessment of Educational Progress (NAEP) and the National Education Longitudinal Survey (NELS)—girls perform better than boys on reading tests. In the High School and Beyond Survey (HSB), boys perform better than girls on reading and vocabulary tests. In all three surveys, the sex differences are very small.

NAEP is the most comprehensive survey of achievement. A congressionally mandated project of the National Center for Education Statistics (NCES), it measures the proficiency of nine-year-olds, thirteen-year-olds, and seventeen-year-olds in a variety of disciplines. In all age groups, girls have consistently received higher test scores in reading and writing since the 1970s. Since 1971, however, boys have made gains relative to girls, particularly in the seventeen-year-old group.

The NELS is a longitudinal survey of eighth-graders also being conducted under the auspices of NCES. The first wave of eighth-graders were interviewed and tested in 1988. Mean test scores for girls were higher than those for boys, although the difference was modest. Girls were less likely to score below "basic" and more likely to be rated as "advanced" when compared to boys. This sex difference is found for all racial and ethnic groups.

The HSB, also sponsored by NCES, is a longitudinal study of high school sophomores and seniors begun in 1980. Contrary to the other studies, boys consistently score better than girls on the HSB reading tests. This is true of sophomores and seniors, and for whites, blacks, and Hispanics. One possible explanation for the differences in these surveys is that sex differences narrow as children grow older. This would be consistent with the very small difference found for seventeen-year-olds in the NAEP and the gains boys make relative to girls in the follow-up of the HSB cohort.

Another explanation is that these differences may reflect differences in the tests given for each survey. The HSB tests were shorter and the NAEP tests much more comprehensive. This could prove to be another case where apparent sex differences may instead reflect test differences rather than differences in the test-takers knowledge or ability.

Even within the NAEP reading test, the performance of boys relative to girls varied, depending on the type of reading exercise. Boys did as well as girls on the expository passages and were most disadvantaged relative to girls in the literary passages. This is consistent with the finding that boys read more nonfiction than girls, and girls read more fiction than boys. This is also consistent with the finding that boys do slightly better than girls on other NAEP tests in subjects requiring good skills in expository reading and writing: civics, history, and geography.

If, as some suggest, boys regard fiction as more "feminine," any advantage girls experience relative to boys in the NAEP may reflect culturally defined biases against boys reading certain kinds of material. It has been suggested that even if the small gender difference favoring girls is *statistically significant,* it may not be *educationally significant.* Boys still do better than girls in almost every other subject tested by NAEP, and the difference in reading scores appears to narrow and possibly even favor boys in older age groups.

Finally, it has also been argued that gender differences in reading favoring girls may be more pronounced among low-achieving or low-income students. This is particularly relevant given the recent heightening of concern about the education of low-income minority boys. An examination of achievement by race, sex, and social class is presented later in this section.

## Writing

Writing skills are tested less frequently. NAEP data do indicate that girls consistently outperform boys on writing-skills assessment. Smaller studies of particular populations do not always support these national findings. A seven-year longitudinal study comparing the development of written language skills of boys and girls from kindergarten through grade six found that—at least in the population studied—neither sex had an advantage over the other.

## Mathematics and Science

The past fifteen years have seen an explosion of research on the relationship between gender and mathematics. While there has been less study on the linkage of gender and science there still is sufficient information to draw preliminary conclusions. However, the usual cautions apply. Most of the research does not break down the data by both race/ethnicity and gender. Furthermore, the interactions of race/ethnicity and gender are rarely studied, and most conclusions based on predominantly white respondents cannot be generalized to women and girls of color.

**Achievement in Mathematics** Gender differences in mathematics achievement are small and declining. Recent meta-analyses have found only very small differences in female and male performance in mathematics. Furthermore, meta-analyses comparing recent research with studies done in 1974 indicate a significant decline in gender differences. The High School and Beyond study of high school sophomores and seniors also shows that gender differences favoring boys in mathematics are declining.

Gender differences in mathematics do exist but are related to the age of the sample, how academically selective it is, and which cognitive level the test is tapping. Indeed these three variables were found to account for 87 percent of the variance in one meta-analysis. For example, no gender differences were found in the problem-solving ability of elementary- and middle-school girls and boys, but moderate to small differences favoring males emerged in high school. Large research studies support these results, finding no gender differences in math performance at age nine, minimal differences at age thirteen, and a larger difference favoring males at age seventeen. The most recent National

Assessment of Educational Progress (NAEP) report finds few gender-related differences in math ability in grades four and eight other than a higher average proficiency in measurement and estimation for boys. However, by grade twelve males showed a small advantage in every content area except algebra.

Larger differences are found at the higher academic and cognitive levels. For example, an earlier NAEP report stated that 8.2 percent of the males but only 4.5 percent of the females were at the highest math levels, while 54 percent of the males and 48 percent of the females could do moderately complex procedures and reasoning. The College Board reports that males in 1988 scored an average of 37 points higher than females on the Level I Math Advanced Placement Test and 38 points higher on the Level II Math Advanced Placement Test. Another study revealed that nearly all differences in math performance between girls and boys at ages eleven and fifteen could be accounted for by differences among those scoring in the top 10–20 percent, with boys more often in the top-scoring groups. However, in classroom work, girls' math grades are as high or higher than boys'.

Gender differences on the SAT-Math have decreased, although they are still large. Between 1978 and 1988 female scores increased by eleven points while male scores increased by four points. However, males still outscored females 498 to 455. The Educational Testing Service does test a demographically matched sample of girls and boys on the Preliminary Scholastic Aptitude Test (PSAT) each year. From 1960 through 1983 gender differences in math from this group declined, although males still slightly outscored females.

A smaller body of research tying both gender and ethnicity to math achievement indicates that the patterns may differ for various groups. A study in Hawaii found non-Caucasian girls outperforming boys in math and outnumbering boys in the highest-achieving groups. Other studies have reported fewer gender differences in mathematics for minority students than for white students.

Gender differences in tests of spatial skills are also declining. For example, a large study found that girls and boys gained equally from instruction in spatial-visualization skills, despite initial differences.

The research results reported here must be examined in light of the achievement of all American students, female and male, in mathematics. An international assessment of the mathematics skills of thirteen-year-olds found United States students scoring below students in the other four countries and four Canadian provinces participating. Korean students had the highest average score (567.8), while the U.S. students scored 473.9. In addition, the most recent National Assessment of Educational Progress reports that more than a quarter of fourth-graders failed to demonstrate the ability to do arithmetical reasoning, and only 5 percent of high school seniors demonstrated the skills needed for high technology or college-level work.

**Achievement in Science** Gender differences in science achievement are not decreasing and may be increasing. While no meta-analyses of studies linking gender and science achievement have been done, the National Assessment of Educational Progress does track science performance. Its results indicate that for nine- and thirteen-year-olds, gender differences in achievement increased between 1978 and 1986, due to the combination of a lag in performance for females and significant increases in the performance of males. According to the NAEP, gender differences in science achievement are largest for seventeen-year-olds, and these differences have not changed since 1978. The areas of largest male advantage are physics, chemistry, earth science, and space sciences.

In addition, gender differences exist at various levels of achievement. NAEP found only 5 percent of seventeen-year-old girls as compared to 10 percent of seventeen-year-old boys scoring at or above NAEP's "highest cognitive level," defined as students' ability to integrate specialized knowledge. Advanced placement (AP) test scores show a similar pattern. The Educational Testing Service reports that in 1988, males scored on average 29 points higher than females on AP biology tests. This, incidentally, was the only science area tested by ETS where gender differences declined; the spread between male and female test scores shrunk eleven points from the forty-point gap measured in 1981. Males also scored about fifty-six points higher than females on the 1988 AP physics tests. However, once again girls receive grades in science that are as high or higher than those of boys.

As with gender differences in mathematics achievement, gender differences in science should be looked at in a larger context. American students, both female and male, are not doing well in science. Their low levels of scientific knowledge, even at the factual level, have been documented in both national and international studies. One international assessment of the science skills of thirteen-year-olds found United States students placing ninth among the twelve nations and provinces participating.

**Mathematics Participation** Gender differences in math-course participation are small, occur only in higher-level courses, and appear to be stable. In 1989 the National Science Board of the National Science Foundation reported that from 1982 to 1987, the average number of math credits that a male high school student received increased from 2.61 to 3.04. During the same time period, the average number of math credits that a female student received increased from 2.46 to 2.93. In 1982 males received .15 more math credits than females; in 1987, .11 more. The National Science Board found that approximately the same percentages of females and males took the same math courses up to calculus, which was taken by 7.6 percent of the boys but only 4.7 percent of the girls. The 1991 NAEP reports that for the District of Columbia and the thirty-seven states participating in the study "Up to Algebra III/Pre-Calculus and Calculus" there were no gender differences in either course-taking or average proficiency. These results are similar to the findings of a 1990 survey by the Council of Chief State School Officers.

**Science Participation** Gender differences in the number of science courses students take are small. However, the pattern of course-taking differs, with girls being more apt to take advanced biology and boys being more apt to take physics and advanced chemistry. In 1989 the National Science Board of the National Science Foundation reported that from 1982 to 1987, the average number of science and computer-science credits a male high school student received increased from 2.25 to 2.69. During the same time period the average number of science credits a female student received increased from 2.13 to 2.57. In both 1982 and 1987, males received .12 more science credits than did females. Another study based on 1987 data reports young women taking .2 fewer science courses than young men (2.93 versus 3.13). Using 1988 data, the National Science Foundation reported girls taking an average of 3.1 science courses compared to boys' 3.3.

All three studies found approximately the same numbers of females and males taking Biology I and Chemistry I but more males taking physics. In 1987 the National Science Board reported 25.3 percent of the males but only 15 percent of the females took physics. This is, however, an improvement. In 1982, 18.2 percent of the males but only 10 percent of the females enrolled in physics.

These results are mirrored by a 1991 survey by the Council of Chief State School Officers. The survey reports that 60 percent of the students enrolled in first-year high school physics are male and that 70 percent of second-year physics students are male.

**Career Plans** Gender differences show up in career plans as well....

High school girls, even those with exceptional academic preparation in math and science, are choosing math/science careers in disproportionately low numbers. A study of Rhode Island seniors found that 64 percent of the male students who had taken physics and calculus were planning to major in science or engineering in college compared to only 18.6 percent of the female students who had taken these courses.

Girls who do go on in scientific fields after high school report that the encouragement provided by their teachers is very important. One study reports that girls who went on to study engineering felt that teachers encouraged them; unfortunately they also felt that counselors discouraged them. Clearly, differential treatment on the basis of sex contributes to the student choices reported here, but there are other factors as well.

**Math and Science Influences** As they grow, girls and boys have different science experiences. Girls are more apt to be exposed to biology-related activities and less apt to engage in mechanical and electrical activities. One study found that by third grade, 51 percent of boys and 37 percent of girls had used microscopes, while by eleventh grade 49 percent of males and 17 percent of females had used an electricity meter. Gender differences in science-related activities may be reinforced in schools if children are allowed always to select science topics based on familiarity or interest.

Eighth-grade boys have been found to use more science instruments in class, particularly physical-science tools, such as power supplies. Although nine-year-old girls express interest in many science activities, they do not *do* as many as boys. This gender difference continues through ages thirteen and seventeen and is paralleled by an increasingly negative view of science, science classes, and science careers on the part of girls.

Gender differences in confidence are strongly correlated with continuation in math and science classes. Math confidence is the surety a student has of her or his ability to learn and perform well in mathematics. Math confidence has been found to be more highly correlated with math performance than any other affective variable.

Females, more than males, have been found to doubt their confidence in math. The Educational Testing Service reports that gender differences in perceptions of being good at math increase with age. Third-grade girls and boys think they are good in math in about the same percentages (64 percent versus 66 percent); by seventh grade, 57 percent of the girls agree, compared to 64 percent of the boys; by eleventh grade the gap widens to 48 percent of girls versus 60 percent of boys. In a classic study, researchers Elizabeth Fennema and Julia Sherman found a strong correlation between math achievement and confidence. Their research revealed a drop in both girls' math confidence and their achievement in the middle-school years. The drop in confidence *preceded* a decline in achievement.

One result of this diminished confidence is a lowering of the role that competence plays in girls' decisions about continuing in math and science. Researchers have found that competence is a more important prerequisite for the attainment of male career ambitions than it is for females. That is, females and males abandon math and science for different reasons. Males who drop out of math and science tend to do so because of a lack of competence—they cannot do the work; many females who drop out do so even though they can do the work.

Other researchers have also found that males are more apt than females to attribute their success to ability, while females are more apt to attribute failure to lack of ability. As boys get older, those who do not like math are more likely to attribute this feeling to the subject itself: they don't like math, they say, because it is "not useful." Girls, instead, interpret their problems with math as personal failures.

Concern about the difficulty or competitiveness of the field can also be an issue. One study found that the perceived competitiveness of engineering was seen by girls as a major barrier to women entering the field. This finding is supported by research that shows girls who see themselves as highly competitive to be more interested in taking math and science courses than other girls. For boys, the degree of competitiveness is not related to interest in taking math and science.

While most students who dislike math do so because they consider it too hard, most students who dislike science say science is "not interesting." Adolescent girls are more likely than adolescent boys to find science uninteresting. Adolescent boys are more likely than girls to discount the importance of science itself.

In general, students' interest in and enthusiasm for math and science decline the longer they are in school. The poll commissioned by the American Association of University Women in 1990 found that all students' enthusiasm for math and science was greatest in the elementary years and dropped as they got older. However, losses for girls were larger than were those for boys.

In addition, males are more apt than females to envision themselves using math as adults. In assessing what factors they used to decide whether or not to continue math study, students listed the usefulness of math, followed by their confidence in their ability and their enjoyment of the subject.

Gender stereotyping also appears to influence whether girls persist in mathematics. Data from the National Assessment of Educational Progress indicate that girls who reject traditional gender roles have higher math achievement than girls who hold more stereotyped expectations. Moreover, girls in advanced math classes tend not to see math as a "male" subject.

Meta-analysis of affective variables associated with taking math courses indicate that gender differences are all small with the exception of the view of math as "something men do." Boys see math as very "male." A longitudinal study that tested students at sixth, eighth, tenth, and twelfth grades found that for girls a view of math as "male" was negatively correlated with math achievement at each grade level. This was the only affective variable for which consistent gender differences were found.

## Implications

It is important that equal attention be given to both girls and boys in teaching reading and writing skills. The assumption that boys are in greater need of instruction in these areas should not be made. Furthermore, girls need particular encouragement to read more broadly in nonfiction areas and boys should be encouraged to read more fiction.

The gender gap is closing in math achievement but not in science achievement. Issues of gender and math have received more attention than issues of gender and science. Much of the work that has been done in science—beyond counting who is taking what courses—has been done in biology, a field in which there are many women, as opposed to physics, a field with very few women.

Since the growing gender gap in science is clearly related to males' climbing test scores, we need to ask why reforms in science education are apparently working for males and not for females. Just as the SAT-Math has been studied and found to underpredict women's achievement, science tests need to be checked for bias as well.

Building on the work done in math, we need to study more fully the possible causes of the gender gap in the sciences. Particular emphasis should be placed on issues of confidence.

Once students satisfy math and science requirements for graduation and college admission, gender differences in science and math course-taking emerge. More students are taking more science and math, but at the advanced levels the gender gap remains constant. It appears that messages about math and science as critical assets for later employment have been somewhat successful, at least for middle-school students. However, while we have more girls taking more math and science, the numbers and percentages of girls interested in careers in math and science [are] increasing minimally, if at all. During senior high school and college, female students drop out of the math/science pipeline because they choose not to pursue scientific careers.

Changing the public images of physics and chemistry to reflect the diversity of these fields and the way they tie in to our everyday lives can provide more girls with the "inside information" that daughters of scientists appear to get. Meeting, getting to know, and working with scientists also reduces negative and intimidating stereotypes about the field. Providing students, especially girls, with more real-life experiences with science and scientists may make a big difference.

Teaching methods to decrease or eliminate the gender gaps in math and science already exist. Having students read and try out math and science problems before they are covered in class appears to narrow the "experience" gap between girls and boys, thus helping to reduce gender differences in class performance. Providing a structure in which all students answer questions, pose questions, and receive answers, rather than one that emphasizes target students or those who call out answers loudest, increases girls' opportunities and interest. Girls also respond well to special programs where they work cooperatively in a relaxed atmosphere where math is fun. Such programs significantly increase the number of math and science courses girls take. However, while hands-on experience is more successful than the lecture approach, such experiences must allow sufficient time and opportunities for girls to reach the same level of performance that teachers expect from boys.

Schools can learn much from out-of-school programs that encourage girls in math and science. Girls are not required to take special out-of-school programs. Designers of successful out-of-school math and science programs have learned how to get girls to attend and, more important, how to keep them interested so that they will keep on attending. We need to continue and expand programs like those developed by Girls, Incorporated; the Girl Scouts; and several AAUW [American Association of University Women] branches. These offer unique opportunities for girls to learn together to overcome stereotypes. What's more, such programs also act as laboratories for developing effective techniques to keep girls involved in math and science. We can't rely on these programs alone, however. Compared to the school system, they can reach only small numbers of girls for relatively short periods of time. Since all girls go to school and go for many years, we must focus most of our effort there, incorporating techniques that work for girls throughout our schools, and doing so in ways that continue to work for girls systemwide.

# POSTSCRIPT

## Are Boys Better in Math Than Girls?

Mills, Ablard, and Stumpf tested mathematical reasoning ability in children in grades two through six. They found that boys performed better than girls at all five grade levels. This particular study differs from previous studies in that gender differences were found as early as second grade. This had not been previously reported. The researchers also found that math ability differences were more evident in academically talented students.

The AAUW report concluded that an analysis of studies done since 1975 shows that gender differences in math achievement have narrowed. Gender differences that do exist depend on the ages of the students tested, how academically selective the sample is, and what cognitive level the test is tapping. Math achievement and ability are correlated with confidence. Girls report having less confidence in their math ability and thus do not perform as well on math tests. In addition, because there are fewer girls in advanced math classes, they are not exposed to the same type of math education as boys.

When girls have trouble in math, is it considered normal? Why is there controversy over girls being discriminated against in math when boys are more likely to make lower grades in most other subjects, more likely to be in special education classes, and more likely to drop out of school?

What difference does it make if girls and boys differ in math skills? Math ability paves the way for a variety of lucrative careers; could there be a feeling of superiority in being able to master the skills of mathematics? Could this feeling be generalized to other aspects of a person's life? Whether a difference in math achievement is real or perceived, children are being done a disservice if their potential for learning in any subject is not maximized.

## Suggested Readings


Bracey, G. (1994, January). Sex and math revisited. *Phi Delta Kappan, 75,* 417–418.

Byrnes, J., & Takahira, S. (1993). Explaining gender differences on SAT-math items. *Developmental Psychology, 29,* 805–810.

Nichols, R., & Kurtz, V. R. (1994, January). Gender and mathematics contests. *Arithmetic Teacher, 41,* 238–239.

# ISSUE 10

## Are Stepfamilies Inherently Problematic for Children?

**YES: David Popenoe**, from "The Evolution of Marriage and the Problem of Stepfamilies: A Biosocial Perspective," in Alan Booth and Judy Dunn, eds., *Stepfamilies: Who Benefits? Who Does Not?* (Lawrence Erlbaum, 1994)

**NO: Lawrence A. Kurdek**, from "Remarriages and Stepfamilies Are Not Inherently Problematic," in Alan Booth and Judy Dunn, eds., *Stepfamilies: Who Benefits? Who Does Not?* (Lawrence Erlbaum, 1994)

### ISSUE SUMMARY

**YES:** Professor of sociology David Popenoe contends that children from single-parent families and stepfamilies are more likely to have emotional problems and health problems and to do poorly in school than children from intact families with two biological parents.

**NO:** Psychologist Lawrence A. Kurdek maintains that multiple-divorce families, not stepfamilies, differ from two-parent families and that stepfamilies are not inherently problematic for children.

Asking the question, Are stepfamilies inherently problematic for children? triggers memories of the fairy tale "Cinderella," with her wicked stepmother and stepsisters. Although professional family associations such as the National Council of Family Relations and the Stepfamily Association have worked to dispel the Cinderella stepfamily myth, it is still a powerful image. Most people grow up believing that they will marry, have their own biological children, and live happily ever after. This does not always happen. All kinds of events can happen to change the way lives unfold. Changes in physical and mental health, abuse, loss of income, and changing needs of spouses are just a few of the things that can alter the fairy-tale ending of which many people dream.

For the past 20 years divorce has become more common, and, as a result, there is an increasing number of stepfamilies being formed. Most of these families result from divorce and remarriage, but some are formed due to the death of a spouse, single-parent marriage, or other circumstance. Because the research on divorce and stepfamilies is clouded with conflicting findings and research design flaws, how these family forms affect the development of children is also unclear.

Studies of children from divorced families and stepfamilies often take a negative approach. Researchers study what is wrong with the behavior of children from different family types rather than how children have adapted their behavior to survive life transitions. Conversely, society may have become so accustomed to validating divorce and remarriage that the needs of children have become ignored.

In the following selections, David Popenoe and Lawrence A. Kurdek present opposing views on the stepfamily's effect on children. Popenoe proposes that stepfamilies are not a useful alternative to the intact family and that they are a breeding ground for all kinds of problems for children. Kurdek refutes Popenoe's argument with four specific points of his own. He maintains that family life has changed and that family stability for stability's sake is not an appropriate societal value.

**David Popenoe**

# The Evolution of Marriage and the Problem of Stepfamilies: A Biosocial Perspective

One of the fastest growing family types in every advanced industrial nation has been the stepfamily....

Since 1960... the chances of spending part or all of one's childhood outside an intact family have grown dramatically. According to various estimates, the chances that a child born around 1980 will not be living at age 17 with both biological parents have increased to over 50% (Hernandez, 1993).... In 1960, an estimated 83% of all children are living with their two married, biological parents; by 1990, this figure was 58%.... More than 9 out of 10 stepchildren live with their biological mother and a stepfather....

## The Problem of Stepfamilies

Many, and perhaps most stepfamilies today lead contented home lives and produce happy and successful children. But a growing body of evidence suggests that the increase of stepfamilies has created serious problems for child welfare.... Contrary to the view of some social scientists in recent years, who believed that the effects of family fragmentation on children were both modest and ephemeral, there is now substantial evidence to indicate that the child outcomes of these alternative family forms are significantly inferior to those of families consisting of two biological parents. Compared to those in intact families, children in single-parent and stepfamilies are significantly more likely to have emotional and behavioral problems, to receive the professional help of psychologists, to have health problems, to perform poorly in school and drop out, and to leave home early. Moreover, some of these negative effects have been shown to persist into adult life.

Social scientists used to believe that, for positive child outcomes, stepfamilies were preferable to single-parent families. Today, we are not so sure. Stepfamilies typically have an economic advantage, but some recent studies

From David Popenoe, "The Evolution of Marriage and the Problem of Stepfamilies: A Biosocial Perspective," in Alan Booth and Judy Dunn, eds., *Stepfamilies: Who Benefits? Who Does Not?* (Lawrence Erlbaum, 1994).  Notes and some references omitted.

indicate that the children of stepfamilies have as many behavioral and emotional problems as the children of single-parent families, and possibly more (e.g., Kiernan, 1992)....

Certain problems are more prevalent in stepfamilies than in other family forms. A common finding is that stepparents provide less warmth and communicate less well with their children than do biological parents (Thomson, McLenahan, & Curtin, 1992). A number of studies have found that a child is far more likely to be abused by a stepfather than by the biological father.... Compared to children in intact and single-parent households,... "stepchildren are not merely 'disadvantaged,' but imperiled" (Wilson & Daly, 1987, p. 230).

As in single-parent families, a major problem of the stepfamily phenomenon is the net loss of fathering in children's lives.... Many studies have shown that stepfathering acts to diminish contact between original fathers and their biological children (Furstenberg & Nord, 1985; Furstenberg, Nord, Peterson, & Zill, 1983; Mott, 1990; Seltzer & Bianchi, 1988). In their turn, stepfathers take a considerably less active role in parenting than do custodial biological fathers, according to many studies, and frequently become disengaged from their stepchildren following the establishment of a stepfamily....

Another problematic aspect of stepfamilies is their high breakup rate, higher than that of two-biological-parent families. According to the most recent census data, more than 62% of remarriages among women under age 40 will end in divorce, and the more that children are involved, the higher the redivorce rate.... By one estimate, about 15% of all children born in recent decades will go through at least two family disruptions before coming of age (Furstenberg, 1990).

In summary, according to the available evidence, stepfamilies tend to have less cohesive, more problematic, and more stressful family relationships than intact families, and probably also than single-parent families. Put more strongly by a recent article in *Psychology Today*, stepfamilies "are such a minefield of divided loyalties, emotional traps, and management conflicts that they are the most fragile form of family in America" ("Shuttle Diplomacy," 1993).

## Biosocial Bases of Family Life

In order to better understand the special problems that stepfamilies pose, it is necessary to delve into the fundamental biosocial nature of human family life....

From the perspective of evolutionary biology, the organization of the human nuclear family is based on two inherited biological predispositions that confer reproductive success, one that operates between parent and child, and the other between parent and parent. The first is a predisposition to advance the interests of genetic relatives before those of unrelated individuals.... With respect to children, this means that men and women have likely evolved to invest more in children who are related to them than in those who are not....

The second biological predisposition is for males and females to have some emotional affinity for each other beyond the sexual act, and to establish pair bonds. We tend to fall in love with one person at a time. Although we think of love attachments as being highly social in character, they also have a strong biological component. There exists an "affective attachment" between men and women that causes us to be infatuated with each other, to feel a sense of well-being when we are together with a loved one, and to feel jealous when others attempt to intrude into our relationship. Around the world today, almost all adults pair-bond with someone of the opposite sex for at least a portion of their lives, and monogamous relationships are the rule....

One fundamental reason for family instability is that, at heart, human beings are probably more self-interested than truly altruistic, even toward our own relatives and intimates. We act, first and foremost, in the interest of self-survival. But another reason is that the male–female bond, especially when compared to the mother–infant bond, is notoriously fragile. Although marriage is universal, divorce has also been a central feature of human social life....

Possibly the most disintegrating force acting on the human pair bond is the male sexual drive.... Universally, men are the more sexually driven and promiscuous, while women are more relationship-oriented....

## Sexual and Reproductive Strategies

... Biologically, the primary reproductive function for males is to inseminate, and for females is to harbor the growing fetus.... Males, therefore, have more incentive to spread their numerous sperm more widely among many females, and females have a strong incentive to bind males to themselves for the long-term care of their more limited number of potential offspring.

The woman's best reproductive strategy is to ensure that she maximizes the survivability of the one baby she is able to produce every few years through gaining the provision and protection of the father.... The man's best strategy, however, may be twofold. He wants his baby to survive, yes, and for that reason he may provide help to his child's mother. But, at the same time, it is relatively costless to him... to inseminate other women, and thereby help to further insure that his genes are passed on....

Why aren't all men promiscuous cads? Because, in addition to the pull of the biological pair-bonding and parenting predispositions discussed previously, virtually all human societies have established strong cultural sanctions that seek to limit male promiscuity and protect the sanctity of the family....

If a man is to stay with one woman rather than pursue many different women, according to sociobiologists, the "paternal certainty" of his offspring is extremely important. A woman can be certain about her own offspring, but a man cannot be.... [A] male tends to invest in his mate's children only when his paternal confidence is high....

## Cultural Contexts

... During the most recent stages of the development of the human species, rapidly paced cultural evolution has overtaken slow-moving biological evolution as the main force of social change (Hallpike, 1986; Scott, 1989). One result is that family structures around the world today are widely variable, determined more by cultural differences than by biological predispositions. . . .

Associated with the rise of horticultural and agrarian societies was fundamental shift in people's attitudes toward reproduction (Lancaster & Lancaster, 1987). . . .

[W]ith increased density of population and wealth, people came to perceive that resources were limited, that major differentials existed between who survived and who did not, and that survival was very much dependent on who controlled the most resources. It was no longer sufficient merely to rear as many offspring as possible and hope that they would survive to reproduce. Reproductive strategies became individually tailored to maximize the use and control of resources. It was necessary to try to guarantee children access to resources in the form of education or inheritance, for example, so that they would have an advantage over other parents' children.

## Marriage and Divorce in Premodern Societies

The new perception of resource scarcity in complex societies generated a dramatic transformation in family life and kinship relations, including concern for the "legitimacy" of children, the rise of inheritance laws, and the careful control of female sexuality. The nuclear family gave way to the complex, extended family; the conjugal unit became imbedded in an elaborate kinship network. The father role of authority figure and head of household grew in importance, whereas the status of women deteriorated. . . .

Through the institutionalization of cultural norms and sanctions, complex societies have become heavily devoted to socially controlling male and female sexual strategies. The most important social institution serving this purpose is marriage. Marriage can be defined simply as "a relationship within which a group socially approves and encourages sexual intercourse and the birth of children" (Frayser, 1985, p. 248). . . . Throughout most of recorded history, until recently, most marriages were arranged (although the principals typically had a say in the matter); they were less alliances of two individuals than of two kin networks, typically involving an exchange of money or goods.

Various theories have been put forth to explain the fundamental purposes of marriage. But certainly one purpose is, as noted previously, to hold men to the pair bond, thereby helping to ensure high quality offspring and, at the same time, helping to control the open conflict that would result if men were allowed unlimited ability to pursue the "cad" strategy with other men's wives. . . .

## Marriage and Divorce in Urban-Industrial Societies

. . . In urban-industrial societies, reproductive concerns about the quantity of children have largely given way to concerns about quality. Children in these societies require massive parental investments if they are to succeed, and child-rearing has become extraordinarily expensive in terms of time and money. . . .

The modern nuclear family that accompanied the emergence of urban-industrialism and cultural modernity in the West was distinctly different from its preindustrial predecessor. . . . The new family form was emotionally intense, privatized, and child-oriented; in authority structure, it was relatively egalitarian; and it placed a high value on individualism in the sense of individual rights and autonomy. . . .

The big winners from the emergence of the modern nuclear family . . . were . . . children. In preindustrial Europe, parental care of children does not seem to have been particularly prominent, and such practices as infanticide, wet nursing, child fosterage, and the widespread use of lower status surrogate caretakers were common (Draper & Harpending, 1987). . . . Draper and Harpending (1987) suggested that one of the greatest achievements of the modern nuclear family was the return to the high-investment nurturing of children by their biological parents, the kind of parenting characteristic of our hunter-gatherer ancestors. . . .

Family stability during this era, together with parental investments in children, may have been greater than at any other time in history. Cultural sanctions concerning marriage were powerfully enforced, and thanks to ever lowering death rates and low divorce rates, both parents were typically able to see their children through to adulthood. This remarkably high family stability helps to explain why the family situation in the United States today appears so troubled, particularly in the minds of the older generation.

## Recent Family and Cultural Change in America

In the past half century, the U.S. family has been on a social roller coaster. The ups and downs have been quite astonishing. Following World War II, the United States entered a two-decade period of extraordinary economic growth and material progress. Commonly referred to as simply "the 50s," it was the most sustained period of prosperity in U.S. history. Together with most other industrially developed societies of the world, this nation saw improvements in the levels of health, material consumption, and economic security that had scant historical precedent. For most Americans, the improvements included striking increases in longevity, buying power, personal net worth, and government-sponsored economic security.

The 1950s was also an era of remarkable familism and family togetherness, with the family as an institution undergoing unprecedented growth and stability within the middle and working classes. The marriage rate reached an all-time high, the birth rate returned to the high levels of earlier in the century, generating the baby boom, and the divorce rate leveled off. Home, motherhood, and child-centeredness reigned high in the lexicon of cultural values. A higher proportion of children were growing up in stable, two-parent families than ever before in U.S. history.

Beginning in the 1960s, however, a series of unanticipated social and cultural developments took place that shook the foundations of the modern nuclear family. . . . Men abandoned their families at an unprecedented rate, leaving behind broken homes and single-parent, female-headed households. Women relinquished their traditional mother/housewife roles in unexpectedly large numbers and entered the labor force. The percentage of births taking place outside of marriage skyrocketed. Highly permissive sexual behavior became acceptable....

Not only did the modern nuclear family become fragmented, but participation in family life went into a precipitous decline....

Underlying these family-related trends was an extraordinary shift in cultural values and self-definition.... Trust in, and a sense of obligation toward, the larger society and its institutions rapidly eroded; the traditional moral authority of social institutions such as schools, churches, and governments withered. What emerged, instead, was a new importance given by large segments of the population to the personal goal and even moral commandment of expressive individualism or "self-fulfillment" (Bellah, Madsen, Sullivan, Swidler, & Tipton, 1985)....

The institution of marriage was particularly hard hit....

The marriage rate has steadily declined over the past few decades, from 76.7 marriages per 1,000 unmarried women in 1970, to 54.2 in 1990. The divorce rate, although it has leveled off, remains at an historically high level. Marriage has become a voluntary relationship which individuals can make and break at will. As one indicator of this shift, the legal regulation of marriage and divorce has become increasingly lax. In summary, fewer people ever marry, those who marry do so at a later age, a smaller proportion of life is spent in wedlock, and marriages are of a shorter duration (Espanshade, 1985).

... One of the significant attitudinal changes of recent years is the rising acceptance of divorce, especially when children are involved....

The high voluntary dissolution of marriages might not be a serious problem if only adults were involved although, even then, it certainly generates considerable instability and anxiety. The problem is that young children, if they are to grow up successfully, still need strong attachments to parents. The evidence strongly suggests that parental bonds with children have suffered in recent years, and that the tremendous parenting advantages of the modern nuclear family are on the wane....

## The Social Response to Stepfamilies

The decline of marriage and the increase of divorce are, of course, the major contributors to the recent growth of stepfamilies....

It is surely the case, especially in view of the diminution of kinship and neighborhood groupings, that stepfamilies need our collective help and understanding more than ever. But we should not confuse short-run actions aimed at helping stepfamilies with long-run solutions. If the argument presented [here] is correct, and the family is fundamentally rooted in biology and at least partly activated by the "genetically selfish" activities of human beings, childrearing by nonrelatives is inherently problematic. It is not that unrelated individuals are unable to do the job of parenting, it is just that they are not as likely to do the job well. Stepfamily problems, in short, may be so intractable that the best strategy for dealing with them is to do everything possible to minimize their occurrence.

Unfortunately, many members of the therapeutic and helping professions, together with a large group of social science allies, now take the view that the trend toward stepfamilies cannot be reversed....

A close companion to this belief in stepfamily inevitability and optimum fit with a changing society is the view that we should now direct most of our attention toward understanding the familial processes of stepfamilies, and seek to develop social policies and interventions that will assist children's adjustment to them.... Once stepfamilies become more common and accepted, it is argued, and once our society comes to define the roles of stepparenthood more clearly, the problems of stepfamilies will diminish.

This may be a largely incorrect understanding of the situation. The reason why unrelated stepparents find their parenting roles more stressful and less satisfying than biological parents is probably due much less to social stigma and to the uncertainty of their obligations, as to the fact that they gain fewer intrinsic emotional rewards from carrying out those obligations....

If, as the findings of evolutionary biology strongly suggest, there is a biological basis to parenting, we must question the view, widespread in the social sciences, that parenthood is merely a social role anyone can play if only they learn the part....

The biosocial perspective presented in this essay leads to the conclusion that we as a society should be doing much more to halt the growth of stepfamilies. It is important to give great respect to those stepfamilies that are doing their job well, and to provide both assistance and compassion for those that are experiencing difficulties. But such efforts should not overshadow the paramount importance of public policies designed to promote and preserve two-biological-parent families, and of endeavors to reverse the cultural drift toward radical individualism and the decline of marriage.

## References

Bellah, R. N., Madsen, R., Sullivan, W. M., Swidler, A., & Tipton, S. M. (1985). *Habits of the heart: Individualism and commitment in american life.* Berkeley: University of California.

Daly, M., & Wilson, M. (1987). The Darwinian psychology of discriminative parental solicitude. *Nebraska Symposium on Motivation.*

Draper, P., & Harpending, H. (1987). Parent investment and the child's environment. In J. B. Lancaster, J. Altmann, A. S. Rossi, & L. R. Sherrod (Eds.), *Parenting across the life span: Biosocial dimensions* (pp. 207–235). New York: Aldine De Gruyter.

Espenshade, T. J. (1985). The recent decline of american marriage. In K. Davis (Ed.), *Contemporary marriage* (pp. 53–90). New York: Russell Sage Foundation.

Frayser, S. (1985). *Varieties of sexual experience: An anthropological perspective on human sexuality.* New Haven, CT: HRAF Press.

Furstenberg, F. F., Jr. (1990). Divorce and the American family. *Annual Review of Sociology, 16,* 379–403.

Furstenberg, F. F., Jr., & Nord, C. W. (1985). Parenting apart: Patterns of childbearing after marital disruption. *Journal of Marriage and the Family, 47*(4), 893–905.

Furstenberg, F. F., Jr., Nord, C. W., Peterson, J. L., & Zill, N. (1983). The life course of children of divorce: Marital disruption and parental contact. *American Sociological Review, 48*(2), 656–658.

Hallpike, C. R. (1986). *The principles of social evolution.* Oxford: Clarendon.

Hernandez, D. J. (1993). *America's children.* New York: Russell Sage Foundation.
Kiernan, K. E. (1992). The impact of family disruption in childhood on transitions made in young adult life. *Population Studies, 46,* 213–234.
Lancaster, J. B., & Lancaster, C. S. (1987). The watershed: Change in parental-investment and family formation strategies in the course of human evolution. In J. B. Lancaster, J. Altmann, A. S. Rossi, & L. R. Sherrod (Eds.), *Parenting across the life span: Biosocial dimensions* (pp. 187–205). New York: Aldine de Gruyter.
Mott, F. L. (1990). When is father really gone? Paternal-child contact in father absent homes. *Demography, 27*(4), 499–517.
Scott, J. P. (1989). *The evolution of social systems.* New York: Gordon & Breach.
Seltzer, J. A., & Bianchi, S. M. (1988). Children's contact with absent parents. *Journal of Marriage and the Family, 50,* 663–677.
Shuttle diplomacy. (1993, July/August). *Psychology Today,* p. 15.
Thomson, E., McLanahan, S. S., & Curtin, R. B. (1992). Family structure, gender, and parental socialization. *Journal of Marriage and the Family, 54*(2), 368–378.
Wilson, M. I., & Daly, M. (1987). Risk of maltreatment of children living with step-parents. In R. J. Gelles & J. B. Lancaster (Eds.), *Child abuse and neglect: Biosocial dimensions* (pp. 215–232). New York: Aldine de Gruyter.

**Lawrence A. Kurdek**

# NO

# Remarriages and Stepfamilies Are Not Inherently Problematic

My strongest reactions to [professor of sociology David] Popenoe's chapter ["The Evolution of Marriage and the Problem of Stepfamilies: A Biosocial Perspective," in Alan Booth and Judy Dunn, eds., *Stepfamilies: Who Benefits? Who Does Not?*] were disappointment and irritation.... I had expected a critical review of the factors that determine both relationship commitment (e.g., Kurdek, 1993a) and relationship stability (e.g., Kurdek, 1993b) in remarriages involving children. No such review was presented.

Instead, Popenoe uses a biosocial perspective to make sweeping claims about the nature of family life that result in the conclusion that society should do more to halt the growth of stepfamilies....

## Children of Stepfamilies Have as Many Behavioral and Emotional Problems as the Children of Single-Parent Families, and Possibly More

My response to this claim has four parts: (a) comparisons between family structures should include mention of the size of any obtained differences between these family structures, (b) comparisons among divorce-related family structures need to take into account the number of parental divorces experienced, (c) the key family structure comparison involves stepfamilies and single divorced-parent families, and (d) comparisons involving stepfamilies need to consider the structural heterogeneity of stepfamilies. I expand on each of these parts.

In their influential meta-analysis of parental divorce and children's well-being, Amato and Keith (1991) presented information on the nature of differences between children in intact families and children in stepfamilies. True to the pattern Popenoe describes, relative to children in intact families, those in stepfamilies had more conduct problems, lower psychological adjustment, and

From Lawrence A. Kurdek, "Remarriages and Stepfamilies Are Not Inherently Problematic," in Alan Booth and Judy Dunn, eds., *Stepfamilies: Who Benefits? Who Does Not?* (Lawrence Erlbaum, 1994).  Some references omitted.

lower self-esteem.... Although reliable, the differences between the two groups are fairly weak....

Based on evidence from the life events, attachment, and family process literatures, there is reason to expect that the children and adolescents most at risk for behavioral and emotional problems are not those in stepfamilies, but those who have experienced multiple parental divorces and, consequently, multiple parenting transitions. Although evidence on this point is limited, it is consistent.

Studies that have examined the effects of parenting transitions on child and adolescent outcomes have typically compared four groups. These are children living continuously with both biological parents, children who have experienced one parental divorce and live with a single mother, children who have experienced one parental divorce and have made the additional transition to living with a mother and stepfather, and children who have experienced more than one parental divorce. Because of their relatively small numbers, children living with single divorced fathers and children living in stepmother families are usually excluded (see Kurdek & Fine, 1993).

Across a range of outcome variables and sources of information, it is the multiple divorce group—not the stepfamily group—that differs most strongly and negatively from the two-parent group. In fact, few differences emerge between children living continuously with both biological parents and either children living with a singly divorced mother or children living in a stepfather family. These findings lead to the plausible conclusion that what negatively affects children's well-being is not so much the kind of family structure in which they happen to reside, but the history of the quality and consistency of the parenting they receive....

Despite the emphasis Popenoe places on family structure, he fails to recognize that stepfamilies themselves are quite structurally diverse. To his credit, he does note that stepfamilies may result from parental death, parental abandonment, or parental divorce. However, he does not mention that there may be important differences between stepfather families and stepmother families, or that the remarriage history of each spouse may affect the stability of the remarriage. Nor does he state that a joint consideration of the husbands' and wives' parent and custody status relevant to previous marriages leads to at least nine types of stepfamilies, and highlights the distinction between residential and nonresidential stepfamilies, or that a substantial number of children—as many as 300,000 children for women in second marriages alone—are born into stepfamilies (Wineberg, 1992). Given such diversity within stepfamily structures, the general and unqualified claim that stepfamilies are no better than single-parent families is unfounded.

## Stepfamilies Are More Unstable Than Intact Families

Popenoe claims that one problematic aspect of stepfamilies is their high breakup rate. However, a close reading of the limited data on this topic reveals that the findings on this issue are actually inconsistent. Most of the evidence concerns the stability of second marriages. Some of these studies report no difference in the marital stability of second marriers with and without children. Others report slightly higher instability rates for second marriers with children compared to those without children. Still others report that for second-marriers, a slightly increased instability rate occurs only for dissolutions occurring within the first 5 years of remarriage and that the birth of children to a mother in a second marriage increases the stability of that remarriage (Wineberg, 1992).

In short, because stepfamilies are a diverse group, it is misleading to characterize their stability as if they represented a homogeneous group. The current evidence gives every reason to expect that stability rates of remarriages vary by divorce history and parent history of each spouse; length of remarriage; age, gender, and pattern of residence for stepchildren; and whether mutual children are born to spouses in the stepfamily.

## A Biosocial Perspective Leads to the Conclusion That Stepfamilies Are Intractably Problematic

Popenoe claims that in order to understand the special problems posed by stepfamilies, one must consider the biosocial nature of human family life. Based on an evolutionary biology perspective, Popenoe states that the organization of the human nuclear family is based on two inherited biological predispositions that confer reproductive success. The first predisposition operates between parents and children and entails advancing the interests of genetic relatives over those of unrelated individuals. The second predisposition operates between parents and concerns affective attachments between males and females. These seem like reasonable propositions.

Popenoe further notes that family instability can be linked to the fact that human beings are more interested in themselves than in their own relatives, results from men being more sexually driven and promiscuous than women, and that because human pair bonds are fragile, men and women follow different reproductive strategies: Men inseminate as many women as possible, whereas women withhold reproductive access until they can be certain that the male will commit his resources to his offspring.

I see two major problems with using these points to support the argument that childrearing by nonrelatives is inherently problematic. First, Popenoe ignores evidence that although the roles consistent with each gender's reproductive strategy do a reasonable job of accounting for differences between men and women in sexual attraction and mate selection, these same roles actually contribute to relationship problems and relationship instability. In what he termed the *fundamental paradox,* Ickes (1993) noted a tension between what genes predispose us to do in finding a mate and what current culture prescribes us to do in living happily with that mate. That is, although our evolutionary past may account for partner attraction, our cultural present accounts for how nonexploitative, equal partner relationships are established and maintained.

Second, Popenoe does not use the term *paternal investment* very clearly, but I assume he means that biological fathers in stable marriages are directly

—and not just genetically—involved in childrearing. However, most of the normative descriptive data on this topic indicate that although fathers believe they should be directly involved in their children's lives, most are not (Thompson & Walker, 1989)....

Thus, the bystander role played by some stepfathers may be functionally similar to the indirect parenting role played by some biological fathers....

## Family Life in the 1950s Was Better Than Contemporary Family Life

I agree with Popenoe that it is important to place family life within a larger sociocultural context. Further, no one could disagree that divorce rates began to accelerate in the 1960s. However, I strongly disagree with Popenoe's claim that the 1950s were an era of remarkable familism and family togetherness. Certainly, marital stability rates were high at this time in history. Nonetheless, there is ample evidence that stable marriages are not necessarily happy or healthy marriages. In addition, prospective longitudinal studies that have assessed the same group of children when they lived with both parents as well as when they lived with a divorced single parent indicate that the relatively adverse functioning of children who have experienced parental divorce is predicted by conditions in the intact family that existed well before the divorce....

What irritates me most about the claim of familism in the 1950s is that it seems to value marital stability for stability's sake. Home, motherhood, and children did rank high among U.S. cultural values, yet current data on middle-aged persons who were children during this era strongly suggest that what transpired in many of these families belied these values. That is, the culture of the family was at odds with the conduct of the family. How can Popenoe extol the somewhat superficial endorsement of familism during this era in light of evidence that many children in these highly stable families were exposed to an interconnecting web of family conflict, domestic violence, harsh and inconsistent discipline, alcoholism, and, in some instances, abuse and neglect? Two biological parents were physically present in many of these families, but at what cost?

## The Family Is Being Deinstitutionalized

Popenoe rightly notes that marriage as a social institution has evolved in form and function to adapt to new economic, social, cultural, and even psychological settings. But for some reason, Popenoe does not seem to think that the current nature of the institution of marriage reflects this continuous process of economic, social, cultural, and psychological change. One of the most peculiar aspects to Popenoe's chapter is that although he endorses a grand model of change (the biosocial, evolutionary perspective), he urges us as members of society to put an end to a family form that could be viewed as the result of the very economic, social, cultural, and psychological changes that preceded it.

... Like it or not, women are no longer economically dependent on their husbands. Like it or not, women no longer need to define themselves in terms of their social roles as wives and mothers. Like it or not, women benefit from participating in roles other than or in addition to that of mother. Like it or not, men and women are going to renege on vows of lifetime commitments to one person because life with that one person sometimes reaches intolerable limits that could not be foreseen at the time of marriage. Finally, like it or not, as a result of these economic, social, cultural, and psychological dimensions of contemporary life, many children will experience the stresses associated with parenting transitions.

## References

Amato, P. R., & Keith, B. (1991). Parental divorce and the well-being of children: A meta-analysis. *Psychological Bulletin, 110,* 26–46.

Ickes, W. (1993). Traditional gender roles: Do they make, and then break, our relationships? *Journal of Social Issues, 49,* 71–85.

Kurdek, L. A. (1993a). *Determinants of relationship commitment: evidence from gay, lesbian, dating heterosexual, and married heterosexual couples.* Manuscript submitted for publication.

Kurdek, L. A. (1993b). Predicting marital dissolution from demographic, individual-differences, interdependence, and spouse discrepancy variables: A 5-year prospective longitudinal study of newlywed couples. *Journal of Personality and Social Psychology, 64,* 221–242.

Kurdek, L. A., & Fine, M. A. (1993). The relation between family structure and young adolescents' appraisals of family climate and parenting behavior. *Journal of Family Issues, 14,* 279–290.

Thompson, L., & Walker, A. J. (1989). Women and men in marriage, work, and parenthood. *Journal of Marriage and the Family, 51,* 845–872.

Wineberg, H. (1992). Childbearing and dissolution of the second marriage. *Journal of Marriage and the Family, 54* 879–887.

# POSTSCRIPT

## Are Stepfamilies Inherently Problematic for Children?

Popenoe maintains that the intact, two-biological-parent family is the only type of family that is appropriate for children. He goes a step further by saying that stepfamilies are so harmful to children that they should be stopped.

Are stepfamilies inherently problematic for children? How do children in stepfamilies fare compared to families in which the mother lives with a number of boyfriends? This type of family form is not considered a stepfamily but could be very unstable for children. How do children from stepfamilies compare to children with two biological parents who are abusive to them? Is it better to be with stepparents who may not treat you warmly, as Popenoe argues, than to be with biological parents who beat you?

On the other hand, history is full of examples in which blood relatives were treated differently than relatives who came into the family through marriage or some other means. Inheriting land or a title as the first-born son or as the lineage associated with royalty has always depended upon being related by blood versus being adopted or being an in-law. Popenoe recognizes that having a son or daughter that is part of one's genetic material is a powerful concept. Whether or not this genetic tie interferes with parenting styles is debatable.

## Suggested Readings


Amato, P. R. (1993). Children's adjustment to divorce: Theories, hypotheses, and empirical support. *Journal of Marriage and the Family, 55,* 23–38.

Cherlin, A. J., & Furstenberg, F. F. (1994). Stepfamilies in the United States: A reconsideration. *Annual Review of Sociology, 20,* 359–381.

Ganong, L. H., & Coleman, M. (1994). *Remarried family relationships.* Thousand Oaks: Sage Publications.

McLanahan, S., & Sandefur, G. (1994). *Growing up with a single parent: What hurts? What helps?* Cambridge, MA: Harvard University Press.

# ISSUE 11

## Will School Vouchers Improve Children's Education?

**YES: Kevin Walthers**, from "Saying Yes to Vouchers: Perception, Choice, and the Educational Response," *NASSP Bulletin* (September 1995)

**NO: John F. Lewis**, from "Saying No to Vouchers: What Is the Price of Democracy?" *NASSP Bulletin* (September 1995)

### ISSUE SUMMARY

**YES:** Teacher Kevin Walthers argues that the pro-school-voucher movement has emerged because parents and taxpayers seriously question the efficacy of the public education system. He cites professionalism among teachers, declining academic standards for students, and disenchantment among taxpayers and parents as justification for changing how public education is administered.

**NO:** Attorney John F. Lewis counters that the perceived problems of the schools—such as drug use, premarital pregnancy, crime, and violence—are really societal problems *in* the schools, not problems *with* the schools. Lewis contends that public education has, in fact, improved over the last few decades.

Using a voucher system as a means for improving the education of children in the United States has been under consideration for nearly 50 years. Over the years, it has enjoyed support from conservative groups. Only recently, however, has this issue gained national attention as a viable option for overhauling the public education system. States such as Wisconsin and Florida have implemented limited school voucher programs as pilot programs. Other state legislative bodies have hotly debated the topic. For example, the governor of New Mexico was recently quoted as saying that he would withhold approval of the entire state budget unless state lawmakers approved a school voucher program. Even after the measure was soundly defeated in the legislature, the governor vowed to continue to fight for the passage of a school voucher program because he strongly believes that it would be an effective approach to improving children's education.

Proponents of school voucher systems believe that current public education systems are not producing graduates who are competitive on an international level, especially in the areas of mathematics and science. They point to declining educational standards for children in the public schools and argue that more emphasis should be placed on reading, writing, and arithmetic. They believe that parents should be given vouchers redeemable for educational services for their children. In this system, parents would be free to choose among public, private, or parochial schools in using these vouchers. Vouchers would therefore allow parents to send their children to better schools than they are required to attend in the current public school system.

Opponents of school voucher programs do not believe that such a system will truly benefit children. They maintain that although children in private schools appear to achieve better than those in public schools, this is largely because students are carefully screened for admission to these schools. When they do not measure up, they are returned to the public system. Critics also argue that a voucher system would produce a larger disparity between low-income and upper-income families because low-income parents are more likely to be unaware of schooling alternatives for their children. Finally, critics argue that if sectarian schools are included in voucher plans, it would be unconstitutional because there would be a mingling of church and state.

In the following selections, Kevin Walthers voices his support for the school voucher program. He contends that it is time to develop more effective approaches to providing quality education for children. He asserts that a school voucher system will restore the confidence of parents and taxpayers as well as produce students who have been prepared more rigorously. John F. Lewis decries the use of a voucher system for public education, suggesting that public education has, in fact, been improving over the years. He argues that there will be no significant improvement in the vast majority of children who are schooled under a voucher system and that such a system will not benefit lower-income children.

**Kevin Walthers**

**YES**

# Saying Yes to Vouchers: Perception, Choice, and the Educational Response

In many ways, perception is reality. The 1992 presidential election turned on voter perceptions regarding the state of the U.S. economy. The public believed that an economic malaise gripped the nation, dismissing George Bush's claims that there were no economic problems. That the economy grew in 1992 (albeit at a slower pace than in previous years) was immaterial. Bush failed to properly gauge voter perception, and lost the election.

Public educators now face the same situation George Bush faced: The people perceive that public education is not fulfilling its mission and they are demanding change. Educators and education associations continue to ignore this prevailing negative perspective, claiming that virtually all criticism is motivated by political opportunism or personal vendettas.

## What Is the Public Perception?

Unfortunately, the criticisms leveled at public education contain more than a kernel of truth. It is time to analyze the public perception, determine the facts and fallacies of that perception, and initiate a debate that will focus on improving education.

Critics of public education abound. Adults bemoan the lax standards of modern schools, industry leaders complain that students lack basic work skills, college professors decry the lack of logical reasoning in student writing, parents cry out for more and better programs, and taxpayers reject increased funding for schools that are retreating academically while expanding fiscally.

With all this criticism, it seems logical that educators would defend themselves by offering evidence that schools are not failing the public trust. Instead, an amazing set of paradoxes exists in the area of educational criticism.

Schools teach higher order thinking skills, yet fail to perform unbiased self-evaluations. Educators support debate and speech activities designed to develop student abilities to reason and respond to information, yet recoil in dismay if someone claims there are serious problems in education. "Even though educators consider themselves to be 'thinking people,' there is a remarkable

From Kevin Walthers, "Saying Yes to Vouchers: Perception, Choice, and the Educational Response," *NASSP Bulletin* (September 1995), pp. 52-61. 

absence of substantive arguments in their response to critics. These responses include evading the specifics of the criticism and arbitrarily attributing Utopian beliefs to critics" (Sowell, 1993, p. 249).

Educators must take an objective look at the charges against them without resorting to partisanship and name calling. Refuting false accusations is a simple task. More difficult and more important is creating a remedy for the true problems, even if that means entirely revamping the U.S. education system.

To accomplish this, educators must evaluate the three main areas of education that receive a majority of the criticism: lack of professional standards among educators; lack of appropriate academic standards for students; and the alienation of parents and taxpayers from the educational process.

## Barriers to Professionalism

Teaching as a profession is a widely debated concept. Many believe teachers lack the critical attributes necessary to claim the title of professional. "Hallmarks of a profession include mastery of a body of knowledge and skills that lay people do not possess, autonomy in practice, and autonomy in setting standards for the field" (Wise and Leibbrand, 1993, p. 135).

These are the steps to building a profession: Upon mastering a particular body of knowledge, a group may begin to practice unfettered by government regulations, obtaining the authority to establish standards for others to enter the profession. Medical doctors are the ultimate example of an autonomous profession. Doctors are required to complete a rigorous preprofessional curriculum as undergraduates, make an acceptable score on a difficult exam for entrance to medical school, graduate from an accredited medical school, pass another difficult professional exam, and complete an accredited residency (Sykes, 1989).

Not all professions require a structure this rigid, but lawyers, pharmacists, architects, and engineers have established standards that exclude the unqualified, restrict the underqualified, and raise the standard of the profession. The impetus for professionalism in the field of teaching must come from internal sources, as there is no external agency that can bestow such a title on any endeavor.

The National Commission on Excellence in Education (1983) addressed the needs of education in A *Nation at Risk.* The commission offered several recommendations regarding teachers designed "to make teaching a more rewarding and respected profession" (National Commission on Excellence in Education [NCEE], 1983, p. 30). The commission stated that education colleges should require prospective teachers to meet high academic standards and that salaries should be market-sensitive and performance based. These are basic elements of professionalism, yet educational leaders have erected barriers to keep these elements out of the educational process.

The NCEE realized that a need existed for better qualified students to enter the field of education. Historically, students enrolled in colleges of education consistently scored below the national average on standardized tests such as the ACT, SAT, and GRE (Sowell, 1993). The brightest students entering universities were choosing not to enroll in colleges of education, depriving schools of a resource considered very valuable in the private sector: bright, young, educated talent. The NCEE recommended awarding grants and loans to attract outstanding students to the teaching profession (particularly in areas of critical shortage such as science and mathematics), as well as developing strategies such as an 11-month contract that would make teaching more attractive financially (NCEE, 1983).

Enhancing the financial aspect of teaching is a key to building professionalism. One characteristic that all professionals share is the right to negotiate contracts on their own behalf, based on their worth to the employer. Friedman notes that "[p]oor teachers are grossly overpaid and good teachers grossly underpaid" (1982, p. 94). The problem with teacher salaries, the economist/author claims, is not that they are too low but that they are too rigid (Friedman, 1982).

If they are to be considered professionals, teachers should be compensated based not only on their value to the school but also on their value to others who seek to employ them. A lack of market incentives for salaries and the penalizing effect of the certification system lead to critical shortages in education. For example, highly qualified scientists, mathematicians, and language specialists are lured away from teaching because of financial disincentives to enter the classroom, and prevented from entering the educational field by legal barriers requiring a teaching certificate. The teaching certificate is designed to ensure that all teachers meet professional standards, but it is rarely more than a "union card":

> Certification raises problems not just because it fails to screen out the mediocre and the bad. It also raises problems because it sets up formidable barriers to entry that keep many excellent prospects out of the job pool. People who are well educated, bright, enthusiastic, creative, and good with children cannot simply pursue a latent interest in education by simply giving it a try. Nor can talented people already working in other lines of endeavor shift into teaching, or perhaps move in and out of it, as they might in other jobs. Instead, potential teachers are asked by the state to foreclose other options, make a substantial investment of time and resources, and jump through formal hoops. Our society is full of people who could make excellent teachers, but burdensome certification requirements are the best way to ensure that most of them never teach (Chubb and Moe, 1990, p. 196).

## Academic Standards

While some question the professionalism of educators, others fear a lack of appropriate academic standards for students. Adults remember "how tough it was when I was in school," but growing evidence supports the public's position that school, while getting easier, ignores the increasing knowledge base needed to compete in a high tech marketplace. Parents and taxpayers see falling test scores, inclusion, affective learning, self-esteem training, and values clarification lessons as proof that schools are not teaching as much material as they used to. Furthermore, they believe the material being taught is not as difficult as it should be.

> 'Sex education' courses and textbooks, for example, seldom involve a mere conveying of biological or medical information. Far more often, the primary thrust is toward re-shaping of attitudes, not only toward sex, but also toward parents, toward society, and toward life. The same pattern is found in many other programs claiming to be about drug prevention, smoking prevention, and many other worthy purposes (Sowell, 1993, p. 35).

Parents and taxpayers demand that "basic skills" regain the attention of educators. They wonder how a person who lacks the skill to complete an employment application managed to graduate from a public high school. This is a strong perception in the community, one educators would be unwise to dismiss as "hate-mongering from the radical right."

The lack of academic standards in the public school is profound. According to the U.S. Census Bureau, in 1930: "... most of the 1 million white illiterates and 2 million black illiterates were people over the age of 50 who had never been to school. By 1990, 30 to 35 million (American) citizens could not read. Most are people under 50 who have been to school for at least eight years" (Wood, 1992, p. 51).

Educators often dismiss this evidence as anecdotal and isolated, but the news, and the public mind set, is filled with studies showing drops in skills in all academic areas. Until educators meet the challenge, the public will not have faith in the abilities of the public education system.

## Alienation

A correlating factor to watered-down curricula is the feeling of alienation held by many taxpayers and parents. Educators cry out for parent and community involvement, then complain when these forces initiate change in school policy. Educators, when asked to identify their "customers," often respond that students or their parents are their clients. One overlooked public school client, however, is the taxpayer. Citizen funding of the educational process creates "a stable and democratic society (that) is impossible without a minimum degree of literacy and knowledge on the part of most citizens" (Friedman, 1982, p. 86). In refusing to acknowledge the role of the community in education, schools are alienating the portion of the population that pays the bills. Therefore, "citizens everywhere, whether or not they have children in school and whether or not they live in the local school district or even the state, have a legitimate hand in governing each and every local school" (Chubb and Moe, 1990, p. 30).

Parents, of course, possess a natural right to be involved directly in the education of their children. The Family Educational Rights and Privacy Act of 1974 arms parents with the legal means to force educators to divulge information regarding course content, among other things. Even without federal law, parents have direct local access to principals, teachers, administrators, and even school board members. This close tie to the schools does not mean, however, that parents should have any more influence on school policy than any other tax-paying member of the community (Chubb and Moe, 1990). The community establishes the schools and sets policies in accordance with the public good, not the individual preference.

## A Workable Solution

The public is growing increasingly dissatisfied with public education. This is in no small way due to damaging media coverage that focuses on the negative aspect of events. It is more newsworthy when a gun is fired in a school building (which happens so infrequently as to be statistically insignificant) than it is when thousands of students successfully complete high school and receive scholarships to major universities—which happens in virtually every district every year.

The media are not the sole cause of dissatisfaction, however, when it comes to the public attitude toward public education. Educators must find a way to convince parents that schooling is a professional endeavor. It is unlikely, however, that continuation of the current system will force a change in U.S. attitudes. Our industry thrives because of its competitive nature, and an infusion of capitalism into education would be a fitting remedy for the ailment of complacency in the classroom.

Nobel Prize-winning economist Milton Friedman developed a plan that, though a radical departure from the status quo, would empower parents as well as quality educators. "Free market vouchers" embody the application of Friedman's plan for what Zerchykov (1987) calls "unregulated vouchers." If Friedman did not coin the term vouchers as it relates to school choice, he certainly may be credited with the universal acceptance of the term as it relates to educational policy.

Vouchers, according to Friedman, would provide a mechanism for equalizing educational opportunities: "Governments could require a minimum level of schooling financed by giving parents vouchers redeemable for a specified maximum sum per child per year if spent on approved educational services" (Friedman, 1982, p. 87).

He begins his argument by noting that while it is a responsibility of the government to provide funding for education (which promotes the common welfare), the government is not required to administer education. This could be done much more efficiently in the private sector, with only minimal regulations that would concern health and safety issues (Friedman, 1982). He does not advocate the abolition of the modern public school, but challenges them to compete for students with private and parochial schools.

Thomas Ascik, executive director of the Clearinghouse on Educational Choice, agrees that free market vouchers give parents the liberty to raise their children as they see fit: "Child rearing is the whole and schooling is only a part. Parents have the authority over the whole and, therefore, they should have the ultimate authority over the part" (Ascik, 1986, p. 109).

Ascik and Friedman also claim that free market vouchers will be a greater benefit to the poor than to the wealthy. Friedman explains that a parent in a low income job can save money and buy the same car that the wealthy drive. In like manner, the parent can work an extra job to send his child to private school so that he can get an education on a par with that of a child in a public school in a wealthy neighborhood. A voucher would enable the family to send the child to a better school and devote economic resources to other aspects of making a better life such as home ownership or providing for otherwise unaffordable extracurricular activities.

Opponents of the free market voucher plan call this plan "welfare for the rich," asserting that private schools would merely raise the cost of tuition by the amount of the voucher, keeping the school as unreachable for the poor as it was before. They also claim that the poorest segments of our society are the least educated, so they would not know how to find the best school for their child. Ascik confronts the latter problem by comparing school funding to the food stamp program:

> Annually, governments invest as much in health as in education. Nutrition is a big part of health. Using the same rationale used to justify the status quo in public education, we may wonder why the government should not fund grocery stores directly rather than deliver food stamps to individuals (Ascik, 1986, p. 111).

In response to the first objection, the market theory used by Friedman to advocate free market vouchers holds that if private schools raise their tuition by the amount of the voucher, someone will fill the gap in the market and provide an alternative of equal quality for a lower price. This basic principal of economic efficiency will bring down the tuition price of the other schools as well, creating more educational opportunities for those on the lower end of the economic scale.

## Why Should Educators Support Choice?

Educators claim to support choice. They point to alternative schools, open enrollment policies, magnet programs, and GED classes as evidence. When students are restricted to choosing from the programs offered by a single entity (usually the local school district), the promise of choice remains unfulfilled. By implementing a true choice plan, educators would elevate the stature of their field, allow for specialized, relevant academic standards, and intimately involve parents in the education of their children.

Unfortunately, teacher associations and unions adamantly oppose any form of choice that would allow students to attend nonpublic schools. Unions cite student welfare as the reason for their opposition to choice, but self-serving political motives are the driving force against any plan that undermines the power of the unions, especially the National Education Association.

The NEA claims to be interested in student success, yet opposes allowing students to leave the monopolistic school district in search of better schools. Association president Keith Geiger asserted that "the solution to the funding and social inequities that condemn children in inner cities and other impoverished areas to inferior schools is not to encourage the flight of the most promising students" (Dunne, 1991, p. 14).

Geiger fails (or refuses) to see that all students would have access to better schools, not just the top prospects. There is a strong inverse link between economic disadvantage and educational achievement. For this reason, federal block grant funds are distributed based on the income level of the students attending a particular school or district. Wealthy districts get little while poor districts receive a substantial supplement.

This would continue under a voucher plan by giving financial incentives to schools that educate children from economically depressed areas. By increasing the financial value of the child's education, inner-city children would become highly desirable members of the student body (Rinehart and Jackson, 1991). Choice plans in Cambridge, Mass., have increased overall student achievement while closing the educational gap between white and black students. East Harlem, N.Y., has seen a five-fold increase in the rate of students reading at or above grade level since initiating a school choice plan (Nathan, 1990). One study of interdistrict choice plans shows that parents want better schools for their children, even if it means taking the student to a school in another district:

> It would be a mistake to dismiss interdistrict school choice as a phenomenon driven by family convenience. Enrollment patterns in districts where significant numbers of transfers occurred (20 students or more from one community to another) show a strong and unmistakable trend. Families enrolled their children in districts that had higher median family incomes and better educated adult populations than their home communities. They also went to districts that had better standardized test scores at the high school level, lower out-of-school suspension rates, lower dropout rates, and higher per-pupil funding (Fossey, 1994).

The plan that Geiger assails as damaging to the minority student has in fact, proved to work just as Milton Friedman said it would more than 30 years ago, even though the programs are limited in scope. Lower-income parents in Massachusetts choice districts are empowered to seek out an education for their children that is equal to that of families with higher income while the taxpayers are blessed with a young population that will have increased earning power due to an improving educational system.

Even if free market vouchers are not the best option, those who oppose choice refuse to engage in thoughtful debate. Many advocates of choice are intelligent, prominent, and eloquent. They count among their ranks politicians, professors, journalists, and at least one Nobel Laureate. Hurling invective at a group with these credentials, as the education associations continue to do, only strengthens the choice position.

The arguments presented by voucher supporters are solid, gaining widespread acceptance from lawmakers in both major parties (Lieberman, 1990). Educators must look at the issue impartially, realizing that the best way to educate children may not be through a government-run monopoly. If educators are to be considered professionals, they must allow for dissent, innovation, and input from the community. Arrogantly claiming to be the sole possessors of educational knowledge and demanding ever-growing infusions of tax money to support public schools is no longer politically viable.

## Conclusion

Vouchers hold the promise of elevating teaching to professional status, raising levels of student achievement, and restoring the confidence of the tax paying public. If teachers do not embrace this idea, they should at least develop thoughtful arguments that show why the plan is unworkable. Until educators and their associations agree that dissent is not only acceptable but encouraged, the public will continue to perceive education as just another in a long list of non-performing, over-bureaucratized, autocratic government programs that usurp individual liberty.

## References


Ascik, T. In *Content, Character, and Choice in Schooling.* Washington, D.C.: National Council on Educational Research, 1986.

Chubb, J., and Moe, T. *Politics, Markets, and America's Schools.* Washington, D.C.: The Brookings Institution, 1990.

Dunne, D. *School Choice: Pros, Cons, and Concerns.* Washington, D.C.: ASPIRA Issue Brief, 1991.

Fossey, R. "Open Enrollment in Massachusetts: Why Families Choose." *Educational Evaluation and Policy Analysis* 3(1994): 320–34.

Friedman, M. *Capitalism and Freedom.* Chicago, Ill.: University of Chicago Press, 1982.

—. *Public School Choice: Current Issues/Future Prospects.* Lancaster, Pa.: Technomic, 1990.

Nathan, J. "Progress, Problems, and Prospects of State Education Plans." In *Choice in Education: Potential and Problems,* edited by W. Boyd and H. Walberg. Berkeley, Calif.: McCutchan, 1990.

National Commission on Excellence in Education. *A Nation at Risk.* Washington, D.C.: U.S. Department of Education, 1983.

Rinehart, J., and Jackson, L., Jr. *American Education and the Dynamics of Choice.* New York: Praeger, 1991.

Sowell, T. *Inside American Education: The Decline, the Deception, the Dogmas.* New York: The Free Press, 1993.

Sykes, G. "Teaching and Professionalism: A Cautionary Perspective." In *Crisis in Teaching: Perspectives on Current Reforms,* edited by L. Weis, P. Altbach, G. Kelly, H. Petrie, and S. Slaughter. Albany, N.Y.: State University of New York, 1989.

Wise, A., and Leibbrand, J. "Accreditation and the Profession of Teaching." *Phi Delta Kappan* 2(1993): 135.

Wood, R. "That's Right—They're Wrong." *National Review* 18(1992): 50–53.

Zerchykov, R. *Parent Choice: A Digest of Research.* Boston, Mass.: Institute for Responsive Education, 1987.

**John F. Lewis**

**NO**

# Saying No to Vouchers: What Is the Price of Democracy?

The year 1995 began with at least 14 state legislatures exploring "school choice" as the answer to the ills facing public education. This surge of activity belies the fact that the idea has been sputtering around since the early 1960s when economist Milton Friedman argued that public schools should not be a government monopoly, and conceived a "voucher" equal to a certain number of public dollars.[1] The voucher would be given to parents who in turn could deliver it as an equivalent to dollars to any school, public or independent, of the parents' choice.

Those who believe in the applicability of market economics to public education believe that parents will use their vouchers to choose the "best" schools —whatever that means. It follows that schools not chosen will either improve to meet the competition or go out of existence.

Since Professor Friedman's suggestion, "school choice" has been heralded as the answer to all kinds of problems facing education. That the idea finds nourishment in this country is not at all surprising, for the soul of "school choice"—allowing parents to use public school funds to enroll their children in any independent school they choose—seems the essence of democracy.[2] Who in a democracy can argue with freedom of choice?

In point of fact, "school choice" is a strategy that does not deal with the problems facing our schools, but in fact runs from them.

## The Myth of Choice

Underlying the idea of "school choice" is the fundamental, all-American belief in rugged competition. Simplistically, the argument runs, "If we give parents a choice, they will pick the best. Schools not chosen will improve or get out of education. Those chosen will grow. Ultimately, choice will bring out the best." Note, however, that it is not the actual consumer who makes the choice. Rather it is the consumer once-removed, the child's parent or guardian, who chooses on behalf of the student. This fact may have a significant if not controlling impact on why the choice is made.

From John F. Lewis, "Saying No to Vouchers: What Is the Price of Democracy?" *NASSP Bulletin* (September 1995), pp. 41-51. 

This kind of marketplace "choice" is what undergirds the private sector. There, the motivator is dollars. The profit motive, Adam Smith long ago pointed out, will produce the best product.[3] Why? Because the only way you can make money is to produce something others choose to buy. More than that, if people have a choice, they will buy the best. So, if you want to make money, produce the best.

But money is not the primary motivator in education. Motivations come in soft packages: Self-satisfaction? Seeing your students succeed? Intellectual stimulation? Indeed, a principal motivation that undergirds "choice" is fear, the threat of losing students. And students may be lost whether or not you are delivering the "best" educational product you can deliver.

What, then, makes us believe that an economic model rooted in Adam Smith's assumptions and called "choice" will improve education?

Of course the inner cities' social problems are horrendous. Dropout rates exceed a third of the class. Scholastic Aptitude Test scores are widely reported to have dropped. We are repeatedly told graduates are unable to add and subtract.[4] Crime is up and on the rise. So is drug use. So also is teen pregnancy.[5]

Because these problems undeniably feed upon themselves and have an impact on one another, does that make the school the source of the problems? Do schools cause cycles of poverty and despair? Is it the fault of schools that crime and drugs and pregnancy are on the rise? Will going to an independent school solve the problem? These are problems *in* the schools but not *with* the schools. *In* the schools means problems in our society—in our cities—in our suburbs—in our families that are brought into the schools. These are not problems amenable to a "school" solution modeled after classic economic theory. The schools are the community operating tables upon which our deeper sicknesses are displayed.

What, in short, makes anyone believe choice will make the slightest difference in the product we turn out? What makes us think it will reduce crime? Slow down drugs? Stop teen pregnancy? Answer? It will not.

## Improving Education

In the past several years, we have explored every conceivable approach to improving education: new curricula, scholarships, vocational supplements, magnets, fast tracks, slow tracks, team teaching, school-within-a-school, and every variation of all the above and more. Nothing has worked to our satisfaction.

Who said schools worked in the 1970s when sex and race discrimination, desegregation, due process, and classroom prayer dominated the Supreme Court agenda? Who said public education worked in the 1960s when desegregation, free speech, armbands, and long hair were the battle cry? Or in the 1950s when we were riding an after-war boom and jobs were plentiful? Who said it worked in the 1940s during World War II? Who paid any attention during the Great Depression of the 1930s when no one had jobs?

The social problems of poverty, crime, drugs, pregnancy, and race relations have grown exponentially during that time. But surely not because of the education being delivered.

In fact, on a number of key international measures U.S. schools do quite well. According to the National Center for Education Statistics, the great majority of U.S. students finished at or near the top of the most recent international comparison of the 19 developed nations in mathematics. Mathematics is, of course, a subject in which our national performance is reported as dismal. Top finishers:

1. Asian students (in the U.S.)—287
2. Taiwan—285
3. Korea—283
4. Advantaged urban students (in the U.S.)—283
5. White students (in the U.S.)—277
6. Hungary—277.[6]

Finally, the United States in 1994 had a 4.5 percent economic growth rate, a gain of three million jobs, and an inflation rate reminiscent of the 1960s. We are the envy of the industrialized world.

The amount the average U.S. worker can produce, already the highest in the world, is growing faster than in other wealthy countries, including Japan. The United States has become the world's low-cost provider of many sophisticated products and services, from plastics to software to financial services.[7]

In July 1992, the International Association for the Evaluation of Educational Achievement (IAEEA) released a report comparing reading skills of 200,000 students in 31 countries. The study found U.S. 9-year-olds reading better than anyone in the world except Finnish 9-year-olds. Using a scale identical to that of the SAT (a mean of 500 and a standard deviation of 100), U.S. 9-year-olds averaged 547, while the Finns came in at 569. Our 14-year-olds finished ninth, with an average score of 535. Interestingly, the U.S. 14-year-olds actually scored almost as close to first place as did the 9-year-olds.[8]

In December 1994, Rand published a monograph, "Student Achievement and the Changing American Family," which throws into substantial question the statistics relied on by so many who would have us believe public education is in free fall. Rand acknowledges SAT scores have dropped significantly since 1970, but points out that the SAT is a totally inappropriate measure. It is not designed to compare student performance over time because it is taken only once or twice and even then not by a statistically representative sample. Moreover, it is taken by a different mix of students each year and even then only by students who intend to go on to college.

A far more reliable measurement of student performance is the National Assessment of Educational Progress (NAEP). Why? Because NAEP is designed to, and does, measure student achievement over time with a standardized test of students at ages 9, 13, and 17. Scores from this test show 13-year-olds' mathematics achievement has, in fact, improved by 6 percent during the 20-year period, and that of 17-year-olds by 4 percent; something is working. Reading scores are also improving with the most dramatic gain being shown by black students (19 percent) and Hispanic students (11 percent).[9]

Ah, but these achievements don't address the dropouts, the crime, the drugs, pregnancies, the decline in moral values. There is no question these are conditions that need to be corrected. But how?

## Opting Out of Democracy

"Choice" is currently a popular answer. It is in the jumbled tradition of so many quick-fix answers—with a dangerous twist: It undermines the very democratic value system it celebrates.

For example, it troubles "choice" advocates that the Supreme Court will not permit the simplest prayer to start the day. This concern is quickly linked to the requirement that students, all students, must by law go to school. And they must go with everyone else regardless of religious persuasion—or lack thereof—with derelicts, with drug addicts, and with immoral mothers and fathers.

It bothers choice advocates that a youngster carrying a gun or drugs is entitled to due process. How can it be a democracy with metal detectors and safety guards? First it surprises, then it angers them that administrators must spend precious hours conducting due process hearings for each student before disciplining the student with a three-day suspension.[10]

It angers them that the school board must do everything in public—that's right, nothing, not even private discussions, can be done in private. They do not understand the significance of public records that are there for all to examine. They are exasperated by Sunshine Laws that require everything in the open.

It frustrates them that students who have had nothing to eat can act up and disrupt a classroom, or that a youngster who needs a urinary catheter can interrupt the normal course of the day and take the teacher from the classroom.

And what is this business about free speech and wearing buttons, and armbands and long hair? "Where is the discipline?" "Why don't you just sit the kid down?" "You mean if you touch him he gets a due process hearing?"

It infuriates the advocates of choice that public schools in most states must by law deal with unions. (It infuriates me, too.) They do not understand that this democracy they wish to brag about to the rest of the world comes with a price—a steep price, and problems—lots of problems. Living together under majority rule, running a public school is not easy.

Consider the fact that a teacher with 10 years' experience and a master's degree in a *public school* will earn twice as much as his or her counterpart in an *independent* school. Moreover, the benefits package in a public school simply has no parallel in private sector education. You bet there are savings. And guess what? An independent school principal simply reassigns a teacher to another class, or directs the teacher to coach soccer. The public school principal has to sit down and *bargain,* and nothing happens unless the union says "O.K." Worse, because of democratically adopted legislation, the termination of an incompetent or inefficient public school teacher costs lots of money and countless administrative hours. And if you do the sensible and courageous thing and spend the money, the public climbs all over you for fiscal irresponsibility. So, no one terminates anyone.

None of this happens in independent schools.

But you know what? As [Walt Kelly's cartoon character] Pogo used to say, "We have met the enemy and he is us." The Constitution and the rule of law are what this country is all about. We put them there. That's what democracy means. That's precisely what our Constitution says.

I do not quarrel with concerns about lack of prayer and rock-hard values in our public schools. I do say the way to address them in this country is not by running to an independent school and asking me to pay. It is by confronting them head-on. This is the heart of the debate. It is not an answer to say that one is entitled in a democracy to choose one's school even if it is independent. I reply "But why should I pay for your independent school?"

It is no answer to our public school problems to set up a dual system and watch as one set of youngsters receives an education unfettered by the bad part of what a democracy means, while others—usually impoverished—must go to schools where the rules of democracy do apply and must, by law, be applied. This is no choice as I understand choice. Capitalistic choice is predicated on an even playing field. If you have problems and you want to change them, you are treated the same as everyone else. Because of laws democracy has thrust upon them, public schools cannot change most of the very reasons that underlie decisions by choice advocates to find fault with them.

Even while opting out of many of democracy's restrictions, independent schools already receive substantial public support. As one compares the efficiencies of public versus independent schools, one often meets the argument that independent school budgets are markedly less.

They are less, first, because teacher compensation (salary and benefits) is dramatically less; second, because the enormous cost of operating under the Constitution and the unfunded mandates of Congress requires public schools to spend more; and third, because the general everyday operating costs are less simply because the clientele wants to be there.

In making the comparisons the pro-choice advocates often forget to add the per-pupil cost of transportation and auxiliary services provided to independent schoolers by the public schools. Not only does this mean the independent schools do not pay the cost, it also means the public schools do pay the cost. In Ohio, that number a year ago was approximately $800 per pupil.

How about auxiliary services? Again in Ohio, a large and representative state, costs grew from $13.26 per pupil in 1967–68 to $338 per pupil in 1992–93. Total cost over those 25 years grew from $5 million to $76 million.[11] In short, at a time when public schools are blamed for costing more, they are subsidizing independent schools.

## We Have Tested "Choice"

Bear in mind that a number of U.S. communities already have some experience with a variety of "choice" models. The jury is still out on the very *raison d'être* of school choice advocates: that given a "choice," parents will pursue educational quality. The early data do not support this claim.

Two years ago, emulating Minnesota's much-heralded public school open enrollment law, Ohio inaugurated such a program on a voluntary basis. Of 612 districts, 49 participated in the first year, 178 in the second year.

- The principal reason parents gave for selecting another district was *proximity to work.* This is [classical economist] Adam Smith once removed: The parent, not the students attending school, makes the economically-driven decision because of proximity to the parent's work.[12]
- Of the 618 participating students at the beginning of the second year, only 21 listed a greater academic opportunity or a special teacher.[13]
- In Minnesota statewide open enrollment is mandatory. *Only* one-half of 1 percent (1 of every 1,000 students) took advantage of the opportunity to make a "choice" and geography was again the driving factor.[14]
- The Arizona Department of Education repeatedly determined that only one-third of parents made "choice" decisions for academic reasons.[15]
- The Carnegie Foundation's *School Choice: A Special Report* declares: "Many parents who do decide to send their children to another school appear to do so for non-academic reasons."[16]
- The same report notes only one-third of Iowa parents listed "educational benefits" as the most important reason for changing schools. Indeed, Carnegie's own survey found that only 15 percent of parents wishing to send their children to other schools cite "academic quality" as the reason.[17]

Even where educational quality is cited as a reason in choosing a different inner-city school, it would be no surprise to learn that at least one "quality" of which parents were speaking was the quality of fear from crime or the related quality of discipline.

I would argue that crime and discipline must be confronted head-on. It is no answer to seek freedom from crime by taking public money to supplement private dollars in private education. So also, public money ought not be spent to accommodate proximity to work. Essentially what choice advocates are doing is opting out of the laws, regulations, and restrictions imposed on public education, or they are taking advantage of "choice" options for reasons other than academic excellence.

## Vouchers Don't Work

Let us forget for the moment *why* the choice is made. Is it worthwhile? After all the hoopla, with all the claims that the private sector does it better, do we have any voucher experience showing the impact on students who have opted for a private education?

Of the few experiments, the one most talked about, perhaps because it has been around the longest, is the nonreligious Milwaukee Parental Choice Program. Twelve private schools—one of which went bankrupt in its first year—participate. By law, no more than 1,500 students may participate. (There are 45 million elementary and secondary public school students in the United

States.)[18] They must come from families whose incomes are no greater than 1.75 times the federal poverty rate. At present, 830 participate. They are selected at random.[19]

In the Milwaukee program, according to the latest report, parents of the participating students are much more involved in their children's schooling than are their public-side counterparts. They have fewer children per family and are better educated, with higher educational expectations and a greater likelihood to work on homework with their children. According to Professor John Witte of the University of Wisconsin, despite this trend in parental involvement, the children showed no significant improvement in attendance.[20] As important, there has been no significant improvement in test scores in reading or math in the first three years.[21]

## The Real Choice

There is still another reason choice won't work. A professor of educational leadership at Stanford, Edward Bridge, found that a quarter of low-income parents in a district allowing choice were totally unaware of any schooling alternatives.[22] Nor should this be a surprise: In the inner city, where poverty reigns, the illustrations are legion of youngsters who do not have mentors. There are few, if any, role models who even know about primary and secondary school much less who can show the youngsters why they should go to school in the first place. No one they know completed school. No one they know got a job because of completing school. Indeed, the few successful ones moved out, mentors departing just when they are of value.

As to those whose parents are literate, motivated, driven by high expectations, and who make a carefully reasoned choice to select an independent school, their departure drains the very stuff, the backbone needed to make public schools work. By definition they will, or should, take advantage of such an opportunity. Why, if they have the option, shouldn't they take the easier road? Why should they stay and fight to make this country understand the problem is democracy itself? That's an impossible mission. Yet, when these parents leave, they leave behind an ever-present and growing underclass. The nation is truly at risk if, in the name of democracy, or "choice," it blames the public schools for their inability to deal with the problem.

One cannot argue that the independent school, unfettered by any of the rules and laws that control public schools, backed by literate parents who are determined to see their children succeed and funded with public dollars, ought to succeed.

If they do not succeed, these parents and their new schools are not confronted by tenure. They can, at the blink of an eye, terminate the teachers who are at fault. If that is not enough, they are not hobbled by mandatory education requirements.[23] Perhaps most significant of all, they can remove the troublesome students, or the students who are not interested or won't learn, and return them—where? To the public school, which must take them.

In the final analysis, why are we wasting time, money, and effort heading toward a dead end on a wrong-way street? I quote from a passage written at a different time:

> All children, like all men, rise easily to the common level. There the mass stop; strong minds only ascend higher. But raise the standard, and, by a spontaneous movement, the mass will rise again and reach it. Hence the *removal* of the most forward scholars from the schools is not a small misfortune.... All this inevitably depresses and degrades the public school... until the public school is left to the management of those who have not the desire nor the power to improve....[24]

Horace Mann wrote this in 1830.

> Choice is not a new idea. Leaving aside questions of whether many students will switch schools, whether those that do will switch for convenience or curriculum, and whether their new schools can sustain themselves ultimately, the newness is in who pays for it.
>
> As a nation, we are rightly absorbed with improving education. We cannot do it by isolating its problems, and pretending to leave those problems behind to be dealt with by those least able to solve them.
>
> The problems of our public schools lie deep in the American experience—poverty, racism, decades of public apathy, drugs, and the growing inability of the family, the church, and the neighborhood to nurture many of our children. These problems—and not the attractively sounding 'solution' of private school choice—need to be addressed.[25]

Choosing to put our shoulders to the harness—to turn and address the problems head-on, not run from them—that is the choice we must make.

## Notes

1. Milton Friedman, *Capitalism and Freedom,* 1st ed. (Chicago, Ill.: University of Chicago Press, 1962).
2. The author does not take issue with offering "choice" between public schools, or even within a single public school district.
3. Adam Smith, *The Wealth of Nations* (Edwin Cannan ed., Modern Library, 1937) (1776).
4. Louis V. Gerstner, Jr., et al., *Reinventing Education* (New York: Dutton Books, 1994).
5. Davis and McCaul, *The Emerging Crisis: Current and Projected Status of Children in the United States* (University of Maine, 1991).
6. Gerald W. Bracey, "The Fourth Bracey Report on the Condition of Public Education," *Phi Delta Kappan,* October 1994.
7. Sylvia Nassar, "The American Economy: Back on Top," *New York Times,* February 27, 1994, Sec. 3, p. 1.
8. Gerald W. Bracey, "The Fourth Bracey Report on the Condition of Public Education," *Phi Delta Kappan,* October 1994.
9. Rand, 1994, pp. 16–23.
10. Goss v. Lopez. 419 US 565 (1975).
11. Source: Ohio Department of Education, Department of School Finance.

12. Susan Urahn, *Open Enrollment Study: Student and District Participation,* 1989–90 (St. Paul Minn.: House Research Office, Minnesota House of Representatives, 1990).
13. *Id.*
14. *Id.*
15. School Choice: A Special Report (Princeton, N.J.: Carnegie Foundation for the Advancement of Teaching, 1992).
16. *Id.*
17. *Id.*
18. U.S. Bureau of the Census, *Statistical Abstract of the United States: 1994,* 114th ed. (Washington, D.C.: U.S. Government Printing Office, 1994).
19. John F. Witte, et al., *Third-Year Report, Milwaukee Parental Choice Program,* University of Wisconsin-Madison, December 1993.
20. *Id.*
21. *Id.*
22. Jack McKay, School Choice May Cheat Students of "Democratic Ideals," *School Administrator,* December 1992.
23. Some argue persuasively that if public money is channeled into independent education, it will only be a matter of time before the education requirements, laws, regulations and collective bargaining are imposed on independent schools.
24. Lawrence A. Cremin, *The Republic and the School,* pp. 111–12, 1957.
25. Robert W. Carr, "A Responsibility to Speak Out Against Choice," *The School Administrator,* October 1992.

# POSTSCRIPT

## Will School Vouchers Improve Children's Education?

At the close of the twentieth century, American society finds itself in the throes of a hotly debated topic: whether or not voucher plans are appropriate or even feasible for the public education of its children. Several critical questions emerge from the selections on this topic:

- Do voucher plans cross the line of the separation of church and state?
- Will children find themselves more homogeneously grouped in their parents' schools of choice under voucher plans? If so, will this impede their attainment of cultural sensitivity and respect for various cultures?
- Is the current public school system as ineffective as those who support vouchers suggest?
- Are voucher plans the remedy for a failing public education system?

## Suggested Readings


School Vouchers. `http://www.tcom.ohiou.edu/OU_Language/project/voucher.html`

Policy Support and Studies Hot Topics Page: Vouchers. `http://www.wested.org/policy/hot_top/sch-vouchers/ht_tp_schl`

Teacher Magazine on the Web: Choice and Vouchers. `http://www.teachermag.org/context/topics/choice.htm`

# ISSUE 12

## Should Bilingual Education Programs Be Abandoned?

**YES: Rosalie Pedalino Porter**, from "The Politics of Bilingual Education," *Society* (September/October 1997)

**NO: Donaldo Macedo**, from "English Only: The Tongue-Tying of America," *Journal of Education* (Spring 1991)

### ISSUE SUMMARY

**YES:** Rosalie Pedalino Porter, director of the Research in English Acquisition and Development Institute, cites several research studies to support her contention that funds for programs for non-English-speaking children have been largely misguided.

**NO:** Linguistics professor Donaldo Macedo asserts that English should not be the only language used for educating children. He maintains that bilingual education programs are effective for educating children who cannot speak or read English and that they improve the academic performance of non-English-speaking children.

There are several types of bilingual education programs in the United States, each with its own strengths and shortcomings. For example, in one type of bilingual curriculum, a child who does not speak English is placed in a class taught by a teacher who speaks both English and the child's original language. The intent is to teach the child in English and in his or her native tongue, as well as to maintain the child's appreciation of the native culture of his or her parents. Problems can arise in such a program, however, when a language is common to many cultures. Consider the teacher who is from one Spanish-speaking country–Guatemala, for example–and who teaches a class composed of Spanish-speaking students from diverse countries, such as Spain, Mexico, San Salvador, Bolivia, and so on. These children may enter high school with a thorough understanding of the Spanish language and Guatemalan culture, but they will likely have little idea of their own culture. To further exacerbate the problem, these children often lack sufficient immersion in the dominant, American culture. As a consequence, these children, who may be just as intelligent as their English-speaking counterparts, could do poorly on culturally relevant standardized tests and thus become discouraged.

Some bilingual education programs give the parents of non-English-speaking children the choice of enrolling their children in a completely native-speaking classroom or a completely English-speaking classroom, where they will receive no extra help or assistance. The problem here is that neither option may benefit the children. If children go to native-speaking classrooms, it can impede their acquisition of English. If they are put into English-only classrooms, they may become frustrated and discouraged.

Some bilingual programs, however, seem to be enjoying great success in recognizing a child's native culture and language and teaching them about American culture. In so-called English immersion programs, children are enrolled in classrooms where they are "immersed" in the English language, but only after they have been oriented to the language and the happenings of an American classroom. However, these immersion programs seem to work best in preschool curricula, since children acquire language more readily in early childhood.

In the following selections, the authors offer different arguments regarding the efficacy of bilingual education. As you read each selection, make note of the vast differences of opinion held by Rosalie Pedalino Porter and Donaldo Macedo. Also make mental notes of the ways in which you believe that non-English-speaking children can be integrated most effectively into the educational system. Taking into account the points made by Porter and Macedo, consider the questions, Which arguments seem to be most closely aligned with the best interests of the children in question? and, Which methods appear most feasible for effective integration into an English-speaking society?

**Rosalie Pedalino Porter**

# The Politics of Bilingual Education

In the United States, the efforts being made and the money being invested in the special programs to help immigrant, migrant, and refugee schoolchildren who do not speak English when they enter U.S. schools is still largely misguided. The current population of limited-English students is being treated in ways that earlier immigrant groups were not. The politically righteous assumption is that these students cannot learn English quickly and must be taught all their school subjects in their native language for three to seven years while having the English language introduced gradually. Twenty-seven years of classroom experience with this education policy and a growing body of research show no benefits for native-language teaching either in better learning of English or better learning of school subjects. These facts have hardly dented the armor of the true believers in the bilingual education bureaucracy.

Yet some changes and improvements have occurred in this most contentious area of public education. Research reports contribute additional evidence on the poor results of native-language instruction as the superior road to English-language competency for classroom work. But the successful results from programs emphasizing intensive English are beginning to appear, now that some small measure of funding is being allocated to these so-called alternative model programs.

All too often, it remains almost impossible to voice criticism of bilingual education programs without being pilloried as a hater of foreigners and foreign languages and of contributing to the anti-immigrant climate. Another area in which little positive change has occurred in the past few years is in reducing the established power of state education departments to impose education mandates on local school districts. The power of the bilingual education bureaucracy has hardly diminished, even in states like California where the state bilingual education law expired in 1987. However, there are counterforces opposing the seemingly settled idea that native-language programs are the single best solution for limited-English students, and these challenges are growing at the local school level.

## Updating the Research

The basic questions posed in the early years of bilingual education still have not found clear-cut answers. Are there measurable benefits for limited-English students when they are taught in their native language for a period of time, both in their learning of the English language for academic achievement and in their mastery of school subjects? Has a clear advantage emerged for a particular pedagogy among the best-known models—transitional bilingual education, English as a Second Language [ESL], structured immersion, two-way, dual immersion, or developmental bilingual programs? There is no more consensus on the answers to these questions than there was five years ago. However, there is growing evidence of an almost total lack of accountability in states that have invested most heavily in bilingual education for the past fifteen or twenty years and have not collected data or evaluated programs to produce answers to the questions raised above. The research that has been published in recent years includes a study by the General Accounting Office, the ALEC [American Legislative Council] Study, a review of the El Paso Bilingual Immersion Project, a longitudinal study of bilingual students in New York, a report of a two-year study of California's bilingual education programs, and a report of a state commission on Massachusetts's bilingual education.

## The GAO Study

Every year since the late 1970s, the school enrollment of limited-English students has increased at a faster rate than the rest of the school population, and the costs of special programs nationwide are beginning to be tallied. The U.S. General Accounting Office (GAO) published a study in January 1994 titled *Limited-English Proficiency: A Growing and Costly Educational Challenge Facing Many School Districts* at the request of the Senate Committee on Labor and Human Resources. The GAO study provides an overview of the serious problems confronting U.S. public schools in meeting the needs of limited-English students, new demographics on where these students are concentrated, and a detailed description of five representative school districts with rapidly growing limited-English proficient (LEP) populations.

Briefly, the GAO report highlights these problems in the five districts that are common to all public schools with LEP students:

- Immigrant students are almost 100 percent non-English speaking on arrival in the U.S.
- LEP students arrive at different times during the school year, which causes upheavals in classrooms and educational programs.
- Some high school students have not been schooled in their native lands and lack literacy skills in any language.
- There is a high level of family poverty and transiency and a low level of parental involvement in students' education.
- There is an acute shortage of bilingual teachers and of textbooks and assessment instruments in the native languages.

The information gathered by the GAO study is valuable to educators, researchers, and policy makers. An alarming fact reported in this study is mentioned only in passing and never explained: *Immigrant children account for only 43 percent of the limited-English students in our schools.* Who, then, make up the other 57 percent and why are such large numbers of native-born children classified as limited- or non-English proficient and placed in native-language instruction programs? In a private conversation with one of the GAO regional managers, I was unable to get an explanation for the high percentage of native-born students classified as limited-English. I was told that the GAO had not found an agreed upon definition of what a "limited-English person" is and that they have included in this category children who speak English but who may not read and write it well enough for schoolwork. In that case, there surely are a large number of students who are wrongly enrolled in programs where they are being taught in another language when what they urgently need is remedial help in reading and writing in English....

## The ALEC Study

The ALEC Study makes a bold attempt to unravel the mysteries of exactly how many students are served by special programs that aim to remove the language barrier to an equal education, what kinds of programs they are enrolled in, where these students are concentrated—by state—and how much is actually being spent in this special effort. As a former school administrator, I know firsthand that it is quite possible to account for special costs. In the Newton, Massachusetts, public schools annual budget there is an account for bilingual/ESL programs that covers all the costs incurred for the LEP students: teachers, teacher aides, books, materials, transportation, and administration. One knew what was spent each year, over and above the school costs for general education, and in Newton this averaged about $1,000 per student per year for LEP students. Not all school districts keep such information, and it is not collected consistently by all state education departments because this is not required by the federal government.

Analyzing data from the National Center for Education Statistics, the Office of Bilingual Education and Minority Languages Affairs (OBEMLA), and various other federal and state sources, the ALEC study synthesizes the data to arrive at these conclusions for the 1991–1992 school year:

- On average, all federal funding for education amounts to 6 percent; state and local sources provide roughly 47 percent each.
- Federal funding for bilingual education, $101 million in 1991 and $116 million in 1992, was mostly allocated to native-language instruction programs, giving only 20–30 percent to ESL programs.
- There were 2.3 million limited-English students enrolled in U.S. public schools while only 1.9 million were enrolled in any special language program, leaving 450,000 LEP students without any special language help.

- Of the 1.9 million students in special programs, 60 percent were enrolled in bilingual programs, 22 percent in ESL, and 18 percent in a category labeled "unknown" because states could not describe their special language programs.
- Candidly explaining the difficulties of collecting strictly accurate data, the costs of programs for LEP students are estimated to be $5.5 billion (56 percent) for bilingual programs, $1.9 billion (20 percent) for ESL, and $2.4 billion (24 percent) for unknown programs, totaling $9.9 billion for 1991–1992.
- Projecting that increases in enrollments in 1993 would be the same as recent increases, spending on special language programs would amount to $12 billion in 1993.

The ALEC study draws some tenable conclusions from the data summarized above while it admits that the approximate cost figures may be over- and under-estimations of what is actually spent. Both federal and state agencies do give preference to native-language instruction programs over ESL in funding decisions by a wide margin, even though "there is no conclusive research that demonstrates the educational superiority of bilingual education over ESL." Even if the ALEC cost estimates were overestimated, this is only one of several recent reports that point out the widespread lack of accountability in bilingual education. Twenty-seven years of heavy investment in mainly bilingual programs has not produced exact data on how much these programs cost or how successful they are in realizing their goals in student achievement. . . .

## The El Paso Bilingual Immersion Project

In 1992, the Institute for Research in English Acquisition and Development (READ) published a monograph by Russell Gersten, John Woodward, and Susan Schneider on the final results of the seven-year longitudinal study of the Bilingual Immersion Project; the results were summarized by Gersten and Woodward in *The Elementary School Journal* in 1995. This evaluation clearly demonstrates advantages for the immersion approach over the traditional bilingual education (TBE) model.

- The Iowa Test of Basic Skills (in English) results for grades 4 and 5 do show superior performance in all academic areas for students in the immersion program over students in the transitional bilingual program.
- By grade 6, 99 percent of immersion students were mainstreamed; at end of 7th grade, 35 percent of TBE students are still in the bilingual program.
- Well-designed bilingual immersion leads to more rapid, more successful, and increased integration of Latino students into the mainstream, with no detrimental effects in any area of achievement for students who took part in this program. The increased integration may lead to

a decrease in high school dropout rates among Hispanic students. Subsequent research is needed to explore the possibility of this effect of immersion programs.

- The major strengths of the bilingual immersion program are its use of contemporary thinking on language acquisition and literacy development and its relatively stress-free approach to the rapid learning of English in the primary grades.
- Teacher questionnaires revealed much greater satisfaction with the early, systematic teaching of English in the immersion program than with the slow introduction of English in the bilingual program.
- Student interviews indicated no significant differences in reactions to the two programs. No evidence emerged, from students, parents, or teachers, that native-language teaching produces a higher level of self-esteem or that early immersion in a second language is more stressful, two of the common beliefs promoted by bilingual education advocates.

Research such as that conducted in El Paso is invaluable in the ongoing debate on program effectiveness. Because the comparison was made between two radically different teaching methods in the same school district with the same population of limited-English students, this study provides incontrovertible proof of the benefits to students of early second-language learning. More recently, the New York City public schools published a report that threw a metaphorical bombshell into the bilingual education camp.

## The New York Study

*Educational Progress of Students in Bilingual and ESL Programs: A Longitudinal Study, 1990–1994,* was published in October 1994 by the Board of Education of the City of New York. New York City invested $300 million in 1993 in bilingual programs where the instruction was given in Spanish, Chinese, Haitian Creole, Russian, Korean, Vietnamese, French, Greek, Arabic, and Bengali—an investment that was not only misguided but harmful to the student beneficiaries, as the results of the longitudinal study show.

The New York City study is important because, like the El Paso study, it examines student achievement in basically different programs in large, urban school districts and because it charts student progress over a period of years. The criteria of student success measured included number of years served in a special language program before exiting to a mainstream classroom, reading level in English, and performance in math. The two groups of limited-English students whose achievement was monitored were (1) Spanish speakers and speakers of Haitian Creole who were enrolled in bilingual classrooms where they received mostly native-language instruction in reading, writing, and school subjects, with brief English-language lessons, (2) students from Russian, Korean, and Chinese language backgrounds who were placed in ESL classes where all instruction is provided through a special English-language curriculum. The study included children who entered school in fall 1990: 11,320 entering kindergarten, 2,053 entering 1st grade, 841 entering 2nd grade, 797 entering 3rd grade, 754 entering 6th grade, and 1,366 entering 9th grade.

As any disinterested observer might have anticipated, there is strong evidence showing that the earlier a second language is introduced, the more rapidly it is learned for academic purposes. Surprising? Not at all, but it flies in the face of the received wisdom of Jim Cummins's theories that were developed, after the fact, to justify bilingual education: the facilitation theory and the threshold hypothesis. With appropriate teaching, children can learn a new language quickly and can learn subject matter taught *in* that language. Reading and writing skills can be mastered, and math can be learned successfully in a second language; here are the proofs from thousands of New York City schoolchildren.

The most riveting outcome of this research reported in the New York study is the fact that "at all grade levels, students served in ESL-only programs exited their programs faster than those served in bilingual programs." The three-year exit rates were as follows: For ESL-only programs, the exit rates were 79.3 percent, 67.5 percent, and 32.7 percent for students who entered school in grades kindergarten, 2, and 6, respectively; for bilingual programs, the exit rates were 51.5 percent, 22.1 percent, and 6.9 percent, respectively.

The three-year exit rates for LEP students who entered kindergarten from different language groups, whether they were in ESL or bilingual programs, [were] reported as follows: 91.8 percent for Korean, 87.4 percent for Russian, 82.6 percent for Chinese, 58.7 percent for Haitian Creole, and 50.6 percent for Spanish.

Differences among language groups remained steady even for students entering the New York schools in the higher grades. Critics of the study, including Luis O. Reyes of the New York City School Board, allege that Korean, Russian, and Chinese background students are from middle-class families and that the social class difference invalidates the study. Socioeconomic data is not reported in the study. We do not know how many of the children in any of the language groups are from poor, working-class, or middle-class families, and we should not make unwarranted assumptions. One could hazard a guess that most immigrant, migrant, and refugee children attending the New York City public schools do not come from affluent families. The undeniable facts are that children from Spanish and Haitian Creole speaking families are mostly funneled into bilingual classrooms, and children from other language groups are mostly assigned to ESL classrooms. I firmly believe that the type of schooling these children receive makes a large difference in their ability to achieve at their own personal best. I believe, even more firmly, that Haitian and Latino children would succeed in mastering English-language skills better and faster and, therefore, join their English-speaking peers in mainstream classes much sooner than is now the case *if they were given the same opportunity given to Russian, Korean, and Chinese students.*

Exiting the special program classrooms more expeditiously is not only a cost consideration but a matter of integration and opportunity. Remaining in substantially segregated bilingual classrooms for several years does not equip students to compete in the broader life of the school and community—in fact it has the opposite effect. . . .

## The California Study and Others

... New York City's willingness actually to monitor the progress of LEP students and report the results to the public is much to be praised when we survey the lack of accountability in other parts of the country. The State of California, with 1.2 million limited-English students (43 percent of all LEP students in the United States) and a twenty-year history of involvement with bilingual education, commissioned an evaluation of educational programs for these students. *Meeting the Challenge of Language Diversity: An Evaluation of Programs for Pupils with Limited Proficiency in English,* the published report of a two-year study, 1990–1992, shows generally poor results for bilingual education programs in California and essentially evades the legislature's requirement that it provide "information to determine which model for educating LEP pupils is most effective and cost effective."

Major findings of this study are the following:

1. California public schools do not have valid assessments of the performance for students with limited proficiency in English. Therefore, *the state and the public cannot hold schools accountable for LEP students achieving high levels of performance* (emphasis added).
2. Many schools do not reclassify students (that is, move them from the bilingual programs with appropriate skills to work in mainstream classrooms), keeping them in native-language classrooms well beyond the time when they are fluent in English. "It is not surprising that many students may wait years to be formally retested for program exit and that many others may never be reclassified, going on to the middle school still bearing the LEP label."
3. Junior and senior high school LEP students do not have access to core academic subjects through Sheltered English or ESL. Long stays in bilingual programs in elementary schools delay the effective learning of the English-language literacy skills that are so important for secondary school work.

*Meeting the Challenge* presents a bleak picture of the disappointing results of twenty years of bilingual education in California. When the Chacon-Moscone Bilingual Bicultural Act of 1976 expired in 1987, the California State Department of Education sent notification to each school district that the intent of the act would still be promoted by state regulations, principally, "that the primary goal of all [bilingual] programs is, as effectively and efficiently as possible, to develop in each child fluency in English." *Meeting the Challenge* fails to tell us how or if this goal is being properly met but offers a variety of excuses for not fulfilling its mission. The weaknesses in this giant instructional system for limited-English students—one out of every five students in California—are of huge proportions. The fact that the State Department of Education has allowed school districts to evade their responsibility to assess and report on student progress shows an unconscionable lack of accountability by this powerful bureaucracy. If we cannot hold the schools responsible for program outcomes after twenty years, then perhaps the responsibility for this failure rests squarely on the state agency that has forcefully promoted the bilingual education policy.

California's high school dropout rates reported in June 1995 amounted to a statewide average of 5 percent per year, or a four-year average of 20 percent of students leaving school before graduation. Discouraging as that seems, the dropout rate for Latino students statewide is even higher—28 percent, compared to 10 percent for Asian students and 12 percent for white students. The four-year dropout rate for the Los Angeles Unified School District, the district enrolling the highest percentage of LEP students in the state, is a shocking 43.6 percent.

In 1993 the Los Angeles Unified School District embarked on a plan to improve its bilingual education programs, partly through expanded teacher training in the native languages of the students (actually, in Spanish only). Clearly, the increased emphasis on native-language instruction has not had any positive effect on the dropout rates for LEP students in the Los Angeles schools. The latest Los Angeles figures on dropout rates by ethnic breakdown, as reported by the State Department of Education in October 1994 for the 1993–1994 school year, are 44.4 percent for Hispanic students, *three-fourths of whom are enrolled in bilingual classes in the district....*

## Massachusetts Revisited

Ironically, the Commonwealth of Massachusetts, which passed the first state law mandating native-language teaching in 1971, Chapter 71-A, has an even more dismal record than California in the area of public accountability. Efforts to reform the Transitional Bilingual Education law have been successfully resisted, even though there can hardly be one legislator who has any documented proof for the effectiveness of bilingual education in Massachusetts. A state commission was appointed by Governor Weld to survey the status of bilingual education in the state, and in December 1994 it reported this conclusion:

> We do not know, on the basis of measured outcomes, whether TBE programs in Massachusetts produce good results or poor results. There are no comprehensive data that evaluate the performance of TBE pupils compared with pupils from other groups. This specialized program which accounts for 5% of all pupils in Massachusetts public schools and 17% of all pupils in Boston public schools is not held separately accountable for its performance.

Apparently, the commission has recommended that the state department of education develop new guidelines on accountability as soon as suitable tests are developed. As a veteran Massachusetts educator who has seen many a set of "guidelines" arrive with a flourish and disappear without a trace, I reserve judgment on the latest pronouncements.

Massachusetts probably leads the country in zany educational experiments. I reported earlier on the Cape Verdean project to try to encourage the use of a nonstandard dialect as the classroom language of instruction. The Boston public school system, in its infinite wisdom, now maintains a K–12 bilingual program in Kriolu, a dialect of Portuguese spoken in the Cape Verde Islands that has no alphabet, no written language, and no books. Massachusetts is thought to be the only place in the world to have schoolrooms in which Kriolu is the language of instruction, with Kriolu programs in Boston, Brockton, and New Bedford schools. Portuguese is the official language of education in Cape Verde.

Aside from the minor matters of alphabets, a written language, or books, there are these exquisite complications. Cape Verdean students may speak one of many dialects and not understand Kriolu, as explained by a science teacher in the Dearborn School, Boston, who says: "Sometimes a student gets upset because he's not understanding the Fogo dialect so you have to go back and help him in Kriolu or Portuguese." Communication between the schools and Cape Verdean parents is not improved either. Massachusetts law requires that all paperwork be sent to parents in the student's native language. A teacher at the Condon School, Eileen Fonseca, says it frustrates parents to receive a notice written in Kriolu: "When we send home report cards and matriculation papers in Kriolu, parents complain. This is new to them. They have to have it read three times, or they just ask for Portuguese or English, often so it can be read to them by family or friends." One parent made this comment: "They sent me a letter apparently to tell me something. I never understood what it was trying to say. I called to say that if the intent of the letter is to communicate, it would be better in Portuguese."

The Kriolu Caper makes an amusing, now-I've-heard-everything anecdote, but the enormity of such folly in education policy is no laughing matter. This program neither helps students learn the language or acquire the literacy skills necessary for school achievement, nor does it facilitate communication between school and family. What it does do is foster resentment in the Cape Verdean community, which does not feel respected or understood, a situation similar to the misguided attempt to make black English the language of instruction for African-American schoolchildren two decades ago. The Peoples Republic of Massachusetts is in serious need of a reality check.

Let me conclude with the review of a chapter in *The Emperor Has No Clothes: Bilingual Education in Massachusetts* by Christine Rossell and Keith Baker that summarizes the major studies on the effectiveness of bilingual education and analyzes those studies that are methodologically acceptable.

Social science research in education is, at best, an approximation of true scientific research. Schoolchildren cannot be isolated in laboratory test tubes and studied under pristine conditions, controlling for minute variables. In the area of bilingual education research, the quality of the product is generally acknowledged to be especially low. The elements of a scientifically valid evaluation of a special effort must include, at the minimum:

- random assignment of subjects to avoid self-selection bias
- a control group to compare with the group receiving the special program (treatment)
- pretesting to establish that students in different groups are starting with the same traits—i.e., that all are limited or non-English speakers—or statistical adjustments to account for pre-treatment differences
- posttesting to determine the effect of different treatments

- assurance that one group does not receive extra benefits, aside from the difference in treatments, such as after-school programs or a longer school day.

In the area of bilingual education research, there is the added problem that the label is applied to a range of educational varieties, from the classic model, in which native language instruction is given 80–90 percent of the school day, to the other extreme, in which the teacher may use a word or two of another language on occasion. This complicates the work of analyzing the effects of bilingual programs.

Rossell and Baker read over five hundred studies, three hundred of which were program evaluations. The authors found seventy-two methodologically acceptable studies, that is, studies that show the effect of transitional bilingual education on English-language learning, reading, and mathematics, compared to (1) "submersion" doing nothing, (2) English as a Second Language, (3) structured immersion in English, and (4) maintenance bilingual education. The authors' overall finding, which is of crucial importance as this is the most current, comprehensive analysis of the research, is that "*there is still . . . no consistent research support for transitional bilingual education as a superior instructional practice for improving the English language achievement of limited-English-proficient children*" (emphasis added).

**Donaldo Macedo**

**NO**

# English Only: The Tongue-Tying of America

During the past decade conservative educators such as ex-secretary of education William Bennett and Diane Ravitch have mounted an unrelenting attack on bilingual and multicultural education. These conservative educators tend to recycle old assumptions about the "melting pot theory" and our "common culture," assumptions designed primarily to maintain the status quo. Maintained is a status quo that functions as a cultural reproduction mechanism which systematically does not allow other cultural subjects, who are considered outside of the mainstream, to be present in history. These cultural subjects who are profiled as the "other" are but palely represented in history within our purportedly democratic society in the form of Black History Month, Puerto Rican Day, and so forth. This historical constriction was elegantly captured by an 11th-grade Vietnamese student in California:

> I was so excited when my history teacher talked about the Vietnam War. Now at last, I thought, now we will study about my country. We didn't really study it. Just for one day, though, my country was real again. (Olsen, 1988, p. 68)

The incessant attack on bilingual education which claims that it serves to tongue-tie students in their native language not only negates the multilingual and multicultural nature of U.S. society, but blindly ignores the empirical evidence that has been amply documented in support of bilingual education.... [T]he present overdose of monolingualism and Anglocentrism that dominates the current educational debate not only contributes to a type of mind-tied America, but also is incapable of producing educators and leaders who can rethink what it means to prepare students to enter the ever-changing, multilingual, and multicultural world of the 21st century.

It is both academically dishonest and misleading to simply point to some failures of bilingual education without examining the lack of success of linguistic minority students within a larger context of a general failure of public education in major urban centers. Furthermore, the English Only position points to a pedagogy of exclusion that views the learning of English as education itself. English Only advocates fail to question under what conditions English will be

From Donaldo Macedo, "English Only: The Tongue-Tying of America," *Journal of Education,* Boston University School of Education, vol. 173, no. 2 (Spring 1991). 

taught and by whom. For example, immersing non-English-speaking students in English as a Second Language [ESL] programs taught by untrained music, art and social science teachers (as is the case in Massachusetts with the grandfather clause in ESL Certification) will hardly accomplish the avowed goals of the English Only Movement. The proponents of English Only also fail to raise two other fundamental questions. First, if English is the most effective educational language, how can we explain that over 60 million Americans are illiterate or functionally illiterate (Kozol, 1985, p. 4)? Second, if education solely in English can guarantee linguistic minorities a better future, as educators like William Bennett promise, why do the majority of Black Americans, whose ancestors have been speaking English for over 200 years, find themselves still relegated to ghettos?

I want to argue in this paper that the answer lies not in technical questions of whether English is a more viable language of instruction or the repetitive promise that it offers non-English-speaking students "full participation first in their school and later in American society" (Silber, 1991, p. 7). This position assumes that English is in fact a superior language and that we live in a classless, race-blind society. I want to propose that decisions about how to educate non-English-speaking students cannot be reduced to issues of language, but rest in a full understanding of the ideological elements that generate and sustain linguistic, racial, and sex discrimination. That is, educators need to develop, as Henry Giroux has suggested, "a politics and pedagogy around a new language capable of acknowledging the multiple, contradictory, and complex subject positions people occupy within different social, cultural, and economic locations" (1992, p. 27). By shifting the linguistic issue to an ideological terrain we will challenge conservative educators to confront the Berlin Wall of racism, classism, and economic deprivation which characterizes the lived experiences of minorities in U.S. public schools. For example, J. Anthony Lukas succinctly captures the ideological elements that promote racism and segregation in schools in his analysis of desegregation in the Boston Public Schools. Lukas cites a trip to Charlestown High School, where a group of Black parents experienced firsthand the stark reality their children were destined to endure. Although the headmaster assured them that "violence, intimidation, or racial slurs would not be tolerated," they could not avoid the racial epithets on the walls: "Welcome Niggers," "Niggers Suck," "White Power," "KKK," "Bus is for Zulu," and "Be illiterate, fight busing." As those parents were boarding the bus, "they were met with jeers and catcalls 'go home niggers. Keep going all the way to Africa!'" This racial intolerance led one parent to reflect, "My god, what kind of hell am I sending my children into?" (Lukas, 1985, p. 282). What could her children learn at a school like that except to hate? Even though forced integration of schools in Boston exacerbated the racial tensions in the Boston Public Schools, one should not overlook the deep-seated racism that permeates all levels of the school structure....

Against this landscape of violent racism perpetrated against racial minorities, and also against linguistic minorities, one can understand the reasons for the high dropout rate in the Boston public schools (approximately 50%). Perhaps racism and other ideological elements are part of a school reality which forces a high percentage of students to leave school, only later to be profiled by the very system as dropouts or "poor and unmotivated students." One could argue that the above incidents occurred during a tumultuous time of racial division in Boston's history, but I do not believe that we have learned a great deal from historically dangerous memories to the degree that our leaders continue to invite racial tensions as evidenced in the Willie Horton presidential campaign issue and the present quota for jobs as an invitation once again to racial divisiveness.

It is very curious that this new-found concern of English Only advocates for limited English proficiency students does not interrogate those very ideological elements that psychologically and emotionally harm these students far more than the mere fact that English may present itself as a temporary barrier to an effective education. It would be more socially constructive and beneficial if the zeal that propels the English Only movement were diverted toward social struggles designed to end violent racism and structures of poverty, homelessness, and family breakdown, among other social ills that characterize the lived experiences of minorities in the United States. If these social issues are not dealt with appropriately, it is naive to think that the acquisition of the English language alone will, somehow, magically eclipse the raw and cruel injustices and oppression perpetrated against the dispossessed class of minorities in the United States. According to Peter McLaren, these dispossessed minority students who

> populate urban settings in places such as Howard Beach, Ozone Park, El Barrio, are more likely to be forced to learn about Eastern Europe in ways set forth by neo-conservative multiculturists than they are to learn about the Harlem Renaissance, Mexico, Africa, the Caribbean, or Aztec or Zulu culture. (McLaren, 1991, p. 7)

While arguing for the use of the students' native language in their educational development, I would like to make it very clear that the bilingual education goal should never be to restrict students to their own vernacular. This linguistic constriction inevitably leads to a linguistic ghetto. Educators must understand fully the broader meaning of the use of students' language as a requisite for their empowerment. That is, empowerment should never be limited to what Stanley Aronowitz describes as "the process of appreciating and loving oneself" (1985). In addition to this process, empowerment should also be a means that enables students "to interrogate and selectively appropriate those aspects of the dominant culture that will provide them with the basis for defining and transforming, rather than merely serving, the wider social order" (Giroux & McLaren, 1986, p. 17). This means that educators should understand the value of mastering the standard English language of the wider society. It is through the full appropriation of the standard English language that linguistic minority students find themselves linguistically empowered to engage in dialogue with various sectors of the wider society. What I must reiterate is that educators should never allow the limited proficient students' native language to be silenced by a distorted legitimation of the standard English language. Linguistic minority students' language should never be sacrificed, since it is the only means through which they make sense of their own experience in the world.

Given the importance of the standard English language in the education of linguistic minority students, I must agree with the members of the Institute for Research in English Acquisition and Development when they quote Antonio Gramsci in their brochure:

> Without the mastery of the common standard version of the national language, one is inevitably destined to function only at the periphery of national life and, especially, outside the national and political mainstream. (READ, 1990)

But these English Only advocates fail to tell the other side of Antonio Gramsci's argument, which warns us:

> Each time that in one way or another, the question of language comes to the fore, that signifies that a series of other problems is about to emerge, the formation and enlarging of the ruling class, the necessity to establish more "intimate" and sure relations between the ruling groups and the popular masses, that is, the reorganization of cultural hegemony. (Gramsci, 1971, p. 16)

This selective selection of Gramsci's position on language points to the hidden curriculum with which the English Only movement seeks to promote a monolithic ideology. It is also part and parcel of an ongoing attempt at "reorganization of cultural hegemony" as evidenced by the unrelenting attack by conservative educators on multicultural education and curriculum diversity....

In contrast to the zeal for a common culture and English only, these conservative educators have remained ominously silent about forms of racism, inequality, subjugation, and exploitation that daily serve to wage symbolic and real violence against those children who by virtue of their language, race, ethnicity, class, or gender are not treated in schools with the dignity and respect all children warrant in a democracy. Instead of reconstituting education around an urban and cultural studies approach which takes the social, cultural, political, and economic divisions of education and everyday life as the primary categories for understanding contemporary schooling, conservative educators have recoiled in an attempt to salvage the status quo. That is, they try to keep the present unchanged even though, as Renato Constantino points out:

> Within the living present there are imperceptible changes which make the status quo a moving reality.... Thus a new policy based on the present as past and not on the present as future is backward for it is premised not on evolving conditions but on conditions that are already dying away. (1978, p. 201)

One such not so imperceptible change is the rapid growth of minority representation in the labor force. As such, the conservative leaders and educators are digging this country's economic grave by their continued failure to educate minorities. As Lew Ferlerger and Jay Mandle convincingly argue, "Unless the educational attainment of minority populations in the United States improves, the country's hopes for resuming high rates of growth and an increasing standard of living look increasingly dubious" (1991, p. 12).

In addition to the real threat to the economic fabric of the United States, the persistent call for English language only in education smacks of backwardness in the present conjuncture of our ever-changing multicultural and multilingual society. Furthermore, these conservative educators base their language policy argument on the premise that English education in this country is highly effective. On the contrary. As Patrick Courts clearly argues in his book *Literacy for Empowerment* (1991), English education is failing even middle-class and upper-class students. He argues that English reading and writing classes are mostly based on workbooks and grammar lessons, lessons which force students to "bark at print" or fill in the blanks. Students engage in grudgingly banal exercises such as practicing correct punctuation and writing sample business letters. Books used in their classes are, Courts points out, too often in the service of commercially prepared ditto sheets and workbooks. Courts's account suggests that most school programs do not take advantage of the language experiences that the majority of students have had before they reach school. These teachers become the victims of their own professional ideology when they delegitimize the language experiences that students bring with them into the classroom.

Courts's study is basically concerned with middle-class and upper-middle-class students unburdened by racial discrimination and poverty, students who have done well in elementary and high school settings and are now populating the university lecture halls and seminar rooms. If schools are failing these students, the situation does not bode well for those students less economically, socially, and politically advantaged. It is toward the linguistic minority students that I would like to turn my discussion now.

## The Role of Language in the Education of Linguistic Minority Students

Within the last two decades, the issue of bilingual education has taken on a heated importance among educators. Unfortunately, the debate that has emerged tends to recycle old assumptions and values regarding the meaning and usefulness of the students' native language in education. The notion that education of linguistic minority students is a matter of learning the standard English language still informs the vast majority of bilingual programs and manifests its logic in the renewed emphasis on technical reading and writing skills.

I want to reiterate in this paper that the education of linguistic minority students cannot be viewed as simply the development of skills aimed at acquiring the standard English language. English Only proponents seldom discuss the pedagogical structures that will enable these students to access other bodies of knowledge. Nor do they interrogate the quality of ESL instruction provided to the linguistic minority students and the adverse material conditions under which these students learn English. The view that teaching English constitutes education sustains a notion of ideology that systematically negates rather than makes meaningful the cultural experiences of the subordinate linguistic groups who are, by and large, the objects of its policies. For the education of linguistic minority students to become meaningful it has to be situated within a theory of cultural production and viewed as an integral part of the way in which people produce, transform, and reproduce meaning. Bilingual education, in this sense, must be seen as a medium that constitutes and affirms the historical and existential moments of lived culture. Hence, it is an eminently political phenomenon, and it must be analyzed within the context of a theory of power relations and an understanding of social and cultural reproduction and production. By "cultural reproduction" I refer to collective experiences that function in the interest of the dominant groups rather than in the interest of the oppressed groups that are objects of its policies. Bilingual education programs in the United States have been developed and implemented under the cultural reproduction model leading to a de facto neocolonial educational model. I use "cultural production" to refer to specific groups of people producing, mediating, and confirming the mutual ideological elements that merge from and reaffirm their daily lived experiences. In this case, such experiences are rooted in the interest of individual and collective self-determination. It is only through a cultural production model that we can achieve a truly democratic and liberatory educational experience. I will return to this issue later.

While the various debates in the past two decades may differ in their basic assumptions about the education of linguistic minority students, they all share one common feature: they all ignore the role of language as a major force in the construction of human subjectivities. That is, they ignore the way language may either confirm or deny the life histories and experiences of the people who use it.

The pedagogical and political implications in education programs for linguistic minority students are far-reaching and yet largely ignored. These programs, for example, often contradict a fundamental principle of reading, namely that students learn to read faster and with better comprehension when taught in their native tongue. The immediate recognition of familiar words and experiences enhances the development of a positive self-concept in children who are somewhat insecure about the status of their language and culture. For this reason, and to be consistent with the plan to construct a democratic society free from vestiges of oppression, a minority literacy program must be rooted in the cultural capital of subordinate groups and have as its point of departure their own language.

Educators must develop radical pedagogical structures which provide students with the opportunity to use their own reality as a basis of literacy. This includes, obviously, the language they bring to the classroom. To do otherwise is to deny minority students the rights that lie at the core of a democratic education. The failure to base a literacy program on the minority students' language means that oppositional forces can neutralize the efforts of educators and political leaders to achieve decolonization of schooling. It is of tantamount importance that the incorporation of the minority language as the primary language of instruction in education of linguistic minority students be given top priority. It is through their own language that linguistic minority students will be able to reconstruct their history and their culture.

I want to argue that the minority language has to be understood within the theoretical framework that generates it. Put another way, the ultimate meaning and value of the minority language is not to be found by determining how systematic and rule-governed it is. We know that already. Its real meaning has to be understood through the assumptions that govern it, and it has to be understood via the social, political, and ideological relations to which it points. Generally speaking, this issue of effectiveness and validity often hides the true role of language in the maintenance of the values and interests of the dominant class. In other words, the issue of effectiveness and validity becomes a mask that obfuscates questions about the social, political, and ideological order within which the minority language exists.

If an emancipatory and critical education program is to be developed in the United States for linguistic minority students in which they become "subjects" rather than "objects," educators must understand the productive quality of language. James Donald puts it this way:

> I take language to be productive rather than reflective of social reality. This means calling into question the assumption that we, as speaking subjects, simply use language to organize and express our ideas and experiences. On the contrary, language is one of the most important social practices through which we come to experience ourselves as subjects.... My point here is that once we get beyond the idea of language as no more than a medium of communication, as a tool equally and neutrally available to all parties in cultural exchanges, then we can begin to examine language both as a practice of signification and also as a site for culture struggle and as a mechanism which produces antagonistic relations between different social groups. (Donald, 1982, p. 44)

It is to the antagonistic relationship between the minority and dominant speakers that I want to turn now. The antagonistic nature of the minority language has never been fully explored. In order to more clearly discuss this issue of antagonism, I will use Donald's distinction between oppressed language and repressed language. Using Donald's categories, the "negative" way of posing the minority language question is to view it in terms of oppression—that is, seeing the minority language as "lacking" the dominant standard features which usually serve as a point of reference for the minority language. By far the most common questions concerning the minority language in the United States are posed from the oppression perspective. The alternative view of the minority language is that it is repressed in the standard dominant language. In this view, minority language as a repressed language could, if spoken, challenge the privileged standard linguistic dominance. Educators have failed to recognize the "positive" promise and antagonistic nature of the minority language. It is precisely on these dimensions that educators must demystify the standard dominant language and the old assumptions about its inherent superiority. Educators must develop liberatory and critical bilingual programs informed by a radical pedagogy so that the minority language will cease to provide its speakers the experience of subordination and, moreover, may be brandished as a weapon of resistance to the dominance of the dominant standard language of the curriculum.

In this sense, the students' language is the only means by which they can develop their own voice, a prerequisite to the development of a positive sense of self-worth. As Giroux elegantly states, the students' voice "is the discursive means to make themselves 'heard' and to define themselves as active authors of their worlds" (Giroux & McLaren, 1986, p. 235). The authorship of one's own world also implies the use of one's own language, and relates to what Mikhail Bakhtin describes as "retelling a story in one's own words" (Giroux & McLaren, 1986, p. 235).

## A Democratic and Liberatory Education for Linguistic Minority Students

In maintaining a certain coherence with the educational plan to reconstruct new and more democratic educational programs for linguistic minority students, educators and political leaders need to create a new school grounded in a new educational praxis, expressing different concepts of education consonant with the principles of a democratic, multicultural, and multilingual society. In order for this to happen, the first step is to identify the objectives of the inherent colonial education that informs the majority of bilingual programs in the United States. Next, it is necessary to analyze how colonialist methods used by the dominant schools function, legitimize the Anglocentric values and meaning, and at the same time negate the history, culture, and language practices of the majority of linguistic minority students. The new school, so it is argued, must also be informed by a radical bilingual pedagogy, which would make concrete such values as solidarity, social responsibility, and creativity. In the democratic development of bilingual programs rooted in a liberatory ideology, linguistic minority students become "subjects" rather than mere "objects" to be assimilated blindly into an often hostile dominant "common" culture. A democratic and liberatory education needs to move away from traditional approaches, which emphasize the acquisition of mechanical basic skills while divorcing education from its ideological and historical contexts. In attempting to meet this goal, it purposely must reject the conservative principles embedded in the English Only movement I have discussed earlier. Unfortunately, many bilingual programs sometimes unknowingly reproduce one common feature of the traditional approaches to education by ignoring the important relationship between language and the cultural capital of the students at whom bilingual education is aimed. The result is the development of bilingual programs whose basic assumptions are at odds with the democratic spirit that launched them.

Bilingual program development must be largely based on the notion of a democratic and liberatory education, in which education is viewed "as one of the major vehicles by which 'oppressed' people are able to participate in the sociohistorical transformation of their society" (Walmsley, 1981, p. 74). Bilingual education, in this sense, is grounded in a critical reflection of the cultural capital of the oppressed. It becomes a vehicle by which linguistic minority students are equipped with the necessary tools to reappropriate their history, culture, and language practices. It is, thus, a way to enable the linguistic minority students to reclaim "those historical and existential experiences that are devalued in everyday life by the dominant culture in order to be both validated and critically understood" (Giroux, 1983, p. 226). To do otherwise is to deny these students their very democratic rights. In fact, the criticism that bilingual and multicultural education unwisely question the traditions and values of our so-called "common culture" as suggested by Kenneth T. Jackson (1991) is both antidemocratic and academically dishonest. Multicultural education and curriculum diversity did not create the S & L scandal, the Iran-Contra debacle, or the extortion of minority properties by banks, the stewards of the "common culture," who charged minorities exorbitant loan-sharking interest rates. Multicultural education and curriculum diversity did not force Joachim Maitre, dean of the College of Communication at Boston University, to choose the hypocritical moral high ground to excoriate the popular culture's "bleak moral content," all the while plagiarizing 15 paragraphs of a conservative comrade's text.

The learning of English language skills alone will not enable linguistic minority students to acquire the critical tools "to awaken and liberate them from their mystified and distorted views of themselves and their world" (Giroux, 1983, p. 226). For example, speaking English has not enabled African-Americans to change this society's practice of jailing more Blacks than even South Africa, and this society spending over 7 billion dollars to keep African-American men in jail while spending only 1 billion dollars educating Black males (Black, 1991).

Educators must understand the all-encompassing role the dominant ideology has played in this mystification and distortion of our so-called "common culture" and our "common language." They must also recognize the antagonistic relationship between the "common culture" and those who, by virtue of their race, language, ethnicity, and gender, have been relegated to the margins. Finally, educators must develop bilingual programs based on the theory of cultural production. In other words, linguistic minority students must be provided the opportunity to become actors in the reconstruction of a more democratic and just society. In short, education conducted in English only is alienating to linguistic minority students, since it denies them the fundamental tools for reflection, critical thinking, and social interaction. Without the cultivation of their native language, and robbed of the opportunity for reflection and critical thinking, linguistic minority students find themselves unable to re-create their culture and history. Without the reappropriation of their culture, the valorization of their lived experiences, English Only supporters' vacuous promise that the English language will guarantee students "full participation first in their school and later in American society" (Silber, 1991, p. 7) can hardly be a reality.

## References

Aronowitz, S. (1985, May). "Why should Johnny read?" *Village Voice Literary Supplement,* p. 13.

Black, C. (1991, January 13). Paying the high price for being the world's no. 1 jailor. *Boston Sunday Globe,* p. 67.

Constantino, R. (1928). *Neocolonial identity and counter consciousness.* London: Merlin Press.

Courts, P. (1991). *Literacy for empowerment.* South Hadley, MA: Bergin & Garvey.

Donald, J. (1982). Language, literacy, and schooling. In *The state and popular culture.* Milton Keynes: Open University Culture Unit.

Ferlerger, L., & Mandle, J. (1991). *African-Americans and the future of the U.S. economy.* Unpublished manuscript.

Giroux, H. A. (1983). *Theory and resistance: A pedagogy for the opposition.* South Hadley, MA: Bergin & Garvey.

Giroux, H. (1991). *Border crossings: Cultural workers and the politics of education.* New York: Routledge.

Giroux, H. A., & McLaren, P. (1986). Teacher education and the politics of engagement: The case for democratic schooling. *Harvard Educational Review, 56*(3), 213–238.

Gramsci, A. (1971). *Selections from Prison Notebooks,* (Ed. and Trans. Quinten Hoare & Geoffrey Smith). New York: International Publishers.

Jackson, D. (1991, December 8). The end of the second Reconstruction. *Boston Globe,* p. 27.

Jackson, K. T. (1991, July 7). Cited in a *Boston Sunday Globe* editorial.

Kozol, J. (1985). *Illiterate America.* New York: Doubleday Anchor.

Lukas, J. A. (1985). *Common ground.* New York: Alfred A. Knopf.

McLaren, P. (1991). Critical pedagogy: Constructing an arch of social dreaming and a doorway to hope. *Journal of Education, 173*(1), 9–34.

Olsen, L. (1988). *Crossing the schoolhouse border: Immigrant students and the California public schools.* San Francisco: California Tomorrow.

Silber, J. (1991, May). *Boston University Commencement Catalogue.*

Walmsley, S. (1981). On the purpose and content of secondary reading programs: Educational and ideological perspectives. *Curriculum Inquiry, 11,* 73–79.

# POSTSCRIPT

## Should Bilingual Education Programs Be Abandoned?

Macedo blames an ineffective bilingual education program for the fact that the vast majority of the high school dropouts in the United States are minorities. He maintains that learning English alone will not assist minority students in becoming equal members of society. Bilingual programs must do more to acculturate students.

Is bilingual education effective? Although Macedo thinks it can be, some studies suggest that bilingual programs may be ineffective. What can society do? Can we, in good conscience, take a "sink or swim" attitude and do nothing while some children become so frustrated and discouraged that they no longer want to go to school? Is society willing to continue to support people who cannot earn a living because they cannot read and write in English? Is it possible that current bilingual programs are not very effective because they are designed in such a way that children are actually taught little English and instead spend their time in special "transitional" classes?

A. M. Thernstrom, in his article "Bilingual Miseducation," *Commentary* (February 1990), encourages bilingual educators to teach the English language while emphasizing the culture of the students' new country. This could prevent the children from feeling like strangers in a foreign land.

The debate on the utility of bilingual education rages on in courtrooms, school boards, and families. However, as we engage in these arguments, we must not lose sight of the true focus of our discussion—the children. What approach will provide the most expedient way to give non-English-speaking children the best possible education?

## Suggested Readings


Citrin, J. (1990). Language, politics, and American identity. *Public Interest, 99*, 96–109.

Hokuta, K. (1992). At issue: Do bilingual education programs help Hispanic children learn English and assimilate into American culture? *CQ Researcher, 2*, 945.

Miller, J. A. (1990). Native-language instruction found to aid L.E.P.'s. *Education Week, 10*, 1, 23.

Office of Bilingual Education and Minority Languages Affairs: Q&A. `http://www.ed.gov/offices/OBEMLA/q_a.html`

# ISSUE 13

## Will Stricter Dress Codes Improve the Educational Environment?

**YES: Jessica Portner**, from "Uniforms Get Credit for Decrease in Discipline Problems," *Education Week* (February 14, 1996)

**NO: Karon L. Jahn**, from "School Dress Codes v. the First Amendment: Ganging Up on School Attire," Paper Presented at the 78th Annual Convention of the Speech Communication Association (October 30, 1992)

### ISSUE SUMMARY


**YES:** Jessica Portner, a writer for *Education Week*, argues that uniforms are good for schools. She states that after a policy on uniforms was adopted by schools in Long Beach, California, teachers and administrators saw a decrease in violence and an increase in academic achievement.

**NO:** Karon L. Jahn, dean of students at Chaminade University, Honolulu, Hawaii, contends that strict dress code policies interfere with students' First Amendment right of freedom of speech.


Dress codes have always been a part of school policy in public and private schools. But the issue of school dress took a political turn in 1996 when the president of the United States, Bill Clinton, took a stand in favor of school uniforms for all children by mentioning the Long Beach, California, school uniform policy in his State of the Union address. The president signed an executive order to send all school districts in the country a manual on school uniforms. Schools were not mandated to implement the policy of uniforms but were encouraged to consider the advantages of school uniforms and were asked to use the *School Uniform Manual* to guide them in the process.

In 1994 Long Beach became the first city in the United States to require a uniform dress policy in the public elementary and middle schools. The Long Beach school district found that after students started wearing similar outfits there was a decrease in student drug cases, sex offenses, assault and battery, and fights. It was felt that the reason for the change was that uniform dress created a positive environment and that this new environment allowed teachers to focus on education instead of spending all their time on discipline issues. Many states have since followed this trend by instituting mandatory or suggested forms of school dress.

School districts are under pressure from community groups and parents to adopt stricter dress codes, and this pressure is usually translated into requiring some type of school uniform. In 1996 Peter Caruso summarized the arguments for and against school uniforms. Reasons for uniforms: attendance increases because students maintain that it is easier to come to school when a "fashionable wardrobe" is not required; students' concentration on school work increases; students' self-esteem increases because students all look the same and differences are not so apparent; school spirit increases in the same way that team uniforms promote unity; clothing costs for families decrease; classroom behavior improves; gang member clothing and gang activity are eliminated; and academic performance increases.

Reasons against school uniforms: First Amendment rights of personal expression are denied; students feel controlled and prevented from expressing themselves; economic hardship for families; gang violence is not deterred; social class differences are not eliminated; and there is no empirical data that uniforms have a positive impact on school and children.

As you think about how you dressed in school and how students dress now, are there real differences? Do students want to look very different from their peers? Do you believe that simply having students wear the same thing to school makes it a better and safer place to be? Are there other factors that accompany a school uniform policy that could be affecting the school environment?

In the following selections, Jessica Portner details the dressing rules for the districtwide K–8 uniform policy in Long Beach, California. She supplies statistical evidence indicating that the wearing of uniforms does indeed provide a solution to school disorganization and violence. Conversely, Karon L. Jahn questions the legality of setting dress codes and requiring uniform dress of children. She wonders if it sends the wrong message about individual freedom. She also provides information about gang dress, its relationship to gang violence, and how it fits into questions about universal school dress codes.

**Jessica Portner**

# Uniforms Get Credit for Decrease in Discipline Problems

Linda Moore has been feeling especially proud lately.

And she has President Clinton to thank.

In his State of the Union Address last month, Mr. Clinton praised student uniforms as a way to promote safety and discipline in public schools. Ms. Moore, the principal of Will Rogers Middle School here, felt a particular satisfaction in the endorsement.

"Everybody is looking for answers, and here is a district that is doing something that is working," she said. For more than a year, the 83,000-student Long Beach system has required its elementary and middle school students to dress in uniform fashion. It was the first public school district in the nation to do so.

Mr. Clinton may have had this Southern California school system in mind when, in his speech, he challenged public schools to mandate uniforms "if it meant that teenagers [would] stop killing each other over designer jackets."

## Dramatic Results

Since the mandatory-uniform policy was launched in 56 elementary and 14 middle schools here in fall 1994, violence and discipline problems have decreased dramatically, a recent survey by the district shows.

From the year before uniforms were required, 1993–94, to last year, assault and battery cases in grades K–8 have dropped 34 percent. Physical fights between students have dropped by 51 percent, and there were 32 percent fewer suspensions.

Though each school in the district can choose its own uniform, most Long Beach students are required to wear black or blue pants, skirts, or shorts with white shirts. Nearly 60,000 K–8 students are affected by the policy.

Parents have the option of excusing their children from the requirements. But, so far, only 500 parents have filled out petitions to exempt their children, according to Dick Van DerLaan, a spokesman for the district.

In addition to Long Beach, a few other districts in California and across the country are testing the benefits of requiring students to come to school in color-specific, and sometimes style-specific, clothing.

The Oakland, Calif., schools began a similar uniform policy last September. And a small number of other districts—including Dade County, Fla.; Seattle; and Charleston, S.C.—allow schools to decide for themselves whether to require uniforms.

But Long Beach appears to be the first school system to have documented measurable success in improving student behavior.

Since students at Rogers Middle School started wearing black bottoms, white tops, and red jackets or sweaters, fights have declined by 40 percent, and academic performance has improved, school officials said.

Uniforms are an effective method of reducing unwanted behavior, she said, because the more formal clothing puts students in the right mind-set to learn.

"It's about dressing for success," said Ms. Moore, who said she wears the school uniform as a gesture of solidarity with her students. She has a selection of bright red blazers in her home closet.

Not one parent at Rogers Middle School has opted out of the plan this year, and a quick look around campus at the unbroken stream of red, white, and black shows that students are largely compliant. But there are some exceptions.

Last week, as Ms. Moore darted down the hall between classes, the former basketball coach was scanning the crowds.

"Tuck in that shirt," she called out to one disheveled teenager who was slouching against a locker. She looked disparagingly at another whose sweatshirt was clearly purple, not red.

In addition to choosing uniform colors, each of the district's schools is allowed to choose the fabric and style of dress. One elementary school requires its pupils to wear ties, and a few others prefer plaid, but most stick with blue or black and white.

"This isn't a private, prep school, with a coat-of-arms and saddle shoes look," Mr. Van DerLaan said. "It's a little more California casual."

## Generation Gap

A catalyst for adopting uniforms in Long Beach was parents' fears over students being attacked for inadvertently wearing a wrong color scarf or hat that might provoke rivalry among local gangs.

The district adopted a dress code more than a decade ago that prohibits gang-related attire, as well as caps, bandanas, baggy pants, and electronic pagers. But many felt the district had to take a more drastic approach.

When Judy Jacobs had two children attending Rogers Middle School, she was among the organizers of the effort to bring uniforms to that school. She now has a child in a district elementary school and has remained enthusiastic about uniforms. "There are so few boundaries for kids these days, with the drug use and violence, so if we can give them some limits, that's good," she said.

The uniformity tends to bolster safety because it makes it easier to spot people who may not belong on campus, school leaders say.

Many who teach in areas where gangs are prevalent argue that students are safer walking to school when dressed in uniform.

"If gang members see one of our students in uniform, they'll leave them alone," as if they belong to a different clique, said William Ferguson, who has been a gym teacher at Franklin Middle School here for 14 years.

But a large portion of the district's students aren't as upbeat as parents and teachers appear to be. And the older they get, the less they seem to like it —which may not bode well for talk in the district of expanding the uniform requirement to high schools.

"It's like we're all in jail," said Hector Gonzalez, a 7th grader at Rogers.

"It's totally bogus," said Gan Luong, an 8th grader at Franklin. "If you wear decent clothes, you shouldn't have to wear uniforms."

Alicia Nunez, also an 8th grader at Franklin, complained that the regimented attire stifles her creativity. "You come to school to get your education, not for them to tell you how to dress," the 14-year-old said as she strode across campus wearing a chocolate-brown T-shirt and jeans.

## Legal Challenge

The U.S. Supreme Court hasn't directly addressed the question of whether public schools can impose dress requirements on their students. Lower courts, however, have generally upheld school dress codes.

Last fall, in one of the first legal tests of a mandatory-uniform policy, an Arizona state judge upheld a Phoenix middle school's policy, even though it does not give students the right to opt out of the requirement.

Most public schools and districts offer a parent or guardian the opportunity to excuse a child from wearing a uniform. And most do not impose harsh penalties on students who are supposed to wear uniforms but don't.

"Schools generally feel they need to exercise latitude when they put their foot down," said Gary Marx, a spokesman for the American Association of School Administrators in Arlington, Va.

The American Civil Liberties Union of Southern California, on behalf of a group of low-income families, filed a lawsuit in state court last October against the Long Beach Unified School District, claiming that the district's uniform policy is a financial burden on poor families. The ACLU also claimed that the district has violated state law by neglecting to adequately inform parents about their right to exempt their children from the program.

The law signed in 1994 by California Gov. Pete Wilson to allow state public schools to require uniforms also says that parents must have a way to opt out of such requirements.

The ACLU lawyers say many parents can't afford the cost of school uniforms. About 66 percent of the district's elementary and middle school students qualify for free or reduced-price lunches. The case is currently in mediation.

Hope Carradine, who dresses three of her five children in uniforms, said she had to ask other family members to help pay for them. "I shop thrift and buy in bulk, and you can't do that with uniforms," she said.

## Other Strategies

But district officials say that parents can buy the essential items—a white shirt and a pair of pants—for $25 from several area stores. In addition, many schools sell sweatshirts or shorts for $6 each. Many local charities also provide free uniforms, backpacks, and shoes to needy students.

And if parents find the costs too burdensome, Mr. Van DerLaan, the district spokesman, said, they can always opt out. A flier explaining this right was sent to parents nine months before any uniform policies became effective, he said.

Despite their commitment to the school-uniform policy, Long Beach officials don't view it as a panacea for discipline problems.

Other efforts, such as stepped-up parent involvement and additional conflict-resolution classes also have contributed to the more peaceful climate on campuses, school leaders here say.

The district is continuing to evaluate the benefits of uniforms to determine whether last year's improved numbers for behavior were more than a blip on the screen.

And while some Long Beach students complain that the regulation dress is monotonous and dampens their personal style, many also see a positive side.

"The good thing is people judge you on your inner characteristics rather than what you wear," said Nick Duran, an 8th grader and the student-body president at Rogers Middle School. Plus, he said, it's easier to choose what to put on in the morning.

**Karon L. Jahn**

# School Dress Codes v. the First Amendment

Teenagers, clothes and gang behavior—what can school administrators do, or not do, with this volatile combination? Nation-wide educators and parents are watching their schools become increasingly an arena of serious and constant violence. No longer a concern limited to the inner city emotional and physical safety of students has become an issue on all campuses. While violence stems from many causes—racial tensions, use of illegal drugs, lack of security at home—school administrators consistently point to student dress as an important element in propagating violence at school.

Few things are more personal than an individual's body and its appearance. Throughout a lifetime, individuals may create their own realities by managing their appearance—which includes developing ideas and actions—and acting toward other people on the basis of the meanings their appearance offers. Communication scholars argue that all behavior, both verbal and nonverbal, communicates. The U.S. Supreme Court (Court) has agreed, protecting speech that contains elements of nonverbal behavior such as leafleting, picketing, flag burning, and contribution of money. At one end of the spectrum is behavior that is entirely symbolic, that which functions only to create meanings inside of people. Such behavior is usually easy to identify because it employs traditional symbols of words, gestures, pictures, flags, and emblems. Wearing green, for example, on St. Patrick's day because one is Irish—or would like to be. On the other end of the spectrum is conduct that is not communicated as merely symbolic, but is made symbolic because of the manner in which it is communicated. A student's dress or hair length, for example, can be chosen for personal pleasure or style or to advertise an attitude or culture.

If schoolchildren truly are not required to "shed their constitutional rights at the schoolhouse gate" then why have school administrators nation-wide, and in particular Anchorage School District in Anchorage, Alaska, taken one giant step backward by writing and enforcing stricter dress codes whose goal is to provide a safe environment for education by banning clothing or items associated with gangs or ganglike behavior? They are, as C. Edwin Baker would argue, "imagining the worst case scenarios and then proceeding to base analyses on the need to prevent it."

The worst case scenarios of gang behavior and the violence associated with such, implies that without dress codes students will be inundated with offensive behavior. The assumption is that students will not be inclined to exhibit, engage, or be harmed by violent behavior if they do not see or wear clothing that glorifies gangs. Wearing an unapproved Raiders jacket or ball cap, therefore, sends a message that the student is a member of a gang (which may be the intent of the message) rather than a message that the student needs to stay warm, likes the team spirit of the Raiders, or was given the clothing by his grandmother and is obligated to wear it.

The basic question this essay attempts to answer is whether school dress codes written with the specific purpose of limiting individual dress preferences, including dress associated with gangs, infringe on speech freedoms granted to individuals by the First Amendment. Can school officials reconcile their responsibility to provide a safe environment to educate all with the First Amendment mandate that government has "no power to restrict expression because of its message, its ideas, its subject matter, or its content"? Does a student have the right to select clothing for his or her body if others fear that selection of certain articles of clothing may suggest that the individual is a member of a gang, or lead to gang behavior and/or violence? Does a student have the right not to see what he or she considers an offensive article of clothing? If so, does the unwillingness of any student to receive a message outweigh another's right to offer such? Do school administrators have the power to write and enforce dress codes that permit certain types of clothing and deny other types? Are these codes to be uniform across the district, or left up to each individual school principal to decide based on the unique circumstances—and preferences—of the principal and his or her school? The answer to these questions requires examination of the literature on gang behavior, school dress codes, and First Amendment doctrine of specifically that of the captive audience.

School officials have a responsibility, often spelled out in their respective state constitutions, to provide an education for students in a safe environment. Suspension of students from school for violent action, including fighting, must be administered by school authorities. But administrative action, which often includes suspension for nonverbal speech acts which include, for example the wearing of red suspenders, ball caps, buttons, or "gang" colors, which have *not* led to violent conduct skids across the line of school safety concerns and crashes on the doorstep of the First Amendment.

Although the Court has extended its protection of political speech to nonverbal acts of communication, it has refused to decide for the nation as a whole whether there are elements of freedom of expression in the way public school students wear their hair or clothing. The Court has addressed other issues for students including protest, and right to organize, cautioning that authorities could interfere with the exercise of basic free-speech rights of elementary and secondary school students for good reason, such as to prevent disruption of the educational enterprise, but emphasizing that students in school are "persons" under the Constitution.

The Court's choice to let the issue lie with individual states has meant for students that their choice of dress and expression can be regulated by the current attitude of the officials in charge of their school. This attitude often reflects the perceived mind-set of the state and nation at large, giving preference to the majority viewpoint at the expense of minority expression. Changes may occur, as they did in a limited fashion during the late 1960s and early 1970s when schools eventually allowed boys to wear long hair and became more tolerant of dress. At least one court stated that students rights "will not be denied in deference to governmental benevolence or popular social theories." During the Reagan years of the 1980s, hair styles for boys became more conservative and boys who chose to let their hair grow were barred from attending school, or forced to sit in a booth or other sequestered area facing a wall, in order to complete their studies.

Over the last two decades, dozens of federal judges have carefully considered whether the guarantees of privacy and free speech apply to a teenager's choice of dress. They have divided roughly evenly on the question, with those courts who have struck down arbitrary rules insisting on a balance of the rights of the student against the need of the school to make reasonable health and safety regulations. Thomas Tedford writes that the "result is a continuing division among the twelve circuits of the federal courts of appeal, for some circuits have discovered constitutional issues whereas others have not."

Theorists George Herbert Mead and Herbert Blumer suggest that individuals come to social contexts with a storehouse of meanings, and this storehouse is developed and refined over time based on social interactions. Individuals use the cues provided by the appearance of others, interpret these cues, and attempt to organize their actions toward others accordingly. Meanings derived from appearance, therefore, are not passively received, on the contrary, each individual must learn, discover, or develop a meaning on his or her own. If every action that an individual takes, or fails to take, is behavior capable of being understood as communication, the question begging to be answered is: what happens when individuals attempt to offer their ideas and actions by choosing dress which falls out of mainstream acceptance?

There is no argument that adolescents are stealing the clothes off of other's backs, or in extreme instances, killing their peers for Nike shoes and Triple FAT Goose parkas. "Dressing for success has never been so risky. The combination of crack-quickened tempers, availability of guns and the flashy clothes of the drug culture has taken fashion awareness to a wicked level," wrote one author in a popular news magazine. While very little of this violence is taking place in the schoolyard, school officials are not taking any chances. They are reacting swiftly to the media's coverage and police information which details an increase in armed robbery and shootings over clothing and other gang dress by establishing dress codes. Many schools, like Crenshaw High School in Los Angeles have banned gang dress which includes bandannas and dangling earrings for boys. Other schools have banned excessive jewelry, shearling coats and decorative gold caps for teeth. In January 1990, the Detroit Board of Education required all of its 259 schools to design and enforce their own mandatory dress codes. During the summer of 1991, the Anchorage school district changed its dress code to include a sentence declaring "students may not wear clothing or items that are associated with gangs or gang-like groups."

Characteristics of gangs are certainly not limited to dress. Scholars and police investigators have recorded everything from the fact that white gangs (known as "stoners" or "heavy metalers") perform Satanic rituals, to the importance of the neighborhood (known as "the 'hood" to Hispanics). Certainly a gang's name (Miami's Mazda Boys who steal Mazda cars) is important, as is its graffiti, gang dress and colors. Today's gang member may wear baggy khaki pants riding low on the hips (known as "busting a sag"), patterns shaved into their heads, bandannas or colored rags hanging from their back pockets, or untucked flannel shirts. Their dress sends a message to others of who they are or who they want to be. They persist in using dress as a message even though it assists police in keeping track of them.

Despite the fact that there is obviously more to gang behavior than dress, school officials are targeting dress as the focal point in determining gang behavior. They are using the goals of their dress codes as a platform to support specific ban of gang, and other "inappropriate" attire. A review of school dress codes nation-wide reveals three distinct goals. First is the goal of individual preference. Most school districts have recognized that a student's dress and grooming is a "manifestation of personal style and individual preference." Administrators, apparently, will not interfere with the right of the students and their parents to make decisions regarding their appearance *except when their choices affect the educational program of the school or the health and safety of others.* Most codes include a discussion of "tight fitting, sheer, brief, low cut, or revealing attire that can cause embarrassment or indecency," and "graphics that are suggestively obscene or offensive on any garments," as examples of unacceptable dress that would violate the health or safety of others.

A second goal which emerges is that of personal hygiene, which again hinges on whether the student will disrupt the educational process by his personal grooming and cleanliness, or lack thereof. Again, most codes include language such as "Good grooming promotes pride and good behavior" or "Each student shall attend school clothed in a manner which is clean." School officials interviewed state that students are rarely sent home for poor grooming, most are given clean clothes available at school, or an opportunity to take a shower or wash their clothes.

A third, and perhaps the most important, goal is whether the student's dress and grooming "are within the limits of generally accepted community standards." School Boards are supporting School District Administrator's decisions to allow individual school officials to set the community standards for their schools. Some school officials, therefore, within a district may require uniforms for its students while others may allow shorts or more casual clothes —and both may claim to support existing community standards. The dress code of the Oakland Unified School District, for example, relies on the mandate provided by Article 1, section 28(c) of the California Constitution which states: "All students and staff of public primary, elementary, junior high and senior high schools have the inalienable right to attend campuses which are safe, secure and peaceful." The Board of Education, therefore, has an obligation, legally and morally, to establish a policy which "insures that schools are a safe and secure learning environment free from violence or the threats of violence and intimidation by gangs, gang regalia, gang gestures, weapons, the sale of dangerous and illegal drugs, drug or alcohol use, profanity, and bigotry and/or intolerance against people on the basis of race, ethnicity, religion, sex, or sexual preference." The code also states that students who dress in an "appropriate manner" (without defining what appropriate means) "make a statement by their appearance that they are in school to learn and that their behavior will be consistent with the serious goals of an academic environment." The code lays out specific articles of dress which may not be worn—T-shirts with designs or wording that demeans people on the basis of race or sex or jewelry which incorporates swastikas; smooth fabric jogging suits, "which are a leading symbol worn by gang members and drug dealers." In addition, students are not allowed to wear clothing designating membership in non-school organizations but official school sweaters jackets, athletic suits, ROTC uniforms, etc. are permitted.

Of these three goals, the desire for a well-groomed student seems to run the least risk of interfering with a student's free speech protection. Poor grooming habits (assuming long hair and/or braids for boys is not considered poor grooming) is probably not speech—symbolic or otherwise. The student's individual preference, however, when it comes in conflict with the school's community standards and safety responsibility would appear to create problems for speech rights. An examination of Anchorage's dress code can shed some light on the difficulties administrators face when balancing the rights of students speech with the responsibility of a safe place for education.

The Anchorage dress code does not list, as the Oakland school district and others have, what specific articles of dress are banned. The code is broadly written to allow each principal to determine what dress is acceptable for his or her school as long as the district's ban of gang clothing and items are prohibited. In-service training provided information on the procedure for reporting dress code violations to secondary education administrators, who would notify the school board, who would handle the final decision of whether the behavior was gang related or not. Few other characteristics of gangs were discussed, but principals were able to discuss among themselves at district meetings some of the particular problems that arose within their schools with the enforcement of the new code. In general, most of the principals agreed that it was difficult last year to determine what is "gang-like behavior" or "gang-like groups." After a one year effort, the district dropped the phrase "gang-like groups" from the code. The phrase "gangs," however, remains and with it the difficult challenge of supporting speech choice from inappropriate action.

Anchorage's secondary schools are a mixed bag of choices. Students who have had a difficult time meeting the attendance and education requirement of the district's six more traditional high schools scattered throughout the city and outlying area may choose to attend SAVE I or SAVE II, schools that give students a second chance—with very strict requirements. Students who choose to get a head start on the work world may attend King Career Center. Students who have had problems with law enforcement authorities may attend McLaughlin high school or REACH. Like most schools across the nation, each school boasts of its own distinct student population which reflects both the geographic and economic location as well as the school's curriculum choices.

Principals of each of the schools have the freedom to decide what is appropriate dress for his or her students. The code allows them to reinforce their requirements of good grooming and dress. Many stated that the behavior of students is "better" when the dress is appropriate—clean, no torn clothing, and "all body parts covered." All principals had no difficulty prohibiting clothing worn in a suggestive manner or clothing offering suggestive, or pornographic phrases. Each had different ways of handling the issue, some would provide a new t-shirt, others would allow the student to cover the message or turn the shirt inside out, and still others would call the parent to come to the school and take the child home to change. Principals in charge of a smaller number of students have an advantage because they are able to work-one-on-one with a student to arrange a clothing "compromise." Some principals may decide to institute total bans, for example, on baseball caps because the students grab them from the heads of others or throw them in the hallways, thereby creating a safety issue. Another principal, however, might not ban all ball caps, only those with an X or other racial or gang symbol.

Many of the principals were adamant about banning specific items that are symbols of racial hatred—swastikas, red suspenders—or gang dress—colored bandannas, black clothing. While they may be tolerant up to a point with students' "testing" behavior, they are quick to enforce the code if they suspect school safety problems. One Junior High principal suspended a student for wearing a button that displayed a racist message. He stated that the "button caused the suspension—not the behavior" because the student "refused to give up racist ideas." Despite his attempts to educate the student and her friends through counselors, special programs, support groups and leadership workshops, she continued to wear the button. He stated that any symbols or dress that sends a message "hateful to minorities" will not be tolerated in his school.

While some expressed discomfort in deciding what was a "gang" most focused on the actual behavior of the student, irrespective of the dress. Some principals have suspended students, for example, who attend school wearing red suspenders, leather boots and a shaved head, citing protection for the safety of the "skinhead" and other students. Most principals stated that they would speak with the student wearing skinhead attire, and his or her peers and teachers prior to taking discipline procedures. At least one principal during the 1991–92 school year had a difficult decision to make regarding a student who had improved his school track record during his high school years, but had taken to dressing in the attire of skinheads his Senior year. While his peers and teachers were convinced he just wanted to "dress that way," had not made any statements that offended anyone, and had kept his grades and job responsibilities up to school standards, the principal took seriously the school dress code mandate that "students may not wear clothing or items that are associated with gangs." After meeting with the principal, the student changed his dress choice and was allowed to stay in school and graduate.

Currently a principal at another high school has used the dress code and other school policies to suspend students dressed as skinheads. Several of these students have chosen to go beyond merely wearing the dress to blocking hallways and engaging in fights which has resulted in disciplinary actions. Physically prohibiting other students from attending class or fighting with other students is behavior which warrants discipline. Students who "show up" on campus dressed as skinheads are immediately sent home.

Most of the principals interviewed see their roles as a "firefighter" for angry students. They watch for behavior that takes the dress out of passive, nonverbal speech and moves it into action before enforcing disciplinary actions. All indicated that it is the behavior—and they generally do not associate dress with behavior—which they discipline. They are willing to tolerate students individual preferences for dress as long as it meets the grooming standards of the school (which shows that students take pride in themselves and their school) and that their preferences do not interfere with school safety goals. A few state that the code is "a very good deterrent" in preventing gang behavior, others say they have no reason to use the code, and yet others feel the code leaves too much choice up to the principals for deciding a student's fate.

The actions of Anchorage principals mirror those of the rest of the nation. Tolerance for student dress varies with the school and individual in charge of administering the code. When questioned about certain First Amendment issues that may arise when enforcing dress codes, most school officials are insistent that there is a "time, place and manner" for everything—and school may not be the place. They suggest that students are held "captive" at the location and look to administrators for education and safety. Despite numerous Court cases invoking the captive audience doctrine, a clear definition of this doctrine has not been articulated. One conclusion which can be drawn, however, is that the captive audience doctrine is more likely to be invoked to restrict speech when the individual is viewed as captive in a home rather than on the street, and if the speech is spoken, rather than written.

Individuals encounter daily unwanted messages. Because of the inevitability of undesired speech outside the protection of our home, the burden is placed on the recipient of information to avoid "further bombardment of his sensibilities." In some instances the Court has ruled that the viewer, when outside the home, has responsibility to turn away or avert his or her eyes to the message. This is almost always the case if the message is written. Marcy Strauss cautions that regulators and courts must not confuse "captivity in a *place* with being captive to *speech*." Students, for example, could solve the problem of unwanted dress messages by requesting different seat assignments in classrooms, selecting lockers in a different hallway, or turning their head at the first glance of an offensive message. While some students will certainly find some dress messages offensive, others may be more willing viewers and would presumably not want their right to view messages denied because the sender has been suspended from school. The question becomes: what is a reasonable burden in the context of school classrooms, cafeterias, libraries or hallways? Is it too much for students to glance at an offensive mural or poster and to turn away? Is it too difficult for those who don't want to read an offensive button to not get close enough to the student to do so? Should the burden of turning one's head when passing someone in the hallway wearing red suspenders and a shaved head outweigh the right of the individual to use dress as a message?

Strauss argues that the captive audience doctrine is "an elastic theory that could expand to curtail most free expression rights." The audience, all too often, acquires "veto power," and the doctrine could be used to prohibit freedom of speech, particularly with "respect to unorthodox views." School officials who regulate dress messages, i.e. deny gang colors, accessories, allow "clean-cut" clothing, violate content-neutral requirements. They are deciding that some messages are more worthy than others. In banning gang dress, school officials have not demonstrated that there is no less restrictive means available to achieve their objective of a safe educational environment.

The Court has ruled that schools may restrict the speech of students who urge the use of drugs to others—and could presumably ban the wearing of dress advocating such. But clothing that does not identify an illegal or pornographic message, should not be banned. Banning dress—or verbal speech—of students who advocate unpopular ideas in a place meant for educational purposes strikes at the very heart of learning and the First Amendment.

Those students who ask to be "left alone" and not be forced to view messages that may cause them discomfort are failing to participate in the democratic process. The right to make choices is essential if students are going to be free thinking, independent, autonomous individuals. Forced listening or viewing of a prescribed, sanitized message removes decision-making choices for the student. Students who do not see the student wearing red suspenders, because the student, if he or she chooses to wear that dress, has been banned from campus, cannot make a decision for themselves to speak, or not to speak, to the student about the meaning of his or her red suspenders. Is the student's right to choose to see or not to see certain messages one worth protecting? If we believe that speech is powerful, and that dress is a manifestation of speech, then this form of communication has the opportunity to inform, convince, persuade and possibly hurt everyone.

To provide for greater freedom we should permit the predictably occasional offensive uses of that freedom. When students send a message of dress or hairstyle they are telling others that their values and preferences have changed, or that their values and preferences have been suppressed. Regulations are created to maintain the status quo—and to prevent people from creating a new status quo. "When people feel compelled to engage in disruptive activity, the greatest need is for the government to respond appropriately to this dissatisfaction, not to suppress the dissidents," writes Baker. Public schools have legitimate interests in the free and open communication of ideas; they are in the learning business. School administrators are charged with the responsibility to provide an atmosphere of education for all. This responsibility includes allowing students to speak freely on issues of the day, to question ideas and concepts they are unsure—or too sure—about, and to wear clothing that may represent statements that are designed to shock or offend. School administrators do not have the right to decide for others which speakers are dressed appropriately and therefore fit to be heard and deserve to take place; they should exhibit greater, not less, freedom of expression than prevails in society at large.

Learning is not a spectator sport. Students have an obligation to attend classes and attend to discussions that will increase their knowledge—no matter how painful that may be. To limit the communication of some, because others find the dress message disgusting or the context unacceptable, dead-ends an avenue for debate. Dress codes may keep unwelcome attire out of the schools, and ultimately suppress what students think. Such a prescribed standard for speech ignores the uniqueness of speech and each person's interest in his or her personal selection of dress. Prohibiting dress will not solve the problems of cultural, economic, or educational differences. To force students to dress in lock-step fashion—as is evidenced by those schools advocating wearing of uniforms and those who determine from month to month what is acceptable "because clothing that is neutral one month may suddenly cause trouble the next"—because of the effect dress may have on their peers is to deny an opportunity for exploring the meaning of equality and understanding. More speech, rich in the vibrant colors, textures, and meanings, dress can provide, is the answer, not less.

# POSTSCRIPT

## Will Stricter Dress Codes Improve the Educational Environment?

Portner reports that significant changes in the school environment were documented after elementary and middle-school students started dressing uniformly. Jahn addresses several problems that school systems are beginning to face as they adopt stricter dress code policies. Controlling the way students dress will not solve the problems of envy, hatred, or intolerance for differences. Only education, discussion, and critical thinking can change students' views. Jahn maintains that uniform dress suppresses the one instrument that can combat violence and tolerance–individual thought and freedom of expression.

One wonders why conservatives like the idea of school uniforms when it represents an intrusion into personal lives by the government. As the introduction to this issue points out, the reasons espoused in favor of school uniforms are very similar to the reasons stated against them. There appear to be many opinions surrounding this issue but very little concrete data to support either view. The issue needs to be studied empirically.

## Suggested Readings


Caruso, P. (1996, September). Individuality vs. conformity: The issue behind school uniforms. *NASSP Bulletin, 80*, 83–88.

Evans, Dennis. (1996, October). School uniforms: An unfashionable dissent. *Phi Delta Kappan, 78*, 139.

Grantham, K. (1994, October). Restricting student dress in public schools. *School Law Bulletin, 25*, 1–10.

Holloman, L. (1995, Winter). Violence and other antisocial behaviors in public schools: Can dress codes help solve the problem? *Journal of Family and Consumer Sciences, 87*, 33–38.

McCarthy, C. (1996, March). Uniforms not a cure for school's ills. *National Catholic Reporter, 32*, 22.

McDaniel, J. (1996, September). Can uniforms save our schools? *Readers Digest, 149*, 79–82.

Should you have to wear a school uniform? (1996, March). *Current Events*, 95, 3.

Will school uniforms help curb student violence? (1996, April). *Jet, 89*, 12–16.

# On the Internet . . .

## Positive Parenting On-Line

This Positive Parenting site contains information and articles related to how parents and educators can communicate more effectively with children and adolescents. Most of the linked information is specific to adolescence.

http://www.positiveparenting.com/features.html

## CYFERNet

The Children, Youth, and Families Education and Research Network (CYFERNet), sponsored by the U.S. Department of Agriculture's Cooperative Extension Service, provides practical research-based information in health, child care, family strengths, science, and technology.

http://www.cyfernet.org

## The American Academy of Child and Adolescent Psychiatry Home Page

Here the American Academy of Child and Adolescent Psychiatry provides information as a public service to assist families and educators in socializing children and adolescents.

http://www.aacap.org

## COHIS: Teen Pregnancy and Maternal/Neonatal Health

The Teen Pregnancy and Maternal/Neonatal Health site of the Boston University Medical Center's Community Outreach Health Information System (COHIS) contains facts and summaries related to adolescent pregnancy.

http://www.bu.edu/cohis/teenpreg/teenpreg.htm

## Adolescent Health On-Line

This Adolescent Health On-Line site of the American Medical Association (AMA) provides extensive information on adolescent health issues and the AMA's Guidelines for Adolescent Preventive Services (GAPS) program. It also links to numerous other sites related to adolescent health issues.

http://www.ama-assn.org/ama/pub/category/1947.html

# PART 4

## Adolescence

*Many people use the term* teenage years *to describe adolescence. This is the period of time from ages 13 through 19. During this period of developmennt the child experiences puberty, and there are dramatic physical changes that occur as the child becomes a young adult. Much less obvious than the physical changes are the cognitive and emotional changes in children at this stage of development. In early adolescence the child is increasingly able to think on an abstract level. Adolescents also undertake the process of identity development, defining who they are. This final section considers some of the key issues related to decisions about values and sexuality that teens make as they move through adolescence.*

- Should Children Who Are at Risk for Abuse Remain With Their Families?
- Is the Welfare of Disadvantaged Children Improving?
- Is Abstinence Education the Best Sex Education?
- Can Memories of Childhood Sexual Abuse Be Recovered?

# ISSUE 14

## Should Children Who Are at Risk for Abuse Remain With Their Families?

**YES: Lisa Kolb**, from "Family Preservation in Missouri," *Public Welfare* (Spring 1993)

**NO: Mary-Lou Weisman**, from "When Parents Are Not in the Best Interests of the Child," *The Atlantic Monthly* (July 1994)

### ISSUE SUMMARY

**YES:** Lisa Kolb, a public information specialist, asserts that the family preservation model is the best way to help families in crisis. Family preservation keeps all the family members together in the home while helping the family solve its problems.

**NO:** Freelance writer Mary-Lou Weisman argues that orphanages and out-of-home placements are necessary for children whose parents abuse or neglect them. She maintains that society has an obligation to take children away from parents who are doing serious harm to them and that some children have their only real family experience when living in an institutional setting.

Newspaper headlines and television accounts of parents who neglect, abuse, or even kill their children show that the unthinkable does happen. Parents, the very people who are obligated to nurture and protect their children, do not always meet their children's needs. Parents may forfeit their responsibility to nurture and provide for their children because of drug addiction, mental illness, an abusive childhood, or poor parenting skills.

In the past, children who did not have parents or family members to care for them were sent to orphanages, but presently these children are placed in foster homes, residential treatment centers, or small group care homes. In addition to these types of placements, another alternative, family preservation, has emerged. In the 1980s the large numbers of children who needed foster care exceeded the number of foster homes available. Thus, the idea of family preservation became a popular alternative to out-of-home placement for needy children.

Family preservation is a model of intervention that is family centered and available 24 hours a day, seven days a week. Social workers spend a lot of time with families in their caseload and try to build on the strengths of the family to help create a more functional family unit. At first family preservation was seen to be a cost-effective answer to helping battered children. Now it has come under fire from some critics, who contend that it does more harm than good because the characteristics and standards of the programs have become so varied.

Can all families be served by the family preservation model, and are children protected from abuse during the treatment period? Are children in out-of-home placements or foster care protected from abuse? Studies provide conflicting answers to these questions. Proponents from each side point to cases of abuse and poor care in foster care as well as in family preservation situations.

How can society best care for children who are at risk for abuse or worse? Should the whole family (including children) be kept together and worked with in that context? Should children be placed in foster care until the family's problems are solved? Should children be taken away from parents entirely and sent to an institution for the rest of their childhood?

What do the children think about these choices? When faced with being removed from their home, no matter what the reason, most children probably want to stay at home. Often children will defend their parents before authorities even if their home situation is not safe. In these cases, who intervenes for children when parents cannot meet their responsibilities and when the children themselves want what may be harmful to them? How can society keep its children safe?

In the following selections, Lisa Kolb states that children are further damaged when they are removed from their homes as their families deal with crises. She sees family preservation as a successful way to solve families' problems while keeping children at home and argues that it works because parents value the family unit. On the other hand, Mary-Lou Weisman presents evidence that some children are not safe with parents who physically and emotionally scar their children. She maintains that society must bite the bullet, take children out of their abusive homes, and put them where they will survive and thrive.

**Lisa Kolb**

# Family Preservation in Missouri

It's 3:00 A.M. in a small, rural town in southwest Missouri. Vanessa Johnston, a family preservation services (FPS) worker, is combing the streets looking for Heidi, one of her clients. Earlier that night, Vanessa learned that Heidi, a 19-year-old single mother, had been accosted by "Stacey," a "friend." Stacey had heard a rumor that Heidi was involved with Stacey's boyfriend, so she had set out to even the score: she surprised Heidi in the dark stairwell leading to her apartment and beat her up.

Heidi has a habit of running when things get rough. Finding no trace of her client, and knowing Heidi's penchant for hitching rides with truckers, Vanessa heads for the local truck stop. She has to talk with only a few drivers to find out that Heidi, with her infant son in tow, has hitched a ride to Oklahoma City.

Vanessa goes back to her office and waits. She knows the rumor about Heidi and Stacey's boyfriend is unfounded, and she wonders how Heidi has been affected by Stacey's assault. She knows that Heidi has felt that Stacey was her only friend, the one person she could trust.

After several hours, the telephone rings: it's Heidi, asking for help to get back home. Vanessa arranges for the bus ride back to Missouri, goes home, and gets ready for work.

Welcome to the world of an FPS worker. The work is harried, and time is a precious commodity. The job is frustrating: one step forward can be followed by two steps backward. And it is emotionally draining–six weeks of being on 24-hour call can take its toll. But it is encouraging: to see a family learn from its mistakes is what this job is all about. Frustrated and eager for a change, many social workers, caseworkers, and others are willing to accept the challenge and take on the daunting job description that comes with FPS.

. . .[F]amily preservation services are designed to protect children who are at immediate risk of out-of-home placement, by providing immediate, intensive, comprehensive, 24-hour, in-home services to these children and their families. FPS is guided by these premises:

- Children have a right to their families.
- The family is the fundamental resource for nurturing children.

From Lisa Kolb, "Family Preservation in Missouri," *Public Welfare,* vol. 51 (Spring 1993), pp. 8–19.  Notes omitted.

- Parents should be supported in their efforts to care for their children.
- Families are diverse and have a right to be respected for the special cultural, racial, ethnic, and religious traditions that make them distinct.
- Children can be reared well in different kinds of families, and one family form should not be discriminated against in favor of another.

Operating statewide since October 1992, FPS is working for a large number of Missouri families. The state measures success by the number of children who remain safely in their homes rather than being removed and placed in foster care. From October 1991 to September 1992—roughly the year before FPS was operating statewide—the program reported serving 656 families. According to the Department of Social Services, Division of Family Services (DFS), which administers the program, 128 of those families ended up having children placed outside the home.

Since it began operating statewide, the program has succeeded in diverting about one-third of the children who otherwise would have entered foster care. Statewide preliminary data show that in the six months to a year following completion of FPS, 81.93 percent of FPS families are intact. A year or more following FPS, 77.89 percent of FPS families are intact.

Vanessa started with the program in November 1991 and had worked with only eight other families before Heidi and her baby. Vanessa identifies the benefits of a program like FPS, which is designed to deal with long-term issues by meeting immediate needs: "We know families will still cycle [in and out of various services] after they've gone through the program, but we hope that what they learned through FPS will help them to pull themselves up and not sink so low the next time."

For Vanessa, one of the most attractive qualities of FPS is the program's flexibility. FPS allows her the latitude to tailor her services to meet the specific needs of her client families. Typically, FPS workers

- teach problem-solving skills to family members;
- teach families how to cope with future crises without relying on harmful behavior;
- provide information to families regarding other sources of assistance;
- teach family members life skills, such as finding an apartment, bargain hunting, nutrition, and money and management;
- focus all services on empowering families to solve their own problems and avert crises.

Statewide, FPS has 114 full-time workers: 36 are employees of DFS, and 78 are working under contract. FPS also has four part-time workers, three in-house and one contractual.

FPS workers must meet a number of requirements:

- They must have a master's degree in social work, counseling, psychology, or a related field. Or, with the approval of DFS, they can have a bachelor's degree and extensive experience in treatment of families in crisis. Vanessa has a bachelor of arts degree in psychology and five and a half years' experience with DFS in investigations, foster care, and casework.
- They must have experience working with children and their families.
- They must demonstrate knowledge of crisis intervention, communications skills, and family education methods.
- They must demonstrate a willingness to work a nonstructured, flexible schedule, routinely including evenings and weekends.
- Contracted workers must meet applicable state licensing criteria.

FPS workers are assigned two families at a time and work with those families for six weeks. The two assignments rarely begin and end at the same time, so there is frequent overlap of cases. Though she could use as much as two weeks between cases to complete the required paperwork—since she has little time to work on anything but the family's needs while the case is in progress —the demand for FPS is so great that Vanessa usually gets no more than two to five days between family assignments.

Vanessa's personality is ideally suited for FPS's nondirective approach. Her ability to act as mother, confidant, and counselor, coupled with her innate sense of when to advise, when to pull back, and when to listen, are key to her rapport with families in crisis. Vanessa admits she works best when encouraging family members to identify their problems and arrive at their own solutions. Although each FPS worker has his or her own style, Vanessa emphasizes that the priority in each FPS case is the same—to make all families safe. If she accomplishes nothing else in her six weeks with a family, Vanessa strives to instill one vitally important attitude: "respect for the kids and their view of the world."

The six-week time frame forces FPS workers to prioritize the elements that are critical to keeping a family together. Vanessa's work with Heidi on parenting and other life skills had to wait until mother and son had a roof over their heads. Kima and Jerry, Vanessa's other FPS family, were not searching for food and shelter, but rather salvation for their marriage.

## Heidi and Zach

Like many clients, Heidi chose FPS as the less of two evils. Faced with the removal of her son, Heidi reluctantly allowed FPS into her life for one simple reason: "Zach is all I have." Many of Vanessa's clients have a history of physical or sexual abuse, and Heidi's background is no different. Her childhood in Alabama was little more than a series of new addresses and new guardians, and she did not develop relationships with any of them. Her parents divorced when she was very young. The few times she lived with them were brief, unpleasant interruptions in her travels from one foster home to another. When she turned

18, Heidi aged out of the Alabama foster care system and finally escaped the instability of foster care; but she found that life in an Alabama group home was not much better. She soon ran away to Arkansas, then to Mt. Vernon, Missouri, where she met Micky.

Within a year, Heidi found herself homeless and pregnant with Micky's child. She delivered Zach while living in an area home for unwed mothers. But, restless and longing for her old lifestyle, Heidi soon left to run with her baby's 15-year-old father and his friends. The drugs, alcohol, and delinquency of the group led to the intervention of DFS and Vanessa.

Immediately, Vanessa learned that, with Heidi, she would have to shelve her counselor's hat. Heidi's past had left her stubborn and independent, with a deep mistrust of adults and no tolerance for advice. Heidi likes the fact that FPS allows her to retain control over her own life: "Vanessa doesn't tell me what to do—the decisions are mine to make. I'm learning to trust in myself. I'm a good person."

With Vanessa's help, Heidi was able to begin pursuing her lifelong dream of becoming a nurse. Daycare, provided by FPS, allowed Heidi to work on her general equivalency diploma (GED); and she scored well in preliminary testing. For the first time in her life, she not only is setting goals but also is working to meet them. "I'll do it," she says, "if it takes me till I'm 80."

Vanessa's teaching methods allowed Heidi to learn by example. "My families learn much more from what I do," she says, "than from what I say." For Heidi, many of life's most mundane tasks—including looking for an apartment—were a mystery; and, as Vanessa explained, "You can't ask about something you know nothing about." Armed with a newspaper, a telephone book, and a map, Vanessa talked Heidi through the procedure—looking in the classified section, calling apartment managers for details, and filling out applications.

The scarcity of rental housing in the area limited Heidi's options, and her monthly income—$234 from Aid to Families with Dependent Children and $200 in food stamps—prevented her from qualifying for federal housing. Finding nothing more suitable, Vanessa and Heidi were forced to make do with a small, windowless basement apartment for $100 a month. With money from the Crisis Intervention Fund, an FPS emergency fund earmarked for high-priority needs, Vanessa took Heidi to garage sales, teaching her to bargain-shop for kitchen items, other household goods, and baby clothes for Zach. One of Vanessa's FPS coworkers obtained a used sleeper sofa, chairs, and a lamp to complete the apartment's furnishings.

Although the apartment soon looked livable, Vanessa worried about the steep, dark stairwell leading to the apartment and the lack of heating or air conditioning. Heidi objected to turning on the gas stove for fear of an explosion, but Vanessa explained that utilities are a good way to establish credit. Meanwhile, Vanessa would look for a used microwave oven.

Vanessa also subtly tried to change Heidi's nutritional habits and attitudes about medical care. Heidi, a frail 80 pounds, frequently skipped meals; and this sometimes would carry over to 4½-month-old Zach, who needed regular feedings of formula. Vanessa was concerned that Heidi would not prepare balanced meals for Zach as his nutritional needs changed. She learned that Heidi occasionally would fix instant soup or other one-step preparation foods if she had access to a microwave. Vanessa knew that Heidi was concerned about Zach staying on target with his weight gain, and she hoped this would entice Heidi to do more cooking.

Whereas Heidi did not seem very concerned about her own health, Vanessa did begin to see improvements in her concern for Zach's health. Heidi would become defensive at the suggestion of seeking medical care for herself, and she ignored her doctor's diagnosis of strep throat and recommendation for a tonsillectomy. With Vanessa's encouragement, however, Heidi began to understand the importance of regular checkups for Zach, who had developed a chronic cough soon after he was born. Heidi was afraid of the "hurt" that doctors cause and the bad-tasting medicine they prescribe, but Vanessa helped her to see that these were the only ways to make Zach better. Watching Heidi follow Zach's medication schedule gave Vanessa a renewed sense that mother and son would make it—together.

As determined as she was to become a better mother, Heidi experienced an equally strong pull to return to her old lifestyle on the streets, running with Micky and his friends. Vanessa had to suppress her own maternal instincts. As a mother of three, she knew that if Heidi were her own child, she likely would have reacted to Heidi's involvement with Micky and his friends by criticizing their behavior and prohibiting Heidi from seeing them. But Vanessa knew that reaction not only would be a waste of time, but also would damage her relationship with Heidi.

As an FPS worker, Vanessa strongly believes that it is neither her position nor beneficial to her clients for her to judge them. She realizes that Micky's role as Zach's father is important to Heidi and that it is unlikely that his influence and that of his friends will diminish.

During a scheduled visit, Vanessa found Micky and his friends at Heidi's apartment. Vanessa's theory is that every moment spent with a family is "teachable," so she turned what could have been a wasted afternoon into a group counseling session by including the entire group in her discussion with Heidi. By opening a discourse about their influence on Zach's well-being, Vanessa believes Micky, and perhaps some of his friends, came away with a sense of the consequences of their actions. Heidi says Micky likes her involvement with FPS and that he admits he has gained a new perspective through Vanessa.

Vanessa's presence gradually began to have a calming effect on Heidi's life. Heidi describes her past experiences with the Department of Social Services (DSS) as having had a "bad thing" with the agency. But she says her relationship with Vanessa is "okay"—a glowing endorsement from the reserved teenager. "DDS has always been rude," Heidi says. "They make me feel like they don't have the time. FPS is making me think some of them do care. Maybe they do."

## Kima and Jerry

Vanessa met Kima and Jerry as their two-year marriage was showing signs of breaking up. Jerry, a 25-year-old unemployed welder, was starting to drink; and drinking made him mean. Kima had plenty of experience with abusive men, and she wasn't going to risk Jerry's angry words turning to violence. Fed up, she had filed for divorce; and, as a would-be single mother of three with no job, she saw FPS as the only way to keep her family together.

Kima's nightmare had begun in her early teens. After months of sexually abusing her, Kima's stepfather one day had escalated his assault to a violent rape, after which he had left her tied in an abandoned barn. She escaped by breaking a window and sawing herself free with a shard of glass. The stepfather, serving an eight-year sentence for the crime, was threatening Kima from prison. Family members who were in contact with him warned her about his plans to find her when he was released. In fact, shortly after his release early in 1993, he was rearrested for attempting to poison the water supply of Sarcoxie, Missouri, a town close to where Kima lived.

Although her stepfather's incarceration gave Kima a sense of release from the pain he had caused, she had had other equally devastating relationships in the years since—sadly, a common occurrence for sexual abuse victims. Kima's oldest son, Travis, 7, was born out of a later rape. Then a boyfriend killed his and Kima's 6½-month-old son. Kima has two other children, Megan, 5, and Miles, 11 months; only Miles is Jerry's child.

Kima and Jerry's first contact with DFS came after Jerry jerked a crying Miles out of his crib, breaking his arm. Although the doctor who treated Miles's injury originally suspected abuse, his final report called the incident "accidental." Jerry now feels DFS is suspicious of him, and his disdain for what he believes was an unfair investigation has left both Kima and Jerry with a blatant distrust of DFS.

Despite this mistrust, Kima saw FPS as the only way to save her marriage, something she very much wanted to preserve. Middle-class values are important to Kima. Her father, killed when she was 11, was a positive influence on her life; and she wants the same for her children. Referred to the program by a DFS worker, the couple was willing to work with FPS because they saw it as an answer to their marital troubles, not acknowledging that the children were at issue.

"I just wanted Jerry to realize he is an equal partner," Kima said. "You can't take 90 percent and give 10. I realize he had a lot of problems growing up. I guess I just wanted us both to start fresh. It's easier for Jerry to talk with someone else present—he's not as apt to walk out."

Jerry says he and Kima immediately accepted Vanessa by "detaching" her from DFS. "I kind of had feelings . . . I didn't know Vanessa or anything about her. I wasn't sure if I was ready to talk to an outsider. But she's strong on offering suggestions. She's even told us several times she'd leave if we wanted her to. I thought we'd have to sit in a circle and play a game. Everything was to our advantage, because it helped."

Kima and Jerry's problems escalated after Kima lost her job with a local trucking company. Until then, it had not been important to Kima that Jerry work—she was willing to do almost anything to keep the peace: "When Jerry is unhappy, the whole house suffers." But when the loss of Kima's paycheck forced Jerry to look for employment, the tension began to mount. Although

Jerry eventually landed a job at an area factory, one with good wages and benefits as well as safe working conditions, he found many excuses to skip work. After three weeks, Jerry had clocked in for only seven shifts.

Now that Kima was unemployed, she had time to begin work on her GED, and FPS enabled her to do that. Since Travis was in the first grade and Megan was enrolled in Head Start, Miles was the only child needing daycare. Unfortunately, Mt. Vernon happens to have the highest teen pregnancy rate in Missouri, which makes state-funded daycare scarce. After Kima completes her GED, she plans to attend college full-time. Through Vanessa, Kima learned that many area colleges have daycare facilities on campus. "FPS points out opportunities," Kima says. "I always knew I had college potential, but until I met Vanessa, I wasn't aware what was available in this area."

Kima and Jerry seemed to be getting past the communication barriers that had caused so many of their problems. "Overall, I feel Jerry has more consideration and respect for me," Kima said. "He has learned to voice his anger rather than just letting it build up. He has been harsh with the kids in the past; but he has learned that if we are to respect his feelings, he has to respect ours. You can't solve your problems when you're angry."

Vanessa points out that FPS's nondirective approach doesn't always work for her. Sometimes, she explains, the atmosphere is just right for physical violence to erupt: "After all, FPS strives to build a rapport while family members are learning to vent their frustrations. Some families become so comfortable with my presence that they forget I'm there and start swinging. That's the time to become very directive."

During counseling, Jerry admitted that he often became frustrated with the children when they would not help Kima around the house. Vanessa helped turn a major point of conflict between Kima and Jerry into a workable solution by developing a chore chart with a reward system for the children. "They learned that there are certain things that have to be done," Kima said. "Now they know that Mom isn't going to do everything for them."

Jerry admitted he had been self-centered and that his moods had made life hard for Kima and the children, but he seemed unwilling to share the decision-making with his wife. Money management had been a problem, and Jerry's new role as the breadwinner gave him a sense of ownership over his paycheck. For instance, the rent was due and the family needed a second car; but Jerry went out and bought a motorcycle. Vanessa worried that Kima and Jerry would be evicted since they were already behind on their rent. Their finances for the coming month looked no better. Because Jerry had missed so much work, his paycheck was going to be short; and, though they had applied, the family was not yet receiving food stamps.

Vanessa's first inclination was to dip into the program's Crisis Intervention Fund. FPS workers have discretion over how and when to use the money, and they do not usually make clients aware that the money is available, so that families do not become dependent on it. FPS workers spend an average of $350 from this fund per family, and Vanessa already had nearly depleted Kima and Jerry's share. Vanessa thought better of bailing Kima and Jerry out of their financial troubles. "Jerry lost his safety net when Kima lost her job," Vanessa said.

"These are hard lessons for Jerry, and it's too bad the whole family has to suffer. He needs to learn." The family did manage to scrape by, but later had to move when the landlord raised the rent.

Most FPS workers are women, but Jerry's respect for male authority made Vanessa wonder if he would be more inclined to open up with a male counselor. Jerry dispelled those fears, however: "To me it doesn't matter whether it's a male or female counselor as long as they are helping. Vanessa taught me to stop and think before I say anything—but there are still times I wish I would do more thinking."

"I can't speak for all families, but it's been very beneficial for us," Kima said. "Jerry and I talk more than we ever would have before. Jerry's focus used to be on the bad side of things. He would always focus on the bad things the kids did. I guess something from his childhood made him feel like he didn't measure up. Vanessa has helped him see the good things."

FPS workers and their families often develop a closeness that makes it difficult to let go at the end of six weeks. This was the case between Vanessa and Kima and Jerry. When asked if he felt that the progress he and Kima had made with Vanessa would continue, Jerry said, "She's not going to leave our lives—we know where she lives." Vanessa's first FPS family still calls her on occasion, she says, just for reassurance that what they are doing is okay.

After leaving the FPS program, families are assigned aftercare (AC) workers from their home counties. AC workers continue the case plan that the FPS worker has started with the family. To make the transition easier for families, Vanessa is in constant communication with the AC workers to prepare them for the next phase of a family's treatment. "From the very first day I'm with a family, I begin pulling in other services that they can rely on when I'm gone," Vanessa says. "Actually, I guess you could say aftercare begins with that very first session."

Vanessa winds up a whirlwind week with Heidi, Kima, and Jerry with a trip to McDonald County, Missouri, where she will attend a "staffing"—a periodic screening of clients to determine progress and alternative services. The two-hour drive will account for part of the 2,000 miles she puts on her family van each month. Accompanying Vanessa are Angela, a private provider of outpatient therapy from a nearby county, and Keith, an FPS coworker.

The room is filled with social workers, FPS workers, and private providers such as Angela, all of whom offer additional insight to the cases they hear. Amid the often horrifying stories of the plight of area families are the occasional lighthearted jokes and repeated trips to the coffeepot—both necessary for the long meetings. Vanessa relates Heidi's progress, and all are impressed. Vanessa appreciates the recognition from her colleagues, but she warns that Heidi has much work ahead of her. Then Vanessa says she is not taking any more FPS families until she returns from a much-needed vacation. Everyone in the room nods in enthusiastic agreement.

Having already had its final staffing, Kima and Jerry's case is closed for Vanessa. She speaks hopefully of their chances for success, knowing they are better prepared for the inevitable rough turns their lives will continue to take. The AC worker has taken over and will continue to guide them toward services should they need assistance.

Families receive a follow-up survey up to one year after they have completed FPS, and this is an FPS worker's final barometer of the program's impact on each family. Vanessa is not ready to say that FPS has succeeded in Kima and Jerry's case. If the survey shows that the children still are living with their family, and if Kima and Jerry are talking and not yelling, then she can say that FPS was successful for this family.

Meanwhile, Vanessa steals a few minutes each day for her own family's needs. Her private life is sandwiched between FPS families, but she has no complaints; and the sparkle in her eye reveals her firm belief that she is doing the right thing. She smiles as she relates how her clients' gratitude is rewarding, but misguided. "It's great that some families say they are doing it for me," says Vanessa. "But if I'm the motivation, then I'm out of there, and where do they go? Believe me, they are doing all the work, and they are doing it for their family."

**Mary-Lou Weisman**

# When Parents Are Not in the Best Interests of the Child

Orphanages are not what they used to be. They aren't even called orphanages anymore. The residents no longer sleep in metal beds, twenty to a dormitory room. At the Boys Town campus, just outside Omaha, Nebraska, children live eight to a suburban-style home, two to a bedroom. Bureaus have replaced lockers. Uniforms and standardized haircuts are gone. So are the long wooden tables where, in the orphanages of legend, children sat awaiting their portions of cornmeal mush for breakfast, or bread and gravy for dinner. For instance, at the former St. James Orphanage, in Duluth, Minnesota, known since 1971 as Woodland Hills, young people wearing clothes from places like The Gap and Kmart push plastic trays through a cafeteria line, choosing baked chicken or shrimp and rice. The weight-conscious detour to the salad bar.

In 1910 some 110,000 orphans lived in 1,200 orphan asylums throughout the United States. At the end of 1990, according to data from the American Public Welfare Association, there were approximately 406,000 children in out-of-home placements. About three-quarters of these children were in adoptive and foster homes. About 16 percent, or 65,000, were emotionally disturbed children in need of therapy, most of whom lived in the group homes and residential treatment centers that are the institutional descendants of the orphanage. (The remainder, less than 10 percent, were cared for by a variety of temporary and emergency services.) What little research is available indicates that most of this smaller subset of "homeless" children have been physically or sexually abused, often by the adults charged with their care. At Boys Town, now a residential treatment center—and no longer just for boys—virtually all the girls and nearly half the boys have been sexually abused. The director, Father Val J. Peter, tells of a teenager who asked him on the day she arrived, "Who do I have to sleep with to get along here?"

Child-care workers agree that children in residential treatment today are likely to be far more disturbed than the children who were in need of protective services twenty years ago and who, in turn, were probably more disturbed than the good-hearted orphans with chips on their shoulders who preceded them. These kids have had it with parents—biological, adoptive, or foster—and the feeling is usually mutual. These kids do not trust adults, especially parents. They cannot tolerate the intensity of family life, nor do they behave well enough to attend public school. During a first screening at a residential treatment center a psychiatrist often asks a child, "If you had three wishes, what would they be?" Twenty years ago a typical answer was "I want a basketball," or "I wish my father didn't drink." Today, according to Nan Dale, the executive director of The Children's Village, a residential treatment center for boys in Dobbs Ferry, New York, one is likely to hear "I wish I had a gun so I could blow my father's head off." Child-care professionals call these young people "children of rage." Some of them take antidepressants and drugs to control hyperactivity. In addition to the behavior and attachment disorders common to children who have been abused and moved around a lot, some suffer from having been exposed *in utero* to crack and some from other neurological problems.

Most of the children who live in institutions are between the ages of five and eighteen. According to a 1988 study 64 percent of children in residential treatment centers were adolescents thirteen to seventeen years old. Approximately 31 percent were younger than thirteen, a percentage that has been increasing. According to the same study, the majority, about 70 percent, were male, a factor attributed to the more aggressive nature of the sex. Approximately 25 percent of the children were black, and eight percent were Hispanic.

A group home may house as few as four children, whereas a residential treatment center may be home to a hundred or more, although in either facility usually no more than eight to twelve are housed together, supervised by house parents or by child-care personnel working eight-hour shifts. At Woodland Hills an old three-story red-brick orphanage building has been renovated so that the first floor can be used for administration, classrooms, and the cafeteria. The second- and third-floor dormitory rooms have been divided into meeting rooms, staff offices, and apartments with bedrooms that sleep two.

Unlike the orphanages from which they are descended, most group homes and residential treatment centers are not meant to be long-term abodes. A typical stay at such a center lasts from several months to two years, after which most children return to their birth, foster, or adoptive families. A significant minority, those who either have no homes to return to or do not wish to go home, move on to less restrictive group homes or to independent living arrangements, also under the aegis of the child-welfare system.

## History

The first orphan asylum in the United States was established in 1729 by Ursuline nuns, to care for children orphaned by an Indian massacre at Natchez, Mississippi. Thereafter the number of orphanages increased in response to wars, especially the Civil War, and to epidemics of tuberculosis, cholera, yellow fever, and influenza. (Contemporary epidemics such as AIDS, the resurgence of tuberculosis, and the rampant use of crack cocaine have the potential to create another orphan crisis in the twenty-first century. By the year 2000, it is estimated, 100,000 children, most of them from female-headed households, will lose their mother to AIDS. Senator Daniel Patrick Moynihan, among others, foresees the return of the orphanage as inevitable.)

In spite of the Dickensian reputation that outlives them, orphanages, which began to proliferate in this country in the mid-1800s, represented a significant social reform for their time, just as the group homes and residential treatment centers that took their place are now seen as reforms. Before orphan asylums were common, orphaned, homeless, and neglected children, if they were not living, stealing, and begging on the streets, were housed, along with adults, primarily in almshouses, but also in workhouses and jails. The Victorian conviction that childhood was a time of innocence influenced attitudes toward destitute children. People came to believe that even street urchins could be rescued—removed to a better environment and turned into productive citizens.

Most orphanages were private institutions, the result of the combined efforts of passionately committed "child savers," children's-aid societies, and a variety of mostly religious but also ethnic organizations that raised the money to build and maintain them. But even as the orphanage was becoming the nation's dominant mode of substitute child care, an anti-institutional effort called "placing out" was under way, setting the stage for a debate that continues to this day. By the mid-1800s children were being transported on "orphan trains" from crowded eastern slums and institutions to the West, where they were adopted by farm families in need of extra hands. By the late nineteenth century, in a further move away from institutionalization, cottage-style "homes," which more closely mimicked family life and each of which housed about twenty-five children, began to take the place of large orphanages.

In the twentieth century, psychology—first psychoanalytic theories and then behaviorism—has dominated the field of child welfare. Unlike psychoanalytic theories, which focus on the child's inner personality, behaviorism emphasizes the way the child interacts with his world. In this view a child is not "bad"; his unacceptable behavior is. By changing the behavior, so the thinking goes, one changes the child. Behavioral theories replaced psychoanalytic theories, which were used only to limited effect by Bruno Bettelheim and others in the "homes" and "schools" for emotionally disturbed children which appeared mid-century. The therapeutic hour remains important, but what goes on in the child's life during the other twenty-three hours of the day is seen as potentially even more valuable. (A book by that name, *The Other 23 Hours,* by Albert E. Trieschman, James K. Whittaker, and Larry K. Brendtro, is the classic text of residential treatment.) The goal of residential treatment is to create a "therapeutic milieu," an environment in which everyday events are turned to therapeutic use. Any activity in a child's day—from refusing to get dressed in the morning to answering a question correctly at school to picking a fight—offers the child-care worker an opportunity to teach, change, or reinforce behavior through therapeutic intervention. Residential treatment aims to seize the moment while it is happening and the child's feelings are still fresh.

## Policy Versus Reality

Orphanages as such had virtually disappeared by the late 1970s as a result of a decrease in the number of orphans and a growing conviction that children belong in families. That every child needs parents and a home has become an article of faith and a guiding principle for social-policy makers and a matter of federal law as well. The philosophy of "permanency planning," as set forth in the Adoption Assistance and Child Welfare Act of 1980, considers the goal of the foster-care system to be keeping children in families. The law allows for but discourages "out-of-home placement"—institutionalization in group homes or residential treatment centers—and calls for the return of the children to a family, biological or otherwise, whenever possible and as quickly as possible. But for many practitioners in residential treatment the law has become increasingly irrelevant.

Richard Small is the director of The Walker Home and School, in Needham, Massachusetts, a residential and day treatment center for severely disturbed pre-adolescent boys. Writing recently in a professional journal with Kevin Kennedy and Barbara Bender, Small expressed a concern shared by many of his colleagues.

> For at least the past decade, we in the field have been reporting, usually to each other, a worsening struggle to work with a much more damaged group of children and families, and a scramble to adjust our practice methods to meet both client needs and policy directives that may or may not have anything to do with client needs.... Those of us immersed in everyday residential treatment practice see these same guidelines as less and less applicable to the real children and families with whom we work. Many of our child clients and their families suffer from profound disruptions of development that we believe are likely to require long-term, multiple helping services, including (but not limited to) one or more time-limited stays in residential treatment. Despite a policy that seems to see clear boundaries between being "in care" (and therefore sick and vulnerable) and "reunified" (and therefore fixed and safe) our experience tells us that many of our clients are likely to live out their lives somewhere between these poles.

In keeping with the goal of permanency planning, institutions are supposed to maintain close communication with the parents of the children they treat. Many centers offer counseling for parents and for the entire family. The Children's Village runs evening and weekend programs especially for parents who have abused their children. At institutions that adhere most closely to the goal of reuniting parent and child, parents are encouraged to visit, and good behavior on the part of children is rewarded with weekend visits home. Green Chimneys, a residential treatment center that serves primarily inner-city kids, regularly transports parents and children in vans between New York City and its campus in Brewster, New York. Nationally, nobody really knows how many families are reunited, for how long or how successfully. Those who work with children in institutions complain that the pressure from departments of social service to reunite parent and child is so intense that the workers sometimes yield to it despite their better judgment.

The objective of residential care is to discharge healthier children into the care of healthier parents—an outcome that authorities agree is desirable in theory but not always likely in fact. In their recent casebook for child-care workers, *When Home Is No Haven,* Albert J. Solit, Barbara Nordhaus, and Ruth Lord write that "one of the hardest tasks for a new worker is becoming reconciled to the inherent contradictions in the Protective Services worker's role. The worker is expected to aim for two goals, which in some instances may be mutually exclusive: reunification of the family, and protection of the child and the child's best interests." . . .

## Institutional Family Values

In the paradoxical world of "child protective services," an institution may be the first home some children have ever known, providing their first chance to sit down to meals with other people at regular times, blow out birthday candles, and be taken care of by adults who do not hit or even yell. All but one of the staple ingredients of a happy home life are replicated in the best group homes and treatment centers. Intimacy is purposely missing. Love and family bonding may be what these children will need and be capable of having eventually, but for the moment the emotional thermostat must be set at neutral. These children are believed to be too disturbed to handle the intensity of real family life; that is precisely why they have been institutionalized.

The best institutions offer emotionally disturbed children a chance at a second childhood. They are given the opportunity to shed cynicism, develop self-esteem, and grow back into innocence and vulnerability. Candy will become a treat. This time they will be protected from harm. This time they will come to think of adults as kind and dependable. They will learn to play. They will learn to care about others.

Treatment communities teach Judeo-Christian values—the work ethic and the golden rule. Institutions offer vocational training and courses in computer literacy. At The Children's Village the best computer students teach their new-found skills to other children and adults in the surrounding communities, and The Children's Village has its own Boy Scout troop. The kids at Woodland Hills collect and pack supplies for national and international relief efforts. In addition, they split wood and deliver logs to the elderly in the Duluth community. Boys Town children host Special Olympics games.

A highly controlled environment is required to create a second childhood for severely disturbed children. Safety is the key issue. Keeping these children from harm involves more than keeping them safe from sexual abuse, physical abuse, drugs, and crossfire; they must be kept safe from themselves and their peers. Newly institutionalized children often try to run away. When a young person at Woodland Hills forgets to bring the appropriate book to class, two peers accompany the student back to the dormitory to retrieve it, thereby minimizing the possibility of an escape attempt. At The Children's Village burly guards equipped with walkie-talkies and trained in firm but gentle techniques of physical restraint stand ready to intervene should fights or tantrums develop beyond the regular staff's ability to control them. Children are never left unattended, not even when they sleep. In every one of the twenty-one cottages at The Children's Village one staff member remains awake throughout the night. The children in these cottages are sometimes suicidal. The bedroom doors in all the cottages open into the corridor, so that youngsters cannot barricade themselves in their rooms. Sexually abused children sometimes become sexual predators. At The Villages in Kansas some young girls will not allow anyone to comb their hair; for girls who have been sexually abused, even grooming can be too threatening.

This antidotal second childhood must be highly structured and predictable as well as safe. Treatment communities impose rules, chores, and schedules, and emphasize neatness, cleanliness, and order. "Everybody wakes up at 7:30 in the morning," writes eleven-year-old Robert, describing his day at The Children's Village, where hairbrushes, combs, toothbrushes, and toothpaste tubes are lined up with military precision on bureau tops. "The first thing we do is make our bed, wash our face, brush our teeth, last but not least put on some clothes. We eat our breakfast by 8:15 and do our chores. At 8:45 we go to school. In school the first thing we do is math, then reading and spelling. We go to lunch at 12:00 noon...." Homer, the orphan hero of John Irving's *The Cider House Rules,* thrives on the routine of orphanage life. He enjoys "the *tramp, tramp* of it, the utter predictability of it." "An orphan," Irving writes, "is simply more of a child than other children in that essential appreciation of the things that happen daily, on schedule." A well-structured day serves the child as a kind of armature within which to build a new, less chaotic, inner self. "How to succeed and how to fail is very clear here," says Daniel Daly, the director of research at Boys Town. "These children are looking for consistency and for an environment they can understand."...

## Paradigms and Politics

[Five] years ago legislation called the Family Preservation Act was vetoed by President George Bush. The bill asked for about $2 billion to strengthen families. About half of that amount was earmarked for "family preservation" —programs to preserve troubled families *before* they broke up, so that fewer children would enter the foster-care system in the first place. Families in crisis would be assigned a licensed social worker, who would be available to them around the clock for a period of about three months, for help with problems ranging from substance abuse to landlord-tenant relations. Parents in imminent danger of abusing their children could find relief in a "respite program." Last year's [1993] budget legislation provided $1 billion for similar purposes, with a substantial portion also to be spent on family preservation. It had the backing of leading child-advocacy groups, including the Child Welfare League of America, the Children's Defense Fund, and The National Association of Homes and Services for Children. The Edna McConnell Clark Foundation has produced media kits claiming that family-preservation programs cost less per family ($3,000 for one family for a year) than family foster care, which it says costs $10,000 per *child,* or institutional care, which costs $40,000 per child.

Directors of some children's institutions are convinced that "family preservation" will take money directly out of institutional pockets. Sam Ross, [founder and executive director of Green Chimneys,] likes to point out that the family, theoretically the best way to rear children, also happens to be the least expensive. He calls this coincidence good news for advocates of family preservation, whom he calls "the liberal-conservative conspiracy." The way Ross sees it, liberal family preservationists believe that residential treatment centers are warehouses for children who could best be served in homes in their own communities. Conservative preservationists are horrified by the cost of residential treatment and are looking for a cheaper alternative. "For once in their lives," Ross says, "they agree on something: let's get rid of residential treatment."

"It makes about as much sense as closing down emergency rooms and intensive-care units in order to lower hospital costs," says Brenda Nordlinger, the executive director of the National Association of Homes and Services for Children.

"Family preservation? Who can be opposed to that?" says David Coughlin, of Boys Town. "But," he warns, "some kids are going to be in trouble all their lives. These kids are always going to need help. You can't just blow across the top of a family for three months and expect their woes to go away."

As of this year [1994] The Villages in Kansas will be responding to pressure from the state, which provides 78 percent of its operating expenses, to institute a family-preservation program in addition to its group-foster-care program. One of the eight Kansas residences will be rededicated as a ninety-day "home away from home" for abused children. Meanwhile, therapists trained by The Villages will work with the abusing parents and the abused children in an effort to reunite the family. "We want to provide the services that the state wants to purchase. We'd be foolish not to," says Mark Brewer, who has been the executive director since last June [1993].

Nan Dale, of The Children's Village, thinks that the fervor to reduce the numbers of children in residential treatment is reminiscent of what is now generally considered the disastrous policy of de-institutionalizing adult mental patients in the 1970s. Program directors are very skeptical about whether preventive-intervention programs are really as successful as their advocates claim. Those who believe that family preservation is being oversold see an ally in John Schuerman, a professor of social work at the University of Chicago. Schuerman has studied preventive-intervention programs and believes that many of the families that were treated and did not split up were not likely to split up in the first place.

Nan Dale is feeling the anti-institutional heat and resenting it. "We're as pro-family a place as you can find. The fact that we serve a child who has been removed from a family does not make us anti-family. We involve parents." Nevertheless, she says, "the lines have been drawn. When the words 'preventive service' got applied to everything up to the doorstep of residential care, some of us had apoplectic fits. We all would have told you that what we did here *was* preventive. We prevent lifetimes in mental hospitals, lifetimes in prisons. All of a sudden some bureaucrat in Washington defines preventive service as preventing placement outside the home, and we become the thing to be prevented." For the first time in anyone's memory The Children's Village, one of the largest and considered one of the best residential treatment centers in the country, has no waiting list. Dale says that children who might once have been sent there are being diverted to less restrictive, less expensive, and less appropriate options, such as foster-home care, on the presumption that a family setting is always better.

"What's in vogue right now is family preservation," says Father Val, of Boys Town. "Just follow the trend. Watch the little lemmings dashing toward the sea. They will tire of family preservation the way they tired of de-institutionalization. It's as if they just discovered that it's a good idea to try to keep kids in families. It's an exegesis of the obvious." Father Val thinks that the need to frame the debate as either anti-family or anti-institution is inevitable, given the longing that human beings feel for simple answers to complex questions. Certainly the people who make child-welfare policy, as well as those who carry it out, believe that the either-or approach is self-defeating. Nevertheless, it persists. Earl Stuck, who was one of the supporters of the Family Preservation Act, acknowledges the problem. "When you try to sell something politically, you have to oversell your case."

David Fanshel was until retirement a professor at the Columbia University School of Social Work. A leader in the field of social work, and foster care in particular, Fanshel was the principal investigator in two major longitudinal studies on foster children in homes and institutions. At a time when many experts are questioning the value of residential treatment and promoting family preservation, Fanshel is going against the tide. He foresees a greater need for residential care in the near future. In fact, Fanshel, for decades one of the leading proponents of permanency planning, has modified his views. He now believes that permanent placement with a family is not an appropriate goal for about a quarter of the older, more seriously damaged and criminally inclined children in the system. He would like to see foster care reorganized into a two-tiered system in which permanent placement would remain the goal for the larger group, and the forestalling of criminal behavior through treatment would be the goal for the other group, which he calls "Subsystem B." He sees institutions playing a significant role in treating such dangerous children. The creation of two subsystems, Fanshel argues, "might help to avoid the inappropriate underfunding of Subsystem B now taking place in the interest of permanency planning."

The debate between family preservationists and those who advocate the wider use of institutions has been going on for decades. Until as late as the 1920s pro-family reformers used the "orphan trains" to place children with farm families. Today their anti-institutional counterparts, in their determination to provide a home for every child, sometimes resort to "adoption fairs," where difficult-to-adopt children are viewed by prospective parents. The social worker who organized one such event told a reporter from *Vogue* that although these fairs can result in the adoption of as many as half the children, "it felt like a slave auction."

Richard Small tells prospective adoptive parents, "If you're going to adopt a child from The Walker School, you're going out of your way to ask for trouble." Small is uncertain about whether it will be possible to find parents for six of the eight children at the school who were recently freed for adoption. One is a very disturbed twelve-year-old boy who has already suffered two failed adoptions. Small is faced with the opposite of King Solomon's conundrum: this time no mothers want the child. How hard should he try to find another adoptive family?

"Another adoption with this boy would be likely to fail," says Small, who also knows that another rejection might harm the boy more than a lifetime without parents. On the other hand, can he consign the child to such permanent and profound loneliness? "He has no one," Small says, "absolutely no one."

Small talked at length with the boy about the pros and cons of risking another adoption. Together, they had just about made up their minds in favor of life without parents when the boy wondered out loud, "Then who will take me for my driver's license?"

"I wish," Small says, "that there were a place, a group home, where kids could live at those times when they couldn't live at home. We've got a number of youngsters in this society—who knows how many?—who are capable of being connected to people, who wish to be connected, who should be connected, but who can't live full-time with the people they're connected to. When they do, terrible things happen to both sides, the kids and the caretakers. These kids get placed in families repeatedly and they repeatedly fail. What are we going to do with these children? Right now we either put them in an institution or we put them in a family."

## Going Home

A good children's institution is a hard place to leave. In the institutional world the child has the advantage; in the real world the child does not. The experts consult. Parents and children consult. Is the family ready? Is the child ready?

Twenty-five years ago 80 percent of the children who "graduated" from The Children's Village went home to some family member, most likely the mother. But starting about five years ago the percentage began to drop. Today only 55 percent go home to family. Nan Dale, citing her own subjective standard of measurement, the "GFF" (gut-feeling factor), estimates that half of that narrow majority are returning to a home situation that is fragile. At Woodland Hills, where most of the kids are released to the care of their families, David Kern says he feels uneasy about the prospects for success almost half the time. He calls sending vulnerable children home the worst part of the job. While he was at The Villages, Don Harris felt uneasy about returning kids to their parents about 80 percent of the time. "The reality is we can help these kids build some bridges to their families, but they probably will never be able to live with them."

Not sending vulnerable children home can also be the worst part of the job. People who work with institutionalized children continually face a quandary to which they have no satisfactory solution: What should they do when, in spite of everyone's best efforts, family seems not to be in the best interests of the child? What the system has to offer is life in a group home followed by independent apartment living, and then nothing.

Life without parents is a difficult sentence to pronounce upon a child, but it's happening more and more often. "Sometimes children have gone beyond the opportunity to go back and capture what needed to be done between the ages of three and eight," says Gene Baker, the chief psychologist at The Children's Village. "Sometimes the thrust of intimacy that comes with family living is more than they can handle. Sometimes the requirement of bonding is more than they have the emotional equipment to give. As long as we keep pushing them back into what is our idealized fantasy of family, they'll keep blowing it out of the water for us."

# POSTSCRIPT

## Should Children Who Are at Risk for Abuse Remain With Their Families?

Kolb summarizes the family preservation model and documents its success in Missouri. In that program family preservation workers teach family members problem-solving skills and ways to cope with family crises while keeping family members, including children, together as a unit. Family preservation workers in Missouri meet certain educational and experiential requirements and work with two families at a time for six weeks.

Parents choose the family preservation treatment to avoid removal of their children from the home and, according to Kolb, want to preserve the family unit because they value it and want to make it work. Whereas traditional social service focuses on the individual for an indefinite amount of time, Kolb reports that family preservation is more successful because it focuses on the family system for a specific amount of time–four to six weeks.

Policymakers have been instrumental in child welfare in that they have diverted funds from one treatment program to another. When family preservation became a lower-cost alternative to foster care in the 1980s, money was diverted into the family preservation model in lieu of other child protection programs. Was this action in the best interests of the children? Who should decide? Parents? Policymakers? Protective service workers?

## Suggested Readings


Berliner, L. (1993, December). Is family preservation in the best interest of children? *Journal of Interpersonal Violence, 8*, 556–557.

Carp, E. W. (1996, June). Two cheers for orphanages. *Reviews in American History, 24*, 277–284.

Craig, C. (1995, Summer). What I need is a mom. *Policy Review, 73*, 41–49.

Ingrassia, M. (1994, April). Why leave children with bad parents? *Newsweek, 123*, 52–58.

McKenzie, R. (1996, May). Revive the orphanage (but don't expect help from child care professionals). *American Enterprise, 7*, 59–62.

Shealy, C. (1995, August). From Boys Town to Oliver Twist: Separating fact from fiction in welfare reform and out-of-home placement of children and youth. *American Psychologist, 50*, 565–580.

Van Biema, D. (1994, December). The storm over orphanages. *Time, 144*, 58–62.

# ISSUE 15

## Is the Welfare of Disadvantaged Children Improving?

**YES: Lisbeth B. Schorr**, from "Making the Most of What We Already Know," *Public Welfare* (Spring 1994)

**NO: William J. Bennett**, from "What to Do About the Children," *Commentary* (March 1995)

### ISSUE SUMMARY


**YES:** Lisbeth B. Schorr, director of the Harvard University Project on Effective Services, contends that organized intervention programs are working to circumvent social problems such as teen pregnancy, juvenile crime, and school dropout rates.

**NO:** William J. Bennett, former secretary of education and former director of the Office of National Drug Control Policy, sees the decline of the two-parent family and moral confusion as the primary reasons for children's poor living conditions.


Since the 1960s social programs have been established by schools, civic organizations, local agencies, and the federal government to reduce the risk factors that disadvantaged youth face. These programs provide intervention treatments such as after-school activities, counseling programs, and tutoring to reduce the incidence of juvenile delinquency, teen pregnancy, and dropping out of school. Some of these programs, such as Head Start and, more recently, the midnight basketball program, have become well known, but others are less familiar to the public. All the programs have good intentions, and some have evaluation results to confirm their success, but questions are being raised about their efficacy. Are intervention programs really improving the lives of disadvantaged children, or are they masking a larger societal problem?

The Federal Interagency Forum on Child and Family Statistics issued a report in July 1997 on key national indicators of child well-being. Not only are the results of the report useful, but this also marked the first time that national agencies collaborated on trends in the health and education of America's children. The forum was founded in 1994 and includes the Departments of Agriculture, Commerce, Health and Human Services, Housing and Urban Development, Justice, and Labor; the National Science Foundation; and the Office of Management and Budget. Specifically, the National Institute of Child Health and Human Development, National Maternal and Child Health Bureau, and National Center for Education Statistics were listed as contributors to the report.

The report states that more children know where their next meal is coming from, more children are being read to by parents, more children are being enrolled in preschool programs and also graduating from college, immunization rates are up, and the rate of infant and childhood deaths has decreased. Not all the trends for children were positive, however. The use of illicit drugs and cigarette smoking is up, and crimes against youths have increased. Children in families with annual incomes below $15,000 were 22 times more likely to experience abuse and neglect than families with annual incomes above $30,000.

In the following selections, Lisbeth B. Schorr reports that programs for disadvantaged children are working and have the support of those in power in Washington, D.C. She lists a number of intervention programs that have met their goals and are considered worth the money being spent on them. William J. Bennett takes an opposing view of the status of children in America, pointing to many societal ills that continue to keep children in the lower class and underclass at a disadvantage.

**Lisbeth B. Schorr**

# Making the Most of What We Already Know

Human-service administrators probably have the toughest jobs in America. When I reviewed the agenda for your meeting [of the American Public Welfare Association], I was delighted that both welfare reform and health care reform would be so expertly covered, so that I would be free to talk about what we know about the needs of children and families that go beyond income, employment, and access to health care, as well as my favorite subject: what we know about what works in meeting those needs.

I began collecting information that sheds light on this subject almost by accident. In the early 1980s, I was struck with a prevailing sense of helplessness in the face of urgent social problems; and I set out to find examples of programs that worked. I wanted to show that organized interventions–in early education, schooling, health services, social services, and family supports–did indeed change life outcomes among disadvantaged children.

I decided at the outset that I would look for programs that were successful in dealing with problems of consequence–problems that were seen as important because of the enormous toll they take on individual youngsters, their families, and society as a whole: school-age child-bearing, school dropout, delinquency, and long-term welfare dependence. I called these "rotten outcomes."

I then looked at the risk factor research and discovered a strong convergence around the finding that because risk factors interact and multiply the effects of one another, the reduction of any risk factor improves the odds of a favorable outcome. The more risk factors in a particular situation, the greater the damaging impact of each. But the impact is not just additive–risk factors multiply one another's destructive effects.

Youngsters who become pregnant or delinquent or who drop out of school already have been in trouble for many years; many of the troubles that surface in adolescence can be predicted from poor school performance and truancy as early as third or fourth grade. We also know that trouble in elementary school

From Lisbeth B. Schorr, "Making the Most of What We Already Know," *Public Welfare,* vol. 52 (Spring 1994), pp. 22–26. 

correlates with a number of antecedent risk factors. In addition to poverty, these include

- being born unwanted or to a teenage mother;
- low weight at birth;
- untreated childhood health problems;
- lack of language, reasoning, and coping skills at school entry; and
- failure to develop trusting relationships with reliable and protective adults early in life.

The important news about these risk factors is that every one of them has been successfully attacked through interventions we know how to provide. We now have evidence of

- school-based health clinics that have reduced the rate of teenage childbearing, raised the average age at which youngsters became sexually active, and reduced the number of unwanted births;
- comprehensive prenatal care and nutrition programs that have reduced the proportion of low birth weight babies;
- intensive family support, nurse home-visiting, and childcare programs that have resulted in lower rates of child abuse, fewer children removed from their homes, and fewer mothers dependent on welfare;
- quality preschool programs whose participants, when they become young adults, include fewer dropouts, fewer delinquents, fewer teenage mothers, and fewer youngsters without jobs; and
- reformed elementary schools that were able to so change the climate of the school that whole populations of children who had been failing began to succeed.

As one synthesizes the evidence, it becomes clear that the contention that in the world of social programs "nothing works" is in fact a canard—a myth that cannot be maintained in the face of the research and experience now at hand.

## Common Elements

The good news, then, is not only that there are programs that work, but that we now know a lot about how and why they work. As I analyzed the information I had collected to identify common patterns among successful programs, several characteristics emerged:

**Successful programs are comprehensive, intensive, flexible, and responsive** Staffs in these programs have extensive repertoires and extensive community networks. They have the capacity to respond flexibly to concrete needs for help with food or housing or a violent family member. Sister Mary Paul, who runs a family services program in Brooklyn, says that no one in her program ever says, "This may be what you need, but helping you get it is not part of my job."

Many of these programs provide their staffs with a pool of flexible funds, which they can use at their discretion to help a family buy a wheelchair or a washing machine or to get the car repaired. They respond to the needs of families at times and places that make sense to the family, often at home, at school, or in neighborhood centers and at odd hours, rather than in distant offices once a week on Wednesday afternoons. Job descriptions are broad, boundaries are permeable, and professionalism is redefined.

In my book, *Within Our Reach: Breaking the Cycle of Disadvantage,* I tell the story of a Homebuilders family preservation worker who appeared at the front door of a family in crisis, only to be greeted by a mother's declaration that the one thing she did not need in her life was one more social worker telling her what to do. What she needed, she said, was to get her house cleaned up. The Homebuilders therapist, a master's-level clinical psychologist with supplemental training by Homebuilders, responded by asking the mother if she wanted to start with the kitchen. After they worked together for an hour, the two women were able to talk about the issues that were at the heart of the family's difficulty. It may have been an unorthodox way of forging a therapeutic alliance, but it worked.

I told this story at a meeting some months ago, and a distinguished professor of psychology interrupted to say that that was going too far. What the psychologist had done, she claimed, was unprofessional.

In a sense, of course, she was quite right. In most professions, highest status is conferred on those who deal with issues from which all human complexity and messiness have been removed. Narrowly drawn boundaries that limit what is expected of a professional may be the traditional essence of professionalism, yet they often interfere with professional effectiveness.

**Successful programs deal with children as parts of families** They recognize that a mother's needs cannot be dealt with in isolation from her children's, and vice versa. They work not alone with one generation, but with two, and often three. Successful Head Start programs and family support centers nurture parents so they can better nurture their children.

Successful programs take into account the real world of those they serve. The clinician treating an infant for recurrent diarrhea sees beyond the patient on the examining table to whether the family needs help from a public health nurse or social worker to obtain nonmedical services. I visited a health center in Mississippi that actually delivers clean water to families who cannot get it any other way.

The effective job-training program knows that unstable childcare can stop a transition to self-sufficiency cold, and that poor-quality child care is likely to interfere powerfully with a young child's chances to climb out of poverty.

**Successful programs deal with families as parts of neighborhoods and communities** Most successful programs have deep roots in the community. They are not imposed from without—they are not "parachuted" into communities—but are carefully integrated with specific local community needs and strengths so that local communities have a genuine sense of ownership, and programs are in fact designed to respond to the real needs of that particular community.

**Staff in successful programs have the time, skills, and support to build relationships of trust and respect with children and families** They work in settings that allow them to develop meaningful personal relationships over time and to provide services respectfully, ungrudgingly, and collaboratively. Psychiatrist James Comer points out that relationship issues are particularly important among low-income people who have given up on helping systems.

None of the programs that succeed are "lean and mean." They have been able to establish a climate that is warm, welcoming, and supportive. The quality and continuity of relationships and support are what make many other activities effective. Home visitors say that respectful, trusting relationships make parent education work.

A careful evaluation of an enhanced prenatal care program in Washington, D.C., found that the most important element that kept women in the program and utilizing health services properly was not the program's cash incentives or even easy access to care; rather it was the "friendly support" of "someone to talk to about pregnancy and other life stresses" that was valued most highly.

Smallness of scale at the point of service delivery also seems to be crucial. Large schools, massive outpatient clinics, and large caseloads vastly complicate the job of personalizing services to respond to individual and family needs. For many children, life trajectories have been changed through a relationship with a caring, attentive adult. And, as those who work as volunteers or as professionals can attest, a caring, attentive adult can come in many forms.

**Successful programs have long-term, preventive orientations and continue to evolve over time** The people responsible for these programs have no illusion that they can implement the perfect model program. They allow their programs to evolve continually to maintain their responsiveness to individual, family, and community needs over time and to respond to feedback from both front-line staff and participants.

Successful programs combine a highly flexible mode of operation with a clearly articulated sense of mission. They operate in an organizational culture that is outcome oriented rather than rule bound. Their approach is long-term, inclusive, preventive, and empowering.

## Countering the System

The successes of these interventions are of enormous importance despite the fact that many of the most successful programs operate in special—and sometimes idiosyncratic—circumstances. But these successes show that something can be done to address social problems previously considered intractable. They provide a vision of what can be achieved. They refute the contention that families in the so-called underclass are beyond the reach of organized services. They show that when high-risk populations get the best of services rather than the worst, life trajectories change. And, by revealing the attributes of success, they contain the information we need to take successful programs to scale.

These attributes of success, of course, are neither counterintuitive nor surprising. When I go around the country making speeches about how effective programs are characterized by flexibility, comprehensiveness, responsiveness, front-line discretion, a family focus, community rootedness, and respectful relationships, practitioners never seem surprised. This is the stuff that most people on the front lines know works—the stuff they know is important.

It is also the stuff that the good ones have to lie, cheat, and connive in order to be able to do.

Recently I received a letter from the director of a community health center who had heard me discuss the attributes of effective programs. She wrote that these attributes describe precisely what she does each day—and that they are precisely the opposite of what she's told to do each day by the large hospital under whose auspices her center operates.

Marc Tucker of the National Center on Education and the Economy says, "When you find an individual school that works, it's almost always because it's running against the grain. You find a teacher or a principal who really doesn't give a damn about the system. They are willing to ignore or subvert every rule in the book in order to get the job done for the kids." You hear the same thing from child protection workers and the staff of job training programs.

Unless we come to grips with the mismatch between the attributes of effective programs and the pressures placed on programs by prevailing systems, successful models will continue to flourish briefly and then disappear or become diluted when special funding and special political protection end, or when they can no longer find a leader who combines the talents of a Mother Theresa, a Machiavelli, and a certified public accountant.

The attributes of effective programs that are now supported by theory, a convergent body of research, and front-line experience in many different disciplines turn out to be totally at odds with the systems within which most programs must function—and which chief executive officers must administer. Successful programs remain the exception and not the rule because existing systems undermine precisely the elements that are the hallmarks of effective programs.

With the tools you are issued, which include categorical financing, rigid rules, hierarchical management techniques, and input-based accountability, of course the front-line practitioners complain that they cannot provide comprehensive, flexible, family-centered, responsive services.

## Bright Prospects

So what are the prospects for change, the prospects that you will get some help in operating systems in which ordinary people can achieve superior outcomes, in which effective programs can be sustained—systems that do not depend on a single charismatic leader?

I think the prospects are bright—even though money may be short. Let me tell you why I believe this:

First, I think we have the best shot we have had in a generation to break the cycle of disadvantage, because we have the information we need to do better; and we have a growing consensus that we must do better.

There is increasing recognition that teenage pregnancy, violence, and school failure are not isolated problems that have either isolated or standardized solutions. We know we have the elements of past success to build on, and we know that we cannot do it at bargain basement prices and that we cannot do it overnight. But we can be certain that if it is done well, it will make a difference in the life of this nation.

Marian Wright Edelman of the Children's Defense Fund likes to say that we are at a point in this country today when doing what is right coincides with what we have to do to save our national skins! The people who are committed to social justice can join with those whose highest priority is a workforce that can increase American productivity and win the international economic competition.

Second, I am optimistic about what can be done because human service administrators now have a lot of friends in Washington. From the president on down, the new leadership in Washington is not only competent, but it is respectful of state competence. They see the differences among states and communities not as inconvenient impediments to standardized rule making but rather as critical strengths.

So we have the president declaring

> We're going to give the states, the counties, and the cities the right to design what we call "bottoms-up" initiatives. In other words, you decide what it is you need, tell us what you need, and if it's in a grant proposal that's anywhere under $10 million—or over $10 million if you get approval for it —we will design something to give you the money you need instead of you having to figure out how to walk through the hoops of all the rules and regulations of the hundreds and hundreds of grants in the federal government.

To carry out this charge, the president has created a "community enterprise board" to identify neighborhoods across America, both urban and rural, that are in trouble. These neighborhoods, in the president's words, "will say what they want done. Then my cabinet will sit down and work together and figure out how to do it—not how to tell them how to comply with our rules, but how to do what people need done at the local level."

As columnist Neal Pierce points out, when a city is struggling to assist homeless people, for example, it will now be able to capture not only federal funds earmarked for the homeless, but also monies appropriated for housing, transportation, job training, childcare, health, mental health, and alcohol and drug abuse—keeping just one set of books and adhering to one set of rules.

In exchange for greater flexibility, we will surely see a greater emphasis on outcome accountability, which I think we should welcome. I believe that accountability based on outcomes that reflect common sense and common understanding—such as increasing rates of healthy births, school readiness, and school success—may be the most powerful force to

- focus attention on the mission rather than on the rules,
- permit flexibility and autonomy at the front end,
- encourage cross-systems collaboration,
- promote a community-wide "culture of responsibility" for children and families, and
- provide evidence to funders and the public that programs are indeed achieving their intended purposes.

I believe that efforts to obtain new funds, especially public funds, and to use old funds under new and more flexible rules will succeed only if they are coupled with clear commitments that effectiveness will ultimately be demonstrated in improved outcomes. Especially if one considers discretion at the frontlines as critical, and if one believes that local programs must be able to evolve over time to meet unique local needs, the old ways of ensuring accountability become counterproductive. Legislation or regulations that attempt to ensure quality by imposing detailed procedural protocols interfere profoundly with a program's ability to operate flexibly. But the demands for accountability cannot be dismissed; and the most reasonable way of ensuring that funds are in fact accomplishing their intended purposes, while allowing for frontline creativity, is by documenting results in terms of important, real-world outcomes.

In an outcome-oriented climate, it would be easier to combine publicly funded efforts with the initiatives that several national foundations, including The Ford Foundation, The Pew Charitable Trusts, the Rockefeller Foundation, and the Annie E. Casey Foundation, are now targeting on cross-systems, neighborhood-based efforts to turn around both neighborhood and family disintegration in areas of persistent poverty and social dislocation.

The provision of effective services to populations that heretofore have been neglected or poorly served requires collaboration among individuals and agencies that have previously worked in isolation. But collaboration alone will not improve outcomes. Because fragmentation is such a big problem in existing services, many have come to see the coordination and integration of services as the solution.

Collaboration is hard, and it's a crucial step in solving many current problems; but it is futile to put together services that are of mediocre quality, that are rendered grudgingly, or that are rendered by professionals who do not persevere or do not know how to work collaboratively with families.

Whether we are talking about school-based services, one-stop shopping, or new links between education and other human services, putting together formerly isolated services is essential. But we should not be so dazzled by the feat of putting together formerly isolated pieces of service that we forget to pay attention to the contents of those elements.

That is why I attach so much importance to the many . . . geographically based initiatives that would match the concentration of social problems in urban communities and depleted rural areas with a similar magnitude of fiscal resources and problem-solving capabilities. The factors implicated in persistent poverty and concentrated social dislocation are too intertwined and pervasive for narrow, one-shot interventions. What is needed is a broad attack on many fronts at once. This approach combines comprehensive and responsive services and restructured schools with community development and economic development, sometimes even with reforms to improve housing and public safety, so that they will interact synergistically to achieve a visible level of effectiveness in an entire threatened community.

It is virtually impossible for any child to grow up whole in neighborhoods that society has abandoned, that are left without decent health care, schools, parks, libraries, theaters, youth centers, or even washing machines—neighborhoods where no one can count on being able to land a legal job that will support a family and where no one feels safe.

Everyone agrees that it takes a village to raise a child. But in the inner city, the village has disintegrated. That is why we need bold and comprehensive strategies. Incrementalism will not do it. There are chasms you cannot cross one step at a time. So my third reason for feeling confident is that bold thinking is in.

It became hard, in the last decade, to think boldly. We learned to think small and to content ourselves with fiddling at the margins. But it is rapidly becoming clear that some of our most urgent problems will not be solved unless we dare to adopt a bolder vision—a vision that is built on a shared understanding that we cannot allow the richest country in the world to declare bankruptcy in our civic life. That vision could transform into action—public-private, national, state, and local—the widespread yearning that I see in so many American communities to make life better for all of America's children and families.

NO

William J. Bennett

# What to Do About the Children

At the dawn of the 20th century there was every reason to believe that ours would be (in the title of a best-selling book at the time) "the century of the child." From the early part of the 1900's through the 1950's, despite ups and downs, despite Depression and war, things got better in almost every area touching the welfare of American children: economic security improved, material earnings increased, medicine progressed, family structure was stable, children occupied a valued place in society, and our civic institutions were strong and resilient. In retrospect, it seems as if the midpoint of the century was a high point for the well-being of children.

By the 1960's, however, America began a steep and uninterrupted slide toward what might be called decivilization. Although every stratum of society has been affected, the worst problems have been concentrated within America's inner cities. No age group has remained untouched, but the most punishing blows have been absorbed by children.

In assessing conditions today, it is important to keep perspective: America is *not* in danger of becoming a third-world country; the vast majority of children do not live in sewers of disease and depravity; and most are not violent, sexually promiscuous, or drug-takers. At the same time, however, there is no question that as we approach the end of the last decade of this "American century," the condition of too many of our children is not good. The indicators are well-known: low educational achievement, the decline of the two-parent family, moral confusion, and, for a sizable and increasingly large minority, abuse, neglect, and very bleak prospects for the future.

Consider some real-world facts:

- From 1960 to 1991, the rate of homicide deaths among children under the age of 19 more than quadrupled. Among black teenagers, homicide is now by far the leading cause of death.
- Since 1965, the juvenile arrest rate for violent crimes has tripled, and the fastest-rowing segment of the criminal population is made up of children.
- Since 1960, the rate at which teenagers take their own lives has more than tripled.

From William J. Bennett, "What to Do About the Children," *Commentary,* vol. 99 (March 1995), pp. 23–28. 

- The rate of births to unmarried teenagers has increased by almost 200 percent in three decades; the number of unmarried teenagers getting pregnant has nearly doubled in the past two decades.
- Today, 30 percent of all births and almost 70 percent of all black births are illegitimate. By the end of the decade, according to the most reliable projections, 40 percent of all American births and 80 percent of all minority births will be out-of-wedlock.
- During the last 30 years there has been a tripling of the percentage of children living in single-parent families. According to some projections, only 30 percent of white children and only 6 percent of black children born in 1980 will live with both parents through the age of 18.

A useful historical reference point may be 1965, when Daniel P. Moynihan, then an Assistant Secretary of Labor, wrote *The Negro Family: The Case for National Action.* Then, one-quarter of all black children were born out of wedlock; one-half of all black children lived in broken homes at some time before they reached age 18; and 14 percent of black children were on welfare. Moynihan considered this "tangle of pathologies" to be a social catastrophe, and so it was. Today, however, were we to achieve such figures in even one of our major urban centers, we would consider it a stunning accomplishment.

As the figures above demonstrate, these problems are by no means limited to lower-class or minority populations. In addition to everything else, divorce, rampant in all social classes, causes over one million children annually to end up, at least temporarily, in single-parent families. And wherever they live, American children today—especially the teenagers among them—spend relatively minuscule amounts of time with either their fathers or their mothers—or their homework—and vastly greater amounts of time on other things from crime to television.

A few years ago a special commission of political, medical, educational, and business leaders issued a report on the health of America's teenagers titled *Code Blue.* In the words of this report. "Never before has one generation of American teenagers been less healthy, less cared for, or less prepared for life than their parents were at the same age." According to the sociologist David Popenoe, today's generation of children is the first in our nation's history to be less well-off psychologically and socially than its parents.

Nor is the concern limited to the experts. When asked in a recent Family Research Council poll, "Do you think children are generally better off today or worse off than when you were a child?," 60 percent of all Americans—and 77 percent of all black Americans—said children today are "worse off." They are right.

## II

The greatest long-term threat to the well-being of our children is the enfeebled condition—in some sectors of our society, the near-complete collapse—of our character-forming institutions. In a free society, families, schools, and churches have primary responsibility for shaping the moral sensibilities of the young.

The influence of these institutions is determinative; when they no longer provide moral instruction or lose their moral authority, there is very little that other auxiliaries—particularly the federal government—can do.

Among those three institutions, the family is preeminent; it is, as Michael Novak of the American Enterprise Institute once famously said, the original and best department of health, education, and welfare. But the family today is an agency in disrepair. Writes David Popenoe:

> This period [the 1960's through the 1990's] has witnessed an unprecedented decline of the family as a social institution. Families have lost functions, social power, and authority over their members. They have grown smaller in size, less stable, and shorter in life span.... Moreover, there has been a weakening of child-centeredness in American society and culture. Familism as a cultural value has diminished.

And so, too, has fatherhood. Each night in America, four out of ten children go to sleep without fathers who live in their homes, and upward of 60 percent will spend some major part of their childhood without fathers.

In the past, the typical cause of fatherlessness was divorce; its new face is homes headed by never-married mothers. This is "the most socially consequential family trend of our generation" (in the words of David Blankenhorn of the Institute for American Values), and it has seismic social implications. Moynihan warned [more than] 30 years ago that a society which allows a large number of young men to grow up without fathers in their lives asks for and almost always gets chaos. We have come to the point in America where we are asking prisons to do for many young boys what fathers used to do.

---

There are other signs of decay, particularly of the cultural variety. Television shows make a virtue of promiscuity, adultery, homosexuality, and gratuitous acts of violence. Rap music celebrates the abuse and torture of women. Advertisements are increasingly erotic, even perverse. And many of our most successful and critically-acclaimed movies celebrate brutality, casual cruelty, and twisted sex.

None of these trends takes place in a moral or cultural vacuum. During the last 30 years we have witnessed a profound shift in public attitudes. The pollster Daniel Yankelovich finds that we Americans now place less value on what we owe others as a matter of moral obligation; less value on sacrifice as a moral good, on social conformity, respectability, and observing the rules; less value on correctness and restraint in matters of physical pleasure and sexuality —and correlatively greater value on things like self-expression, individualism, self-realization, and personal choice.

How does all this affect young children? A single, simple statistic tells much: if, in 1951, 51 percent of Americans agreed with the statement, "Parents who don't get along should not stay together for the children," in 1985 that figure had risen to 86 percent.

The social historian Barbara Dafoe Whitehead has observed that the Hallmark company now offers two lines of divorce cards: one set for the newly single adults, the other for children of divorced parents. For the latter, a typical message is piercing in its casualness: "I'm sorry I'm not always there when you need me but I hope you know I'm always just a phone call away." By contrast, one adult card reads, "Think of your former marriage as a record album. It was full of music—both happy and sad. But what's important now is . . . YOU! the recently released HOT NEW SINGLE! You're going to be at the TOP OF THE CHARTS!" As Whitehead comments, What had once been regarded as hostile to children's best interests is now considered essential to adults' happiness."

If the self, in the late Allan Bloom's withering assessment, has become "the modern substitute for the soul," we are also living in an era in which it has become unfashionable to make judgments on a whole range of behaviors and attitudes. This unwillingness to judge has resulted in unilateral moral disarmament, as harmful in the cultural realm as its counterpart is in the military. With the removal of social sanctions in the name of "tolerance" and "open-mindedness," and the devaluing of the idea of personal responsibility, is it any wonder, for instance, that in a recent survey 70 percent of young people between the ages of 18 and 34 said that people who generate a baby out-of-wedlock should not be subject to moral reproach *of any sort?*

It would be supererogatory at this late date to catalogue the role of government in giving form and force to these ideas and beliefs through law and policy. Suffice it to say that from the area of criminal justice, to education, to welfare policy, to the arts, to a whole tangle of sexual and family issues, government has increasingly put itself on the side of the forces of decomposition, not on the side of the forces of restoration. The consequence is that the moral universe we are sending our children into today is more harsh, more vulgar, more coarse, and more violent than the moral universe most of us grew up in—and they are less equipped to deal with it.

We should not flinch from admitting this unsettling truth: we live in a culture which seems dedicated to the corruption of the young, to assuring the loss of their innocence before their time. "It dawned on me recently," the anthropologist David Murray has written, "that we have now become the kind of society that in the 19th century almost every Christian denomination felt compelled to missionize."

## III

If the problem is one of moral breakdown, it would be fatuous to suggest that it can be fixed by government intervention. There is, after all, one proposition which has been tested repeatedly over the last three decades and just as repeatedly been found wanting—namely, that we can spend our way out of our social problems. Instead of encouraging government, we need to relimit it—not only, or even primarily, for fiscal reasons, but because the "nanny state" has eroded self-reliance and encouraged dependency, crowding out the character-forming institutions and enfeebling us as citizens.

Still, there are a number of actions government *can* take that would amount to constructive and far-reaching, even radical, reforms. A number of these ideas have been on the table for quite some time, but as the results of the November 1994 elections suggest, Americans may be more ready for fundamental reform today than at any other point in recent history. So we suddenly find ourselves presented with an extraordinary opportunity.

Before getting down to particulars, I would stipulate two general points that should guide any discussion of public-policy solutions to the problems faced by children in America. One of them I borrow from an old principle of medicine: *primum non nocere*—first, do no harm. In many, many cases, the best thing government can do is (to quote Myron Magnet of the *City Journal*) "to *stop* doing what makes the problem worse."

As for the second point, it was well expressed by Alexander Hamilton, who in *The Federalist No. 17* questioned whether "all those things . . . which are proper to be provided for by local legislation [should] ever be desirable cares of a general jurisdiction." To state this in terms of our present situation, there are many responsibilities which would be better handled by states and localities but which have fallen under the jurisdiction of the federal government; they should be devolved back to the smaller "laboratories of democracy."

Within those constraints, government, at one level or another, does have a role to play in improving conditions for the young. Let us look at a few key areas, beginning with the link between welfare and illegitimacy.

Between 1962 and 1992, welfare spending in the United States increased by over 900 percent in 1992 dollars. At the same time, the poverty rate dropped by less than 5 percent—and illegitimacy rates increased over 400 percent. Children are the real victims in this national tragedy. They are being conditioned into the same habits of dependence they are surrounded by, resulting in an almost unbreakable cycle of welfare and "the tangle of pathologies" associated with it. John J. DiIulio, Jr. of Princeton has put this last point well:

> The problem *is* that inner-city children are trapped in criminogenic homes, schools, and neighborhoods where high numbers of teenagers and adults are no more likely to nurture, teach, and care for children than they are to expose them to neglect, abuse, and violence. . . . Children cannot be socialized by adults who are themselves unsocialized (or worse), families that exist in name only, schools that do not educate, and neighborhoods in which violent and repeat criminals circulate in and out of jail. . . .

Quite a number of serious and thoughtful proposals have been advanced for restructuring the entire system of welfare benefits, of which Charles Murray's is among the most thoroughgoing.[1] In a similar spirit, I would endorse full-scale and far-reaching plans to send welfare back to the states, which have proved the best settings for innovative reform and experimentation.

As for the problem of illegitimacy in particular, one year after legislation is enacted I would recommend ending direct welfare payments to women who have children out of wedlock; enforcing existing child-support laws; and terminating the increase in benefits for women who have children while participating in welfare programs. The success of such reforms, it seems to me, depends critically on their sweep and magnitude; incremental steps will not do the necessary job of altering fundamental assumptions and expectations.

To turn to a point that has been heavily controverted since the elections of November 8 [1994]: in my view, situations will arise which may warrant the removal of a child from the care of his parent(s). To be sure, this should only happen in desperate circumstances and as a last resort. But we cannot ignore the plain fact that there are more and more horrifying cases of abuse, neglect, and parental malfeasence.

While adoption is the best alternative in such circumstances, the concept of orphanages, or group-care homes, should not be dismissed. Such institutions pretty much disappeared from the national scene when government began distributing money in the expectation that poor parents, with federal assistance, would do a better job of raising their children. But in far too many cases that expectation has been resoundingly refuted by experience.

When parents cannot care for their children's basic material, psychological, medical, and moral needs, it is time to look to other institutions. The orphanage—call it a boarding school without tuition—may then be in their best interest. Can anyone seriously argue that some boys would be worse off living in Boys Town than in, say, the Cabrini Green housing project in Chicago, considered by its residents a virtual war zone?

---

But adoption is certainly preferable. Only 50,000 children are adopted each year in the United States; half are healthy infants and half are older children or children with disabilities. At any given time, however, one to two million homes are waiting to adopt. Provided only the child is young enough, there is, in effect, no such thing as an unwanted child, and this goes even for babies who are not fully healthy. Unfortunately, most potential adopters (and adoptees) are hamstrung by needless barriers.

In addition to the high cost of a private adoption, often as much as $10,000, many couples are automatically excluded from consideration due to race, financial background, age, disability, or home size. Other potential adopters are scared away by lax confidentiality laws, nonbinding adoptions, and the expanded rights of the biological father to reclaim legal custody.

The barriers to adoption are only one side of the problem. Availability is also severely limited. Unwed mothers are often denied information about adoption in prenatal counseling; others decide to abort their pregnancy for economic reasons. (Indeed, it may be partly for this reason that abortion has increasingly become a problem of juveniles: of the one million teenage pregnancies each year, about 400,000 now end in abortion.)[2] Finally, and perhaps most importantly, with the stigma of illegitimacy all but gone in this country, for many young, unwed, pregnant women single motherhood has become a more attractive option than giving a child up for adoption.

Again, there is a limit to what government can do. But again, too, the greatest hope lies in reforms at the state level, such as:

- prohibiting the use of race and/or ethnicity as a disqualification for would-be foster or adoptive parents (in practice this has affected whites seeking to adopt nonwhite babies);
- expediting adoption procedures for infants and children who have been abandoned by their parents and are living in limbo in hospitals, group homes, and/or foster care;
- terminating parental rights and thus making a child available for adoption if by the age of six months—in the case of infants born with positive toxicology—maternal drug use has not ceased, or if a child has been severely abused by its parents;
- enacting model legislation that will require courts to consider the best interests of the child first in all cases concerning custody;
- establishing uniform rules making voluntary surrender/adoption irrevocable at any point past 72 hours after birth;
- restricting payments to biological parents by adoptive parents to necessary expenses related directly to the pregnancy and adoption;
- ensuring that adoptive families are treated with the same respect as other families, free of the fear of intrusion by the state or other parties after an adoption has been finalized.

Then there is divorce—which, in terms of damage to children, can be the most devastating circumstance of all, yet which is conspicuous by its absence from the agenda of policy-makers.

As Karl Zinsmeister of the *American Enterprise* has written: "We talk about the drug crisis, the education crisis, and the problems of teen pregnancy and juvenile crime. But all these ills trace back predominantly to one source: broken families."

The statistics, indeed, are chilling. Children of single-parent families are twice as likely to drop out of high school, or, if they remain in school, have lower grade-point averages, lower college aspirations, and poorer attendance records than the general population. Girls living with only one parent are two-and-a-half times more likely to become teenage mothers. When it comes to crime, according to some studies, 70 percent of juveniles now incarcerated in state-reform institutions have lived either in single-parent homes or with someone other than their natural parents, and 75 percent of adolescent murderers come from single-parent homes.

The divorce rate has nearly doubled since 1960—not coincidentally, the same period in which no-fault divorce laws became popular. Previously, before a divorce was granted, the law had required a showing of fault, such as cruelty, abuse, adultery, or desertion. The recision of these conditions not only significantly increased the number of divorces but transformed marriage into a simple business contract.

Though the incidence of divorce cannot significantly be addressed through public policy, its effects can perhaps be curbed to some degree. My suggestions include braking mechanisms when children are involved, such as mandatory and substantial "cooling-off" periods as well as mandatory counseling; reinstituting fault as an absolute requirement for divorce and in determining the terms of a settlement; and classifying all property as family property, which would affect the distribution of assets in cases where children are involved.

This brings us to institutions outside the home, starting with the schools. Parents all over the country are increasingly aware that the public-education system in America is an embarrassment. As the federal government has taken over more responsibilities for the nation's schools, the quality of education has plummeted. The response of the education establishment and of the teachers' unions to this situation, and to the growing movement for greater parental involvement and local control that has arisen in response to it, has been to advocate pumping more money into the system. This has only served to perpetuate and even escalate the problem.

The signs of failure are everywhere, and need not be reiterated here.[3] Fortunately, there are many potentially good solutions—though more money is not among them. Instead, and yet again, a devolution is in order: the first step toward genuine education reform should be to rein in the federal government. In my judgment, legislation is called for which would restore decision-making responsibilities to state and local authorities, enabling the federal government to give states a block grant with virtually no strings attached. The state, local school districts, and parents would then be in a better position to make their own decisions regarding curriculum, books, standards, discipline. etc. Not only would this lead to a system more accountable to parents, but it would encourage innovation and experimentation.

The next step is to implement reforms at the state level which would foster excellence in the education system. These include open enrollment; charter schools; privatization; performance-testing for students and teachers; a merit-pay system for teachers and administrators; and, above all, school choice, complete with vouchers redeemable at public, private, and religious schools. And to prevent a future trend toward regulatory authority, the federal Department of Education should be dismantled. The limited functions of the department should be carried out by the executive branch in an office of education policy.

What about crime? Between 1985 and 1991, the annual rate at which young men aged 15 to 19 were being killed increased by 154 percent, far surpassing the rate of change in any other group. Twenty percent of high-school students now carry a knife, razor, firearm, or other weapon on a regular basis. As James Q. Wilson recently pointed out, "Youngsters are shooting at people at a far higher rate than at any time in recent history."[4] Or, in the words of Senator Bill Bradley, "The murderers are younger, the guns more high-powered, and the acts themselves occur more and more randomly." This problem will almost certainly get worse before it gets better, as by the end of the decade there will be a half-million more American males between the ages of 14 and 17 than there are today, 30,000 of whom will probably become high-rate offenders.

The justice system spends $20 billion a year to arrest, rehabilitate, and jail juvenile offenders, only to watch 70 percent of them commit crimes again. Here, too, money is evidently not the panacea. Genuine reform of our juvenile-justice laws, which for the most part should take place on the state level, would involve keeping records of juvenile arrests, fingerprinting offenders, and making these records available to adult courts to prevent juvenile criminals from being treated as first-time offenders when they reach the age of 18. I would also strongly recommend legislation at the state level to allow juveniles, 14 or older, to be charged as adults for certain crimes—such as murder, rape, armed robbery, and assault with a firearm.

Genuine reform would also establish consistent, graduated punishments for every offense. It would insist on building and maintaining the facilities needed to keep violent offenders off the streets. It would speed up the criminal-justice system by enacting and enforcing realistic trial provisions. It would prohibit irresponsible judges from unilaterally imposing measures (such as "prison caps") which release violent and repeat offenders back onto the streets. It would require offenders to pay restitution to their victims. And it would create extended sentences in institutional boot camps for repeat offenders and those who failed to participate in the community-service and public-works programs to which they had been sentenced.

A special subcategory of the overall crime problem is drugs. From the mid-1980's until 1991, significant progress was made on the drug front, with researchers tracking a sharp decline in overall use. But in 1991 use began to rise, and drugs are still a major problem among the young.

According to the latest study from the University of Michigan's Institute for Social Research, one in four students has used illegal drugs before reaching high school; among 8th graders, 13 percent say they have smoked marijuana in the last year, *double* the rate of 1991; and over 40 percent of all 10th graders and nearly 50 percent of all 12th graders have used some illicit drug, including LSD, inhalants, stimulants, barbiturates, and cocaine and crack. This, in the words of the study's principal investigator, Lloyd D. Johnston, is "a problem that is getting worse at a fairly rapid pace," and it is being abetted by a decline in peer disapproval and a general softening of teenagers' attitudes toward drug use.

While the Clinton administration has not formally abandoned the war against drugs, it has abandoned it for all practical purposes. This could have a dire effect on what has already been achieved, incomplete as that is. If we mean to continue our efforts, we will need to do a number of things. They include allowing communities to choose their own antidrug priorities by combining federal antidrug support with that from states and localities; putting the U.S. military in charge of stopping the flow of illegal drugs from abroad, and giving the military control over the entire interdiction process; establishing trade and diplomatic sanctions and eliminating aid to cocaine-source countries that fail to reduce their production of cocaine by 10 percent per year, and by at least 50 percent in five years; and requiring the Attorney General first to identify all major drug-trafficking organizations known to be operating in the U.S. and then to create a plan to dismantle them.

## IV

Drawing up laundry lists of public policy may seem a tedious and academic exercise. It is nevertheless an instructive one, if for no other reason than that it glaringly exposes how *little* has been done, on the most commonsensical level, to address the terrible problems that confront us, and that have accumulated in both number and intensity over the past 30 years. In this sense, thinking concretely about specific, practical reforms offers the hope that, by a concerted national effort, we might yet begin to alleviate some of the worst manifestations of these ills, and even, in time, to reverse course.

And yet, to repeat, even if we were to enact each and every one of the desired reforms in each and every area, we would still be a long way from having healed the broken families of America. Smart, intelligent public policies can and do make a difference. But political solutions are not, ultimately, the answer to problems which are at root moral and spiritual.

"Manners," wrote Edmund Burke two centuries ago,

> are of more importance than laws. Upon them, in a great measure, the laws depend. The law touches us but here and there, and now and then. Manners are what vex or soothe, corrupt or purify, exalt or debase, barbarize or refine us, by a constant, steady, uniform, insensible operation, like that of the air we breathe in. They give their whole form and color to our lives. According to their quality, they aid morals, they supply them, or they totally destroy them.

Can government supply manners and morals if they are wanting? Of course it cannot. What it can supply, through policy and law, is a vivid sense of what we as a society expect of ourselves, what we hold ourselves responsible for, and what we consider ourselves answerable to. There can be little doubt that in this last period of time the message our laws have been sending our young people and their parents has been the profoundly demoralizing one that we expect little, and hold ourselves answerable for still less.

By changing and improving our laws, we might not thereby bring about, but we would certainly *help* to bring about, a climate that would make it easier rather than harder for all of us to grow more civilized; easier rather than harder for us to keep our commitments to one another; easier rather than harder for us to recapture the idea of personal and civic responsibility. This, in turn, would make it easier rather than harder for us to raise our children in safety to adulthood—something which at the moment we are not doing very well at all.

## Notes

1. "What To Do About Welfare," *Commentary,* December 1994.
2. Although abortion *per se* is not one of my subjects in this article, let me register here my belief that 1.5 million abortions a year–of which the overwhelming majority are performed on perfectly healthy women in order to prevent the birth of perfectly healthy children–is a national catastrophe. There is no doubt that such a number must also have a coarsening effect on adults' attitudes toward children and what they need from us.
3. Chester E. Finn, Jr., in "What To Do About Education: The Schools" *Commentary,* October 1994 provides a long list of the appalling details.
4. "What To Do About Crime," *Commentary,* September 1994.

# POSTSCRIPT

## Is the Welfare of Disadvantaged Children Improving?

Schorr collected information on social programs aimed at reducing risk factors for children in the areas of school-age childbearing (teen parenting), school dropouts, delinquency, and long-term welfare dependence. Programs that are working had some common elements, such as flexibility in responding to family needs, dealing with the whole family system, and community ownership.

Both Schorr and Bennett use statistics to support their views on social intervention results for disadvantaged children. Their views reflect the current discussions being conducted on a larger scale about America's welfare system. Welfare reform proponents want social programs to be held accountable for their expenditure of funds and their success rates.

The goals of welfare reform are to reduce the amount of time that some families can receive public assistance and to build incentives to motivate families to improve their own lives. Proponents assume that in the absence of welfare payments, parents will find jobs, support their families, and develop a sense of pride, initiative, and self-esteem, but are these goals realistic for the people involved? Similarly, proponents of social intervention programs for disadvantaged children believe that their programs will work to reduce risk factors and motivate children to seek a better life, but are their goals realistic? Can they be successful within the context of the larger society? Can the long-term effects of these programs be documented, and can the cycle of poverty and family dysfunction be ended by these interventions?

## Suggested Readings


Barry, V. (1995, Winter). What will happen to the children? *Policy Review, 71*, 7–14.

Besharov, D. J. (1996, May). Child abuse reporting. *Society, 33*, 40–46.

Edelman, M. W. (1996, June). Taking a stand. *Emerae, 7*, 58–63.

Murphy, P. T. (1995, May). Preserving chaos. *Commonweal, 122*, 12–15.

Peter, V. J. (1995, November). Welfare reform, the American family, and orphanages: What's best for the children? *USA Today: The Magazine of the American Scene, 124*, 56–60.

Stoesz, D. (1996, June). Suffer the children. *Washington Monthly, 28*, 20–25.

# ISSUE 16

## Is Abstinence Education the Best Sex Education?

**YES: Thomas Lickona**, from "Where Sex Education Went Wrong," *Educational Leadership* (November 1993)

**NO: Peggy Brick and Deborah M. Roffman**, from " 'Abstinence, No Buts' Is Simplistic," *Educational Leadership* (November 1993)

### ISSUE SUMMARY

**YES:** Thomas Lickona, a developmental psychologist, states that Americans need to promote a higher standard of sexual morality in society through "directive" sex education, which promotes abstinence before marriage.

**NO:** Peggy Brick, director of education at Planned Parenthood of Northern New Jersey, and Deborah M. Roffman, a sexuality educator and consultant, refute the directive approach to sex education and argue that a comprehensive approach to sex education is more effective.

The number of adolescent females in U.S. society who bear out-of-wedlock children continues to rise. Most people understand that teenage pregnancy is a serious and epidemic problem. Unwed adolescent mothers lack sufficient skills and education to support themselves and their children. They are unlikely to receive emotional or financial support from the fathers of their children, for the fathers are too young and unprepared for the financial and emotional responsibilities of parenthood as well. The adolescent mother's needs are often met by her parents or, more often, through publicly supported programs. It is no surprise that the cost of providing such services, not only during pregnancy and at the time of birth but often throughout the life of the mother and child, is very high. Teen mothers and their children are at a distinct disadvantage in their ability to function successfully in society. As a consequence, they often turn to welfare programs, such as Aid to Families with Dependent Children, and other social programs for help.

The obvious solution is to lessen the number of out-of-wedlock births that are occurring. Sexuality education is the current method through which

U.S. society confronts the problem. However, what constitutes effective sexuality education? Professionals continue to debate which sex education approach to this emotionally and financially costly societal problem will yield the intended results. The sexuality programs considered acceptable by some researchers, teachers, clinicians, clergy, and parents are seen by others as contributing to the problem. As a result, the arguments about what is appropriate sex education continue, even as we enter the twenty-first century. These arguments might be conceptualized into two extremes: (1) We have been much too liberal in our approach to teaching children about sexuality. In our zeal to be nonjudgmental and open-minded, we have forgotten our responsibility to teach children the morality and safety of abstinence in this world of unwanted infants and sexually transmitted diseases. (2) Comprehensive sex education in the schools, which begins in kindergarten and continues through grade 12, has not been given a chance in America. Virtually no school district has integrated teaching about the social and psychological aspects of human sexuality, along with its physical dimensions, into its curricula from the beginning of a child's school years until the end. If this were to occur, we could make significant progress in solving the problem of adolescent pregnancy.

In the United States, Congress has appropriated $250 million in abstinence education grants to the states. The program is controversial because many sex educators and policymakers at the state level are concerned about the efficacy of abstinence-only programs. Under federal guidelines, these abstinence-only programs must teach that sex outside of marriage is likely to have harmful psychological and physical effects. Other topics include how to reject sexual advances, avoiding drugs and alcohol, and being able to support oneself financially before engaging in sex. This funding is controversial because many sex educators advocate abstinence-plus programs, which discourage premarital sex but also discuss birth control and disease prevention for adolescents who may decide to engage in sex.

In the following selections, Thomas Lickona elaborates the typical rationale for the morality and safety of a program similar to the one currently being adopted in the United States. Peggy Brick and Deborah M. Roffman argue for a more comprehensive approach to sex education that is even broader than the abstinence-plus programs.

Thomas Lickona

# Where Sex Education Went Wrong

Most of us are familiar with the alarming statistics about teen sexual activity in the United States. Among high school students, 54 percent (including 61 percent of boys and 48 percent of girls) say they have had sexual intercourse, according to a 1992 Centers for Disease Control study. The number of 9th graders who say they have already had sex is 40 percent.[1]

In the past two decades, there has been an explosion in the number of sexually transmitted diseases. Twelve million people are infected each year; 63 percent of them are under 25.

Each year, 1 of every 10 teenage girls becomes pregnant, and more than 400,000 teenagers have abortions. One in 4 children is born out of wedlock, compared to 1 in 20 in 1960.

But statistics like these do not tell the whole story. The other side–one that should concern us deeply as moral educators–is the debasement of sexuality and the corruption of young people's character.

## A Legacy of the Sexual Revolution

A 1993 study by the American Association of University Women found that four out of five high school students say they have experienced sexual harassment ("unwanted sexual behavior that interferes with your life") in school. Commented one 14-year-old girl: "All guys want is sex. They just come up to you and grab you."

In suburban Minneapolis, a mother filed state and federal complaints because 3rd and 4th grade boys on the school bus had tormented her 1st grade daughter daily with obscene comments and repeated demands for sexual acts. A 6th grade teacher taking my graduate course in moral education said, "The boys bring in *Playboy,* the girls wear make-up and jewelry, and the kids write heavy sexual notes to each other."

At an Indiana high school, a teacher said, "Kids in the halls will call out –boy to girl, girl to boy–'I want to f— you.' " At Lakewood High School in an affluent Los Angeles suburb, a group of boys formed the "Spur Posse," a club in which participants competed to see how many girls they could sleep with.

Growing up in a highly eroticized sexual environment—a legacy of the sexual revolution—American children are preoccupied with sex in developmentally distorted ways and increasingly likely to act out their sexual impulses. The widespread sexual harassment in schools and the rising rates of teen sexual activity are not isolated phenomena but an outgrowth of the abnormal preoccupation with sex that children are manifesting from the earliest grades.

The sexual corruption of children reflects an adult sexual culture in which the evidence continues to mount that sex is out of control. In 1990, 29 states set records for the sex-and-violence crime of rape. By age 18, more than a quarter of girls and one-sixth of boys suffer sexual abuse. One in four female students who say they have been sexually harassed at school were victimized by a teacher, coach, bus driver, teacher's aide, security guard, principal, or counselor.[2] By various estimates, sexual infidelity now occurs in a third to one-half of U.S. marriages.

Sex is powerful. It was Freud who said that sexual self-control is essential for civilization. And, we should add, for character.

Any character education worthy of the name must help students develop sexual self-control and the ability to apply core ethical values such as respect and responsibility to the sexual domain. Against that standard, how do various contemporary models of sex education measure up?

The history of modern sex education offers three models. The first two are variations of the nondirective approach: the third, by contrast, is a directive approach.

## Comprehensive Sex Education

"Comprehensive sex education," which originated in Sweden in the 1950s and quickly became the prototype for the Western world,[3] was based on four premises:

1. Teenage sexual activity is inevitable.
2. Educators should be value-neutral regarding sex.
3. Schools should openly discuss sexual matters.
4. Sex education should teach students about contraception.

The value-neutral approach to sex soon showed up in American sex education philosophy, as in this statement by the author of the *Curriculum Guide for Sex Education in California:* " 'Right' or 'wrong' in so intimate a matter as sexual behavior is as personal as one's own name and address. No textbook or classroom teacher can teach it."[4]

What was the impact of nondirective, value-neutral, comprehensive sex education on teenage sexual behavior?

- From 1971 to 1981, government funding at all levels for contraceptive education increased by 4,000 percent. During that time teen pregnancies increased by 20 percent and teen abortions nearly doubled.[5]

- A 1986 Johns Hopkins University study concluded that comprehensive sex education did not reduce teen pregnancies,[6] a finding replicated by other studies.
- A 1986 Lou Harris Poll, commissioned by Planned Parenthood (a leading sponsor of comprehensive sex education), found that teens who took a comprehensive sex education course (including contraceptive education) were significantly *more likely* to initiate sexual intercourse than teens whose sex education courses did not discuss contraceptives.[7]

## The "Abstinence, But" Model

Negative results like those cited did not lead comprehensive sex educators to alter their approach—but AIDS did. AIDS led to two modifications: (1) teaching students to practice "safe [or "safer"] sex" through the use of barrier contraception (condoms); and (2) grafting an abstinence message onto the old comprehensive model. These changes resulted in what can be called the "Abstinence, But" approach, which says two things to students:

- Abstinence is the only 100 percent effective way to avoid pregnancy, AIDS, and other sexually transmitted diseases.
- But if you are sexually active, you can reduce these risks through the consistent, correct use of condoms.

This hybrid model, still found in many public and private schools, seems to many like a "realistic" compromise. But closer examination revels fundamental problems in the "Abstinence, But" model.

### *1. It Sends a Mixed Message*

"Don't have sex, but here's a way to do it fairly safely" amounts to a green light for sexual activity. The problem is that "Abstinence, But" is still nondirective sex education. Abstinence is presented as the safest contraceptive option,[8] but "protected sex" is offered as a "responsible" second option. The emphasis is on "making your own decision" rather than on making the right decision.

As a rule, if educators believe that a given activity is ethically wrong—harmful to self and others (as teen sexual activity clearly is)—we help students understand why that is so and guide them toward the right decision. We don't say, for example, "Drug abuse is wrong, but make your own decision, and here's how to reduce the risks if you decide to become drug active."

### *2. An Abstinence Message Is Further Weakened When Schools Provide How-to Condom Instructions and/or Distribute Condoms*

Teachers providing condom instruction will commonly demonstrate how to fit a condom to a model (or students may be asked to put a condom on a banana). In the same nonjudgmental atmosphere, discussion often includes the pros and cons of different lubricants, special precautions for oral and anal sex, and so on. Some schools also take what seems like the next logical step of actually distributing condoms to students. Both actions signal approval of "protected sex" and further undermine an abstinence message.

### *3. Condoms Do Not Make Sex Physically Safe*

For all age groups, condoms have a 10 percent annual failure rate in preventing pregnancy; for teens (notoriously poor users), the figure can go as high as 36 percent.[9] By one estimate, a 14-year-old girl who relies on condoms has more than a 50 percent chance of becoming pregnant before she graduates from high school.[10]

Contraceptive sex educators often cite AIDS as the main justification for "safe sex" education, but research shows that condoms do *not* provide adequate protection against AIDS (and, especially among teens, may generate a false sense of security). In a 1993 University of Texas study, the average condom failure rate for preventing AIDS was 31 percent.[11]

While AIDS is still relatively infrequent among teens, other sexually transmitted diseases are epidemic. Many of these diseases—and 80 percent of the time there are no visible symptoms—can be transmitted by areas of the body that are not covered by contraceptive barriers. Human Papilloma Virus, once very rare, is perhaps the most common STD among teens, infecting 38 percent of sexually active females ages 13 to 21. Victims may suffer from venereal warts, painful intercourse, or genital cancer. The virus can also cause cancer of the penis. Condoms provide no protection against this virus.[12]

Chlamydia infects 20 to 40 percent of sexually active singles; teenage girls are most susceptible. In men, chlamydia can cause infertile sperm; in women, pelvic inflammatory disease and infection of the fallopian tubes. A single infection in a woman produces a 25 percent chance of infertility; a second infection, a 50 percent chance. Medical research has found that condoms do not significantly reduce the frequency of tubal infection and infertility stemming from this disease.[13]

Given teenagers' vulnerability to pregnancy despite the use of condoms and the fact that condoms provide inadequate protection against AIDS and no protection against many STDs, it is irresponsible to promote the myth that condoms make sex physically safe.

### *4. Condoms Do Not Make Sex Emotionally Safe*

The emotional and spiritual dimensions of sex are what make it distinctively human. If we care about young people, we will help them understand the destructive emotional and spiritual effects that can come from temporary, uncommitted sexual relationships.

These psychological consequences vary among individuals but include: lowered self-esteem (sometimes linked to sexually transmitted diseases), a sense of having been "used," self-contempt for being a "user," the pain of loss of reputation, compulsive sexual behavior to try to shore up one's damaged self-image, regret and self-recrimination, rage over rejection or betrayal, difficulty trusting in future relationships, and spiritual guilt if one has a faith tradition that prohibits sex outside marriage (as world religions typically do).[14] Condoms provide zero protection against these emotional consequences.

*5. Nondirective Sex Education Undermines Character*

From the standpoint of character education, the nondirective "Abstinence, But" model fails on several counts:

- It doesn't give unmarried young people compelling ethical reasons to abstain from sexual intercourse until they are ready to commit themselves to another person. Instead, students learn that they are being "responsible" if they use contraception.
- It doesn't help students develop the crucial character quality of self-control—the capacity to curb one's desires and delay gratification. To the extent that sex education is in any way permissive toward teenage sexual activity, it fosters poor character and feeds into the societal problem of sex-out-of-control.
- It doesn't develop an ethical understanding of the relationship between sex and love.
- It doesn't cultivate what young people desperately need if they are to postpone sex: a vision of the solemn, binding commitment between two people in which sex is potentially most meaningful, responsible, and safe (physically and emotionally)—namely, marriage.

## Directive Sex Education

By any ethical, educational, or public health measure, nondirective sex education has been a failure. As a result, schools are turning increasingly toward directive sex education—just as the national character education movement is embracing a more directive approach to promoting core ethical values as the basis of good character.

A directive approach means helping young persons—for the sake of their safety, happiness, and character—to see the logic of an "Abstinence, No Buts" standard, often called "chastity education." This standard says three things:

1. Sexual abstinence is the *only* medically safe and morally responsible choice for unmarried teenagers.
2. Condoms do not make premarital sex responsible because they don't make it physically safe, emotionally safe, or ethically loving.
3. The only truly safe sex is having sex *only* with a marriage partner who is having sex *only* with you. If you avoid intercourse until marriage, you will have a much greater chance of remaining healthy and being able to have children.

There are now many carefully crafted curriculums, books, and videos that foster the attitudes that lead teens to choose chastity—a moral choice and a lifestyle that is truly respectful of self and others. Here are some examples:

*1. Decision-Making: Keys to Total Success*

Facing a serious teen pregnancy problem (147 high school girls known to be pregnant in 1984–85), the San Marcos, California, school system implemented a multifaceted program, which included six-week courses for junior high students on developing study skills, self-esteem, and positive moral values;[15] daily 10-minute lessons on "how to be successful"; a six week course for 8th graders using Teen Aid's curriculum on the advantages of premarital abstinence and how to regain them (for example, self-respect and protection against pregnancy and disease) after having been sexually active; *Window to the Womb,* a video providing ultrasound footage of early fetal development to show students the power of their sexuality to create human life; and summaries of all lessons for parents plus a parent workshop on teaching sexual morality to teens.[16]

After San Marcos implemented this program, known pregnancies at the high school dropped from 20 percent in 1984 to 2.5 percent in 1986 to 1.5 percent in 1988. Meanwhile, scores on tests of basic skills went up, and in 1988 San Marcos won an award for the lowest drop-out rate in California.

***2. Teen S.T.A.R. (Sexuality Teaching in the Context of Adult Responsibility)***

[Teen S.T.A.R.] is currently used with more than 5,000 teens in various regions of the United States and in other countries. The program teaches that fertility is a gift and a power to be respected. Its premise is that "decisions about sexual responsibility will arise from inner conviction and knowledge of the self." More than half of the teens who enter the program sexually active stop sexual activity; very few initiate it.[17]

***3. The Loving Well Curriculum***

[The Loving Well Curriculum], a literature-based program, uses selections from the classics, folktales, and contemporary adolescent literature to examine relationships from family love to infatuation and early romance to marriage. An evaluation finds that of those students who were not sexually active when they started the curriculum, 92 percent are still abstinent two years later, compared to 72 percent abstinent in a control group not exposed to the curriculum.[18]

***4. Postponing Sexual Involvement***

[Postponing Sexual Involvement] was developed by Emory University's Marion Howard specifically for low-income, inner-city 8th graders at risk for early sexual activity. Of students in the program, 70 percent said it taught them that they "can postpone sexual activity without losing their friends' respect." Participants were *five times less likely* to initiate sexual activity than students who did not take the program.[19] . . .

## Answers to Common Questions

Educators committing to directive sex education must be prepared to answer some common questions. Among them:

*What about all the teens who will remain sexually active despite abstinence education? Shouldn't they be counseled to use condoms?* Obviously, if a person is going to have sex, using a condom will reduce the chance of pregnancy and AIDS, but not to an acceptable level. Condoms offer no protection against many other STDs and their long-term consequences, such as infertility. Schools have the mission of teaching the truth and developing right values—which means helping students understand why the various forms of contraception do not make premarital sex physically or emotionally safe and how premature sexual activity will hurt them now and in the future.

*Isn't premarital sexual abstinence a religious or cultural value, as opposed to universal ethical values like love, respect, and honesty?* Although religion supports premarital abstinence, it can be demonstrated, through ethical reasoning alone, that reserving sex for marriage is a logical application of ethical values. If we love and respect another, we want what is in that person's best interest. Does sex without commitment meet that criterion? Can we say that we really love someone if we gamble with that person's physical health, emotional happiness, and future life? Given the current epidemic of sexually transmitted diseases, it's possible to argue on medical grounds alone that premarital sexual abstinence is the only ethical choice that truly respects self and other.

*Isn't the recommendation to save sex for marriage prejudicial against homosexual persons, since the law does not permit them to marry?* All students can be encouraged to follow the recommendation of the U.S. Department of Education's guidebook, *AIDS and the Education of Our Children:*

> Regardless of sexual orientation, the best way for young people to avoid AIDS and other STDs is to refrain from sexual activity until as adults they are ready to establish a mutually faithful monogamous relationship.[20]

*Is abstinence education feasible in places, such as the inner city, where poverty and family breakdown are harsh realities?* Programs like Atlanta's Postponing Sexual Involvement have a track record of making abstinence education work amid urban poverty. Virginia Governor Douglas Wilder has argued that "the black family is teetering near the abyss of self-destruction" and that "our young, male and female alike, must embrace the self-discipline of abstinence."[21] Sylvia Peters, who won national acclaim for her work as principal of the Alexander Dumas School (K-8) in inner-city Chicago, made the decision to tell her students (6th graders were getting pregnant before she arrived), "Do not have sex until you are married—you will wreck your life."[22] These two black leaders know that the problem of black illegitimate births—up from 35 to 65 percent in little more than two decades— won't be solved until there is a new ethic of sexual responsibility.

Sexual behavior is determined by value, not mere knowledge. Studies show that students who have value orientations (for example, get good grades in school, have high self-regard, consider their religious faith important, have strong moral codes), are significantly less likely to be sexually active than peers who lack these values. These internally held values are more powerful than peer pressure.[23]

Our challenge as educators is this: Will we help to develop these values and educate for character in sex, as in all other areas? If we do not move decisively—in our schools, families, churches, government, and media—to promote a higher standard of sexual morality in our society, we will surely see a continued worsening of the plague of sex-related problems—promiscuity, sexual exploitation and rape, unwed pregnancy, abortions, sexually transmitted diseases, the emotional consequences of uncommitted sex, sexual harassment in schools, children of all ages focused on sex in unwholesome ways, sexual infidelity in marriages, pornography, the sexual abuse of children, and the damage to families caused by many of these problems.

Nondirective sex education obviously didn't cause all of these problems, and directive sex education won't solve all of them. But at the very least, sex education in our schools must be part of the solution, not part of the problem.

## Notes

1. Centers for Disease Control and Prevention, (1992), "Sexual Behavior Among High School Students, U. S.," in *Morbidity and Mortality Weekly Report 40,* 51–52.
2. American Association of University Women "Report on Sexual Harassment," (June 1993).
3. D. Richard, (1990), *Has Sex Education Failed Our Teenagers?,* (Colorado Springs: Focus on the Family Publishing).
4. S. Cronenwett, (1982), "Response to Symposium on Sex and Children," in *Character Policy,* edited by E. A. Wynne, (Lanham, Md.: University Press of America), p. 101.
5. R. Glasow, (1988), *School-Based Clinics* (Washington, D.C.: NRL Educational Trust Fund).
6. D. A. Dawson, (1986), "The Effects of Sex Education on Adolescent Behavior," *Family Planning Perspectives* 18, 4: 162–170.
7. L. Harris, (1986), "American Teens Speak: Sex, Myth, TV, and Birth Control," poll commissioned by the Planned Parenthood Federation of America.
8. Thanks to Onalee McGraw for this point.
9. E. Jones and J. Forrest, (May/June 1989), "Contraceptive Failure in the United States." *Family Planning Perspectives.*
10. W. Kilpatrick, (1992), *Why Johnny Can't Tell Right From Wrong,* (New York: Simon & Schuster).
11. Reported by CBS Evening News, 1993.
12. Source: Dr. Joe McIlhaney, Medical Institute for Sexual Health, Austin, Texas. For an in-depth treatment of sexually transmitted diseases, see McIlhaney's 1991 book *Safe Sex: A Doctor Explains the Realities of AIDS and Other STDs* (Grand Rapids: Baker Book House).
13. *Safe Sex: Slide Program Lecture Notes,* (1993), (Austin: Medical Institute for Sexual Health).
14. Thanks to Carson Daly for her contribution to this list.
15. These lessons are available from the Jefferson Center for Character Education, Suite 240, 202 S. Lake Ave., Pasadena, CA 91101.
16. Teen Aid, N. 1330 Calispel, Spokane, WA 99201–2320. For information on a similar program with comparable positive outcomes, contact: SEX RESPECT, P.O. Box 349, Bradley, IL 60915–0349.
17. C. Balsam, (October 1992), "Letter to the Editor," *New Oxford Review.* For information about Teen S.T.A.R., contact Hanna Klaus, P.O. Box 30239, Bethesda, MD 20824–0239.

18. Based on an article by S. Ellenwood in *Character* (April, 1993), the newsletter of Boston University's Center for the Advancement of Ethics and Character. For information about the Loving Well Curriculum, contact Nancy McLaren, Project Coordinator, College of Communication, Boston University, 460 Commonwealth Ave., Boston, MA 02215.
19. M. Howard and J. McCabe, (1990), "Helping Teenagers Postpone Sexual Involvement," *Family Planning Perspectives* 22: 1.
20. *AIDS and the Education of Our Children,* (1988), (Washington, D.C.: U.S. Department of Education).
21. L. D. Wilder, (March 28, 1991), "To Save the Black Family, the Young Must Abstain," *The Wall Street Journal.*
22. S. Peters, (February 1993), comments as a panel member at the annual conference of the Character Education Partnership, Washington, D.C.
23. I am indebted to William Bennett for this point.

# NO 

**Peggy Brick and Deborah M. Roffman**

## "Abstinence, No Buts" Is Simplistic

There are no easy answers to the sexual health crisis afflicting our society, including those advocated by Thomas Lickona. The "Abstinence, No Buts" approach does not adequately address the developmental needs of children and adolescents, the reality of their lives, or the societal forces that condition their view of the world.

First, Lickona undermines rational dialogue by dividing educators into artificial, polar camps: "values-free-intercourse promoters," who push for contraception-based "comprehensive" sex education (the bad guys), and "values-based-intercourse preventers," who espouse chastity-based "character" education (the good guys). It is neither accurate nor helpful for him to imply that one particular interest group has a corner on instilling character, core values, and ethical thought; on wanting young people to grow up emotionally, socially, physically, and spiritually healthy; on working toward a day when developmental and social problems—such as premature sexual activity, teenage pregnancy, abortion, STD, HIV, sexism, and sexual harassment/abuse/exploitation—no longer threaten our children.

Second, Lickona's definition of "comprehensive" sex education bears little resemblance to the actual approach. Comprehensive sexuality education encompasses not only the complexities of sex and reproduction, but the enormously complicated subjects of human growth and development, gender roles, intimacy, and social and cultural forces that influence our development as males and females (Roffman 1992). Such an approach seeks to help young people understand sexuality as integral to their identity and enables them to make responsible lifelong decisions (SIECUS 1991).

More than 60 mainstream organizations support this approach through membership in the National Coalition to Support Sexuality Education. These include the American Medical Association, American School Health Association, American Association of School Administrators, National School Boards Association, and the Society for Adolescent Medicine. The majority of American adults support such a strategy as well. For example, recent surveys in New Jersey and North Carolina found that at least 85 percent of those surveyed approved of comprehensive sexuality education (Firestone 1993, North Carolina Coalition on Adolescent Pregnancy 1993).

A truly comprehensive approach is ongoing and begins during the preschool and elementary years (Montfort 1993). Curriculums of this type educate, rather than propagandize, children about sexuality. Youngsters learn to ask questions, predict consequences, examine values, and plan for the future. They confront real-life dilemmas: What would happen if? What would you do if? By the middle grades, students learn to take action on issues such as: What can we do to reduce teen pregnancies in this school? To educate students about HIV/AIDS? (See Reis 1989, Kirby et al. 1991, Center for Population Options 1992, O'Neill and Roffman 1992, SIECUS 1993). Ideally, this approach to sexuality education will be integrated throughout the entire curriculum (Brick 1991).

## Why Directive Approaches Fail

Those of us committed to comprehensive sex education and to public education in a pluralistic society are not persuaded by the arguments for "directive," ideological sex education for several reasons.

1. It is hypocritical and futile to expect efforts directed at adolescents to solve the nation's myriad sexual problems. Powerful social forces contribute to the early development of unhealthy sexual scripts—about who we are as males or females, how we should act, and issues of right and wrong.

For example, the early learning of male gender roles, often linked with violence and the need to dominate, is fundamentally related to problems of rape and harassment (Miedzian 1991). The manipulation of the sexuality of both males and females from an early age, and the stimulation of sexual desires by advertising and other media, are fundamental to the operation of our economic system (D'Emilio and Freedman 1988). Adolescent child-bearing, sexually transmitted diseases, and the spread of HIV are highly correlated with poverty and lack of hope for the future (National Research Council 1987). Further, many problems attributed to teens are not just teen problems: the majority of *all* pregnancies in this country are unplanned (Heller 1993). Seventy percent of adolescent pregnancies are fathered by adult men (Males 1993).

2. Directive approaches require a delay of intercourse 10 or more years beyond biological maturity, which is contrary to practice in virtually all societies —unless there is a strict tradition segregating unmarried males and females and chaperoning women (Francoeur 1991).

3. The success of these proposals requires an immediate, fundamental change in the sexual attitudes and behaviors of a society through mere educational intervention. Such a radical change has never been accomplished. Traditionally, the majority of American males have accepted premarital intercourse, and as early as 1973, a study showed 95 percent of males and 85 percent of females approved of it (DeLamater and MacCorquodale 1979).

4. Advocates of the directive approach do not prepare youth to make decisions in a highly complex world. They permit no choice but *their* choice and deliberately deny potentially life-saving information to those who do no conform to their viewpoint.

5. The curriculums espoused are fear-based, characterized by devastating descriptions of the dangers of all nonmarital intercourse and medical misinformation about abortion, sexually transmitted disease, HIV/AIDS, and the effectiveness of condoms. For example, the major cause of condom failure is incorrect usage. Knowledge of proper condom use, of the variations in quality among brands, and of the substantial increase in effectiveness when condoms are used in combination with spermicides greatly reduces the risk for those who choose to have sexual intercourse (Kestelman and Trussell 1991). These sex-negative, emotionally overwhelming, and potentially guilt-producing strategies may well induce problems rather than ameliorate them by leading to unhealthy sexual attitudes, irrational decision making, denial, or rebellion (Fisher 1989).

Moreover, these curriculums are promoted by groups such as Concerned Women for America, the Eagle Forum, Focus on the Family, and the American Life League, which are lobbying heavily to impose Fundamentalist Christian doctrine on public schools (Kantor 1993, Hart 1993).

## Distorted and Misrepresented Data

Given these concerns, claims about the success of abstinence-only programs must be examined with extreme caution. Take, for example, the claim that a program in San Marcos, California, greatly reduced teen pregnancies in the mid-80s. In fact, this claim was not based on a scientific study but on the observation of the high school principal reporting the number of students who *told* the school counselor they were pregnant. After a much-publicized program condemning premarital intercourse, far fewer students reported their pregnancies to school staff; actual census figures for San Marcos indicated that from 1980–1990, the birth rate for mothers aged 14–17 more than doubled (Reynolds 1991). Many other evaluators have challenged the integrity of research documenting these extraordinary claims in support of abstinence-only curriculums (Trudell and Whatley 1991, Kirby et al. 1991, Alan Guttmacher Institute 1993). Such programs may change attitudes temporarily (at least as reported to a teacher), but they do not change behavior in any significant way.

Similar statistical distortions have been used to discredit programs that are not abstinence-only in approach. Seriously flawed is the conclusion, based on data collected in a 1986 Lou Harris Poll, that "teens who took a comprehensive sex education course (defined as one including contraceptive education) were subsequently 53 percent more likely to initiate intercourse than teens whose sex education courses did not discuss contraceptives."

First, the survey did not ask when intercourse was initiated in relation to the timing of the program; therefore, the word "subsequently" (implying causation) is patently misleading. Second, the analysis ignored the crucial variable of chronological age. Sexual intercourse among teenagers increases with age, as does the experience of having had a "comprehensive" program. Therefore, causation was implied, when in reality, correlation was the appropriate interpretation.

Besides the use of distorted data, groups demanding an abstinence-only approach dismiss people whose values regarding sexual behaviors differ from their own, asserting that these people are "without values." In fact, comprehensive sex education is based upon core human values that form the foundation of all ethical behavior, such as personal responsibility, integrity, caring for others, and mutual respect in relationships.

Moreover, comprehensive sex education is based on values appropriate to our democratic and pluralistic society—including respect for people's diverse viewpoints about controversial issues.

## A Wake-Up Call for Society

Our entire society, not just sex education, has failed to provide children and youth with the educational, social, and economic conditions necessary to grow toward sexual health. In fact, truly comprehensive K–12 sexuality education, which at most exists in only 10 percent of schools nationwide, has hardly been tried (Donovan 1989). Sexuality education—of whatever kind—is neither the cause, nor the cure, for our nation's sexual malaise.

In a society where children's consciousness is permeated by virulent images of sex—where their sexuality is manipulated by advertising and the media, where few adults provide helpful role models—we cannot expect sex education to perform a miracle. Curriculums that provide as their primary or sole strategy admonitions against nonmarital intercourse are destined to be ineffective and, in fact, insult the real-life needs of children and youth. In a society that conveys complex, confusing messages about sexuality, only comprehensive sexuality education can begin to address the diverse needs of youth and promote healthy sexual development.

## References

Alan Guttmacher Institute. (1993). *Washington Memo,* p. 4.

Brick, P. (1991). "Fostering Positive Sexuality." *Educational Leadership* 45, 1: 51–53.

Center for Population Options. (1992). *When I'm Grown: Vol. II. Grades 3 and 4; Vol. III, Grades 5 and 6.* Washington, D.C.: CPO.

DeLamater, J. D., and P. MacCorquodale. (1979). *Premarital Sexuality: Attitudes, Relationships, Behavior.* Madison: University of Wisconsin Press.

D'Emilio, J., and E. B. Freedman. (1988). *Intimate Matters: A History of Sexuality in America.* New York: Harper & Row.

Donovan, P. (1989). *Risk and Responsibility: Teach Sex Education in America's Schools Today.* New York: Alan Guttmacher Institute.

Firestone, W. A. (1993). "Support of Sex Education Grows." *Family Life Matters* 18: 1.

Fisher, W. A. (1989). "Understanding and Preventing Adolescent Pregnancy and Sexually Transmissible Disease/AIDS." In *Applying Social Influence Processes in Preventing Social Problems* edited by J. Edwards et al. New York: Plenum Press.

Francoeur, R. T. (1991). *Becoming a Sexual Person.* New York: Macmillan.

Harris, L. (1986). *American Teens Speak: Sex, Myths, TV, and Birth Control.* New York: Planned Parenthood Federation of America.

Hart, J. (August 28, 1993). "Battle Lines Drawn on Classroom Sex Education," *The Boston Globe.*

Heller, K. (February 21, 1993). "Out of Control." *Philadelphia Inquirer Magazine:* 18, 20–22.

Kantor, L. M. (1993). "Scared Chaste? Fear-Based Educational Curricula." *SIECUS Report* 21, 2: 1–15.

Kestelman, P., and J. Trussell. (1991). "Efficacy of the Simultaneous Use of Condoms and Spermicides." *Family Planning Perspectives* 23: 226–232.

Kirby, D., R. P. Barth, N. Leland, and J. V. Fetro. (991). "Reducing the Risk: Impact of a New Curriculum on Sexual Risk-Taking," *Family Planning Perspectives* 23: 253–263.

Males, M. (August 9, 1993). "Infantile Arguments." *In These Times:* 18–20.

Miedzian, M. (1991). *Boys Will Be Boys: Breaking the Link Between Masculinity and Violence.* New York: Doubleday.

Montfort, S., P. Brick, and N. Blume. (1993). *Healthy Foundations: Developing Positive Policies and Programs Regarding Children's Learning about Sexuality.* Hackensack: Planned Parenthood of Greater Northern New Jersey.

North Carolina Coalition on Adolescent Pregnancy. (Spring 1993). "New Stateside Poll Shows Overwhelming Support for Sex Education in Schools, for Adolescent Health Care Centers, and Access to Contraceptive Services for Teens." *The Network:* 1.

National Research Council. (1987). *Risking the Future: Adolescent Sexuality, Pregnancy, and Childbearing.* Washington, D.C.: National Academy Press.

O'Neill, C., and D. Roffman, eds. (1992). "Sexuality Education in an Age of AIDS." *Independent School* 51, 3: 11–42.

Reis, B. (1989). *F.L.A.S.H.: Family Life and Sexual Health, 9/10.* (1986). *F.L.A.S.H. 7/8.* (1985). *F.L.A.S.H. 5/6.* Seattle: Seattle-King County Department of Public Health.

Reynolds, N. (December 19, 1991). "So-Called San Marcos Miracle Actually May Be Just a Myth." *San Diego Union.*

Roffman, D. (1992). "Teaching About Sexuality in Independent Schools." *Independent School* 51, 3: 11–18.

SIECUS. (1991). Guidelines for Comprehensive Sexuality Education. New York: Sex Information and Education Council of the U.S.

SIECUS. (1993). "Comprehensive Sexuality Education: A SIECUS Resource Guide of Recommended Curricula and Text Books." *SIECUS Report* 21, 6: 20–23.

Trudell, B., and M. Whatley. (1991). "Sex Respect: A Problematic Public School Sexuality Curriculum." *Journal of Sex Education and Therapy* 17, 2: 125–140.

# POSTSCRIPT

## Is Abstinence Education the Best Sex Education?

Out-of-wedlock births to adolescent mothers have become problematic in U.S. society for several reasons. The onset of the menarche (first ovulation and subsequent menstruation) is coming at increasingly earlier ages for young females. This combined with the tendency for delaying marriage means that the adolescent female faces longer periods of singlehood during her fertile years than did her great-grandmother. Consider, for example, that it was not uncommon for a woman born at the turn of the century to be married at age 17 or 18. Consider, too, that this woman's menarche was a year or more later than that of a contemporary adolescent female. The result is fewer years of singlehood and fewer opportunities for premarital sexual endeavors.

Current notions regarding adolescent sexuality suggest that teens will inevitably express themselves sexually as part of the developmental process of adolescence. Therefore, unless they are taught to exercise restraint and sexual abstinence, they should be apprised of the risks of early sexual activity and empowered with information about how to express themselves sexually while avoiding pregnancy and sexually transmitted diseases. But on the basis of current rates of teen pregnancy, the information that teens are now receiving is not encouraging more responsible behaviors, such as abstinence or the use of contraceptives.

## Suggested Readings


American Academy of Pediatrics, Committee on Adolescence (1995). Condom availability for youth. *Pediatrics, 95*(2), 281–185.

Jacobs, C. D. (1995). School sexuality education and adolescent risk-taking behavior. *Journal of School Health, 65*(3), 91–95.

Kasun, J. (1994, Spring). Condom nation. *Policy Review*, 79–82.

Post, S. (1992, October 17). Adolescents in a time of AIDS: Preventive education. *America*, 278–282.

Sellers, D. E. (1994). Does the promotion and distribution of condoms increase teen sexual activity? Evidence from an HIV prevention program for Latino youth. *American Journal of Public Health, 84*(12), 952–959.

Whitehead, B. D. (1994, October). The failure of sex education. *Atlantic Monthly*, 55–80.

# ISSUE 17

## Can Memories of Childhood Sexual Abuse Be Recovered?

**YES: May Benatar**, from "Running Away From Sexual Abuse: Denial Revisited," *Families in Society: The Journal of Contemporary Human Services* (May 1995)

**NO: Susan P. Robbins**, from "Wading Through the Muddy Waters of Recovered Memory," *Families in Society: The Journal of Contemporary Human Services* (October 1995)

### ISSUE SUMMARY

**YES:** May Benatar, a clinical social worker, argues that the mass media and contemporary culture question the accuracy and truthfulness of survivors of sexual abuse. By doing this the long-term effects of these abuses tend to be minimized.

**NO:** Susan P. Robbins, an associate professor of social work, contends that the reason some professionals are skeptical of recovered memories is that there is no research that supports the accuracy of recovered memory. She cautions that the indiscriminate acceptance of recovered memories can lead to a serious backlash of disbelief when legitimate cases of abuse are reported.

There has been a definite shift in societal thinking about child abuse during the past 20 years. Historically, when an adult would come forth with an account of sexual abuse that was purported to have occurred decades earlier, these accounts were likely to have been considered by mental health professionals as fantasies. In the past decade or so, both the mass media and the helping professions have been much more likely to accept these allegations, which have come to be known as recovered memories of past sexual abuse, as true. It is easy to imagine not only the problems for the person recalling such difficult memories but also the problems that families have had to endure as a result of these disclosures. One controversial question is how valid are allegations that are based upon repressed memories from years ago?

Few people would argue with the notion that human memory is not always accurate; our memories do indeed fail us at times. It has been documented in the literature, however, that traumatic memory is physiologically encoded differently than normal memory in one's brain. If so, should we assume that traumatic experiences are more indelibly etched and can be retrieved with greater accuracy than normal memory? Or is it possible that memories of abuse are not as easily recalled due to the trauma involved? Some mental health professionals believe that therapists can suggest memories to clients and that these memories can become integrated into the client's memory as if they actually happened when they, in fact, did not.

In the following selections, May Benatar argues that we, as a society, do not pay enough attention to these heinous past traumas. Susan P. Robbins contends that perhaps we accept these allegations as fact too readily.

**May Benatar**

**YES**

# Running Away From Sexual Abuse: Denial Revisited

After a period of increased professional and public awareness of how pervasive the sexual maltreatment of children is in our society, we appear to be in danger of vaulting away from hard-won insights into this major public health issue. Both propounding and expressing the prejudices of the culture, the press and other media have taken to indicting the veracity of traumatic memories of survivors of sexual abuse, minimizing the toxic long-term effects of the sexual maltreatment of children, and casting doubt on both the skill and good intentions of clinicians treating both child victims and adult survivors. We have seen front-page articles on the purported "false" memories of adult survivors of abuse; examples of "false" accusations of innocent parents, grandparents, or teachers; or speculations that therapists, many of whom are survivors themselves, intentionally or unintentionally suggest events to their patients that never took place.

A 1993 *Newsweek* cover photograph showed a middle-age couple convicted of molesting their grandchildren. The caption asks: "When does the fight to protect our kids go too far?" Does this strange juxtaposition of material imply that convicting child molesters is "going too far?" The article inside (Shapiro, 1993) reviews a few recent court cases and one reversal and addresses the issue of child testimony; the author asks whether we are panicking over child abuse. Is criminal prosecution tantamount to panic? And if it is, is the abuse of children not worthy of such a response?

In the *New Yorker,* Wright (1993a, 1993b) wrote a two-part article on the case of a Washington state deputy sheriff, who, after being accused of child abuse by his two daughters, confessed to sexually abusing them, prostituting them to family friends, and being part of a satanic cult. The case unraveled when it was discovered that at least some of the accusations and confessions by both parents resulted from overzealous questioning and suggestions by police interrogators on what were alleged to be highly suggestible subjects. The article clearly implies that this case represents one of many instances of modern-day witch hunts—the innocent "witches" in this case being those accused of perpetrating unthinkable crimes such as ritual sexual abuse, torture, and murder.

From May Benatar, "Running Away From Sexual Abuse: Denial Revisited," *Families in Society: The Journal of Contemporary Human Services* (May 1995). 

In *Mother Jones,* a well-regarded if somewhat off-beat publication, Watters (1993) also expressed concern about false memories and false accusations in a report of a young woman's delayed discovery of childhood abuse. The woman entered therapy following a severe depressive episode and while in therapy recovered memories of sexual abuse. Although the facts of the case neither exculpate the accused nor affirm the victim's accusations, the author uses this case to propose that "a substantial segment of the therapy community has charged ahead, creating a *growth* industry around the concept of recovered memories."

Even Carol Tavris (1993), a noted feminist author, cast a skeptical eye on what she termed the "incest-survivor machine," an umbrella term for therapists working with adult survivors, writers of self-help books for survivors, and the grass-roots recovery movement of adult survivors.

For clinicians working with patients to address the post-traumatic effects of childhood sexual abuse and for adult survivors struggling to take their own stories seriously and understand the difficulties of their adult lives as sequelae of and adaptation to violations that occurred during childhood, this emphasis on the "hype" of sexual abuse is deeply troubling.

## Child Abuse: Past and Present Findings

The reality of child abuse is well established. Why then is it currently acceptable, even fashionable, to doubt the victims, those who prosecute for them, and those who treat their post-traumatic illnesses? This backlash against sexual-abuse survivors has social, cultural, political, and psychological roots. One reading is that this backlash is a response to the evolution in law regarding the issue of incest—an evolution that now allows some adult survivors to seek legal redress many years, even decades, after the commission of crimes. Another reason for this backlash may be related to the cultural mysogyny that Faludi (1991) documents in her book *Backlash,* which refers to the social forces that thwart the gains that women have achieved in society. On another level of analysis, we may understand this phenomenon of denial of social realities as "cultural dissociation." As a society we are unable to accept the reality of the cruelty, sadism, neglect, and narcissism that adults inflict upon children. In a world where some people still debate the reality of Nazi death camps, it is not surprising that we have difficulties acknowledging that 1 of every 3 girls and 1 of 7 to 10 boys are "used" by an adult in a manner that brings great harm to them for the rest of their lives.

The epidemiology of child sexual abuse has been carefully documented. Kinsey found in the early 1950s that 24% of his female sample of 4,000 women reported sexual abuse in childhood (before the age of puberty) (Brownmiller, 1975). Dozens of studies have confirmed this finding. Thirty years later, Russell (1986) carefully surveyed a nonclinical population of nearly 1,000 women. She reported that 38% of the sample reported being molested before the age of 18 and 28% before puberty. In addition, she found that most abusers are known to the child as trusted individuals who occupy a position of authority over the child.

In another significant study, Herman and Schatzow (1987) discussed recall of traumatic memories from childhood often dissociated by the child in an effort to maintain secrecy and safety. Fifty-three female patients in group psychotherapy reported delayed recall of traumatic memory; 74% of the women confirmed their memories of abuse by obtaining independent corroborating evidence—physical evidence, diaries, pictures, confirmation by perpetrators and/or corroboration by other family members who had also been victimized. This study appears to strengthen Russell's and Kinsey's data. Even those with delayed recall, when seeking confirmation of the reality of their memories many years after the fact, are able to confirm the memory. To my knowledge, no comparable study demonstrates *false* recall of childhood-abuse memories.

Interestingly, the conflict between the reality of child abuse and the voices of disbelief and disavowal is not unique to the 1990s; a century ago western psychiatry experienced a similar struggle and process. Masson (1984), in *The Assault on Truth,* presented important work done in 19th-century France regarding the criminal brutalization and sexual abuse of children. In setting the stage for his explanation of why Freud first adopted and later abandoned the "seduction theory" to explain the origins of hysterical neurosis, Masson discusses child abuse in Europe during that period. Forensic psychiatrists uncovered shocking facts about child abuse. Ambrose Tardieu, a professor and dean of forensic medicine at the University of Paris and president of the Academy of Medicine in Paris in 1860, published "A Medico-Legal Study of Cruelty and Brutal Treatment Inflicted on Children." He presented case after case of detailed medical evidence indicating severe child abuse, including the sexual abuse of children. He indicated that the phenomenon was not rare and that perpetrators were often parents and that victims were often very young and primarily girls.

Paul Brouardel, Tardieu's successor to the chair of legal medicine in Paris and also a contemporary of Freud, described perpetrators as "excellent family men" who were often the fathers of the victims. Brouardel was a collaborator of Jean-Martin Charcot, a neurologist who demonstrated the efficacy of hypnosis in the treatment of psychiatric patients, particularly female hysterics. Freud was fascinated by Charcot's work and came to Paris to study with him. Masson argues that Freud and his contemporaries were more than likely aware of the work of Tardieu, Brouardel, and other forensic psychiatrists in France through their studies with Charcot. Freud's early struggles to understand the underpinnings of neurosis suggest his awareness of the traumatic origins of psychic disturbance as well as the influence that the French pioneers had on his clinical awareness. In the late 1890s Freud (1984) wrote movingly and persuasively in *The Aetiology of Hysteria* about 18 cases of hysterical neurosis in which an early experience of sexual abuse had led to hysterical symptoms in adult life—symptoms similar to what we categorize today as post-traumatic stress disorder or dissociative disorder.

However, it was Pierre Janet, another visitor to Charcot's seminars, who developed both a complex theoretical understanding and efficacious treatment model for hysteria. Janet published many of his findings the year before Freud's *Aetiology of Hysteria* appeared, but unlike Freud he held fast to the trauma model that Freud renounced. Janet described many cases of what we have come to understand as dissociative disorders and multiple personality disorder. Janet understood his patients' symptoms, much as trained clinicians do today, as ingenious and creative adaptations to overwhelming childhood stress such as physical and/or sexual abuse. He saw hysterical symptoms, not as compromise formations of drive derivatives or expressions of drive conflicts, but rather as fossils from the past, derivatives of traumatic memory, communications of early betrayals and overwhelming affects (van der Kolk & van der Hart, 1989).

Yet for most of the 20th century, Janet was *not* studied and *not* employed in our attempts to understand mental life. Freud's development of psychoanalysis obliterated Janet's work. To read Janet today, 100 years later, is to be struck with how little modern trauma psychology and our understandings of traumatic memory can add to his understandings, how clearly he explicated what we have come to rediscover in the past decade and a half, and how brilliantly he anticipated modern findings on the psychophysiology of memory.

Herman (1992) and others have proposed that Freud and his students moved away from trauma theory or the "seduction theory," because the zeitgeist of the time and place could not support such conclusions. Earlier in the century, in Tardieu's and Charcot's France, the political atmosphere was one of reform: challenges to the monarchy and the church enabled a movement toward understanding mental illness as a rational, not magical, pursuit. They viewed mental illness as a sequela of early experience that could be understood and addressed by science. These sociopolitical forces ushered in an era of more humane treatment of the mentally ill that approached mental illness as trauma based. Freud's science grew in different soil—Viennese soil—where trauma-based theory was unable to take root.

For a brief period in the 1800s, clinicians and students of forensic psychiatry knew that many children were severely abused by their families and that such abuse led to dramatic effects in the mental health of adults. They also understood effective treatment of these symptoms involved revisiting early memory and processing these memories in the context of a solid therapeutic alliance. By the beginning of the 20th century, after Freud had published *The Aetiology of Hysteria,* the political winds had shifted, as had the politics of psychiatry. Traumatic etiology was relegated to the background and endogenous intrapsychic conflicts moved to the foreground. We stopped looking at the environmental surround—the maltreatment of children—and turned our scientific gaze inward toward fantasy formation and the intricate topography of the mind.

## Where Do We Go Today?

It has taken us nearly a century to get back to where we started—the work of Janet. Two concurrent social movements helped to reawaken our awareness of childhood trauma. In the 1970s, the returning Vietnam War veterans became quite active in seeking validation for their catastrophic experiences during the war. They organized themselves to obtain services from veterans hospitals and recognition for their suffering from their communities. Their illnesses became the focus for legal activity and psychiatric attention. Psychiatrists rediscovered "war neurosis" and learned from their patients about the aftereffects of severe, intense, and acute traumatic experience. Post-traumatic stress disorder became a diagnostic entity and was entered into the *Diagnostic and Statistical Manual of Mental Disorders* in 1980.

The other major social change that contributed to the reemergence of our awareness of childhood sexual abuse was the women's movement in the 1970s. Women meeting in consciousness-raising groups, helping one another to name their fears, their frustrations, and their hopes, began telling stories of sexual manipulation, sexual violence, and early experiences of sexual violation at the hands of family members. Women Against Rape centers sprang up across the country; from these centers rape-crisis-counseling centers were developed. Today, a strong grass-roots recovery movement exists, carrying the message about child abuse and dissociative disorders to the public. Individuals help one another in 12-step-type recovery groups, generating art, newsletters, books, workshops, and conferences to help heal themselves as well as educate clinicians and lay individuals.

As a result of these two powerful movements for social change, survivors of childhood sexual abuse found a voice and clinicians began to listen. By the 1980s we began to see new journals devoted to exploring the effects and the treatment of individuals so affected. A whole new subspecialty in psychiatry, psychology, and social work emerged: working with dissociative disorders. Today, however, troubling signs indicate that public and political retrenchment from various interconnecting and interactive factors are contributing to renewed denial and disavowal of the prevalence of child sexual abuse. Moreover, social, legal, political, and psychological pressures are undermining all that we have learned about the etiology and sequelae of this devastating societal problem.

## Factor One

In many ways, the mass media have focused more attention on survivors than has the mental health establishment. Oprah, Phil, and Sally Jesse have featured shows alerting the public to the painful experiences of adult survivors, which has led to a "Geraldoizing" effect. Despite the fact that Geraldo Rivera has actually done a couple of interesting shows on multiple personality disorder and has devoted more time and attention to the consequences of severe childhood trauma than have many mental health professionals, his and other popular talk shows tend to be associated with sensationalism and exploitation. As a result, real problems are trivialized in the public mind. If Geraldo thinks it is interesting, it must be hype. The overall effect is chilling. Clients wonder whether their memories and intense psychic, even physical, pain associated with their abuse histories are merely childish bids for attention. A client who kept her childhood rape secret for 40 years spoke of her dread of being perceived as having the "designer" affliction of our time.

## Factor Two

The effect on memory is one sequela of childhood trauma that muddies the water for both the layperson and professional. How reliable is memory?

Police and prosecutors of violent crime understand that survivors of psychological trauma make very poor witnesses. Janet brilliantly described the differences between what he termed "narrative memory" and "traumatic memory" (van der Kolk & van der Hart, 1989). Narrative memory is what we generally mean when we speak of memory. It involves a complex process whereby new experiences are integrated into preexisting schema or mental categories, along with the slow evolution and expansion of those schema. Traumatic memory is different. Trauma is an event or series of events that lies outside the ordinary, expectable events of life. It is overwhelming in its affective impact on the individual. It does not easily fit into preexisting schema, nor does it evolve easily with other memories. Traumatic memories are "dissociated." To use a computer analogy, narrative memory is stored on drive C, the drive that is generally available to consciousness and voluntary control processes. Although drive C may have subdirectories of unconsciousness as well, that is, memories that are repressed but can be brought into consciousness through psychoanalysis, dream work, free association, and the like, drive B, or dissociated, memories arise unexpectedly when someone or something triggers them into actualization: therapy, a child reaching a developmental milestone, a movie, a book, a television show, a death. Dissociated memories are fragmentary, illusive, uncertain, even terrifying.

If the trauma is not verifiable and if it occurred early in life and was severe, these dissociated states act as containers for memories and pain and assume the coherence of alternative selves, that is, separate personality or ego states that hold particular memories together. During the therapeutic process, the therapist and patient attempt to understand the nature of these drive B materials, retrieve them, and integrate them into drive C consciousness. In so doing, traumatic memory is integrated and assimilated into narrative memory.

For example, a 36-year-old woman who has been in therapy for three years struggling with depression and periodic panic attacks glances at her four-year-old daughter playing at the beach and suddenly remembers being raped by her father when she was four years old. In the following days, she questions her sanity and is unable to understand what is happening to her. Her therapist may also wonder about this bewildering experience. She will likely try to forget or trivalize it.

The impulse to both know the secrets of early trauma, and to tell it most typically fight with the impulse to keep the secret: what emerges is often jumbled and contradictory. That is the nature of traumatic memory! This is why victims are poor witnesses. The most common scenarios for survivors is to want to discredit their dissociated memories, not particularly to elevate them to heroic status. False memories, or memories that are iatrogenically induced during therapy, are not that common. Although some types of memories can be distorted or implanted in the minds of individuals under certain circumstances, evidence does not indicate that this occurs frequently, or even occasionally, in psychotherapeutic work with survivors of trauma.

## Factor Three

Faludi (1991) states that approximately every 30 years a cultural backlash arises against nascent feminism. Even modest status gains by women are quickly followed by a cultural response indicating that these changes and gains are not good for society or women.

Sexual abuse and sexual violence are cast as women's issues, despite the fact that children of both sexes are affected by abuse. Attacks on feminism focus energy on maintaining the *status quo* in power relationships. As a result, child victims and adult survivors may be discredited under the rubric of women's issues. Faludi points to the 1980s as a decade of government retrenchment on women's issues, disproportionate cuts in funding for women's programs, and decreased commitment in government funding for battered women's programs, despite increases in domestic violence. A dramatic rise in sexual violence against women, an increase that outstrips other types of violent crimes, has been met with indifference at all levels of government.

The retreat from renewed awareness of child-abuse problems in general and sexual abuse in particular reflects this backlash. Interestingly, patients' veracity in therapy was never an issue until we began discussing issues of sexual abuse.

## Factor Four

The changing legal climate regarding prosecution in civil incest suits has also affected adult-survivor issues. In the early 1980s, legal scholars began to reconsider the problem of seeking legal redress for crimes involving sexual abuse years after the commission of these crimes and after the statute of limitations had expired. In the *Harvard Women's Law Review,* Salten (1984) persuasively argued, "Given the latent nature and belated detection of many incest related injuries, the parent's special duty of care to his [sic] child, the youth of the incest victim, and the likelihood of psychological disabilities which preclude timely action, a tort suit for latent incestuous injuries is perhaps the paradigmatic example of special circumstances requiring equitable preservation of a potential remedy" (p. 220). As a result of this and other legal arguments, several U.S. state and Canadian provincial legislatures are considering changes in the law that toll the statute of limitations for both criminal prosecution of incest (incest *is* a crime) and civil incest suits from age 21 and/or from the time the facts of the crime are discovered. These changes in the law would acknowledge both the powerlessness of children to bring suit or initiate prosecution and the problem of associative memory, whereby memories of child sexual abuse may not be available to the victim until many years after the victimization.

This "delayed discovery" approach to civil litigation has precedent in cases involving injuries from asbestos and other harmful substances. Perpetrators are now within reach of the law years, even decades, after the commission of their crimes. This evolution in the law, however, has invigorated attacks against delayed memory in adult survivors. The False Memory Syndrome Foundation is dedicated to disseminating information on what its spokepersons describe as the growing threat of false accusations of incest and sexual abuse.

Part of its mission is to provide financial assistance to families in need of legal services or legal counseling.

## Conclusion

Freud anticipated the skepticism and criticism that would greet his views on sexual trauma as a cause of hysteria. Nevertheless, his views are as relevant today as they were 100 years ago. Freud discussed three aspects of work with traumatized patients:

- Patients reexperiencing an early life experience in a dissociative manner clearly demonstrate suffering, pain, shame, terror, and extreme helplessness. Suggested memories do not have this quality.
- Patients resist these memories both consciously and unconsciously and often disavow the memories immediately after the experience. People do not want to believe that they were betrayed by the adults whom they trusted for protection. Typically, such a belief requires a reorientation of one's frame of reference.
- Freud mentions that when he successfully suggested a scene to a patient, even the most compliant patients are unable to reproduce such scenes with the intensely appropriate affect and detail characteristic of dissociated memory. Although Freud did not speak of "dissociated memory" as such, he described it very sympathetically in *The Aetiology of Hysteria.*

Freud's critics had the final say, and Freud changed his mind about traumatic memories. The legacy of this intellectual struggle in psychiatry has affected tens of thousands of people whose early-life trauma has been ignored. For the past 15 years, we have struggled to reverse this legacy. We have made great strides in our understanding of female psychology, trauma, memory, and self-formation. Countervailing reactionary forces that are not grounded in scientific skepticism or informed by a spirit of inquiry would erase these gains. Both professionals and the lay public must meet this challenge by refusing to dishonor the struggles of those who refuse to forget.

## References

Brownmiller, S. (1975). *Against our will: Men, women and rape.* New York: Simon and Schuster.

Faludi, S. (1991). *Backlash: The undeclared war against American women.* New York: Crown Publishers.

Freud, S. (1984). The aetiology of hysteria. In J. M. Masson (Ed.), *Freud: The assault on truth* (pp. 251–282). London: Faber and Faber.

Herman, J. L. (1992). *Trauma and recovery: The aftermath of violence from domestic abuse to political terror.* New York: Basic Books.

Herman, J. L., & Schatzow, E. (1987). Recovery and verification of memories of childhood sexual trauma. *Psychoanalytic Psychology, 4,* 1–14.

Masson, J. (1984). *Freud: The assault on truth.* London: Faber and Faber.

Russell, D. (1986). *The secret trauma: Incest in the lives of girls and women.* New York: Basic Books.

Salten, M. (1984). Statutes of limitations in civil incest suits: Preserving the victim's remedy. *Harvard Women's Law Journal, 7,* 189–220.

Shapiro, L. (1993, April 19). Rush to judgment. *Newsweek,* 54–60.

Tavris, C. (1993, January 3). Beware the incest-survivor machine. *New York Times,* Sect. 7, p. 1.

van der Kolk, B., & van der Hart, O. (1989). Pierre Janet and the breakdown of adaptation. *American Journal of Psychiatry, 146,* 1530–1540.

Watters, E. (1993, January–February). Doors of memory. *Mother Jones,* p. 24.

Wright, L. (1993a, May 17). Remembering Satan, part I. *New Yorker,* pp. 60–81.

Wright, L. (1993b, May 24). Remembering Satan, part II. *New Yorker,* pp. 54–76.

# NO 

**Susan P. Robbins**

# Wading Through the Muddy Waters of Recovered Memory

In her essay "Running Away from Sexual Abuse: Denial Revisited" Benatar (1995) addresses a timely and important topic—recovered memories of childhood sexual abuse. Delayed recovery of memories of traumatic events and the nature, validity, and accuracy of these memories have been at the center of a controversial and bitter debate among mental health professionals and researchers (see Berliner & Williams, 1994; Butler, 1995; Byrd, 1994; Ewen, 1994; Gleaves, 1994; Gold, Hughes, & Hohnecker, 1994; Gutheil, 1993; Lindsay & Read, 1994; Loftus & Ketcham, 1994; Peterson, 1994; Pezdek, 1994; Pope & Hudson, 1995; Slovenko, 1993; Wylie, 1993; Yapko, 1994a, 1994b).

Proponents of recovered memory believe that many victims of repeated childhood sexual abuse repress or dissociate all memory of their trauma as a mechanism for coping. Although conscious memory of the trauma is not available to the victim, it nonetheless is believed to affect one's social and psychological functioning in adulthood. Seeking therapy for various problems such as substance abuse, eating disorders, depression, or marital difficulties, unhappy adults (primarily white, middle- and upper-class women in their thirties and forties) report memories of abuse that usually surface during the course of therapy. Such memories may also surface while participating in recovery groups, attending self-help conferences, reading incest-recovery books, or as the result of a specific trigger event. These memories typically appear as terrifying images or flashbacks that proponents believe are genuine, if not precise, memories of earlier abuse. Professional knowledge about recovered memory is derived primarily from clinical case reports, and most proponents accept these case studies as confirming evidence.

Critics are skeptical of recovered memories because no reproducible scientific evidence supports these claims. They contend that the growing body of research on memory has consistently shown memory to be subject to inaccuracy, distortion, and fabrication. They have also raised serious questions about the therapeutic methods used to help clients "recover" memories, and some claim that the real feminist issue is the victimization of clients by their therapists who, either knowingly or unconsciously, are suggesting, implanting,

From Susan P. Robbins, "Wading Through the Muddy Waters of Recovered Memory," *Families in Society: The Journal of Contemporary Human Services* (October 1995).  References omitted.

and reinforcing memories of abuse that never happened. Many critics have expressed concern that indiscriminate acceptance of recovered memories will lead to a serious backlash of disbelief in authentic cases of abuse.

In the past five years, a rapidly growing body of literature has supported both sides of this contentious debate. Although social workers are often cited as central figures in this debate, leading social work journals have not previously addressed this controversy. Benatar's essay, although timely, adds little to this debate and is a prime example of practice prescriptions based on ideology and theoretical conjecture. In addition to a woefully inadequate review of the current literature in this area, the essay suffers from a lack of conceptual clarity, unwarranted assumptions, and factual inaccuracy.

At the outset, the issue of child sexual abuse is confused with that of "recovered memories" of abuse. These are, in fact, two different issues that have recently come to be associated with each other. The former deals with a well-documented phenomenon—the sexual abuse of children by parents, relatives, other adult caretakers, friends, acquaintances, and strangers. The latter involves the debate about traumatic memory, including the repression of traumatic events and delayed recovery of these memories. According to Loftus and Ketcham (1994), this is a debate about memory and not a debate about childhood sexual abuse.

Benatar expresses disdain for the popular media's skeptical stance about delayed memory, the techniques used to uncover such memories, and the growing incest-survivor industry. Casting this skepticism as an antifeminist backlash against sexual-abuse survivors, she discounts the crucial issue of "false memories" and asserts that those who even question the veracity of traumatic memories are eroding the important gains made in our recognition of childhood abuse. Throughout, she improperly equates skepticism about recovered memories with denial of child sexual abuse.

Adding to this conceptual confusion, Benatar fails to draw distinctions among children who are current victims of abuse, adults who have always remembered traumatic incidents of childhood abuse, and those who have only recently recovered previously amnesic memories. Because this important point is neither addressed nor explored, all client reports of childhood abuse (which she refers to as "their own stories") are inferentially cast as being equally valid descriptions of historical events.

## Child Abuse: Past and Present Findings

Benatar correctly notes that "the reality of child abuse is well established." Given the increasing empirical evidence substantiating the reality of child abuse, it is most unfortunate that her ensuing discussion is based on specious analogies, incomplete data, and the use of unverified historical theories.

For example, labeled as "cultural dissociation," she equates the denial of the reality of Nazi death camps to what she believes is a prevalent societal denial of child abuse. In comparing the widely discredited beliefs of a relative few to a broader cultural misogyny that disavows child abuse, she engages in fallacious and distorted logic based on improper generalization and false analogy (see Fischer, 1970).

More problematic is the narrow sample of studies Benatar cites to support her discussion on the epidemiology of child sexual abuse, a problem further compounded by the lack of any critical analysis or discussion of the methodological limitations of these studies. A more thorough review of the literature reveals a broad range in the estimated prevalence of childhood sexual abuse. Although studies on child sexual abuse date back to 1929, few systematic studies utilizing careful statistical analyses were done before the late 1970s and early 1980s (see Demause, 1991). Retrospective surveys have reported base rates ranging from 6% to 62% for women (Burnam, cited in Peters, Wyatt, & Finkelhor, 1986; Wyatt, 1985) and between 3% and 31% for men (Landis, 1956; National Committee for the Prevention of Child Abuse, cited in Goldstein & Farmer, 1994). Researchers attribute the wide disparity in prevalence rates to the varying methodologies and definitions of sexual abuse used in each study. Studies that broadly define sexual abuse to include verbal propositions, for example, yield much higher estimates than do those using narrower definitions that only include forced sexual contact. Other definitions have included exposure, peeping, masturbation, unwanted kissing, and fondling (see Baker & Duncan, 1985; Finkelhor, Hotaling, Lewis, & Smith, 1990; Lindsay & Read, 1994; Russell, 1986, 1988; Williams & Finkelhor, 1992). Further complicating this problem, some studies fail to clarify the definition of sexual abuse being used (see Wassil-Grimm, 1995).

Because the primary focus of Benatar's essay is on recovered memories of abuse, the data she cites are also shaded by her failure to distinguish between incestuous and nonincestuous abuse. This is a critical point because the pathogenic and traumagenic nature of child sexual abuse has been linked in numerous studies to incest by a biological parent in general and, more specifically, to repeated molestation by fathers involving contact abuse and the use of force specifically (see Conte & Berliner, 1988; Elliott & Briere, 1992; Herman, 1981; Russell, 1986). Significantly, recovered memories typically involve repeated incest (see Bass & Davis, 1994).

It is difficult to obtain reliable data on incest because most studies do not make sufficient distinctions in their categorization of abusers. Based on a small number of retrospective studies, estimates indicate that approximately 4% to 5% of girls have reported being abused by a father, adoptive father, or stepfather before the age of 18 (Wassil-Grimm, 1995). Data from Williams and Finkelhor (1992) and Russell (1986) indicate that between 1% to 2.8% of girls are abused by a biological father. The rates are higher, of course, when abuse by other family members is included. Further, most cases of sexual abuse involve exhibition, masturbation, and both nongenital and genital touching rather than forced penetration (Lindsay & Read, 1994; Wakefield & Underwager, 1992). Russell's (1986) data showed a marked trend toward stepfathers abusing more frequently, using verbal threats, and being more severely abusive.

Two separate reviews of retrospective studies of childhood sexual abuse (Lindsay & Read, 1994; Wassil-Grimm, 1995) concluded that the preponderance of surveys indicate that the prevalence of intrafamilial incest is lower than the rates reported in the memory-recovery literature. In contrast, Demause (1991) contended that the known rates should be increased by 50% in order to correct for factors that lead to underreporting, including repression. Although the factors he cited are valid, his figures are based on pure speculation. Likewise, Bradshaw (1992) claimed that approximately 60% of all incest is repressed. To date, no replicable scientific evidence supports these claims. In a critique of what she sees as a "cycle of misinformation, faulty statistics, and unvalidated assertions" by incest-recovery authors, Tavris (1993) noted that inaccurate and sometimes concocted statistics are "traded like baseball cards, reprinted in every book and eventually enshrined as fact."

Another issue that is rarely discussed in the recovery literature is that not all children who are sexually abused experience the abuse as traumatic or develop psychological problems as an adult (Browne & Finkelhor, 1986; Kendall-Tacket, Williams, & Finkelhor, 1993; Russell, 1986). A review of recent empirical studies by Kendall-Tacket et al. (1993) found that many women are totally asymptomatic. Contradictory evidence also surrounds the relationship of sexual abuse to high levels of dissociation and multiple personality disorder (see Beitchman, Zucker, Heed, deCosta, & Cassavia, 1992; Brier & Elliott, 1993; Hacking, 1995; Kluft, 1985; Lindsay & Read, 1994; Nash, Hulsey, Sexton, Herralson, & Lambert, 1993a, 1993b). These findings should not minimize the severe trauma and psychological distress that some abuse victims experience; rather, they should alert us to the fact that the sequelae of childhood sexual abuse is not the same for all victims. Not surprisingly, those who demonstrate higher levels of traumatization and psychopathology are more often found in clinical samples than in the population in general (Russell, 1986).

It should be clear from the above discussion that *all* statistics on child sexual abuse should be interpreted very cautiously. Because of its hidden nature, child sexual abuse is seriously underreported. However, data from clinical samples, especially those samples undergoing therapy for childhood sexual abuse, are likely to overestimate its prevalence. Conversely, underestimates are likely if the data are based on retrospective surveys of adults in the general population, because some may choose not to report their abuse and some may not remember it. Despite discrepancies in the data, it is painfully clear that sexual abuse of children is a serious and pervasive problem that occurs more often than previously believed. As Pope and Hudson (1995) have astutely pointed out, even when conservative estimates of 10% for women and 5% for men are used, this means that 14,000,000 adults in the United States are former victims.

## Revisiting Freud and Janet

Benatar gives a brief description of Freud and Janet's theories of repressed or dissociated trauma, supported only by historical case studies. Although case studies are an important source of information, they should not be confused with scientific findings. Despite a widespread belief in the validity of case reports that show repression or dissociation to be a common response to sexual abuse (see Blume, 1990; Chu & Dill, 1990; Courtois, 1988, 1992; Ellenson, 1989;

Erdelyi & Goldberg, 1979; Fredrickson, 1992; Kluft, 1985; Mennen & Pearlmutter, 1993), little support for this belief can be found in empirical studies. In a review of 60 years of research, Holmes (1990) could not find any controlled studies that supported the concept of repression.

The few studies that were initially thought to provide possible evidence of repression (Briere & Conte, 1993; Herman & Schatzow, 1987; Loftus, Polonsky, & Fullilove, 1994; Williams, 1994) have yielded divergent results, with rates ranging from 18% to 59%. Methodological limitations, however, restrict the ability of any of these studies to support fully the mechanism of repression or dissociation (see Lindsay & Read, 1994; Loftus, 1993; Pope & Hudson, 1995). Despite Benatar's assertion that the Herman and Schatzow study supports the claim of delayed traumatic recall, this study has received widespread criticism because of its nonrepresentative sample, lack of specification of methodology (including criteria for confirmation of abuse), the use of composites of cases, little or no amnesia in the majority of cases, and the possibility of suggestion during therapy (see Lindsay & Read, 1994; Pope & Hudson, 1995; Wassil-Grimm, 1995). In short, Herman and Schatzow's study is far from conclusive.

Studies have shown to the contrary that people typically remember their past abuse. Loftus, Polonsky, and Fullilove (1994) found that in their sample of 105 women involved in outpatient treatment for substance abuse, the majority (54%) reported a history of childhood sexual abuse; the vast majority (81%) had always remembered their abuse. In Williams's (1994) study of 100 women with documented histories of sexual abuse, the majority (62%) acknowledged their abuse when asked by the researcher. Because no follow-up interview was conducted in either of these studies, it is impossible to know whether those failing to report their past abuse did so due to repression, ordinary forgetting, normal childhood amnesia, or the desire not to disclose a painful event. Femina, Yeager, and Lewis's (1990) longitudinal study of 69 adults with documented histories of child abuse (primarily physical) found no evidence of total amnesia. The majority (62%) readily reported their abuse to the interviewer. Those who initially denied or minimized their abuse acknowledged in a follow-up "clarification" interview that they did, in fact, remember their abuse but chose to withhold the information for various reasons.

In order for us to validate the clinical impressions gained from current and historical case histories, we need carefully designed studies to test the repression/dissociation hypothesis. Pope and Hudson (1995) suggested that the design of the Williams study is a useful starting point. Strict criteria for inclusion and the use of clarification interviews, similar to those used by Femina et al. (1990) would be a necessary addition to the study design. Pope and Hudson proposed that a series of case reports could be used to present preliminary evidence if they strictly adhered to the research criteria. They noted that given the high prevalence of repression suggested by many authors, this area "begs further carefully designed studies to resolve one of its most critical questions." In sum, both the existence and prevalence of repression have yet to be scientifically validated; the same is true for the type of dissociative amnesia hypothesized in the recovery literature.

## Traumatic Memory

In her discussion of traumatic memory, Benatar exhibits a serious misunderstanding of memory, in general, and memory organization, storage, and retrieval, in particular. Based on a narrow and inaccurate reading of van der Kolk and van der Hart's (1989) article, she presents an oversimplified typology of memory and compounds it with a misleading computer analogy.

Memory researchers widely accept that memory is *constructive* and *reconstructive,* not reproductive (Loftus, 1993; Loftus & Ketcham, 1994; Rose, 1992; Squire, 1987). Neuroscientist Steven Rose (1992) cautioned against the use of a flawed brain/computer metaphor:

> Brains do not work with information in the computer sense, but with *meaning* [which] is a historically and developmentally shaped process . . . because each time we remember, we in some senses do work on and transform our memories; they are not simply being called up from store. . . . Our memories are recreated each time we remember [emphasis added].

In their review of current research on memory processing, encoding, and state-dependent learning, van der Kolk and van der Hart (1989) reappraise Janet's early theory of psychopathological dissociation in an attempt to link it with recent findings. However, in contrast with Benatar's firm assertion that "traumatic memory is different," this is not what the authors conclude. They state that

> [Janet's notion] that traumatic memories are stored in memory in ways different from ordinary events is as challenging today as it was . . . almost 100 years ago. One century later, much remains to be learned about how memories are stored and keep on affecting emotions and behavior.

Likewise, in her ensuing discussion of trauma, dissociation, and memory, Benatar confuses theory with fact, stating that "if the trauma is verifiable and if it occurred early in life and was severe, these dissociated states act as containers for memories and pain and assume the coherence of alternate selves." Numerous studies on verifiable traumas (Leopold & Dillon, 1963; Malmquist, 1986; Pynoos & Nader, 1989; Strom et al., 1962; Terr, 1979, 1983) have shown to the contrary that vivid (although not necessarily accurate) recall of traumatic events is common. No subjects in these studies repressed the event or developed dissociative amnesia. Post-traumatic symptomatology most commonly involves intrusive images, flashbacks, nightmares, and anxiety attacks, such as those seen in Vietnam veterans.

It is also well established that adults rarely have recall of any events prior to the age of two or three and only sketchy memories up until age five (Fivush & Hudson, 1990; Loftus & Ketcham, 1994; Pendergast, 1995; Usher & Neisser, 1993). This normal "infantile amnesia" is developmentally based and is not due to trauma. Traumatic amnesia in adults is a well-documented phenomenon and involves either large portions of the memory (one's name, address, and other personal information) or circumscribed traumatic events, with good recall of everything prior to and subsequent to the event. In both cases, people are *aware* of the fact that they have amnesia (see Loftus & Ketcham, 1994).

In the last decade, with the revival of Freud's seduction theory and Janet's theory of dissociation, some clinicians and researchers have begun *theorizing* that traumatic memories of *repeated* childhood sexual abuse are encoded differently from other traumas and result in a total loss of awareness of not only the events but of the amnesia itself (see Herman, 1992; Terr, 1991, 1994). The idea that these painful memories are somehow "split off" or dissociated into compartmentalized areas of the mind remains an untested hypothesis. To date, attempts to establish a link between dissociated or repressed trauma and current findings in the neurobiology of memory have been speculative at best. Despite her personal conviction that traumatic memories and ordinary memories are qualitatively different, Herman (1992) acknowledged that "the biological factors underlying... traumatic dissociation remain an enigma." To paraphrase Klein (1977), we must avoid confusing what a theorist has merely claimed or believed with what she or he has actually proved or demonstrated. Even van der Kolk and van der Hart (1989) conceded that "we can neither confirm or [sic] contradict most of Janet's observations on memory disturbances following traumatization."

## Veracity of Client Reports

Benatar is partly correct in her assertion that "veracity in therapy was never an issue until we began discussing issues of sexual abuse." However, this conclusion is based on the faulty premise that acceptance of a client's narrative truth is presumed to be an accurate historical account of events, which is not necessarily the case. In most cases, the veracity of a client's narrative report of life events is not an issue unless the therapist becomes aware of contradictions. It is important to note that allegations of sexual abuse, when made by children or adolescents, are now routinely subjected to extensive collateral verification by an independent investigator (Faller, 1988).

Although psychoanalysts since Freud have been trained to believe that memories of seduction and sexual abuse are incestuous wishes (Masson, 1990), the response on the part of most mental health professionals has been to ignore, minimize, or avoid the topic of sexual abuse (Craine, Henson, Colliver, & MacLean 1988; Jacobson, Koehler, & Jones-Brown, 1987; Post, Willett, Franks, House, & Weissberg, 1980; Rose, Peabody, & Stratigeas, 1991). Whether this is a result of disbelief is, according to Rose et al. (1991), a topic of endless debate. The fact that clinicians have routinely failed to inquire about or respond to reports of sexual abuse represents a serious omission, especially given the prevalence of abuse found in clinical populations.

Contrary to Masson's (1984) and Miller's (1984) assertions that Freud abandoned his theory about the primacy of incest in the etiology of hysteria, Demause (1991) argued that an unbiased reading of Freud shows that he continued to believe in his patients' spontaneous reports of *conscious* memories of abuse. Freud concluded that only *unconscious* memories of early infantile scenes of seduction were "phantasies which my patients had made up or which myself had perhaps forced on them" (cited in Demause, 1991). If Demause is correct, it would appear that even Freud came to question the veracity of *recovered* memories of sexual abuse but did not doubt those memories that were always remembered. In a similar vein, Hacking (1995) noted that Janet revised his early formulations and dropped the concept of dissociation in his later writings. He eventually came to believe that double (or multiple) personality was a special and rare case of bipolar disorder, which he termed "les circulaires." It is interesting that the proponents of recovered memory extensively cite his earlier work while ignoring his later ideas.

It is widely acknowledged that it is impossible to verify charges of sexual abuse in the absence of external corroboration. Because of its hidden nature and the tendency for perpetrators to deny their guilt, it is sometimes difficult to find the necessary corroboration, especially decades after the alleged abuse occurred. But we must be clear that clinical judgment alone is not a sufficient predictor of veracity. In his discussion of the child sexual abuse accommodation syndrome, Summit (1983, 1992) acknowledged that "there is no clinical method available to distinguish valid claims from those that should be treated as fantasy or deception." He further cautioned that "the capacity to listen and the willingness to believe . . . is not an admonition to interrogate or assume that every disclosure is real" (Summit, 1992). Clearly, we must be open to listening to our clients and willing to help them explore issues of past abuse. However, we must be cautious about accepting a client's narrative truth as historical fact in the absence of corroboration. This is especially true in the case of recovered memories; some memories may be fully accurate, some may be partly accurate, and some may be totally false. This does not imply that we should disbelieve our clients but rather that we maintain a neutral stance about historical accuracy. Historical accuracy becomes mandatory, however, when this debate is moved from the therapist's office into the courtroom (see Gutheil, 1993; Slovenko, 1993).

A more controversial but intricately related issue that Benatar fails to address is that of recovered memories of satanic ritual abuse, alien abductions, past lives, preverbal body memories, in *utero* trauma, and cellular memory (see Goldstein & Farmer, 1993, 1994; Mack, 1994; Mulhern, 1991; Pendergrast, 1995; Richardson, Best, & Bromley, 1991; Robbins, 1995; Smith, 1995; Victor, 1993). These memories raise interesting questions regarding both the veracity of client reports and the therapeutic methods used to retrieve or recover them: Are all such memories possible? If not, which ones are? Where do we draw the line? Based on what criteria? How can we determine their accuracy? These questions are significant because a growing number of therapists involved in memory-recovery therapy believe in the validity and accuracy of all recovered memories (Loftus, Garry, Brown, & Rader, 1994; Smith, 1995; Yapko, 1994a, 1994b). Not surprisingly, their clients come to believe in them as well.

## False Memories: Fact or Fiction?

Skepticism about "false memories" is often voiced by proponents of recovered memory because it is seen as a backlash to the discovery of childhood sexual abuse and an attempt to silence the victims; as such, false memories are equated with "denial" of abuse (Bloom, 1995; Rockwell, 1995). In the past several years this has become the subject of debate in scholarly journals and professional conferences. Because these issues become tangled and confused, it is important once again to make the distinction between the debate about memory and the documented reality of abuse; the false-memory debate is not about the latter.

A growing body of research has shown that partially and wholly inaccurate memories are not an unusual phenomenon. Because memory is extremely malleable, it is influenced by various factors, and false memories can be created through exposure to misinformation (Loftus, 1993; Terr, 1994). According to Terr, a false memory can be "a strongly imagined memory, a totally distorted memory, a lie, or a misconstructed impression." Numerous studies have shown that people can be led to construct not only inaccurate and confabulated details of past events, but detailed memories of entire events that never happened (see Haugaard, Reppucci, Laurd, & Nauful, 1991; Loftus, 1993; Loftus & Ketcham, 1994; Neisser & Harsch, 1992; Pynoos & Nader, 1989; Spanos, Menary, Gabora, DuBreuil, & Dewhirst, 1991).

Evidence about erroneous memory has sparked concern that memories of abuse are being created by therapists who, through well-intentioned but misguided therapeutic methods, may directly or indirectly evoke specious memories with the use of hypnosis, guided visualization, "truth" drugs, abreactive therapy, dream and body memory interpretation, or suggestive questioning (Byrd, 1994; Gangelhoff, 1995; Gutheil, 1993; Lindsay & Read, 1994; Loftus, 1993; Ofshe & Watters, 1994; Pendergast, 1995; Yapko, 1994a). Although proponents of recovered memory therapy incorrectly believe that false or suggested memories cannot be experienced with the same emotional intensity as can recovered memories of real trauma, evidence suggests otherwise (see Loftus & Ketcham, 1994; Yapko, 1994a). As Loftus and Ketcham noted, reconstructed memories, once adopted, come to be believed in as strongly as genuine memories. Concern about false memory is bolstered by detailed accounts of coercive therapy and lawsuits filed by "retractors"—hundreds of women who have left therapy and recanted their allegations of abuse (see Goldstein & Farmer, 1993, 1994; Pendergrast, 1995).

Studies documenting distorted and confabulated memory in children and adults have been discounted by some proponents of memory recovery because they do not speak directly to the issue of false memories of childhood sexual abuse. Benatar echoes this position along with reservations similar to those noted by Berliner and Williams (1994) and Pezdek (1994) that little scientific evidence supports the claim that false memories of abuse are common or that memory-recovery therapy is widespread. Because little research has been done in this area, this is an accurate appraisal of our lack of scientific knowledge about false memories induced in therapy. However, it is noteworthy that many who accept the "truth" of recovered memories of childhood victimization are not willing to extend the same credibility to those who claim they were victimized by their therapists. Nonetheless, methodologically sound studies are necessary to validate the phenomena of false memory as well as recovered memory; we must rely on the same standard of proof for both.

## Where Do We Go From Here?

Clearly, the reluctance of clinicians to address the reality of child sexual abuse poses a serious barrier to accurate and effective assessment and treatment. Rose et al. (1991) noted that "short- and long-term sequelae result not only from sexual and physical abuse, but from inappropriate treatment and nonrecognition of the abuse." Given social work's commitment to multidimensional assessment and holistic, nondichotomous thinking (see Compton & Galaway, 1989; Haynes & Holmes, 1994; Hepworth & Larsen, 1993; Morales & Sheafor, 1995), it is critical that clinical practitioners gather accurate information about their client's past and present biopsychosocial functioning, strengths and resources, developmental history, significant life events, and reactions to and feelings about these events. In this holistic context, it would be unconscionable to fail to inquire about physical and sexual abuse—past or present. We must be sensitive to the fact that clients may choose initially not to disclose their abuse until a level of trust is developed in the therapeutic relationship. Failure to disclose should not *automatically* be assumed to be due to repression or dissociation.

We must also be cautious about hastily attributing a laundry list of nonspecific symptoms to prior abuse, as this defeats the purpose of a multidimensional assessment. When a previously repressed history of sexual abuse is revealed, it is especially important to consider the use of collateral sources of information because clients may themselves be confused about these memories. However, collateral sources should never be used without the client's express permission. The use of collateral sources does not imply that the social workers should take on the dual roles of investigator and therapist, because doing so represents a serious conflict of interest (Mason, 1991). Instead, collateral information should be used to help both the practitioner and the client gain a well-rounded picture of the situation. Hepworth and Larsen (1993) noted that important factors that may otherwise be overlooked can often be identified by persons close to the client. According to van der Kolk and van der Hart (1989), Janet frequently interviewed his patients' family members and acquaintances in order to get as complete a picture as possible.

## Conclusion

Social workers who work with victims of childhood sexual abuse, especially those whose claim is based solely on recovered memories, should become acquainted with the full range of clinical and social scientific literature on the topic. Clinical case studies must be balanced with scientific findings; both are crucial sources of knowledge. Many clinicians receive only training or information that supports a narrow ideology and practice methodology. As I have suggested elsewhere (Robbins, 1995), social workers must be fully informed in order to "evaluate critically these disparate ideological positions and the adequacy of the research that supports them." This is especially important because a recent study by Feld (1995) found that few social workers are provided with any content about memory or memory retrieval in their academic programs.

In addition, social workers need to be fully aware of their own personal biases in order to prevent them from interfering with assessment and treatment. Preconceived beliefs about repression, dissociation, and recovered memories may lead to an ideological stance that inhibits thorough and accurate assessment. It is imperative that we recognize the serious consequences for our clients and their families when our personal biases lead us to either underdiagnose or overdiagnose childhood sexual abuse. Further, we must remember that the imposition of our personal values and beliefs is antithetical to our deeply held value of client self-determination (Hepworth & Larsen, 1993).

As a result of the lack of scientific verification and the polemical debate shaping research and practice, we must wade cautiously through the muddy waters of recovered memory. Social workers may feel caught between two conflicting sets of claims that demand allegiance to one side or the other. It is doubtful, however, that positioning ourselves at the extremes of this debate will lead to a stance that is in the best interests of our clients. Amid the black and white positions of what Loftus and Ketcham (1994) call the "true believers" and "skeptics," a middle-ground stance is often hard to find, despite the grey areas of uncertainty and ambiguity that exist. Acknowledgment of these grey areas does not mean, however, that one is in "denial" or is uncaring or negligent as a practitioner. We must be open to new findings in this area but we must also be cautious in distinguishing between conjecture and fact.

Finally, when skepticism about the ideology of the recovery movement is based on a thorough review of valid, scientific findings, it must not be cast as antifeminist backlash. As Klein (1977) aptly noted, "Scientific questions are to be settled by appeals to evidence rather than by appeals to authority—even the authority of a Freud."

# POSTSCRIPT

## Can Memories of Childhood Sexual Abuse Be Recovered?

The controversy surrounding the accuracy of recollections of abuse (sometimes called false memories) tends to obscure the issue regarding the susceptibility of human beings to adopt false beliefs at the suggestion of someone else. In typical cases a person establishes a belief that abuse has occurred before any memory of it has surfaced and then looks for evidence to confirm the belief. Robbins uses this explanation to reject the accuracy of these memories, whereas Benatar argues that we should accept them more readily.

Making a revelation about child abuse may leave an individual deeply depressed and even suicidal. Equally problematic is the impact on the family, who is often torn apart psychologically and forced to endure a nightmarish court battle when the alleged perpetrator of the abuse is summoned to court. The challenge is to ascertain the difference between what a person feels and believes versus the literal, physical reality upon which the memories are based. Should we, as a society, turn our backs in disbelief on all those coming forth with repressed memories? Do we continue our present trend of predominant belief and acceptance of these allegations? What about a person who cannot prove such allegations but experiences the pain of the abuses and believes they occurred? Do we merely turn our backs, or do we try to help even though the allegations may not be true? Finally, if we do choose to help, how do we go about providing such assistance?

## Suggested Readings


Berliner, L., & Loftus, E. (1992). Sexual abuse accusations: Desperately seeking reconciliation. *Journal of Interpersonal Violence, 7*(4), 570–578.

Gardner, R. A. (1994). Differentiating between true and false sex abuse accusations in child custody disputes. *Journal of Divorce and Remarriage, 21*(3), 1–20.

Gellert, G. A. (1995). Sensitivity and specificity in child abuse detection. *Journal of Child Sexual Abuse, 4*, 99–104.

Ney, T. (Ed.). (1995). *True and false allegations of child sexual abuse: Assessment and case management.* New York: Brunner/Mazel.

Scotford, R. (1995). Myths, memories and reality. *Contemporary Hypnosis, 12*(2), 137–142.

Yapko, M. (1993, September/October). The seductions of memory. *The Family Therapy Networker*, 30–37.

# Contributors to This Volume

## EDITORS

**DIANA S. DelCAMPO** is the child development and family life specialist with the New Mexico Cooperative Extension Service at New Mexico State University in Las Cruces, New Mexico, and holds the rank of professor. She is a member of the National Council on Family Relations and the National Extension Family Life Specialists' Association. She received a B.S. from Concord College in West Virginia, an M.S. from Virginia Polytechnic Institute and State University, and a Ph.D. in curriculum and instruction from the University of Michigan. She presently develops educational programs in child and family development, supervises grant projects, and coordinates projects with other state agencies in New Mexico. She has published educational guides, chapters in several books, symposium proceedings, and articles in various journals.

**ROBERT L. DelCAMPO** is a professor of family science at New Mexico State University in Las Cruces, New Mexico. He is a licensed marriage and family therapist, clinical member, and approved supervisor of the American Association for Marriage and Family Therapy. He also holds memberships in the International Family Therapy Association and the National Council on Family Relations, and he is a former president of the New Mexico Association for Marriage and Family Therapy. He received a B.S. from the State University of New York, an M.S. from Virginia Polytechnic Institute and State University, and a Ph.D. in family relations and child development from Florida State University. His work has appeared in such journals as *Family Relations* and *Contemporary Family Therapy.*

## STAFF

Theodore Knight List Manager
David Brackley Senior Developmental Editor
Juliana Gribbins Developmental Editor
Rose Gleich Administrative Assistant
Brenda S. Filley Director of Production/Design
Juliana Arbo Typesetting Supervisor
Diane Barker Proofreader
Richard Tietjen Publishing Systems Manager
Larry Killian Copier Coordinator

# AUTHORS

**KAREN E. ABLARD** is a professor in the Center for Talented Youth Research at Johns Hopkins University in Baltimore, Maryland.

**RUDOLPH ALEXANDER, JR.** is a professor in the department of social work at Ohio State University and is the current director of the Social Work Program.

**AMERICAN ASSOCIATION OF UNIVERSITY WOMEN** is an organization of college and university graduates that was founded in 1881 to work for the advancement of women.

**SUSAN A. BEEBE** is in the Department of Pediatrics at the University of Utah Medical Center in Salt Lake City, Utah.

**JAY BELSKY** is a professor in the College of Health and Human Development at Pennsylvania State University. He has published numerous articles on maternal employment, child care, and family issues, and he is the author of *Transition to Parenthood* (Dell, 1995).

**MAY BENATAR** is a clinical social worker in private practice in Montclair, New Jersey. She currently teaches and lectures to professional groups on sexual abuse and the treatment of dissociative disorders.

**WILLIAM J. BENNETT** is codirector of Empower America. He served as secretary of education under President Ronald Reagan and as director of the White House Office of National Drug Control Policy under President George Bush.

**T. BERRY BRAZELTON** is founder of the Child Development Unit at Children's Hospital Boston and has been a practicing pediatrician for 45 years. He has authored many books on children and families.

**PEGGY BRICK** is director of education at Planned Parenthood of Greater Northern New Jersey in Hackensack, New Jersey. She is also president of the Sex Information and Education Council of the United States (SIECUS).

**HELEN L. BRITTON** is an associate professor in the Department of Pediatrics at the University of Utah Medical Center in Salt Lake City, Utah.

**JOHN R. BRITTON** is an associate professor in the Department of Pediatrics at the University of Utah Medical Center in Salt Lake City, Utah.

**K. ALISON CLARKE-STEWART** is a professor of social ecology at the University of California–Irvine. She is the author of several articles and coauthor, with Christian P. Gruber and Linda Fitzgerald, of *Children at Home and in Daycare* (Lawrence Erlbaum, 1994).

**CARLA M. CURTIS** is a professor at Ohio State University. Her areas of research interest include child and family policy, social welfare policy, and regulatory analysis.

**W. J. DOHERTY** is both a professor and marriage and family therapy director at the University of Minnesota in St. Paul, Minnesota.

**DAVID EGGEBEEN** is a professor in the College of Health and Human Development at Pennsylvania State University.

**MARTHA F. ERICKSON** is director of the University of Minnesota's Children, Youth and Family Consortium. She developed the Steps Toward Effective, Enjoyable Parenting (STEEP) and is the author of numerous journal articles and book chapters as well as a weekly parenting column.

**JIB FOWLES** is a professor of communication at the University of Houston–Clear Lake. He is the author of *The Case for Television Violence* (Sage Publications, 1999).

**DAVID GATELY** was a graduate student of psychology at the Ohio State University in Columbus, Ohio, when he coauthored "Favorable Outcomes in Children After Parental Divorce" for the *Journal of Divorce and Remarriage.*

**STANLEY I. GREENSPAN** is clinical professor of psychiatry and pediatrics at George Washington University Medical School.

**LESLIE DOTY HOLLINGSWORTH** is an assistant professor at the University of Michigan in Ann Arbor, Michigan. Her research focuses on the adoption of children and on children's racial identity.

**KARON L. JAHN** is dean of students at Chaminade University in Honolulu, Hawaii.

**MERRILYN O. JOHNSON** is from the Nursing Ph.D. Collaborative Program at the Medical University of South Carolina and the University of South Carolina in Columbia, South Carolina.

**LISA KOLB** is a public information specialist for the Missouri Department of Social Services in Jefferson City, Missouri.

**EDWARD F. KOUNESKI** is currently completing his doctoral dissertation in family social science, with a specialization in marriage and family therapy, at the University of Minnesota.

**LAWRENCE A. KURDEK** is a psychologist at Wright State University in Dayton, Ohio.

**ROBERT E. LARZELERE** is director of Residential Research at Father Flanagan's Boys' Home in Boys Town, Nebraska. The residential research program collaborates with Boys Town campus programs to conduct research on a wide range of Boys Town's residential programs.

**JOHN F. LEWIS** is a managing partner in the Cleveland, Ohio, office of the law firm of Squire, Sanders, and Dempsey.

**THOMAS LICKONA**, a developmental psychologist, is a professor of education at the State University of New York College at Cortland and director of the Center for the Fourth and Fifth Rs (Respect and Responsibility).

**DONALDO MACEDO** is a professor of English and program director for Bilingual English as a Second Language Studies at the University of Massachusetts–Boston.

**LORI A. McGRAW** is the 4-H program coordinator for the Oregon State University Extension Service. Her responsibilities include involvement in the school-age child care programs and the 4-H Adventures Program.

**CAROL J. MILLS** is director of research in the Center for Talented Youth Research at Johns Hopkins University in Baltimore, Maryland.

**GREG PARKS** is an intern program specialist in the Research and Program Development Division at the Office of Juvenile Justice and Delinquency Prevention, which is part of the United States Department of Justice.

**DAVID POPENOE** is a professor of sociology and an associate dean for the social sciences at Rutgers–The State University in New Brunswick, New Jersey. He is the author of *Disturbing the Nest* (Aldine de Gruyter, 1988).

**ROSALIE PEDALINO PORTER** is chairman of the board and acting director of the Research in English Acquisition and Development (READ) Institute in Amherst, Massachusetts.

**JESSICA PORTNER** is a freelance writer in Long Beach, California.

**SUSAN P. ROBBINS** is an associate professor in the Graduate School of Social Work at the University of Houston in Texas. She is the author of *River and Jungle* (Random House, 1993).

**DEBORAH M. ROFFMAN** is a sexuality educator, trainer, and consultant. Since 1975 she has taught human sexuality education.

**LISBETH B. SCHORR** is director of the Harvard University Project on Effective Services in Boston.

**ANDREW I. SCHWEBEL** is a professor in the Department of Psychology at the Ohio State University in Columbus, Ohio. He is coauthor, with Mark A. Fine, of *Understanding and Helping Families: A Cognitive-Behavioral Approach* (Lawrence Erlbaum, 1994).

**MURRAY A. STRAUS** is a professor of sociology and codirector of the Family Research Laboratory at the University of New Hampshire in Durham, New Hampshire.

**HEINRICH STUMPF** is a professor in the Center for Talented Youth Research at Johns Hopkins University in Baltimore, Maryland.

**ELIZABETH H. THILO** is an associate professor of pediatrics at the University of Colorado School of Medicine and the Children's Hospital in Denver, Colorado.

**SUSAN F. TOWNSEND** is an assistant professor of pediatrics at the University of Colorado School of Medicine and the Children's Hospital in Denver. She is also medical director at the University Hospital Newborn Nursery in Denver, Colorado.

**ALEXIS J. WALKER** is both a professor of human development and family sciences and director of the Gerontology Program at Oregon State University.

**KEVIN WALTHERS** teaches government at Mesquite High School in Dallas, Texas.

**MARY-LOU WEISMAN** is a freelance writer who has written about children, ethics, and social issues for the *New York Times* and *The New Republic.*

**KARL ZINSMEISTER** is editor in chief of *The American Enterprise* and the author of a book on the American family to be published soon.

# Index